The Political Economy of the Middle East

Series Editor
Ashraf Mishrif, Humanities Research Centre,
Sultan Qaboos University, Al Khaud, Oman

This series explores the nature of Middle Eastern political regimes and their approaches to economic development. In light of the region's distinctive political, social and economic structures and the dramatic changes that took place in the wake of the Arab spring, this series puts forward a critical body of high-quality, research-based scholarship that reflects current political and economic transitions across the Middle East. It offers original research and new insights on the causes and consequences of the Arab uprisings; economic reforms and liberalization; political institutions and governance; regional and sub-regional integration arrangements; foreign trade and investment; political economy of energy, water and food security; finance and Islamic finance; and the politics of welfare, labor market and human development. Other themes of interest include the role of the private sector in economic development, economic diversification, entrepreneurship and innovation; state-business relationships; and the capacity of regimes and public institutions to lead the development process. The book series is Scopus Indexed.

Ashraf Mishrif · Magdalena Karolak ·
Cameron Mirza
Editors

Nationalization of Gulf Labour Markets

Higher Education and Skills Development in Industry 4.0

Gulf Research Centre Cambridge
Knowledge for All

palgrave
macmillan

Editors
Ashraf Mishrif
Humanities Research Centre
Sultan Qaboos University
Al Khaud, Oman

Magdalena Karolak
College of Humanities and Social Science
Zayed University
Dubai, United Arab Emirates

Cameron Mirza
International Research and Exchanges Board (IREX)
Washington, DC, USA

ISSN 2522-8854 ISSN 2522-8862 (electronic)
The Political Economy of the Middle East
ISBN 978-981-19-8071-8 ISBN 978-981-19-8072-5 (eBook)
https://doi.org/10.1007/978-981-19-8072-5

This Palgrave Macmillan imprint is published by the registered company Springer Nature Singapore Pte Ltd.
The registered company address is: 152 Beach Road, #21-01/04 Gateway East, Singapore 189721, Singapore

To our families, friends, and beloved ones

Acknowledgements

This book is the product of an extensive discussion in a workshop titled Nationalization of GCC Labour Market: The Changing Role of Higher Education in the Era of the 4th Industrial Revolution, in the context of the Gulf Research Meeting 2021, which was held in the University of Cambridge, UK, in July 2021. This original research and invaluable insights brought forward by leading experts and specialists from different disciplines, professions, and backgrounds make this volume truly interdisciplinary and offer new insights into the nature of the higher education system and conditions of the labour market in the Gulf countries.

The editors would like to thank the contributors of this book, without whom this volume would not be possible. We are also grateful to the Gulf Research Center Cambridge for organizing the Gulf Research Meeting in July 2021. Although the Gulf Research Meeting 2021 was held virtually due to the outbreak of COVID-19, the Gulf Research Center had done its utmost to organize their annual meeting and make our workshop possible. We appreciate their commitment to advance knowledge in humanities and social sciences.

We are also grateful to Vishal Daryanomel, editor of Palgrave Macmillan for supporting us to get this volume published. Our thanks also go to three anonymous reviewers who provided thorough reviews and useful comments that allowed us to improve the manuscript.

The publication of this book comes at an important time in history, when both higher education and labour market have to introduce radical changes to mitigate the negative effects of COVID-19 and respond to the emerging skills and needs brought about by Industry 4.0 technologies in the job market. We hope that our contribution to this volume will assist policymakers and stakeholders to initiate and devise the appreciate policies that could support Gulf countries in their social, economic, and digital transformation.

Contents

1 **The Nexus Between Higher Education, Labour Market, and Industry 4.0 in the Context of the Arab Gulf States** 1
Ashraf Mishrif, Magdalena Karolak, and Cameron Mirza

Part I Overview on Higher Education and Human Capital in the Gulf Region

2 **GCC's Higher Education in Industry 4.0: Preparing Lifelong Learners** 27
Thamer Al-Ani

3 **Is Work Integrated Learning a Panacea to Employability of Graduates in GCC Countries?** 59
Shazia Farooq Fazli and Ayesha Farooq

4 **Migrating Human Capital: A Case Study of Indian Migrants in the GCC Countries** 91
Anisur Rahman

Part II Higher Education and Labour Market in Selected Sectors

5 Human Capital Enhancement Through International and On-Line Programs in the Universities of Qatar and the UAE 123
Mariam Orkodashvili

6 Formulating Digital Right-Skilling in the Gulf's Healthcare 4.0 Ecosystem to Enhance Professional Capabilities 149
Náder Alyani

7 A Hospitable Kingdom? Building New Employment Opportunities for Saudi Youth in the Culture, Tourism and Hospitality Sectors 179
Annalisa Pavan

8 Workforce Nationalization in the UAE: Creating a Framework for Training Emirati Nationals for the Banking Sector 203
Sowmya Vivek and Allen Baby

Part III Higher Education and Labour Market in Selected Gulf Countries

9 A Realist Perspective on Agile Policy for Future Skills in a Digital Age—An Example from the Kingdom of Bahrain 227
Annamarie Lawrence

10 High-tech Nationalization of Gulf Employment: A New Labor Market Approach in the United Arab Emirates 255
Robert Mogielnicki

11 Human Capital and Health Education Among Menopausal Emirati Women in Dubai: Implications and Recommendations 269
Linda Smail

12 Emiratization: Challenges and Potential Strategies—An Emirati Youth Perspective 293
Anca Bocanet and Rihab Grassa

13 Bridging the Gap Between Gulf Higher Education and Labor Market in Industry 4.0 319
Ashraf Mishrif, Magdalena Karolak, and Cameron Mirza

Index 333

Notes on Contributors

Thamer Al-Ani is Professor of Econometrics at Baghdad University. He was Head of Economics Department, Baghdad University from 1994 to 2000, before joining the League of the Arab States as Director of Economic Relations Department in 2000 until 2019. He is Member of Iraqi Economist Association, Royal statistical society, and Arab society for Economic research.

Náder Alyani is a learning scientist and a training professional with Siemens Healthineers, Germany, working on digitalization and harmonization of regulatory and statutory compliance processes on a global scale. His previous academic, consulting, and managerial activities had focused on capability development, mitigating risk, and implementing learning and innovation for strategic alignment. Over the last two decades, he has consulted on, managed, or directed projects and programmes with equanimity and integrity covering digital transformation, lean organizational change, digitally enhanced L&D, and developing capabilities including the right-skilling for 4th Industrial Revolution, within sectoral use-cases. Hardly satisfied with the status quo, his passion for learning as empowerment and optimization, and valuing diversity and inclusion lights a fire beneath his professional endeavours.

Allen Baby is the Manager of Center for Training of EIBFS. Dr. Baby was Assistant Vice President-Credit Risk with SBI, Bangalore, India. He holds Ph.D. in Finance from University of Liverpool, UK. He is specialist in investments, credit, and other banking areas, and trained over 3000+ participants at senior levels in banking, finance, and the Investment Industry. He has also expertise in Corporate Banking & Treasury, with India's top Bank (SBI). Handled large, and emerging companies across various sectors of $350mn. He was also an AVP—Treasury with SBI and worked across verticals like Forex, Global market research, Bonds, Derivatives, Stocks.

Anca Bocanet is Assistant Professor and Program Team Leader at the Higher Colleges of Technology in the UAE. She earned her Ph.D. in Science and Technology Management from University of Naples Federico II, Italy. She teaches a variety of courses for the Business Analytics Program. Dr. Anca earned her Ph.D. in Science and Technology Management from University of Naples Federico II, Italy in 2011. Her current research interests include complexity theory and systems, organizational learning, and innovation and entrepreneurship. Her latest research contributes to the debate on corporate innovation–productivity trade-off in the context of new ventures creation.

Ayesha Farooq a Nuffic fellow, is a Professor of Strategy at the Department of Business Administration, Aligarh Muslim University, Aligarh, India. Her significant research themes are strategy, sustainability, and entrepreneurship. Dr. Farooq is a resource person at many management schools, with special mention of the Cadbury Centre, University of Birmingham (UK) and created video content for UOB.

Shazia Farooq Fazli is working as Assistant Professor in the Department of Sociology, Aligarh Muslim University, Aligarh, India. Her areas of interest include reproductive health & reproductive rights of women and counselling to create awareness regarding AIDS. She has worked at Bill & Melinda Gates Foundation working on women-related issues.

Rihab Grassa is Faculty in the Higher Colleges of Technology in Dubai-UAE as well as external associate researcher for the Laboratoire Interdisciplinaire de Gestion Université–Enterprise in the High Institute of Accounting and Business Administration, University of Manouba, Tunisia. She remains actively engaged in the Islamic Finance industry, through preparing reports for governmental and financial institutions, conference contributions, research, publishing, and drafting of reports and case studies. She has published a wide variety of academic papers and conference proceedings, and has presented on topics related to Islamic banking, Islamic finance, economic growth, financial development, Sukuk market, risks, governance. Dr. Rihab serves as associate editor and board editor in high indexed journals such as Journal of Islamic Accounting and Business Research, Journal of Economic Development and Cooperation, Indonesian Journal of Sustainability, Accounting and Management, and Journal of Islamic Monetary Economics and Finance. Also, she is the guest editor of two special issues in Journal of Financial Reporting and Accounting and International Journal of Accounting, Auditing and Performance Evaluation.

Magdalena Karolak is Associate Professor of Humanities and Social Sciences at Zayed University, UAE. She received her Ph.D. in Linguistics, M.A. in Political Science and M.A. in Latin American Studies, and BA in French Language. Prior to working at ZU, Dr. Karolak held Assistant Professor positions in Bahrain and Saudi Arabia. In 2014–2015, she was an American Political Science Association MENA Fellow. Her research interests include transformations of societies in the MENA region and comparative linguistics. Dr. Karolak has published more than 50 journal articles and book chapters on the shifting gender relations, social media, culture and identity, and political system transformations in the MENA countries. She is the author of three scholarly monographs.

Annamarie Lawrence is a Senior Consultant for Tribal Group, a UK-based global education consultancy. Her global experience includes supporting Bahrain Government with establishing work integrated teaching and learning models for employers and higher education to work closer together. Her technical and strategic experience has been utilized in her contributions to national policy offering support for integrated policy that supports both education and labour market interventions. Her policy experience includes contributing to national innovation policy, national research policy, apprenticeships policy, and leading a policy initiative to govern professional standards for applied learning practitioners. Her research interests cover international education policy, EdTech policy gap for industry 4.0, policy impact assessments and the integration of skill policy on the labour market. Annamarie holds a master's degree in Human Capital Development from Gothenburg University, Sweden, and a Senior Fellowship from the UK Higher Education Academy. In addition, Annamarie holds credentials in education policy, quality assurance in education, work integrated learning, policy impact assessments, and Theory of Change models.

Cameron Mirza is the Chief of Party for Pre-Service Teacher Education in Jordan, a USAID programme. In 2021, he launched a new pre-service teaching diploma with 4 public universities. Previously, Cameron was MENA Director for Nottingham Trent University working with governments to close skills gaps and spent several years reforming the higher education sector of the Kingdom of Bahrain. First, as Head of Strategy at the Ministry of Higher Education, then as Director of Strategy for the University of Bahrain. Cameron led the University to its highest position in the QS World, Arab rankings, and Times Impact rankings. In the UK, Cameron was responsible for delivering such programmes as the Respect Action Plan, the youth action plan, young apprenticeships, family intervention programme, review of diversity in the curriculum, and review of child poverty while at the Department for Education and Skills. Cameron was also an advisor to the Ministry of Higher Education for Egypt, supporting the improvement of over 40 Universities in Partnership with the Egyptian Knowledge Bank. Cameron is a board member of BETT MEA and sits on the board of Global Impact Initiative, a Texas-based NGO.

Ashraf Mishrif is Oman Chamber of Commerce and Industry Chair in Economic Studies at Sultan Qaboos University. Prior to that, he was senior lecturer at King's College London, and taught at several universities including Qatar University, Anglia Ruskin University in Cambridge, Greenwich University among others, where he established and led several research clusters and doctoral programmes in economic development, political economy, international trade and investment, economic diversification, and private sector development. Dr. Mishrif assumed several executive posts, including Managing Director of EU-MED International, Cultural Advisor for the Egyptian Embassy Education Bureau in London, and member of the Academic Board of Directors, Boston Business Management School, Singapore. He is the editor of the Palgrave Macmillan Book Series Political Economy of the Middle East. His research interests include economic development; political economy; foreign trade and investment; industrial policy; and private sector development. He recently authored Omani Private Sector and its contribution to sustainable development (SQU Press, 2022), and co-edited the books *Economic Diversification in Gulf Countries: The Private Sector as an Engine of Growth, Vol. I*; and *Economic Diversification in Gulf*

Countries: Comparing Global Challenges, Vol. II (Palgrave Macmillan 2018).

Robert Mogielnicki is a Senior Resident Scholar at the Arab Gulf States Institute in Washington. He manages the institute's political economy research and oversees 'Next Gen Gulf'—a long-term research series that examines how advanced technologies shape Gulf Arab governments and economies. Dr. Mogielnicki is also an Adjunct Assistant Professor at Georgetown University's Center for Contemporary Arab Studies, where he teaches a graduate-level seminar on China–Middle East Relations, and he is the Middle East and North Africa advisor with Freedom House for a year-long research project on global media and technology influence. He published his monograph, A Political Economy of Free Zones in Gulf Arab States, with Palgrave Macmillan's international political economy series in April 2021. Dr. Mogielnicki holds a D.Phil. degree from the University of Oxford's Magdalen College and an MPhil degree in Modern Middle Eastern Studies from the University of Oxford's St Antony's College.

Mariam Orkodashvili has been affiliated with Pennsylvania University; UC Berkley; MIT; California State University; Peabody College of Education, Vanderbilt University, USA; Tbilisi State University, Georgia; Georgian American University; The Parliament of Georgia; Max Planck Institute for Social Anthropology, Halle-Saale, Germany; Education Research Institute in Washington, D.C.; and Edinburgh University, Scotland, UK. Her research interests include education policy; education discourse analysis; media discourse analysis; language change, evolution, and variation; cognitive linguistics, neuroscience, and biolinguistics. Mariam Orkodashvili's publications have appeared in SAGE Encyclopedia of Theory (SAGE publications); Oxford Studies in Comparative Education; International Perspectives on Higher Education Institutions (Peter Lang Publishers); Sociology of Education (SAGE publication); European Education: Issues and Studies (Routledge: Taylor & Francis); Comparative and International Education (Sense Publishers); International Perspectives on Education and Society (Emerald Publishers, UK); The Jon Ben Sheppard Journal of Practical Leadership (UTPB Publication); The Journal of Democratization (Heldref Publications); Peabody Journal of Education (Routledge: Taylor & Francis).

Annalisa Pavan is an International Relations graduate and Ph.D. holder from the University of Padova, Italy, where she is Professor of International Policies on Education. She has been a Visiting Researcher at SOAS, University of London, (2015) and at the King Faisal Center for Research and Islamic Studies, Riyadh (2016). Her research interests and publications include Saudi, Kuwaiti and Emirati government-funded study abroad scholarship programmes, the ongoing socio-cultural changes in Saudi Arabia, the development of the Saudi leisure tourism industry, and the image of Saudi Arabia in Western media. Affiliation: University of Padova, ITALY.

Anisur Rahman is currently Professor and Director, UGC-Human Resource Development Centre, Jamia Millia Islamia, New Delhi (India). He holds Master's in Economics from AMU, Aligarh) as well as Sociology, M.Phil. and Ph.D. from, JNU, New Delhi. He has teaching and research experience of more than 25 years. His area of interest includes South Asian Migration and Diaspora, Gulf Social Demography, Issues of Higher Education and Minorities. He has published 8 books and over 50 Research Papers in Reputed Journals in India and abroad including his contributions as chapters in edited books by well-known scholars. Dr. Rahman has presented over 80 Research Papers in several Conferences/Seminar/Workshops in India and Abroad. He has visited several countries like the USA, the UK, France, Germany, the Netherlands, Sweden, Denmark, Switzerland, Hong Kong, Saudi Arabia, and the UAE. He visited Paris, France as Visiting Professor thrice for research in 2010, 2013, and 2015. He has delivered over 130 invited talks at different institutions of higher learning in India and abroad. He is also a member of several academic committees, bodies, and editorial boards.

Linda Smail is Associate Professor in the College of Interdisciplinary Studies at Zayed University, Dubai, United Arab Emirates where she teaches Mathematics and Statistics courses. She obtained her Ph.D. in Mathematics from the Applied Mathematics Laboratory at Marne-La-Vallée University, France in 2004. Her research interests include graphical models and Bayesian Networks. Dr. Smail is particularly interested in inference in Bayesian Networks and learning in graphical models with a focus on exact inference algorithms for Bayesian networks. Her primary scholarly goal is to conduct research and use Bayesian Networks in different fields from Medical, Entrepreneurship, to decision making under uncertainty. Dr. Smail is active in pursuing research in applied mathematics and statistics, but after she joined Zayed University an unexpected opportunity to work with faculty from the business, Nutrition, and public health departments on their research and their students' senior projects. It ignited in her a passion for interdisciplinary research. Her latest research deals with knowledge of Emirati women and their attitudes toward menopause, the quality of life of Emirati women with breast cancer, and entrepreneurial intentions among Emirati youth.

Sowmya Vivek is Director of Quality Assurance and Institutional Effectiveness in EM Normandie, UAE. Prior to that, she was head of research at Emirates Institute of banking and Financial Studies (EIBFS), UAE, and head of quality for Deposit Operations in ICICI Bank, India. Dr. Vivek is a seasoned banker/academician, with 17 years of work experience in banking and training/academics in India, Kuwait, Bahrain, and UAE. She trained more than 5000 bankers in the areas of operational risk management and controls, credit risk management, retail analytics and finance, retail banking operations, process management, and engineering and quality management. Dr. Vivek holds Ph.D. in Management from University of Liverpool. She is currently working on her second doctorate (DBA) in quality management from SP Jain Global school of Management, Australia. She also earned a master's degree in economics from Delhi School of Economics. Her areas of research include GCC economies, Sectors and Banking environment particularly the areas of operational risk management and Islamic banking.

Abbreviations

4IR	Fourth Industrial Revolution
AI	Artificial Intelligence
CAA	Commission for Academic Accreditation
CPS	Cyber-Physical System
DEL	Digital Enhanced Learning
ECD	Early Childhood Development
EOI	Export-Oriented Industrialization
FDI	Foreign Direct Investment
GCC	Gulf Cooperation Council
GDP	Gross Domestic Product
GIA	Global Innovation Alliance
HEIs	Higher Education Institutions
HRT	Hormone Replacement Theory
IIoT	Industrial Internet of Things
ILP	Individual Learning Portfolio
IMF	International Monetary Fund
IoT	Internet of Things
KASP	King Abdullah Scholarship Program
NCDs	Non-Communicable Diseases
OECD	Organisation for Economic Cooperation and Development
QNRF	Qatar National Research Fund
QSTP	Qatar Science and Technology Park
R&D	Research and Development
SMEs	Small and Medium Enterprises
SWFs	Sovereign Wealth Funds
TAP	Tertiary Action Plan

TEL	Technology Enhanced Learning
TFR	Total Fertility Rate
TVET	Technical and Vocational Education and Training
UAE	United Arab Emirates
WB	World Bank
WEF	World Economic Forum
WIPO	World Intellectual Property Organization

List of Figures

Chapter 3

Fig. 1	Interrelationship among attributes (*Source* Harvey et al. 1997)	68
Fig. 2	Work-integrated practices and employability skills (*Source* Authors)	72
Fig. 3	In-house WIL practices	75
Fig. 4	Outside B-school practices	78
Fig. 5	Leadership development	79
Fig. 6	Teamwork	80
Fig. 7	Initiatives by students	81
Fig. 8	Interpersonal skills	82
Fig. 9	Communication skills	83
Fig. 10	Critical reasoning and analytical skills	83
Fig. 11	Planning and organising skills	84
Fig. 12	Influencing factors on employers	86

Chapter 4

Fig. 1	Crude birth rate in GCC countries (per 1000 people) (*Source* From World Bank Data)	101
Fig. 2	Crude death rate in GCC Countries (per 1000 people) (*Source* World Bank Data)	103
Fig. 3	Fertility rate (births per woman) in GCC countries (*Source* From World Bank Data)	104

Chapter 6

Fig. 1 Combining 'high-tech' and 'high-touch' skills as required by current healthcare era (OECD 2021: 55) 159
Fig. 2 ADE^2 Heuristic Model: Combining three interconnected processes in healthcare professionals' L&D 169

Chapter 8

Fig. 1 Research framework 211
Fig. 2 Demographics of the participants 213
Fig. 3 The top training requirement for UAE nationals 214
Fig. 4 Ranking in terms of skills 214
Fig. 5 UAE nationals' response on the level of training required WRT creativity and innovation 215
Fig. 6 UAE nationals' response on the level of training required WRT Systemic thinking 215
Fig. 7 UAE nationals' response on the level of training required WRT critical thinking 216
Fig. 8 UAE nationals' response on the level of training required WRT agility and lifelong learning 217
Fig. 9 UAE nationals' response on the level of training required WRT communication and collaboration 218
Fig. 10 UAE nationals' response on the level of training required WRT technology, digitization and analytics 218
Fig. 11 UAE nationals' response on the level of training required WRT risk management and compliance 219
Fig. 12 UAE nationals' response on the level of training required WRT customer relationship management 220
Fig. 13 UAE nationals' response on the level of training required WRT core banking products and management and leadership development 221

Chapter 11

Fig. 1 Women by education level 278
Fig. 2 Source of information about menopause 280
Fig. 3 The percentages of women who knew about menopause symptoms 281
Fig. 4 The percentages of women who knew about HRT risks 282
Fig. 5 The percentages of women who knew about HRT benefits 282

Chapter 12

Fig. 1 UAE Unemployment 1991–2020 (% of total labor force) 298
Fig. 2 Top obstacles of Emiratization in the UAE private sector 302

List of Tables

Chapter 2

Table 1	Oil revenue as a percentage of GDP, state budget, and Tax revenue of total revenues in the GCC countries	35

Chapter 3

Table 1	Strategy of systematic review	62
Table 2	In-house WIL practices	76
Table 3	Outside B-school practices	78
Table 4	Leadership development	79
Table 5	Teamwork	80
Table 6	Initiatives by students	81
Table 7	Interpersonal skills	82
Table 8	Communication skills	83
Table 9	Critical reasoning and analytical skills	84
Table 10	Planning and organising skills	84
Table 11	Influencing factors on employers	85

Chapter 4

Table 1	National and foreign populations in the GCC countries from 1975 to 2016	94
Table 2	Total population and percentage of nationals and non-nationals during 2014–2016	95
Table 3	Country rating—quality of education	97

Table 4	Government spending on education as a % of total budget expenditure (2018)	98
Table 5	Gross Enrolment Ratio (GER) in percentage among the GCC countries	99
Table 6	Current healthcare expenditure in the GCC	106
Table 7	Size of Indian workers in the Gulf countries 1991–2017	110
Table 8	Top ten labour sending Indian states during 2010–2017	110

Chapter 5

Table 1	Predominant business directions across universities in Qatar and UAE	145
Table 2	Student perceptions of business education priorities	145
Table 3	Predominant IT directions across universities in Qatar and UAE	145
Table 4	Student perceptions of IT education priorities	145

Chapter 9

Table 1	Agile and its application in education policy making	236

Chapter 11

Table 1	Knowledge of Menopause	279
Table 2	Knowledge and HRT practice	280

Chapter 12

Table 1	Workforce distribution by gender and sector in UAE in 2019	300
Table 2	Demographic characteristics of the sample	306
Table 3	Motivations and preferences for work	307
Table 4	Reasons beyond choosing government of private sector	308
Table 5	Sector preferences	310
Table 6	Relocation	311
Table 7	Reason for refuse of relocation	311
Table 8	Obstacles for Emiratization	312

CHAPTER 1

The Nexus Between Higher Education, Labour Market, and Industry 4.0 in the Context of the Arab Gulf States

Ashraf Mishrif, Magdalena Karolak, and Cameron Mirza

1 Introduction

The nexus between higher education and labour market has been narrowly examined in the Gulf context. The need for re-examining this relationship is urgently required considering the changing demographic structure and socioeconomic conditions in the Gulf region and the increasingly globalized labour market. We also observe the impact of

A. Mishrif (✉)
Humanities Research Center, Sultan Qaboos University, Al Khoud, Oman
e-mail: amishrif@squ.edu.om

M. Karolak
College of Humanities and Social Science, Zayed University,
Dubai, United Arab Emirates
e-mail: Magdalena.Karolak@zu.ac.ae

A. Mishrif et al. (eds.), *Nationalization of Gulf Labour Markets*,
The Political Economy of the Middle East,
https://doi.org/10.1007/978-981-19-8072-5_1

globalization on the region, which has been dependent on the international labour market to a large extent to supply foreign workers to fill the significant shortage in the national workforce. The acceleration of globalization and industrialization resulted in the international energy sector dependence on the Gulf oil. This, in turn, contributed to the creation of wealth accompanied by a remarkable phase of economic and social development in the Gulf region during the 1970s and 1990s. Since then, all member states of the Gulf Cooperation Council (GCC) have been classified as high-income countries.

Wealth creation, economic growth and prosperity, and generous social welfare system have all allowed GCC governments to invest in human capital development. All GCC countries have made such investments in education infrastructure, curriculum development, soft skills, and training. They increased the number of students' enrolment through lifelong education programs that encouraged elementary and secondary school students to continue their education until getting their diplomas certificates or undergraduate degrees. Although education is a long-term investment, the efforts made by the GCC countries have paid off, as the number of citizens joining the labour market has significantly increased, particularly in the government and the public sector that is currently oversaturated. The inability of the government to absorb most of the graduates with undergraduate and postgraduate degrees has posed a serious threat to social stability, forcing the governments to nationalize their labour markets.

The nationalization of the GCC labour markets has yet been limited to replacing foreign workers with citizens in the public and, most recently, in the private companies. It is a highly controversial policy, as almost all GCC countries are still dependent on foreign workers. For example, foreign workers constitute around 95% of the total workforce in the UAE. The situation is quite similar in Qatar, Bahrain, Kuwait, while Saudi Arabia are less dependent on expatriates than the smaller Gulf states. We also notice that the private sector is often not attractive to most local workers for potential employment due to lower wages and

C. Mirza
International Research and Exchanges Board (IREX), Washington, DC, USA
e-mail: cmirza@irex.org

unattractive financial incentives and work packages. Although Omanization has reached its peak in the post-COVID-19 pandemic, the share of Omani workers in the private sector has not surpassed 16% of the total workforce in 2021 (Mishrif 2022). Private sector companies often complain about the lack of skills and experience among citizens, hence still unwilling to sacrifice highly skilled expatriates who accept low wages with inexperienced local workers who demand higher wages.

The controversy and debate over the policy of labour market nationalization has also intensified as GCC labour markets have become highly competitive and the type of skills required such as technical and non-technical skills of Industry 4.0 technologies are not widely available locally. Industry 4.0 technologies illustrate the growing trend towards automation and data exchange in technology and processes in the manufacturing sector, including the industrial internet of things (IIoT), the internet of things (IoT), cyber-physical system (CPS), smart factories, smart manufacturing, artificial intelligence (AI), cloud computing, big data analytics, and cognitive computing. In factories, automation allows the manufacturing system to operate wirelessly, whereby machines are automated with wireless connectivity and sensors to monitor the entire production process. This process provides faster response times and allows for near real-time communication between systems. Today, these technologies are widely used in the advanced industrial countries in North America, Europe, and Japan, but they are relatively new and hardly used outside the supply chain sector in many developing countries.

For the GCC countries, the decision to integrate in Industry 4.0 has long been politically made and the pace of engaging in this advanced revolution is increasing. Political and industry leaders are aware that Industry 4.0 technologies will help solve problems, track processes, and increase productivity. They are also working on digital transformation, where almost all GCC countries have high speed internet and 5G and other related technologies. However, the rate of integrating in Industry 4.0 depends largely on the ability of the GCC countries to optimize the gains of industrialization that began in the 1970s and the 1980s. This requires extensive analysis of the socio-economic conditions that drives policy change and adjustment in education and labour market, the efforts made in the development of higher education, investments in research and innovation (R&D), and creation of a highly skilled national workforce that would reduce the dependency on foreign workers. To address these factors, we need to first comprehend the socioeconomic conditions in the GCC countries, and the relationship between higher education and labour market in the context of Industry 4.0.

2 The GCC Socio-economic Context

Gulf Cooperation Council (GCC) countries, namely, Kuwait, Qatar, the United Arab Emirates, Bahrain and Saudi Arabia entered the 2000s with a consciousness that implementing the necessary reforms that would make their economies independent of oil resources (World Bank 2004, p. 42), innovative and competitive at the world level as well as transforming their societies from passive and highly subsidized citizens to active and economically independent individuals, are a must. Such transformations of the economy and the society are underpinned by the overhaul of the education systems that would promote soft skills such as critical thinking, creativity, leadership, communication, etc. instead of rote learning. Indeed, the economic growth of a country is closely linked to the human capital of its population (Denison 1962; Romer 1987). But the GCC countries present a specific context in this regard, one in which heavy reliance on oil profits, the rentier economic model (Luciani and Beblawi 1987), the existence of a large and easily disposable mass of foreign workers as well as oil surplus distributed among citizens in form of free services and subsidies (Hertog 2010, p. 4) created a unique environment with its unique challenges for the future.

The reliance on oil resources has proved a double-edged sword for the GCC economies. Although oil brought prosperity in the 1970s, in the 1980s the GCC economies suffered from falling oil prices, growing financial strain due to the Iraqi invasion of Kuwait and rising expenditures on arms, security, and defence (Luciani and Beblawi 1987). Subsequently, high demographic growth, the cost of developing infrastructures, rising unemployment, and inflation combined with a growing consciousness of a decline in oil supplies have caused further strain on the GCC economies. In addition, having grown accustomed to extensive social welfare measures, rentier state societies entertain high expectations of their governments. The scenario seems to have repeated itself in 2015 with oil barrel prices plunging almost 50% on a year-to-year basis, while in April 2020 the Covid-19 pandemic economic downturn caused oil prices to crash to never-seen before negative levels. This situation caused deficits in the GCC's budgets. Indeed, IMF and Deutsche Bank estimated that Saudi Arabia requires prices to remain at 104 USD per barrel, UAE at 81 USD, Qatar at 77 USD and Kuwait at 78 USD to balance their budgets. Even though in 2022, international events caused oil prices to rise above 100 USD a barrel due to the invasion of Russia on Ukraine, this is only a short-term fix to the GCC's budgets. The long-term plans must take into account the worldwide move towards sustainable energy sources from which there will be no return to a petroleum-based economy (World Economic Forum 2020; Sillanpää and Ncibi 2017).

Consequently, economic constraints and current demographic pressures linked to a rapid population growth call for a holistic strategy to transform the GCC economies at a faster rate. Soon the dwindling oil wealth will have to be divided among a larger population, and there will be considerable pressure on states' budgets to maintain the same level of social welfare (Gause 1997, p. 67) or to rethink fiscal policy, in particular, to increase taxation, which has already started with the introduction of VAT in the UAE, Saudi Arabia, Oman and Bahrain. The drive towards greater sustainability requires substantial economic contributions of the society. However, within a rentier context, the majority of citizens display "low societal capacities" (Hertog 2010, p. 5), which translates into low productivity and high expectations from state resources. Moreover, population of GCC presents specific characteristics compared to the rest of the world. More than 40% of the region's population are under 15 years of age (De Boer and Turner 2007, p. 10). In the past, national workers would be easily absorbed in the public sector where their jobs would be secured indefinitely. At present, they are already forced to compete for jobs in private sector as the public sector is already saturated with nationals. This poses a problem for GCC labour market since foreign workers who dominate the private sector offer better skills and have lower wages expectations (Kapiszewski 2006, p. 13). Lack of appropriate skills also hampers entrepreneurship through which individuals create their own employment.

Data from Ernst & Young Report (2015) suggests that lack of appropriate skills, among others, becomes a major deterrent in broader participation of the nationals in the skilled workforce. Moreover, students prefer humanities to technical fields of study that are most needed on the job market. Data from Linkedin, for instance, shows that among GCC university graduates in 2017 only 7% of GCC digital professionals studied locally. Thus, those who graduate do not possess adequate skills to compete with expatriates in the private sector. There is also insufficient initiative for startup businesses among nationals. On the other hand, the public sector is saturated. In the UAE, public jobs account for 80% of national employment (WEF 2017, p. 4). Such dependence on public employment leads to major distortions such as: the private sector offers employees greater returns on education in terms of wages; yet the educational system remains disconnected from the requirements of the private sector employment (ibid., p. 9). All in all, there has been little incentive for nationals to seek jobs in the private sector. Consequently, in the early 2000s GCC the problems of youth unemployment (Kabbani and Kothari 2005, p. 4) and structural unemployment, which is unemployment "by choice", exacerbated (McKinsey & Company 2007, p. 6).

The policies of nationalization often led to employment of nationals in areas other than those they are qualified for and to job creation for the sake of the employment of nationals through the quota system, for instance; both leading to decreasing productivity coupled with high costs. Ultimately, a failure to satisfy the population demands, especially in economic terms, threatens the long-term social stability of the region. Former studies concluded that labour market nationalization in the Gulf has been mostly achieved by "quotas and prohibitions" (Hertog 2012a, b, p. 1). This trend was amplified by the pandemic and its fallout with some of the GCC governments reserving specific fields of the economy solely to national employment (Saudi Arabia, Oman), raising the fees of foreign workers hiring or those of their dependents (Saudi Arabia, Oman), as well as sending some of the foreign worker population back to their home countries (Kuwait, Oman, Bahrain, Saudi Arabia) and imposing financial penalties on companies not complying with nationalization quotas (UAE). The results of those policies varied in the past. Qatar and UAE's national population accounted for 10–15% of the private sector employees total but it increased to 62% in Saudi Arabia, the latter reaching the highest percentage scores among the GCC countries (Carvalho et al. 2017). There are also attempts to balance the ratio between men and women in the workforce.

In the past, economic reforms undertaken by the GCC had usually limited results (Al Qudsi 1998). They lacked a comprehensive and holistic approach based on economic policy, sound regulatory frameworks and education and training reform that would combine transformation of "private sector participation, labor markets, financial markets and human resources" to yield significant results (Shochat 2008, p. 6). They also lacked political will (Sick 1997, p. 12). Contrary to the past undertakings, the packages of through economic reforms adopted in the late 2000s by the GCC governments, branded as "Visions", offer a holistic approach. The extensive expenditure on healthcare, education and training ought to increase the human capital in the GCC region (Al Yahya 2010). Indeed, within the context of the transformation of society, education reforms are a key concern in light of digital disruption. Education and innovation could pave the way to the region's sustainability by promoting a shift from oil to knowledge-based economy (Hvidt 2011, p. 51). However, the region's human capital assessment falls significantly behind the world average. UNDP's Arab Human Development Reports and the two Arab World Competitiveness Reports (2002–2003 and 2005) stressed that education, research and development are weak in the region, and that education systems lack relevance through systems focusing on inputs rather than outcomes. This serious shortage "exacerbates other problems associated with importing both foreign workers and technologies" (Davis and Hayashi 2007, p. 2). The World Bank's report, "The Road Not Traveled: Education Reform in the Middle East and North Africa" highlights the fact that despite major investment, the MENA region achieved minimal results in the education. The latter was witnessed in international educational assessment tests such as TIMSS, PISA and PIRLS, while at higher education graduate employability is a key metric often cited. While some GCC countries, notably the UAE and Bahrain (Karolak 2012), experienced improvements in the international test scores results, the Arabian Gulf region falls below the all-participating countries averages and remains way behind the top scorers from Asia (Mullis et al. 2020). The GCC spending on Research & Development, a key component of the economic growth, also continues to lag behind the global averages of developed countries (McKinsey & Company 2020).

3 Higher Education and Labour Market in the GCC Countries

While the region's young people have attained higher education levels than their parents, they have not been able to translate their education attainment to greater income opportunities. Furthermore, the era of Industry 4.0 offers new opportunities but also presents new challenges. The potential for technology to disrupt the GCC labour market is powerful. 45% of existing work activities worldwide are potentially automatable today which cuts across both public and private sector (McKinsey Quarterly 2015). This automation potential could translate into significant economic value, but it also places pressure on education systems to produce graduates with a new set of skills which is beyond academic attainment. According to the IBM Institute for Business Report (2019, p. 6), the shortage of skilled workers by 2030 is expected to reach more than 85 million workers globally. Today the half-life of a learned skill is expected to be five years and even shorter for technical skills. Skills required nowadays take longer to learn because of the focus on behavioural skills and soft skills. Other new technology-related skills also take more time as they are highly technical and change rapidly. The role of education is primordial to prepare graduates to fit in within these new labour market conditions. The Covid-19 pandemic has only accelerated the shift to digital technologies and disrupted the work environments offering flexible online work and requiring lifelong learning from the workforce. In turn, the educational systems are under more pronounced pressure to provide their graduates with the appropriate skills. This is especially true for Higher Education Institutions that "need to create a framework for blended and multi-disciplinary programs in order to meet the demands of the digital economy and continually changing workplaces" (World Government Summit 2022, p. 10).

The need for high and technical skills is also driven by the industrial development in the GCC countries, which experienced a relative increase in the share of manufacturing to gross domestic product (GDP) compared to other non-oil sectors and subsequently the rise in the percentage of the workforce employed in this sector. This is statistically confirmed as the share of the manufacturing sector in total GCC GDP averages 10%, while the rate of urbanization reaches an unprecedented level with almost 80% of the population live in urban areas (Mishrif 2018a, b). For example, the growing demand for advanced knowledge and high skills in engineering is associated with the changes in the physical landscape and built environment. The GCC region is now marked by skyscrapers and smart cities and the economy is increasingly diversified in service industries such as tourism, financial services, insurance, banking, real estate services, transportation, restaurants, and repair and maintenance services.

Mishrif (2018b) attributes the success of Gulf industrialization to three main industrial policy instruments: finance, labour, and innovation. He acknowledges that all GCC countries have developed an efficient financial system that can supply sufficient capital flows constantly and at a short pace of time. The GCC countries possess 14 of the largest 34 sovereign wealth funds globally, with estimated capital and assets worth US$3 trillion, accounting for almost 40% of total global assets of sovereign wealth funds (Mishrif and Akkas 2018). He argues that:

> The strength of the Gulf financial system is evident in its solid financial structure and its capacity to balance between the demand for investment and the supply of capital. The Gulf banking and finance sector has become more diverse to cover all aspects on retail banking, corporate banking, investment banking, bond markets, debts markets, deposits, capital markets, pension funds, insurance, and asset management. (p. 7)

In terms of labour policy, Mishrif (2018a, b) maintains that the current demographic structure reveals high dependency on international labour markets for the supply of labour due to shortage in local workforce. He attributes the segmentation in the labour market between the public and private sector and the imbalance between the national and foreign workforce to the preference of most nationals to work for the government and the public sector because of high salaries and other generous incentives such as short working hours, long holidays, early retirement, and generous pension.

To address these structural challenges in the labour market, Mishrif (2018a, b) suggests the introduction of two major policies, namely the nationalization of labour market and reforming the education system, particularly higher education that deals with innovation and research and development (R&D). Labour market nationalization aims at creating job opportunities for nationals. The second policy is the development of the higher education system. All GCC countries have made huge strides in developing their higher education, with investments in physical infrastructure that include the establishment of numerous education cities and research complexes furnished with advanced laboratories and high-tech equipment. To offer some points of comparison, the first institution of higher education in the UAE opened in 1976, while in 2022 there are 76 such institutions operating in the country. Similarly, in Saudi Arabia, the first university was established in 1957; currently, there are 88 institutions of higher learning in the kingdom.

However, there is an urgency to invest in R&D and develop national innovation systems, as their average of 0.89% of GDP is far below the world average of 3% (Mishrif 2018a, b). When it comes to the nexus between education and Industry 4.0, we need to stress here that these countries should improve their higher education through the creation and development of national innovation systems.

We define national innovation system here as a comprehensive system that comprises political, economic, and social factors affecting innovation such as the education system, financial system, regulatory system, strength of innovation institutions, and organization of private companies. GCC countries have committed themselves to the creation of a knowledge-based economy that is driven by innovation and entrepreneurship. The number of entrepreneurship programs has increased in national and private universities, with the aim of developing entrepreneurial knowledge and skills. Government organizations are established to promote entrepreneurial activities by providing subsidized technical and vocational training, language skills, and financial support to small and medium enterprises (SMEs) and start-up companies throughout their early years of operations. Moreover, publicly funded R&D programs are increasingly directed to new industries and innovating firms to identify, adapt, and transfer technology from their foreign counterparts, through trade or joint ventures as well as to create innovative startups in the GCC spurring technological invention. The Entrepreneurial Nation initiative in Abu Dhabi is a good example of the latter, providing support for entrepreneur with an aim to establish 20 unicorn companies by 2031.

4 Innovation Through Higher Education and Industry 4.0

Since the turn of the twenty-first century, GCC countries have strived to build knowledge economies in order to face challenges such as a growing youth population, volatile oil prices, economic diversification, and the need to build human capital to compete globally (Al-Kuwāirī 2012; Miniaoui and Schiliro 2016). Since entrepreneurship and innovation can play in contributing to national development by generating a number of economic and social benefits, GCC countries have formulated policies to promote entrepreneurship and innovation among its young population as part of their national vision and development agenda (Buckner et al. 2012; Silatech 2010).

For example, the United Arab Emirates (UAE) has encouraged entrepreneurial ambitions of Emirati youth by introducing an innovation policy within the public education sector as part of its national innovation strategy (Miniaoui and Schiliro 2016; UAE Ministry of Cabinet Affairs

2015). Qatar's national development strategy uses the term entrepreneurship 21 times and speaks of innovation 48 times. Consistent with its strategy, the Qatari government created entities such as the Qatar Development Bank and Enterprise Qatar to support and develop the country's small and medium sized enterprises (Silatech 2010). Similarly, Bahrain established the Bahrain Development Bank, Economic Development Board, and Tamkeen to lead private sector growth through innovative and entrepreneurial activities. In fact, outright services, and resources such as financial grants, training and advisory programs, and incubators are directly delivered by various government and quasi-government bodies (Preuss 2011).

Despite such investments to spur entrepreneurship and innovation, GCC countries have nevertheless lagged behind their comparable countries in the world in terms of educational achievement, production of knowledge and research, and development of scientific and technological advances (Tadros 2015). In fact, the GII Report in 2016 showed that GCC countries are situated within the upper middle range of the Global Innovation Index ranking. At the same time, however, the GII Report 2016 also explicitly states that "despite these top ranks, and compared to their level of development, resource-rich countries in the [Arab] region could rank higher" (Dutta et al. 2016).

An area of development within GCC countries that could contribute to increasing innovativeness is higher education. In fact, the triple helix of university–industry–government interactions, where innovation and entrepreneurship are at the centre, has been a model adopted throughout the globe for the development of a knowledge-based economy (Etzkowitz 2008). It draws from the innovative practice of elite American universities where they actively sought after and received government and industry funding for research and development, which in turn, also facilitated economic and technology development of their respective cities and regions (O'Mara 2005). In other words, universities are central to the triple helix approach. They are often considered to be the engine of the economy and are generally positioned at the centre of attention by policy makers desiring to foster technological developments and innovations and to sustain an economy based on knowledgeable and skilled human capital (Weber 2011; Markkula and Kune 2015). A report released in 2019 by the European University Association entitled "The role of universities in regional innovation ecosystems", states that universities' access to international research is a key source of innovation potential and authority in the eyes of businesses and government agencies. The report further asserts that universities play a pivotal role in society as an institution of knowledge creation in post-industrial economies (Reichert 2019). These assertions assume that a quality higher education system that can support and sustain research and development is present. It also assumes that what is being taught in the universities is of quality and relevant to the needs and demands for a knowledge-based economy.

So then, in what ways do universities in the Arab Gulf play a role in contributing to innovation and entrepreneurship development in their respective countries in the context of the 4th Industrial Revolution? To what extent are higher education policies and subsequent activities aligned with national efforts to spur innovation? And how have universities, especially national flagship universities, worked to improve their quality not only to support national development efforts but also be internationally competitive in an increasingly digitally disrupted era and dynamic labour market?

In considering the above questions, it is important to note that it is insufficient for governments and universities to create structures and environments that support innovative and entrepreneurial activities. Equally as important is the presence of individuals who will take advantage of the resources and opportunities. And for rentier contexts like the GCC where the majority of its citizens display "low societal capacities" (Hertog 2010), it becomes even more critical that young people are not only equipped with the skills and knowledge to engage in innovation but also instilled with positive attitudes, motivation, and desire to innovate. So then, to what extent are universities engaged in activities that spur and build a culture of innovation and entrepreneurship among the young? And what opportunities and challenges do universities face in trying to foster a culture of innovation?

5 Industrial Policy and Industry 4.0 in the GCC Countries

The real shift towards Industry 4.0 in the Gulf region has already begun with the introduction of Export-Oriented Industrialization (EOI). Mishrif (2018a, b) argues that GCC countries have embarked on the creation of industrial cities and business clusters with a degree of specialization in each location to reflect comparative cost advantages in terms of exploiting raw materials, transportation, and consumer markets. The Jebel

Ali Free Zones, Dubai Industrial City, and King Abdullah Economic City have not only become major manufacturing powerhouses and hubs for high-tech companies in various industries, but they also serve as means of stimulating economic development, urbanization, and employment generation. The development of integrated transportation and logistics network to support the supply chain system has put the GCC countries closer to Industry 4.0 than ever before. Indeed, GCC countries have established many modern airports and seaports that connect their industrial cities, free zones, and business hubs with the rest of the world (Beblawi 2011), however, it is the introduction and application of advanced technologies such as big data analytics, internet of things, cloud computing and artificial intelligence in the logistics and supply chain system that accelerates the integration of these countries in Industry 4.0.

Finally, we argue that the nexus between higher education, labour market, and Industry 4.0 is best illustrated in the development of a new division of labour in the GCC region. Mishrif (2018a, b) argues that the structure of the labour market stipulates changes in the education system to address the mismatch between the type of educational programs and the requirements of the labour market. He advocates specialization in education programs, which should concentrate more on science and engineering and transferable skills to create a new generation of scientists, engineers, physicists, and economists. This emphasis is vital for specialization in the production process and division of labour, while producing a meaningful outcome of labour market nationalization programs. Mishrif (2018a, b) also argues that the current labour importing strategy must change, as most expatriates are unskilled labour. The next wave of expatriates must concentrate on skilled and high-skilled labour for the innovative and technology-based industries to flourish. The UAE has already extended its long-term residence offer for expatriates in order to attract high-skilled labour, innovators, and entrepreneurs.

6 Motivation, Reasons, and Structure of the Book

6.1 *The Motivations and Reasons of the Book*

This book addresses the critical aspects of the nationalization of labour market in the Gulf countries. The aim is to examine the role of higher education institutions in providing the market with the right skills that are most needed and preparation of the workforce for the types of skills required by Industry 4.0 technologies. The book also explores the new dynamics of technology and information systems in upgrading the skills, changing the work environment, and generating employment for the youth in the Gulf countries. The holistic approach of the subject area makes this volume indispensable for academics, researchers, students, and policy makers in the Gulf region and beyond.

The book covers a broad range of topics including the nationalization of labour market programs such as Emiratization, Omanization, and Saudization, the attitude towards women in the workplace, and the role of high-tech firms in upskilling and enhancing labour productivity. It also provides sector-specific investigations in healthcare, banking, finance, tourism, and hospitality. The analysis is based on original research and primary data collected by a group of scholars from 15 countries and presented in an illustrative, accessible, and concise manner. This book places the Gulf region in the forefront of the debate on the conditions and requirements of labour markets in the age of Industry 4.0.

This book does not only provide a forward-looking approach to the nexus between higher education, labour markets and industrial development for decades to come, but it also provides an educated account and scientific research on the preparedness of the GCC educational systems with regards to the opportunities and challenges posed by Industry 4.0. There has been little assessment so far on how to improve employability of national workers considering the technological change. The discussion on this topic fills in a significant research gap by providing opportunities for assessing and evaluating the current situation, learning from best practices, and providing practical solutions, all of them make this book vital for the future of Gulf economies.

This book also aims at assessing and answering critical questions on the quality of educational reforms. How have Gulf educational institutions and curricula changed to match the current and future needs of the labour markets? With what results? What further steps should be taken to improve the employability of graduates given the changing nature of jobs? How should higher education be changed to meet the demands of Industry 4.0 considering the increasing need for creativity, higher order cognitive thinking, critical thinking, and problem-solving? How does the potential automation of jobs impact nationalization policies? What strategies should universities adopt in light of shifting skills needs and to prepare young people and adults for work rather than for a specific job? What are the strategies to improve female workforce participation given the changing nature of work? What strategies should governments adopt to prepare the workforce for a rapidly changing job market and how can employers be part of an integrated solution? What is the role of universities in upskilling and reskilling employees and wider society as skills become obsolete? What are the outcomes of labour market nationalization strategies in the GCC?

6.2 Structure of the Book

This book is divided into three parts. Part I provides an overview of the higher education system human capital, and labour market in the GCC countries. In Chapter 2, Thamer Al-Ani examines the role of higher education in preparing lifelong learners in the era of Industry 4.0. He argues that the investments made in national projects such as Smart Nation, Skills Future and efforts made by higher education institutions to develop knowledge, soft skills and innovation will upskill the Gulf population and workforce and hence facilitate the nationalization of the GCC labour market. He concludes by arguing that although COVID-19 has caused disruption to the current development process, the ongoing plans to develop more holistic education systems that teach students how to learn, rather than what to learn, are vital to meet the demand of the labour market.

Chapter 3 by Shazia Fazli and Ayesha Farooq examines how Work Integrated Learning (WIL) and experiential learning are recognized as significantly contributing to graduates' transition to the workplace in the GCC context. They conclude by evaluating whether WIL has become a panacea to employability and increases job opportunities for graduates in GCC countries.

Chapter 4 by Anisur Rahman raises a critical question on how migrating human capital affects the mode of production in the context of increasingly globalized economy and rising importance of Industry 4.0. He argues that the migration of skilled labour force from India and other South Asian countries has played an important role in the accumulation of human capital in the GCC region. He tries to assess the potential and volume of skilled and non-skilled workers who migrated from India to the GCC countries. He analyses the role of the National Education Policy of India along with the resulting accumulation of human capital in upcoming years while explaining efforts of the GCC countries such as increasing the share of budgetary allocation on R&D, education, training and, skill-oriented curriculum to enhance the skills of their respective citizens.

Part II covers higher education and labour market in selected economic sectors and industries. In Chapter 5, Mariam Orkodashvili explains human capital enhancement through local, international, and online programs in the universities of Qatar and UAE. She attempts to describe the curricula of the selected universities and novel approaches to business education and information technologies and identifies strengths and weaknesses for future improvements that might turn out essential for the future development of human resource management. She puts special emphasis on business, management, and IT fields since these spheres could be viewed as among the most widely involved areas in human capital production and development. As multinational corporations and international companies look for innovation and leadership skills with cross-cultural awareness and global understanding in their employees, Orkodashvili underscores the importance of study programs with international elements and comparative analysis of cross-country practices in higher education institutions of GCC countries.

In Chapter 6, Náder Alyani focuses on the digital healthcare sector. He argues that progressive technology-mediated developments accentuated by the COVID-19 pandemic in digital health sector have caused digital skill mismatches in healthcare professionals. He utilizes the term "right-skilling" to refer to how the new demands on the healthcare professionals require retraining the professional workforce and often acquiring and developing their capabilities with the right skills to fill the gaps in adding value to the emergent digital activities of the healthcare enterprises. He argues that digital learning and right-skilling tools, such as blended learning within a hybrid corporate academy design and ADE heuristic model can assist in addressing the gap in professional performance, outlined as a policy and practice case anchored on the United Arab Emirates. He concludes by summarizing the possibilities offered by digital right-skilling within the Gulf's healthcare sector to build capability and capacity for continuous and sustainable performance enhancement.

Chapter 7 by Analisa Pavan concentrates on the tourism and hospitality sector in Saudi Arabia. Pavan seeks to address critical questions on the massive investments in the Saudi Leisure tourism industry. What are the economic, social, and political goals behind investments to build from scratch and develop the leisure tourism industry? What plans and actions are being adopted by the Saudi leadership to create new employment opportunities for Saudi youth? How are Saudi higher education policies being adjusted, as concerning education and training for the tourism sector, to comply with the Saudi Vision 2030 mandate "to close the gap between the outputs of higher education and the requirements of the job market"? Does the nascent Saudi leisure tourism industry—now reliant on the Public Investment Fund, the Saudi sovereign wealth fund—have the capability to build the skills and, over time, to nurture and sustain the motivations and aspirations of Saudi youth in the quest for stable and well-paid employment? She argues that the development of the leisure tourism industry in Saudi Arabia is currently a work in progress, and as such, a subject of anecdotal talk inside and outside Saudi Arabia. She concludes that, while the current cultural openness (cultural diplomacy) in Saudi Arabia, inspired and managed by foreign consultancies for the most part, is attractive and helps to appease the young, the reality is that basic red lines are still firmly in place and fully enforced. Cultural and economic renaissance will be neither achievable nor sustainable without promoting the social progress of the country.

Chapter 8 presents the case study of workforce nationalization in the banking sector in the UAE. Sowmya Vivek and Allen Baby argue that although Emiratization has been widely implemented in multiple sectors in the country including private and public sectors, the banking and financial services is one of the major employers of UAE nationals. However, the majority of UAE nationals working in the banking sector are currently working in retail banking where jobs are on a decline due to extensive digitization. They conclude by underlining the urgent need to upskill the employees in line with changing skill sets required for the banking sector in the twenty-first century.

Part Three addresses higher education and labour market in selected GCC countries. In Chapter 9, Annamarie Lawrence discusses the prospect of higher education in Bahrain, where she analyses the "Tertiary Action Plan"(TAP), as a new agile policy approach to education reform. Unlike critics of traditional linear policy processes that they do not consider the cultural, social, and economic complexities of the policy context, Lawrence argues that these factors have become particularly important within the future skills agenda driven by Industry 4.0 and post Covid-19 recovery. She argues that the TAP process highlights key themes that describe the "different" approach, including whole system change and different rhetoric used to describe education "transformation" rather than reform; focusing on educational and labour market outcomes over delivering KPIs; and high-level integrated collaboration and responsibility. She concludes by asserting that there is some evidence of agile policy making, but this could be made more explicit by ensuring realist evaluation and monitoring principles are added to implementation of the various TAP initiatives.

In Chapter 10, Robert Mogielnicki explains the experience of the UAE in encouraging technology-driven economic growth and innovation. He argues that policymakers want to position national citizens at the forefront of this technology-oriented economic development, and consequently, they have pursued traditional workforce nationalization policies to ensure the continued participation of citizenry in the region's labour markets. Using the UAE as a case study, his work explores the prospects for better aligning direct labour market interventions with economic growth and development strategies. An Emiratization policy approach focused on digital and technology-oriented skills is raised as an alternative policy option, subjected to critical evaluation, and considered alongside an initial set of recommendations for harmonizing labour market demands with future-oriented growth.

Chapter 11 is also focused on the UAE. Linda Smail argues that health education is a major factor in designing and helping women and communities, in general, improve their health and productivity in the society, by increasing their knowledge or influencing their attitudes. She conducted a community-based study of a random sample of 497 Emirati women aged 30–64 years attending primary health care centres in the Emirate of Dubai to investigate their knowledge about and attitudes toward menopause and menopause Hormone Replacement Theory (HRT). Her study will enable the delivery of better health education based on increased awareness of health issues while enabling healthcare policymakers to create and formulate a healthcare policy that further increases awareness and has the potential to enhance menopausal women's quality of life and therefore reach their full potential at work.

In Chapter 12, Anca Bocanet and Rihab Grassa focus on the UAE by investigating the Emiratization process from an Emirati youth perspective. They assess the challenges of implementing Emiratization through the analysis of primary data collected from more than 3000 Emirati students. The chapter highlights several issues with the Emiratization initiative, including the Emirati culture, policy instruments and laws, and implementation procedures. They conclude by assessing the challenges identified and recommend the necessary changes in regulations and policy mechanisms to ensure the effective implementation of an Emiratization program in the private sector, which can significantly help to alleviate citizen unemployment and ensure their effective integration into the labour market.

The book concludes with key findings presented in the manuscript and identifies the main channels and dynamics through which GCC countries can bridge the gap between education development and labour market needs. Chapter 13 places the current development in the higher education sector and labour policy in the context of industry 4.0. The chapter also defines the types of jobs associated with industry 4.0, while attempting to foresee the prospect of these jobs and related skills in the Gulf region. As the impact of investment on education may take a generation or two to be realized, we wonder how and to what extent will the Gulf countries be able to lessen their heavy dependence on expatriate workers and build a formidable, skilful national workforce capable of fully engaging in the development process.

7 Concluding Remarks

This chapter provided the research background and conceptual underpinnings that govern the relationship between higher education, labour market and Industry 4.0 in the context of the GCC countries. While explaining the socio-economic conditions that brought about radical changes in the education sector and labour market, we highlighted the ineffectiveness of higher education to supply the job market with graduates equipped with the right skills needed in the increasingly globalized labour market so far. Indeed, the outbreak of the COVID-19 pandemic has accelerated the pace of integrating the GCC countries into Industry 4.0. However, successful engagement in Industry 4.0 depends on the ability of the GCC countries to build on its first phase of industrialization and that new industrial policy must take the optimum gains of the accumulated wealth in the past fifty years, the quality and competence of labour, and innovation and technologies that are fundamental for Industry 4.0.

References

Al-Kuwāirī, A. K. (2012). The Visions and Strategies of the GCC Countries from the Perspective of Reforms: The Case of Qatar. *Contemporary Arab Affairs* 5(1), 86–106. https://doi.org/10.1080/17550912.2011.647417.

Al Qudsi, S. (1998). *Labor Markets and Policy in the GCC: Micro Diagnostics and Macro Profiles*. Abu Dhabi: The Emirates Centre for Strategic Studies and Research.

Al Yahya, K. O. (2010). GCC Human Resource Development and Organizational Reform: HR Empowerment and Utilization in Oman and Saudi Arabia. In ECSR (Ed.), *Human Resources and Development in the Arabian Gulf*. Abu Dhabi: ECSR.

Beblawi, H. (2011). Gulf Industrialization in Perspective. In Jean-François Seznec and Mimi Kirk (Eds.), *Industrialization in the Gulf: A Socioeconomic Revolution*. London and New York: Routledge, pp. 185–197.

Buckner, E. et al. (2012). Social Entrepreneurship: Why is it Important Post Arab Spring? Online Survey Report, CCDRL, Stanford University, Bayt.com, and you gov Sarj. http://img.b8cdn.com/images/uploads/article_docs/white_paper_social_entrepreneurship_stanford_bayt_final_13063_EN.pdf.

Carvalho, A., Youssef, J., & Dunais, N. (2017). *Increasing Private Sector Employment of Nationals in the GCC: Labour Policy Options to the Rescue*. Retrieved May 29, 2022, from https://www.ticg.com.kw/content/dam/oliver-wyman/ME/ticg/publications/Increasing-Private-Sector-Employment-Of-Nationals-In-The-GCC.pdf.

Davis, N., & Hayashi, C. (2007). *The Gulf Cooperation Council Countries and the World: Scenarios to 2025: Implications for Competitiveness*. Retrieved March 26, 2016, from https://pdfs.semanticscholar.org/e01d/0ad60e9243bd6a108dc9d4ebeb23d7ddfcd3.pdf.

De Boer, K., & Turner, J. M. (2007). Beyond Oil: Reappraising the Gulf States. *The McKinsey Quarterly*. Retrieved April 1, 2016, from http://www.mckinseyquarterly.com/Economic_Studies/Country_Reports/Beyond_oil_Reappraising_the_Gulf_States_1902%207.

Denison, E. F. (1962). *The Source of Economic Growth in the United State and the Alternatives before US*. New York: Committee for Economic Development.

Dutta, S., Lanvin, B., & Wunsch-Vincent, S. (Eds.). (2016). *Global Innovation Index 2016: Winning the Global Innovation*. Cornell University, INSEAD, and the World Intellectual Property Organization (WIPO), Geneva, pp. 41–42. https://www.wipo.int/edocs/pubdocs/en/wipo_pub_gii_2016.pdf.

Ernst & Young. (2015). *How Will the GCC Close the Skills Gap?* Retrieved May 1, 2016, from https://pdf4pro.com/cdn/how-will-the-gcc-close-the-skills-gap-ey-2bbd9d.pdf

Etzkowitz, Henry. (2008). *The Triple Helix: University–Industry–Government Innovation in Action*. New York and London: Routledge.

Gause, F. G. III. (1997). The Political Economy on National Security in the GCC. In G. G. Sick & L. G. Potter (Eds.), *Essays in Politics, Economy, Security, and Religion*. New York: St. Martin's Press.

Hertog, S. (2010). The Sociology of the Gulf Rentier Systems: Societies of Intermediaries. *Comparative Studies in Society and History* 52(2), 1–37.

Hertog, S. (2012a). *National Employment, Migration, and Education in the GCC*. Cambridge: Gerlach Press.

Hertog, S. (2012b). *A Comparative Assessment of Labor Market Nationalization Policies in the GCC*. Retrieved September 1, 2019, from http://eprints.lse.ac.uk/46746/1/A%20comparative%20assessment%20of%20labor%20market%20nationalization%20policies%20in%20the%20GCC%28lsero%29.pdf.

http://www.ey.com/Publication/vwLUAssets/EY-gcc-education-reporthowwill-the-gcc-close-theskillsgap/$FILE/GCC%20Education%20report%20FINAL%20AU3093.pdf.

Hvidt, M. (2011). Economic Diversification in the Gulf Arab States: Lip Service or Actual Implementation of a New Development Model. In M. Legrenzi & B. Momani (Eds.), *Shifting Geo-Economic Power of the Gulf. Oil Finance and Institutions*. Farnhate: Ashgate Publishing Limited.

IBM Institute for Business Report. (2019). *The Enterprise Guide to Closing the Skills Gap*. Retrieved from https://www.ibm.com/downloads/cas/EPYMNBJA.

Kabbani, N., & Kothari, E. (2005). *Youth Employment in the MENA Region: A Situational Assessment*. Retrieved from http://siteresources.worldbank.org/SOCIALPROTECTION/Resources/SPDiscussionpapers/Labor-Market-DP/0534web.pdf.

Kapiszewski, A. (2006). *Arab Versus Asian Migrant Workers in the GCC Country*. Paper presented at the United Nations Expert Group Meeting on International Migration and Development in the Arab Region: Challenges and Opportunities. Beirut, Lebanon.

Karolak, M. (2012). Upgrading Bahrain's Tertiary Education to Meet the Challenges of Social Development. Revue des mondes musulmans et de la Méditerranée 131, 167–186.

Luciani, G., & Beblawi, H. (1987). *The Rentier State*. New York: Croom Helm.

Markkula, M., & Kune, H. (2015). Making Smart Regions Smarter: Smart Specialization and the Role of Universities in Regional Innovation Ecosystems. *Technology Innovation Management Review, Canda* 5(10). https://timreview.ca/article/932.

McKinsey & Company. (2007). *GCC Education Breakout: Preparing GCC Youth with Skills to Meet Job Market Needs*, GCC Education Leaders Conference. Retrieved April 6, 2011, from faculty.ksu.edu.sa/…/29/Deck%20GCC%20education%20youth.pdf.

McKinsey & Company. (2020). *Reimagining Higher Education in MENAP*. Retrieved June 1, 2022, from https://www.mckinsey.com/industries/education/our-insights/reimagining-higher-education-in-menap?cid=other-eml-alt-mip-mck&hdpid=e8bc9d51-c6d9-4c14-a029-4935c4fe15cf&hctky=3076926&hlkid=9e6965b6715f4f08ab4e14e9c45a62ba.

McKinsey Quarterly. (2015). *Four Fundamentals of Workplace Automation*. Retrieved from https://www.mckinsey.com/business-functions/mckinsey-digital/our-insights/four-fundamentals-of-workplace-automation.

Miniaoui, H., & Schilirò, D. (2016). Innovation and Entrepreneurship for the Growth and Diversification of the GCC Economies, Munich Personal RePEc Archive, MPRA Paper No. 71898, posted 10 Jun 2016 08:08 UTC. https://mpra.ub.uni-muenchen.de/71898/

Mishrif, A. (2018a). Challenge of Economic Diversification in the GCC Countries. In Ashraf Mishrif & Yousuf Al Balushi (Eds.), *Economic Diversification in the Gulf Region: Comparing Global Challenges*, volume 2. Singapore: Palgrave Macmillan, pp. 1–20.

Mishrif, A. (2018b), Industrialization and Diversification Strategies in the GCC Countries, in International Conference on Innovation and Economic Diversification in GCC's National Development Plans (IED18) Organized by Arab Open University in Kuwait—14th & 15th March 2018, pp. 1–13.

Mishrif, A. (2022). *Omani Private Sector: Its Contributions and Role in Economic Development*. Muscat: Sultan Qaboos University Printing Press.

Mishrif, A., & Akkas, E. (2018). Exploring the Connexion Between Sovereign Wealth Funds and Islamic Finance in the Gulf Countries. *International Journal of Economics and Finance* 10(5), 75–86.

Mullis, I. V. S., Martin, M. O., Foy, P., Kelly, D. L., & Fishbein, B. (2020). *TIMSS 2019 International Results in Mathematics and Science*. Retrieved from Boston College, TIMSS & PIRLS International Study Center website: https://timssandpirls.bc.edu/timss2019/international-results/.

O'Mara, M. (2005). *Cities of Knowledge: Cold War Science and the Search for the Next Silicon Valley*. Princeton, NJ: Princeton University Press. 9780691117164.

Preuss, L. (2011). On the Contribution of Public Procurement to Entrepreneurship and Small Business Policy. *Entrepreneurship & Regional Development* 23(9–10), 787–814. https://doi.org/10.1080/08985626.2010.546433.

Reichert, S. (2019). *"The Role of Universities in Regional Innovation Ecosystems" EUA Study, March 2019*. European University Association, Belgium. https://www.eua.eu/downloads/publications/eua%20innovation%20ecosystem%20report%202019-3-12.pdf.

Romer, P. M. (1987). Growth Based on Increasing Returns due to Specialization. *American Economy Review 77*(2), 56–62.

Shochat, S. (2008). *The Gulf Cooperation Council Economies: Diversification and Reform*. LSE Kuwait Programme Introductory Paper.
Sick, G. (1997). The Coming Crisis in the Persian Gulf. In G. Sick & L. G. Potter (Eds.), *The Persian Gulf at the Millennium: Essays in Politics, Economy, Security, and Religion*. New York: St. Martin's Press.
Silatech. (2010). *The Silatech Index: Voices of Young Arabs*. Accessed from https://silatech.org/wp-content/uploads/2018/12/the-silatech-index-voices-of-young-arabs-nov-2010.pdf.
Sillanpää, M., Ncibi, C. (2017). Legacy of Petroleum-Based Economy. In *A Sustainable Bioeconomy*. Cham: Springer. https://doi.org/10.1007/978-3-319-55637-6_1.
Tadros, M. E. (2015). *The Arab Gulf States and the Knowledge Economy: Challenges and Opportunities*. The Arab Gulf States Institute in Washington. https://agsiw.org/wp-content/uploads/2015/07/Tadros_Knowledge-Economy_Rev1.pdf.
UAE Ministry of Cabinet Affairs. (2015). *UAE National Innovation Strategy*. Accessed from https://www.moei.gov.ae/assets/download/1d2d6460/National%20Innovation%20Strategy.pdf.aspx.
Weber, A. S. (2011). The Role of Education in Knowledge Economies in Developing Countries. *Procedia-Social and Behavioral Sciences* 15, 2589–2594. https://doi.org/10.1016/j.sbspro.2011.04.151.
Wiseman, A. W. (2011). *Impact of Science Education on the GCC Labor Market*. Abu Dhabi: The Emirates Centre for Strategic Studies and Research.
World Bank. (2004). Unlocking the Employment Potential in the Middle East and North Africa: Toward a New Social Contract. *MENA Development Report*. Washington: The World Bank.
World Economic Forum. (2017). *The Future of Jobs and Skills in the Middle East and North Africa: Preparing the Region for the Fourth Industrial Revolution*. Retrieved October 8, 2019, from http://www3.weforum.org/docs/WEF_EGW_FOJ_MENA.pdf.
World Economic Forum. (2020). *Renewable Energy Could Power the World by 2050. Here's What That Future Might Look Like*. Retrieved June 1, 2022, from https://www.weforum.org/agenda/2020/02/renewable-energy-future-carbon-emissions/.
World Government Summit. (2022). *The Future of Higher Education in the Knowledge Economy*. Retrieved May 30, 2022, from https://www.worldgovernmentsummit.org/observer/reports/2022/detail/future-of-work-education.

PART I

Overview on Higher Education and Human Capital in the Gulf Region

CHAPTER 2

GCC's Higher Education in Industry 4.0: Preparing Lifelong Learners

Thamer Al-Ani

1 Introduction

GCC's education system has a reputation for preparing excellent science, technology, engineering, and math (STEM) learners, where students learn to the test. This was useful in creating a workforce that crunches and manages numbers efficiently. Creative and critical thinking did not come from this sort of preparation, however. Now plans are under way to develop more holistic education systems that teach students how to learn, rather than what to learn in order to adjust and continue to have an education system that delivers what the economy needs, as well as what nationalization needs.

T. Al-Ani (✉)
Cairo, Egypt
e-mail: thameralany@hotmail.com

A. Mishrif et al. (eds.), *Nationalization of Gulf Labour Markets*,
The Political Economy of the Middle East,
https://doi.org/10.1007/978-981-19-8072-5_2

The efforts are characterized by three main thrusts. They are working to make a more digitally literate and technologically competent population through the Smart Nation and SkillsFuture initiatives. They are creating cohorts of ideation experts through unique higher education opportunities Finally, GCC are nationalizing its population and creating a more globally savvy and connected citizenry. Nationalization of education is important, and higher education institutions can reach out to peer institutions around the world to establish tighter connections with student and faculty exchanges. This is a very important step toward preparing learners to nationalize GCC labor market.

Governments in GCC countries need to focus on bridging the gap between industry and Research (R) and Development (D) centers and increase knowledge absorption by the industrial sector. Incentives such as tax congestion will not be affective in fostering R and D efforts as the countries already have relatively relaxed taxation systems. Instead, competitive grants and subsides can be utilized to help the government direct R and D efforts into specific sectors as a mean of influencing diversification. The most important challenge for GCC countries is creating jobs for the growing working-age population, and reforms are needed to increase the employment of nationals in the private sector.

There is a particular urgency for GCC to lead Industry 4.0 and to wean themselves off the constraints of oil-derived revenues. The world now finds itself being dramatically altered by a new industrial revolution—Industry 4.0—bringing technological developments that will transform economies and societies far more profoundly than any previous period of rapid development and change. While nations around the world are researching and evaluating how they can harness the potential of technology such as big data, robotics, and AI, there is a particular urgency for countries in the Gulf to lead Industry 4.0 and to wean themselves off the constrains of oil-derived revenues. Fortunately, the nature of this threat has been recognized by GCC governments and is most evident in national social and economic development plans such as Saudi Arabia's Vision 2030, which states that "a sophisticated digital infrastructure is integral to today's advanced industrial activities."

Global society is changing because of the shifts in technological capacity. Higher education must change with it. GCC should be at the forefront of innovation in higher education. GCC serves as a model to nations around the world wanting to prepare their workforce with ways of thinking and working that are in demand in the (4IR). GCC's economic prosperity is closely linked to its successful education system. With a population of approximately 57 million people, outstanding development, good public health, and robust economic growth, the employment prospects for most of its citizens have been strong to date. Most of the workforce will need to be upskilled and retrained in the near future.

Finally, there is a particular urgency for GCC to lead Industry 4.0 and to wean themselves off the constraints of oil-derived revenues. The world now finds itself being dramatically altered by the anew industrial revolution—Industry 4.0—bringing technological developments that will transfer GCC learners to nationalize the GCC labor market to achieve very important goals for their national plans.

Methodology, data used, and source of data:

The study relied on the integrated approach that is based on the fact that there is a link between thought and practical reality about the countries of the Gulf Cooperation Council and the impact of the fourth industrial revolution and the performance of the Gulf Cooperation Council countries, which allows mixing between theories that explain phenomena with their practical applications in order to prepare learners. On the other hand, the study relied on the data Published about the Gulf Cooperation Council countries in everything related to them through the publications of the United Nations, the International Monetary Fund, and the World Bank, as well as from other sources. In the end, the descriptive and analytical approach was adopted in the study.

1.1 Objectives

- The paper tries to explain GCC efforts which Smart Nation, Skills-Future, and the efforts of GCCs institutes of higher education will combine to upskill and educate a workforce and citizenship.
- How GCC countries will have opportunities throughout their lifetime to learn new skills?
- How GCCs countries make use of the extensive expenditure on health care, education, and training ought to increase the human capital in the GCC region?
- How Global society is changed through technological capacity?
- Why the higher education institutions in the GCC countries do not produce skilled workers?

- How Policies of labor nationalization for GCC countries have been largely unsuccessful to compete with the well-qualified expatriates?
- How the GCC can reshape its post-COVID-19 education system?

This study constitutes 6 sections, in Sect. 2 we display economic diversification and reduction risk of fluctuations in international oil prices. While Sect. 3 shade the light on the higher education and labor nationalization in GCC countries besides the impact of COVID-19 on economies and education, especially the technologies and ways of working which are keys to the Industry 4.0 concept. Section 4 explains the fourth industrial revolution via the rule of higher education in GCC countries. While Sect. 5 illustrates the investment in human capital in order to prepare learners to nationalize GCC labor market. Conclusion will be covered by Sect. 6, finally Sect. 7 introduces some recommendations.

2 Economic Diversification and Reduction Risk of Fluctuations in International Oil Prices

The economic growth of a country is closely linked to the human capital of its population (Denison 1962; Romer 1987). GCC countries are at a stage where the transformation of their labor markets remains of utmost importance. The beginning of the twenty-first century marked a turning point as it brought an awareness that major social and economic reforms are a must to avoid future economic decline. So far, the GCC economies have relied heavily on oil profits; the rentier economic model (Luciani and Beblawi 1987) has worked with oil surplus distributed among citizens in form of free services and subsidies. Yet, reliance on oil resources has proved a double-edged sword for the GCC economies.

Although oil brought prosperity in the 1970s, in the 1980s the GCC economies suffered from falling oil prices, growing financial strain due to the Iraqi invasion of Kuwait, and rising expenditures on arms, security, and defense (Luciani and Beblawi 1987). Subsequently, high demographic growth, developing infrastructures, rising unemployment, and inflation combined with a growing consciousness of a decline in oil supplies have caused further strain on the GCC economies. In addition, having grown accustomed to extensive social welfare measures, rentier state societies entertain high expectations of their governments.

The scenario seems to have repeated itself in 2015 with oil barrel prices plunging almost 50% on a year-to-year basis. As in the near future the possibly dwindling oil wealth will have to be divided among a larger population, there will be considerable pressure on states' budgets to maintain the same level of social welfare or to rethink fiscal policy, in particular increase taxation. These demographic considerations are combined with a long-term need for economic diversification and a gradual shift away from oil dependency.

Population of GCC presents specific characteristics compared to the rest of the world. More than 40% of the region's population are under 15 years of age (de Boer and Turner 2007, p. 10). As these youth enter the labor market, the GCC national workforce is expected to increase by 30% in 2020 (Shediac et al. 2010, p. 2). In the past, national workers would be easily absorbed in the public sector where their jobs would be secured indefinitely.

At present, they are already forced to compete for jobs in the private sector as the public sector is already saturated with nationals. This poses a problem for GCC labor market since foreign workers who dominate the private sector offer better skills and have lower wage expectations (Kapiszewski 2006, p. 13). Data from Ernsta and Young Report suggests that lack of appropriate skills, among others, becomes a major deterrent in a broader participation of nationals in the skilled workforce. Moreover, students prefer humanities than technical fields of study that are most needed on the job market.

Data from Linkedin, for instance, shows that among GCC university graduates in 2017 only 7% of GCC digital professionals studied locally. Thus, those who graduate do not possess adequate skills to compete with expatriates in the private sector. There is also an insufficient initiative for start-up businesses among nationals. On the other hand, the public sector is saturated. In UAE, public jobs account for 80% of national employment (WEF 2017, p. 4). Such dependence on public employment leads to major distortions such as: the private sector offers employees greater returns on education in terms of wages; yet, the educational system remains disconnected from the requirements of the private sector employment (ibid., p. 9).

There is little incentive for nationals to seek jobs in the private sector. Consequently, the GCC have already begun facing the problem of youth unemployment and structural unemployment, which is unemployment "by choice." In addition, the policies of nationalization often led to the employment of nationals in areas other than those they are qualified for and to job creation of jobs for the sake of the employment of nationals; both leading to decreasing productivity coupled with high costs. Ultimately, a failure to satisfy the population demands, especially in economic terms, threatens the social stability of the region.

Plans should develop more holistic education systems that teach students how to learn, rather than what to learn to adjust and continue to have an education system that delivers what the economy needs.

The GCC countries are adopting three main approaches to diversification. The first focuses on creating a parallel economy to overcome the existing rigid structure and burdensome regulations. This is the case in Saudi Arabia and Kuwait. The second aims at promoting a competitive position in sectors such as finance, tourism, and education. This is the case in the United Arab Emirates, Bahrain, and Qatar. The third approach, common across all the GCC countries but to varying degrees, is related to the economic reform process.

The GCC countries have all launched an economic reform process that aims at encouraging private sector involvement and stimulating non-oil sectors by removing regulatory and administrative barriers (Saif 2009).

There are several reasons to study enhanced diversification as it unfolds in the Gulf States. As pointed out by Kubursi, "were oil supplies everlasting, and the demand for oil strong and continuous, economic diversification would be pointless. The governments of the region would instead need only to ensure the distribution of oil revenues among the population" (Kubursi 1984). However, in the real world, oil resources are finite, and experience shows that both the price of and the demand for oil have fluctuated considerably. A second factor that has brought diversification to the forefront of economic policy in the Gulf region is the simple fact that oil revenues quickly crowd out any other economic activity

These three challenges—income from oil is finite, fluctuates, and is practically the only source of the wealth—have placed the issue of economic diversification on the political agenda of the Gulf countries (Bahrain, Kuwait, Oman, Qatar, Saudi Arabia, and The United Arab Emirates) since oil was discovered.

Economic diversification is, however, not a new strategy among the GCC countries. It has been on the political agenda since oil and gas became the main and almost sole source of income in these countries some half a century ago. Notable projects were established in the 1970s with the specific aim of diversifying the economies by means of investing oil money in productive assets.

The concepts of diversification and industrialization are very often used interchangeably, even though—obviously—they carry different meanings. It is understandable since a diversification process, especially vertical diversification, implies the accumulation of productive capacity within either the manufacturing or the service sector. Industrialization is a much broader process than merely establishing manufacturing industries, it means diversifying the GCC countries, it also entails the process of creating service industries such as tourism, financial services, insurance, banking, real estate services, transportation, restaurants, repair and maintenance services, etc. The aim of diversification is spreading risk by creating a variety of income sources; industrialization in its broadest understanding is the process of creating these diverse income sources in GCC countries. In the literature on diversification, especially of earlier dates, it seems to be the practice to treat diversification merely as the creation of manufacturing industry (Rajiv et al. 2011).

The development of the oil sector is considered as a part of the diversification. The manufacturing sector has been divided into two parts, oil-based and import substitution industries. Therefore, processing crude oil and using gas as feedstock in petrochemical plants will reduce the risk associated with fluctuations in international oil prices, create jobs, and attain a higher value-added. Furthermore, diversification by using import substitution policy will aim at diversity away from oil. It holds a much better prospect of survival after the oil era.

It is very important to mention that diversification means reducing the leading role of the public sector by promoting the growth of the private sector. Obviously, if private sector invests and operates tourism facilities, manufacturing industries, harbors, food processing, etc.; it can no doubt provide a push toward creating a non-oil economy, non-oil exports, and non-oil revenue sources. There are two reasons for the link between diversification and private sector involvement in the GCC countries economy, first, the emphasis on private sector development is seen to create jobs and involve a large section of the population in production. A second reason relates to the issue of foreign direct investment (FDI). Which brings with it not only capital but also, and more importantly, jobs, new technology, and new management methods, as such the potential for GCC countries to attract FDI is severely limited without a well-functioning private sector.

Even after nearly forty years of diversification policies, oil and gas exports still play a significant role in the GCC economies. Moreover, the manufacturing sector performance is very weak compared to other non-oil Arab countries and in relation to the service and distribution sector, GCC countries have try to develop industries, services, and other sectors, in order to reduce the relative size of the oil sector. Furthermore, non-oil export has an average increased as a proportion of total exports, specially, UAE, Qatar, and Bahrain, while the contribution of oil revenues in decline slightly, Table 1. The contribution of the oil sector to the GDP in all its aspects remains quite high in comparison with other developing and developed countries. The result appear that all these developments are indicative of varying degrees of success in diversification away from dependence on oil, despite the diversification efforts have not yet resulted in a sustainable development pattern.

The discussion of Table 1 envisions a small gradual shift from the allocation state to a more production-oriented policy, where the state, the citizens, and the private sector are encouraged to produce and involved in producing actual goods and services, and where the government relies on proceeds from this production in financing the societies. This shift could be achieved by the diversification process ahead encompasses not only strategic investments in economic assets, infrastructure, and education, but also, broader economic and social reforms aimed at re-establishing the link between effort and reward in the work–life of the nationals in order to stimulate better use of human resources.

The sovereign wealth funds (SWFs) must play massive role in the diversification by investing oil revenues in either local or international industries, to enable GCC countries to convert the volatile and exhaustible oil incomes into a more stable financial stream of wealth that could be used to develop GCC countries. The GCC countries hold an estimated US $2862.51 billion of assets (SWFs), United Arab Emirates, 1214.91 billion, Saudi Arabia, 792.14 billion, Qatar, 304 billion, Oman, 25 billion, Kuwait, 527 billion, and Bahrain, 11.1 billion. Accordingly, investments are undertaken in these economies, they create jobs in the local economies and contribute to further education and training of the local workforce, besides reduction the risk of fluctuations in the international oil prices and make the investment inside and outside GCC countries is the main source of income rather than oil.

One of the key requirements for economic diversification is innovation, which is defined as the ability to achieve change that creates a new

Table 1 Oil revenue as a percentage of GDP, state budget, and Tax revenue of total revenues in the GCC countries

Country	*Oil revenue % of GDP*		*Oil revenue % of state budget*		*Tax revenue % of total revenue*	
	2014	*2020*	*2014*	*2020*	*2014*	*2020*
Bahrain	24.7	9.6	85.7	58.4	3.4	16.8
Kuwait	60.4	47.4	92.1	89.3	1.2	3.1
Oman	47.7	24.4	85.6	71.6	7.0	6.5
Qatar	50.5	25.6	45.2	82.4	13.7	14.6
Saudi Arabia	40.2	15.7	87.8	52.8	7.6	29.0
United Arab Emirates	33.6	11.5	66.8	39.0	8.7	52.0

Source The Joint Arab Economic Report (2021), Arab Monetary Fund, and others Exports including oil only without gas

dimension of performance, at least new to the national economy. The innovation means invention or R and D, but rather the capacity to absorb, implement, and exploit innovation effectively within industrial sectors in order to build competitive strength and generate added value for the economy.

At a national level, innovation performance is a function of the collective capabilities of a range of players and the effectiveness with which they are able to interact. These players, comprising government, industry, education, and research providers and funders, together form a so-called national innovation system. The government has a primary role in setting the regulatory and policy framework that encourages innovation. In the Middle East, many governments still have some way to go to develop and implement an effective regulatory framework. One of the reasons is the lack of an overarching policy aimed at building up innovation capability within the economy.

Governments in the region have launched and implemented various initiatives to foster innovation. However, the innovation output in the region has generally fallen short of expectations. In 2010, Google's managing director for Southern/Eastern Europe, the Middle East, and Africa highlighted the lack of innovation in the Middle East by pointing to the fact that a mere 3224 patents were filed from the Middle East and North Africa (MENA) region in the last 13 years. Japan, in 2008 alone, filed 233,000 patents.

Furthermore, according to the World Intellectual Property Organization (WIPO), 2021 edition, in 2020, Japan filed 288,472 patents, while Saudi Arabia filed 3568 patents, Bahrain 264 patents, Qatar 685 patents, UAE 1908 patents, and Oman 529 patents (patent applications 2020).

Inadequate spending on R and D, a passive approach toward technology dissemination, and a lack of knowledge flow linkages have hampered research efforts undertaken by the GCC countries. According to the Arab Knowledge Report 2009, Arab countries spend around 0.7% of their Gross domestic product (GDP) on R and D activities; in Organization for Economic Co-operation and Development (OECD) countries the average is 2.3% in (2008). Furthermore, Arab Knowledge Report 2014 has shown that spending on scientific research and technology as % of the production in Saudi Arabia is 0.01%, Kuwait 0.03%, Bahrain 0.00%, and UAE 0.00%, while South Korea is 1.00% and Malaysia 0.20%. Moreover, the report explained that the rates of spending on R and D in the Arab countries as a percentage of GDP during the past four decades do not meet the requirements of this sector. In recent years, the Arab countries only allocated modest amounts of their GDP to R and D, at a range between 0.03 and 0.73%. The Arab states' allocations for R and D as a percentage of the GDP, are far below the global average, which reached about 2.13%.

The spending on Research, Development, and Innovation in the GCC countries, is not enough to generate wealth and address the needs related to diversification in the same time, the expenditure of scientific research institutions in the private sector remains very low. According to the Global Knowledge index 2021, among the 131 countries included in the UNESCO study, Qatar ranked 41th, UAE 28th, Saudi Arabia ranked 47th, Oman ranked 82th, Bahrain 94th, and Kuwait ranked 117th. There is no doubt that the low participation of the private production and service sectors in funding scientific research and technological development clarifies, to some extent, the limited innovative activity in the GCC countries which affect negatively on the efforts toward diversification (The Global Knowledge Index, 2021).

3 The Higher Education and Labor Nationalization in GCC Countries

This section is limited to analyzing the quality of higher education in GCC countries in terms of teaching and learning. The objective of this paper is to establish the linkage of quality of education in terms of learning by determining the needs and characteristics of the students, teachers, curricula, and pedagogy of higher education in GCC countries. The more specific objective is to identify and analyze the factors that affect the teaching and learning quality of higher education in the GCC countries.

The quality of higher education stands on three pillars: quality of administrative support services, quality of research, and quality of academics. Institutions provide good administrative support services to produce quality research and academics. The quality of administrative support services is based on management, governance, funding, resources, infrastructure, and other support services. Quality of research is based on motivation, freedom, funding, and a research environment within the institute. Similarly, the quality of academics (teaching–learning) is based on various factors which include quality of faculty, students, curricula, and pedagogy and all these factors are linked with support services on the one hand and with their own needs and characteristics on the other hand. Despite good administrative support services, the quality of academics is a challenge for the GCC countries. The quality of higher education in terms of learning achievements has been a challenge for the GCC countries. This challenge has been linked with various basic characteristics and needs of students, faculty, curricula, and teaching pedagogy.

This section states that the quality of higher education cannot be improved unless it focuses on the needs and the characteristics of students, teachers, curricula, and pedagogy which are necessary for the best teaching–learning environment in the higher education institutions. Various needs and characteristics of the students, faculty, curricula, and pedagogy identified include lack of students' prior knowledge, students' attitude toward hard work, lack of competition among students, a habit of memorization rather than understanding, lack of critical and analytical skills, weak English language, logical and numerical abilities, a socio-culture gap between local culture and expatriate faculty, a lack of local curricula to meet local market and students need, a gap between foreign curricula and student level, less focus on teaching pedagogy and market needs, etc.

The higher education institutions must focus more on the student learning to strengthen their capacities to work progressively through the acquisition of relevant knowledge, useful skills, and appropriate attitudes. The ultimate goal of higher education institutions should be learning achievements. Education policies of the higher education institutions will be effective if better educated, qualified, and skilled people are produced. The higher education institutions must consider and address the basic characteristics of students, teachers, curricula, and pedagogy while making policies. The paper may be useful for the policymaker of the higher education in the GCC countries.

Despite the continuous efforts of (GCC) countries to enhance the quality of higher education and research by investing a huge amount of money to expand education opportunities, provide considerable infrastructure, spread regional higher education institutions, and establish accreditation councils, the quality of education and research remains a major concern. The two major challenges in these countries are the quality of higher education and research. Much has been written on the quality of higher education, but the concern is what are the needs and issues in the teaching–learning process to overcome the challenges of quality of higher education. The objective of the section is to identify and analyze the factors that affect the quality of higher education teaching and learning in the GCC countries.

The quality of higher education is a major and complex issue in the GCC countries various causes and factors which contribute to this concern can be found here later. Generally, the factors influencing the quality of higher education can be grouped into three broad areas. These are quality of administrative support services (management, funding, infrastructure, support services, etc.), quality of academics (teaching–learning environment), and quality of research (knowledge creation and dissemination).

In the case of quality of administrative support services, the GCC countries have made significant developments during the past few decades. There is a considerable improvement in the education infrastructure (Davidson 2010), an increased university enrolment through public and private institutions, a reduced gender gap in education, an ensured equity in education through the regional spread of higher education institutions of all types with diversified programmers and established institutional accreditation councils for quality assurance. Similarly, a number of foreign universities or their branches/campuses have been established in the GCC member countries (Damaj and Chaaban 2014).

Various mega projects such as "Free Education Zones" in UAE (Quality Assurance Agency 2014), "Education City" in Qatar "Knowledge Oasis" in Oman have been established where a number of foreign universities are providing higher education in various fields (Deghady 2008). Similarly, in Saudi Arabia, the King Abdullah University of Science and Technology has been established with a $10 billion endowment coming directly out of the King's purse, which makes this university the sixth richest in the world. There has been tremendous expansion in the educational facilities in all of the six Gulf countries.

Despite of all these efforts in providing quality services in education at country and institutional level, which it was assumed would improve the quality of academics and research, the quality of higher education in the GCC countries still remains an issue and does not correspond to the needs of Gulf societies. The quality of higher education across the GCC region is still not on a par with standards in developed nations and some emerging economies (Sawahel 2012). A large number of studies and reports have confirmed that higher education in the GCC region has fallen short of expectations and has failed to address the aspirations of younger generations (Dakhli and El Zohairy 2013). Several national reports acknowledged that quantitative growth had taken place at the expense of the quality of education.

The gap in the quality of education between GCC member countries and other countries at a similar level of development still exists. The higher education institutions in the GCC countries have been criticized as not producing research in terms of quantity and quality. There exists a severe decline in universities and research centers in the region and none of the GCC institutions is prominent in producing significant research. The poor quality of higher education programs in the Arab world and the level of scientific research are the most important challenges that face higher education in the Arab world (Abedalhakeem and Siddiek 2012). In the whole region, only four Saudi universities are listed among the top 500 universities in 2016, i.e. King Abdulaziz University (150), King Saud University (150), King Abdullah University of Science and Technology (300), and King Fahd University of Petroleum and Minerals.

A good teaching–learning environment is supposed to produce good quality students as per market and society requirements. However, the existing teaching–learning environment in the GCC countries has also contributed to the quality issue and has been widely criticized in the literature. The quality of education—defined as learning achievement (Marlaine and Verspoor 1991) is not encouraging in the Middle East and North Africa region. The higher education institutions in the GCC countries do not produce skilled workers as per market requirements. They have "educated" a growing cohort of students without ensuring that they have desired skills needed by the market and thus are experiencing a shortage of skilled workers in the marketplace. The higher education sector in the GCC countries has failed to meet the needs of either the public or the private sector.

Consequently, strategies for labor nationalization have been largely unsuccessful as a large proportion of the workforce produced is unable to compete with the well-qualified expatriates. Thomas and Mathew (2001) confirmed that when the quality and appropriateness of human capital produced to align with the needs of society, employment opportunities are expanded and economic actors are better able to achieve their goals and objectives. Similarly, in the teaching–learning process, besides students, the other important stakeholder and areas are teachers, curricula, and teaching pedagogy. However, in the GGC countries, the quality of teachers is a concern and according to Gulf education officials and researchers, the elusiveness of teacher quality in the Arabian Gulf states has reached crisis levels. In the same way, the widespread adoption of foreign curricula in higher education institutions to meet the local market needs, students' learning abilities, and skills required for employment are widely criticized in the literature (Shah and Baporikar 2011). Furthermore, program quality, pedagogy, and other elements related to program standards are extensively criticized (Wilkens 2011).

COVID-19 has heightened human suffering, undermined the economy, turned the lives of billions of people around the globe upside down, and significantly affected the health, economic, environmental, social domains, and education. This study aims to provide a comprehensive analysis of the impact of the COVID-19 outbreak on the educational domain, the energy sector, society, and the economy and investigate the global preventive measures taken to reduce the transmission of COVID-19. This analysis unpacks the key responses to COVID-19, the efficacy of current initiatives, and summarizes the lessons learnt as an update on the information available to authorities, business, and industry.

This review found that a 72-hour delay in the collection and disposal of waste from infected households and quarantine facilities is crucial to controlling the spread of the virus. Broad sector by sector plans for socio-economic growth as well as a robust entrepreneurship-friendly economy are needed for the business to be sustainable at the peak of the pandemic. The socio-economic crisis has reshaped investment in energy and affected the energy sector significantly with most investment activity facing disruption due to mobility restrictions. Delays in energy projects in gulf countries are expected to create uncertainty in the years ahead. This report will benefit governments, leaders in education sector, energy firms, and customers in addressing a pandemic-like situation in the future, M. Mofijur and others (2021).

The GCC can reshape its post-COVID-19 education system. Of all sectors in the GCC, education was among the least prepared for a disruption like COVID-19, and the most affected by it. With almost no advance notice, a well-established model of in-person learning was forced to shift entirely online, sending 2.75 million children home. As a result, there is a risk of a decline in long-term learning levels, along with a potential increase in the gap in digital literacy among children. Governments must take short- and long-term measures to prevent such negative outcomes.

Most schools, leaders, and education ministries have already taken significant steps to provide the best education possible under the circumstances. However, those measures have largely been reactive and ad hoc—as the results show. There have been profound challenges with the transition for even those GCC countries that had already started implementing digital learning. In the UAE, teachers reported insufficient digital preparedness levels impeding the teaching process. In Saudi Arabia, many students had problems logging onto e-learning platforms due to poor connectivity. In Oman, public schools were closed, and the school year was terminated. There have been similar issues elsewhere. Countries that had already made major investments in digital learning, such as China, Singapore, and South Korea, also experienced significant problems.

Most education ministries in the GCC are now working hard to set the right conditions for reopening schools after the summer, a critical short-term imperative. However, given the likelihood of ongoing disruptions to in-person learning in the future, governments should adopt longer-term measures to improve online learning. First, governments and schools should improve online learning to minimize the drop in the average learning level. Education ministries should treat e-learning as a supplement that leads to better outcomes, not as a substitute or replacement for classroom learning. That means that education ministries should modernize traditional pedagogical methods by establishing national guidelines and standards for online education. School systems should provide educators with digital literacy training through media campaigns, tailored workshops, training programs, and regular e-learning forums and webinars.

As with traditional education, governments should establish an accreditation scheme for online institutions and programs, to regulate offerings and ensure quality. Teachers who undergo formal training should receive an e-certification, with mandatory staff quotas that increase over time. For example, 20% of a school's educators must be e-certified after one year, 40% after two years, and so on. Governments will need to create digital materials to support online learning, potentially by working with private-sector providers such as Google or Coursera. They should offer tailored online quizzes and exams, with a recording application to ensure academic honesty. A central online platform can provide many of these offerings and feature national curricula, prepared lectures, and segmented levels of access for teachers, students, and parents.

Along with improvements to online education, governments should make long-term efforts to reduce the digital literacy gap between privileged and underprivileged children. A key factor is access. Education ministries should ensure that all students have a laptop or equivalent electronic device to attend online classes. As part of broader digitization agendas, governments should partner with national telecom companies to increase broadband internet coverage, offer discounted rates for low-income families, and establish public Wi-Fi hotspots in areas with high concentrations of students. Schools can provide some classes and content through dedicated television channels, further increasing accessibility. In particular, governments should ensure that all students have access to online resources. Online libraries can give students access to textbooks and other resources. Students should also have the software and tools they need for projects along with subscriptions to leading global newspapers and magazines. For students at university, virtual reality programs can be critical resources. For example, medical students can perform mock surgeries through virtual reality simulations.

The pandemic has been a massive disruption for GCC governments, demonstrating the need to be prepared for future problems. If education ministries are to fulfill their mandate in such circumstances, they need to adjust. By reshaping the education system to mitigate the negative impacts of COVID-19, they can integrate online learning and create an education system that is ultimately better for current and future generations of students. Karim Aly (2020).

4 The Fourth Industrial Revolution (4IR): The Rule of Higher Education in GCC

The Singaporean experience is distinguished in the world and applicable in the Arab Gulf countries, therefore, here, in this research, we simulate the Singaporean experience in an attempt to benefit from it in the six Arab Gulf states. Singapore has always been adaptive, and this is reflected in its approach to education. This chapter explains the current revisions of higher education in Singapore, which are designed to instill lifelong learning tendencies in the Singaporean population. Through the implementation of three ambitious government-led efforts, Singapore is altering the way it educates people. The three specific higher education developments reported upon here are the Smart Nation Singapore, Skills-Future Singapore, and the establishment of several new higher education institutions to prepare the population for living and working in a fully digital era. Through these initiatives, Singapore is preparing for the future economy with remarkable ingenuity (Gleason 2018).

Singapore's 4IR Preparation is explained by the *Report of the Committee on the Future Economy* came out in February 2017 outlining Singapore's economic strategies for 4IR preparation. This effort was a follow-up to the 2010 Economic Strategies Committee's work intended to take into consideration the challenges of the automation economy. The goal of the 2017 strategy is to ensure that Singapore experiences economic growth at 2–3% per year on average, a stronger performance than most advanced economies to which Singapore compares itself. The report recognizes that Singaporeans must constantly retrain and upgrade their skills to stay relevant. The report lays out an innovative 7 Strategy Plan to alter society in preparation for the technological changes pending. Those that explicitly mention higher education and adult learning are:

1. Deepen and diversify our international connections.
2. Acquire and utilize deep skills.
3. Build strong digital capabilities (Ministry of Communications and Information Singapore, "Report of the Committee on the Future Economy.")

Through these three efforts, Singapore is internationalizing its education and creating more experiential learning opportunities.

The first education strategy, "Deepening and Diversifying International Connections," is pursued in education through the Global Innovation Alliance (GIA) initiative intended to build new networks through which youth can facilitate innovation.

The second education strategy relative to higher education and 4IR is to "Acquire and Utilize Deep Skills." Deep skills include analytical and evaluative capacities combined with complex problem-solving and effective team collaboration capabilities.

The third relevant strategy is to "Build Strong Digital Capabilities." In response to the new industries emerging from digitization and the resulting big data production, this effort involves creating strong human capacity in data analytics and cybersecurity.

Three Education-Focused Initiatives to Prepare for 4IR in Singapore, One such initiative, within which Singapore's MOE has invested substantial financial resources, is Yale-NUS College. A collaboration that began in 2011 between Yale University and NUS resulted in the first liberal arts college in Singapore and one of the first in Asia. Yale faculty, together with experts from around the world, designed a unique curriculum linked with a distinctive pedagogical approach. The first cohort of students began studying at Yale-NUS College in August 2013. The unique features of the College include an interdisciplinary international common curriculum, team-based teaching in the common curriculum, small class sizes which are capped at 18 students, extremely diverse student body, and a required four-year residential experience. The residential experience allows the learning to take place outside the classroom, which is important to the development of lifelong learning skills and is practiced elsewhere in Singapore to varying degrees. These efforts are combined with experiential learning opportunities for all students and a robust study abroad program. As noted above these are the sorts of self-organizing learning environments that foster the needed knowledge workers for the 4IR (Karen 2016).

The distinctive pedagogy involves close interactions between faculty and students both inside and outside the classroom. This is something that is relatively new to Singapore's higher education landscape. Teaching at Yale-NUS is learner-centered and problem-based with very few lectures. Seminars last 1.5–3 hours in order to elicit deep discussion. Experiential learning and international experience are integral to the learning experience, which is consistent with Singapore's desire to internationalize its citizen (Hussain et al. 2007).

The majors also provide depth in a given field but typically with an interdisciplinary focus. For example, the Mathematics and Computational Science (MCS) major offers students a unique opportunity to go beyond the frontiers of traditional mathematics education. As the major's website explains, "We encourage students to participate actively in these flourishing developments. Displaying keen interest in this discipline, our students have embarked on projects to design robots, launch software start-ups, analyse big data networks, develop data visualisation tools, and philosophise on randomness and chaos." ("Why MCS?," Yale-NUS College, accessed December 28, 2017.)

The Yale-NUS College example is very different from the goals of developing deep skills through focused, performance-based learning. The development of this college, as well as the others noted in Table 1, demonstrates the efforts to which Singapore's MOE has gone to create the best global learning environments for both Singaporean citizens and global talent. There is a broad range of types of education available, for different types of learners. This will keep Singapore's labour force diverse and agile. Adult learners are also returning to the classrooms of these universities and colleges, to upskill the older population as well. The example of the creation of Yale-NUS College is just one petri dish in Singapore's higher education laboratory. These institutions are the front line of preparation for 4IR, but they are only one piece of a grandeur effort to assist Singaporeans and the economy in the era of 4IR. Two large initiatives, SkillsFuture and Smart Nation, are working with and alongside Singapore's institutions of higher education to prepare the population for living and working in a fully digital era.

The policies and programs being erected to address technological unemployment and to prepare for 4IR are not without their detractors. The ever-present connectivity that automation brings clashes with some notions of privacy. This analysis of Singapore's approach does not address the viability of the effort as a whole in Singapore to apply elsewhere. Rather, the efforts in Singapore are presented as an example of the multi-pronged approach being taken so as to suggest how other nations might adapt such a combination of efforts as is appropriate to their cultural and legislative context.

The three specific higher education developments reported upon here are the Smart Nation Singapore, SkillsFuture Singapore, and the establishment of several new higher education institutions to prepare the population for living and working in a fully digital era. Through these initiatives Singapore is preparing for the future economy with remarkable ingenuity.

SkillsFuture is a national movement to provide Singaporeans with the opportunities to develop their fullest potential throughout life, regardless of their starting points. Through this movement, the skills, passion, and contributions of every individual will drive Singapore's next phase of development toward an advanced economy and inclusive society.—Skills mastery is more than having the right paper qualifications and being good at what you do currently; it is a mindset of continually striving toward greater excellence through knowledge, application, and experience.

SkillsFuture is a government-led initiative to help Singaporeans adjust their mindsets and their capacities for the automation economy. This is important, as many nations are focused on taxing robots and preparing for universal basic income (UBI). Some, including Bill Gates, have suggested that a tax on robots could be used to distribute the economic gains from automation efficiencies that will not be reaching the unemployed. This is not Singapore's approach. The cultural belief in the value and necessity of work is strong, and citizens have a deep-rooted commitment to working for a living. The initiative of SkillsFuture is culturally responsive in that way.

The SkillsFuture initiative is based on four key thrusts. First, it is intended to help individuals make decisions about their education, training, and how this might align with their career. Formerly called the Individual Learning Portfolio (ILP), MySkillsFuture is a one-stop education, training, and career guidance website. The website is intended to align the acquisition and the utilization of skills for Singaporean citizens and is integrated into the nation's job bank. Second, SkillsFuture runs an integrated high-quality system of education and teaching that responds to the shifts in 4IR technology and corresponding industry jobs. Third, the initiative representatives work with the industry to ensure there is employer recognition for upskilling certificates and the corresponding promotion/compensation for mastery of skills. Fourth, SkillsFuture works to foster a culture that supports and celebrates lifelong learning across Singapore. Public messaging through posters, advertisements, and the like is common around the city-state.

SkillsFuture is organized into five levels of support: student, junior level, middle management, senior management, and career switcher. There are multiple opportunities across Singapore for adult learners in particular. Research is expanding into a better understanding of how to engage adult learners as well. For many, re-education and upskilling are expensive. Singapore has three different funding mechanisms in place for this. There are SkillsFuture credits for all Singaporean citizens so that they do not have to have the financial means to afford this upskilling. There are also SkillsFuture qualification awards and student awards and an Earn and Learn program. SkillsFuture works with institutions of higher education but also maintains the Institute of Lifelong Learning, where Singaporeans at all levels can take targeted courses to gain new skills. The intention is that labor disruption will be less socially alarming and economically challenging as a result. Furthermore, Singaporeans will be better prepared for the automation economy, benefiting themselves and the nation's economy.

Smart Nation Singapore is a separate government initiative developed to help citizens ease into the social and economic changes that are already emerging with the automation economy. Singapore launched its Smart Nation effort in December 2014. The approach expands from the idea of a Smart City, which emerged in the 1980s, and today involves the application of technology to sustainable and inclusive ICT connectivity. The technology supporting Smart Cities involves the Internet of Things (IoT) and a Wi-Fi-enabled network of sensors and devices all talking to each other to enhance life for city residents. But the ability of a city community to take advantage of such technologies requires a digitally literate population. Ezra Ho argues that Singapore was already a Smart City by 2014, but that the Smart Nation initiative "is about coordinating and intensifying the effort to develop the institutions, regulations, and talent for a hyper-connected, datafied urbanity." In order for Singaporeans to take advantage of the higher education and SkillsFuture opportunities, they must have digital literacy. Digital literacy is demonstrated as technical and cognitive competence in a variety of areas. It is the "ideas and mindsets, within which particular skills and competencies operate, and about information and information resources, in whatever format"; the most accurate definition of digital literacy is drawn from Allan Martin's work: Digital Literacy is the awareness, attitude, and ability of individuals to appropriately use digital tools and facilities to identify, access, manage, integrate, evaluate, analyze, and synthesize digital resources, construct new knowledge, create media expressions, and communicate with others, in the context of specific life situations, in order to enable constructive social action; and to reflect upon this process.

Having these skills is essential in order for a society to benefit from Smart Nation efforts and 4IR more broadly. As detailed by Hoe Siu Loon, Singapore's digital literacy journey began in the 1980s with the National Computerization Plan.55. Since then there has been a succession of government-led initiatives to upgrade the physical digital capacity as well as the human capacity of the nation including the National IT Plan of 1986, the IT2000 plan of 1992, the Infocom 21 plan of 2000, the Connected Singapore plan of 2003, the Intelligent Nation 2015 plan, and more recently in the Infocomm Media 2025 Plan.56. Smart Nation Singapore identifies five key domains in which digital technology can enhance the lives of citizens. These include transport, home and environment, business productivity, health and enabled aging, and public-sector services.

The networks and structures put in place to implement Smart Nation Singapore are important to understand for those seeking to integrate such a program into their own higher education and lifelong learning national programs. In January 2016, Dr. Janil Puthucheary was appointed as the Minister of State, Ministry of Communications and Information and MOE, and placed in charge of the Smart Nation initiative. This was an important leadership position and is strategically placed across both ministries. In March 2016 the Smart Nation Fellowship program was launched to recruit and create a network of computer scientists and technology experts to collaborate with the government on how best to create projects for the public in line with adapting the population to a new way of living and working. Then, in May 2016, the "Lee Hsien Loong Interactive visible the good efforts of full-time polytechnic students working on interactive digital media projects that contributed to the Smart Nation efforts."

All of this effort on a national scale inevitably resulted in the need for more administration oversight. In May 2017, the Smart Nation and Digital Government Office (SNDGO) was formed under the Prime Minister's Office to prioritize and help deliver digital solutions for citizen and business needs. Collaboration with primary, secondary, and tertiary education has been consistent throughout the development of Smart Nation Singapore and will likely become more important as the digitization process intensifies.

The government has also recognized the security risks associated with the new reality of life being online, plugged in, and always connected. For this reason, cybersecurity is paramount. Safeguarding the relevant systems and networks of Smart Nation for all citizens and compliance with the nation's privacy of data laws is a priority. A key element of Smart Nation is building computational capabilities in cybersecurity and data analytics. Here efforts are five pronged. For the youth of Singapore, IMDA Playmaker program is deployed to expose young children to technology while gaining educational experiences. Also, Code@SG is a movement that introduced coding and computational thinking to students in schools, again working to enhance digital literacy in preparation for 4IR jobs. Starting in 2018 Singapore will add Coding to 19 different schools' "O" Level subject testing in order to measure capacity better in this area.

The six-member nations of the Gulf Cooperation Council (GCC) Kuwait, Saudi Arabia, Bahrain, Qatar, the United Arab Emirates, and Oman—are undergoing an astonishing development of their higher education landscapes that has attracted keen interest on the part of other Arab countries. In line with their increasingly freewheeling and booming private sectors, higher education has been characterized over the last five years by exponential growth in the number of institutions, a dependence on the private sector to provide education that meets the needs of the market, and the unquestioned dominance of the American university model.

The populations of the GCC nations are rising dramatically as the result of an overall annual growth rate of over 3%. Roughly 60% of the population is under 16 years of age. Until the mid-1990s, the governments focused most of their attention and resources on handling the exploding numbers at the primary and secondary levels. The production of university graduates was of considerably less urgency, as these countries had grown accustomed to the luxury of importing foreign experts to perform the necessary technical and managerial functions. Indeed, universities in the Gulf rarely date back more than 30 years. When throngs of secondary graduates began pouring out of the schools in the mid-1990s demanding university training, Gulf governments found themselves hard-pressed to satisfy the demand through existing institutions.

As Gulf nations have sought rapid modernization over the last 30 years, they have all made the education of females a recognized hallmark of modernity and an element of their educational policies, albeit within the strict guidelines of Islam and traditional tribal customs. Females are still very rarely permitted by their families to go abroad for university study, thereby making local study their only option. Thus, while tens of thousands of Gulf males go to universities abroad and relieve local universities of some of their burden, the exploding number of female graduates must be educated in their countries. In general, about 60% of graduates of Gulf universities today are female (although only a small percentage of these graduates ever enter the workforce). And the fact that most public higher education in the Gulf is segregated by sex makes the university enterprise more expensive in terms of its efficient use of faculty, staff, and facilities.

Gulf governments see privatization as more than a simple solution to unmanageable numbers; they have private higher education as a means of ensuring the quality of instruction and the relevance to market needs that have been missing from public universities; the region's secondary and university graduates have always lagged far behind graduates in East Asia and other developing nations. As indigenization of the workforce has become a priority in every GCC country, the fact that local graduates of public universities lack the required skills has become painfully obvious. The prevailing notion today is that private institutions will be in competition with each other and more in tune with the needs of the private sector, thereby guaranteeing courses of study of international standard leading to employment and in the same time, offering a very important solution to bring the learner to replace foreign workforce in the era of the 4IR.

GCC should follow approach that Smart Nation, SkillsFuture, and the efforts of GCC's institutes of higher education will combine to upskill and educate a workforce and citizenship that is uniquely educated for 4IR to nationalize of GCC labor markets. This is how GCC is planning to shift its populations' skill sets. They will have opportunities throughout their lifetime to learn new skills. The efforts are characterized by three main thrusts. First, they are working to make a more digitally literate and technologically competent population through the Smart Nation and SkillsFuture initiatives. Second, they are creating cohorts of ideation experts through unique higher education opportunities. Finally, GCC are nationalizing its population and creating a more globally savvy and connected citizenry.

Nationalization of education is important, and higher education institutions can reach out to peer institutions around the world to establish tighter connections with student and faculty exchanges. This is a very important step toward preparing learners to nationalize the GCC labor market There is a particular urgency for GCC to lead Industry 4.0 and to wean themselves off the constraints of oil-derived revenues. The world now finds itself being dramatically altered by a new industrial revolution—Industry 4.0—bringing technological developments that will transform economies and societies far more profoundly than any previous period of rapid development and change. While nations around the world are researching and evaluating how they can harness the potential of technology such as big data, robotics, and AI, there is a particular urgency for countries in the Gulf to lead Industry 4.0 and to wean themselves off the constraints of oil-derived revenues. Fortunately, the nature of this threat has been recognized by GCC governments and is most evident in national social and economic development plans such as Saudi Arabia's Vision 2030, which states that a sophisticated digital infrastructure is integral to today's advanced industrial activities.

Finally, the aim of this chapter is to present the investment in human capital on preparing lifelong learners to nationalize GCC labor market The latter is based on qualitative education, training, knowledge, technology, and innovation and encompasses a breadth of non-tangible skills that the GCC population possess such as organization, leadership work habits, initiative problem-solving, confidence, etc,. The Singaporean experience is distinguished in the world and applicable in the Arab Gulf countries, therefore, here, in this research, we simulate the Singaporean experience in an attempt to benefit from it in the six Arab Gulf states.

5 Investment in Human Capital in GCC Countries and Preparing Learners to Nationalize GCC Labor Market

The formation of human capital—the knowledge, skills, and health that people accumulate over their lifetimes—is critical for the six Gulf Cooperation Council (GCC) countries. Human capital contributes not only to human development and employment but also to the long-term sustainability of a diversified economic growth model that is knowledge-based and private sector-driven. This approach is critical, given that income from oil and gas will eventually decline and that the nature of work is evolving in response to rapid technological changes, in turn demanding new skill sets. The GCC governments have demonstrated their strong political will for this shift: four of them are among the first countries to join the World

Bank's Human Capital Project—a global effort to improve investments in people as measured by the Human Capital Index (Sameh 2020).

The GCC countries face four main challenges: Low levels of basic proficiency among schoolchildren; a mismatch between education and the labor market; A relatively high rate of adult mortality and morbidity; A unique labor market, in which wages in the public sector are more generous than in the private sector and government employment of nationals is virtually guaranteed. To address these challenges, this chapter outlines four strategies in a "whole-of-government" approach: Investing in high-quality early childhood development; Preparing healthcare, better educated, and skilled youth for the future; Enabling greater adult labor force participation; Creating an enabling environment for human capital formation. These strategies are based on best practices in other countries and feature some of the GCC countries' plans, including their national "Visions," to take their economies and societies further into the twenty-first century.

With the COVID-19 pandemic, the GCC countries face additional challenges that may worsen some pre-existing vulnerabilities and erode human capital. In response, the GCC governments have taken multiple measures to protect their populations' health and their economies. Any country's decision to reopen its economy needs to closely consider public health consequences to avoid a resurgence of infections and any further erosion of its human capital. The COVID-19 crisis underscores that the need to accelerate and improve investment in human capital has never been greater. Once the GCC countries return to a "new normal," they will be in a position to achieve diversified and sustainable growth by adopting, and then tailoring, the strategies presented above (World Bank 2020).

To help improve human capital requirements, the GCC generally needs to focus on these pillars, prioritize public investment in early childhood development (ECD), expand enrolment in early childhood education focus learning on skills rather than credentials, promote female labor force participation and reduce skills mismatch, reduce risk factors of noncommunicable diseases (NCDs), especially among youth and develop all-of-government, whole-of-society actions that motivate behavioral changes and increase value for money in these investments.

Global society is changing because of the shifts in technological capacity. Higher education must change with it. GCC should be, at the forefront of innovation in higher education. GCC serves as a model to nations around the world wanting to prepare their workforce with ways of thinking and working that are in demand in the fourth industrial revolution (4IR).

GCC's economic prosperity is closely linked to its successful education system. With a population of approximately 57 million people, outstanding development, good public health, and robust economic growth, the employment prospects for most of its citizens have been strong to date. Most of the workforce that will need to be upskilled and retrained in the near future. GCC's education system has a reputation for preparing excellent STEM learners, where students learn to the test. This was useful in creating a workforce that crunches and manages numbers efficiently. Creative and critical thinking did not come from this sort of preparation, however. Now plans are under way to develop more holistic education systems that teach students how to learn, rather than what to learn in order to adjust and continue to have an education system that delivers what the economy needs, as well as what nationalization needs.

GCC has always been adaptive, and this is reflected in its approach to education. This research explains the current revisions of higher education in GCC, which are designed to instill lifelong learning tendencies in the GCC population. Through the implementation of three ambitious government-led efforts, GCC is altering the way it educates people. The three specific higher education developments reported upon here are the Smart Nation GCC, SkillsFuture GCC, and the establishment of several new higher education institutions. Through these initiatives GCC is preparing for the future economy with remarkable ingenuity by preparing learners to nationalize GCC labor markets. Lifelong learning has been identified as the essential element for success in the era of 4IR. We do not know what is coming next, so we must prepare minds that are agile, flexible, and cooperative. SkillsFuture and Smart Nation are programs which address the labor disruption pending from automation (Gleason 2018).

GCC are well poised to capture the potential benefits of 4IR. GCC has the financial means to put large sums of money and human capital into the retooling of its entire education system. The overall lesson is that nations need to be prepared for change.

Finally, there is a particular urgency for GCC to lead Industry 4.0 and to wean themselves off the constraints of oil-derived revenues. The world now finds itself being dramatically altered by the anew industrial revolution—Industry 4.0—bringing technological developments that will transfer GCC learners to nationalize GCC labor market to achieve the very important goal for their national plans.

6 Conclusions

One of the key requirements for economic diversification is innovation, but the spending on R and D is not enough to generate wealth and address the needs related to diversification. In the same time, the expenditure of scientific research institutions in the private sector remains very low. These reasons affect negatively the efforts toward diversification, while the contribution of the oil sector to the GDP, exports earings and the state budget in GCC countries remain quite high in comparison with other developing and developed countries, it means that the diversification efforts have not yet resulted in a sustainable development pattern. The purpose of GCC efforts is that Smart Nation, SkillsFuture, and the efforts of GCCs institutes of higher education will combine to upskill and educate a workforce and citizenship that is uniquely educated for 4IR. This is how GCC should plan and implement to shift its populations' skill sets in order to prepare lifelong learners to nationalize GCC labor market.

GCCs higher education is internationalizing its population and creating a more globally savvy and connected citizenry by making use of the extensive expenditure on health care, education, and training ought to increase the human capital in the GCC region.

Global society is changing because of the shifts in technological capacity. Higher education must change with it. GCC countries are, once again, at the forefront of innovation of higher education since the region's human capital assessment falls significantly behind the world average. Policies of labor nationalization for GCC countries have been largely unsuccessful to compete with the well-qualified expatriates. Labour economy confirmed that when the quality and appropriateness of human capital produced to align with the needs of society, employment opportunities are expanded, and economic actors are better able to achieve their goals and objectives.

The pandemic of COVID-19 has been a massive disruption for GCC governments, demonstrating the need to be prepared for future problems.

7 Recommendations

1. The Singaporean experience is distinguished in the world and applicable in the Arab Gulf countries, therefore, here, in this research, we simulate the Singaporean experience in an attempt to benefit from it in the six Arab Gulf states.
2. GCC should focus on Sovereign funds as an important financial source for financing higher education toward achieving the goals of the 4th industrial revolution in order to prepare lifelong learners in GCC countries.
3. The study recommended that the decline in oil prices is an opportunity to reinvigorate the Arab countries efforts to diversity, as well as, to leave oil prices to the law of demand and supply, and the mechanism of the free market, and advise OPEC organization to work on pricing oil against a basket of currencies rather than US dollar only. This is positioned to avoid the decrease of the dollar against other currencies.
4. Governments in GCC countries need to focus on bridging the gap between industry and R and D centers and increase knowledge absorption by the industrial sector. Incentives such as tax congestion will not be affective in fostering R and D efforts as the countries already have relatively relaxed taxation systems. Instead, competitive grants and subsidies can be utilized to help the government direct R and D efforts into specific sectors as a means of influencing diversification.
5. GCC countries will have opportunities throughout their lifetime to learn new skills. The efforts are characterized by three main thrusts. They must work to make a more digitally literate and technologically competent population through the Smart Nation and SkillsFuture initiatives. GCC countries must create cohorts of ideation experts through unique higher education opportunities.
6. Internationalization of education is a very important step for GCC student, and higher education institutions can reach out to peer institutions around the world to establish tighter connections with student and faculty exchanges, which establish infrastructures to prepare learners to nationalize GCC labor market.
7. In preparation for 4IR, GCC countries must deploy policies that merit rigorous appraisal by other countries, developed and developing countries, and institutions of higher education for important

reason which prepare lifelong learners for GCC labor market putting in mind that economic reforms undertook by the GCC had usually limited results.

8. Education ministries are to fulfill their mandate in such circumstances, they need to adjust, by reshaping the education system to mitigate the negative impacts of COVID-19, which they can integrate online learning and create an education system that is ultimately better for current and future generations of students and workforce.

References

Abedalhakeem, T.E., and Siddiek, A.G. (2012). Higher Education in the Arab World and Challenges of Labor Market. *International Journal of Business and Social Science*, 3(9), 146–151. Retrieved from http://ijbssnet.com/journals/Vol_3_No_9_May_2012/16.pdf.

Damaj, I.W., and Chaaban, F.B. (2014). Dhofar University: A Case Study in the Practicalities of Collaboration and Accreditation. *Learning and Teaching in Higher Education: Gulf Perspectives*, 11(1), 1–19.

Dakhli, M., and El Zohairy, D. (2013). Emerging Trends in Higher Education in the GCC: A Critical Assessment. In Alon, I., Jones, V., and John R.M. (Eds.), *Innovation in Business Education in Emerging Markets*. New York. Palgrave Macmillan.

Davidson, C. M. (2010). The Higher Education Sector in the Gulf: History, Pathologies, and Progress. In *The EU and the GCC: Challenges and Prospects under the Swedish EU Presidency*. Koch, Christian and Stenberg, Leif. Dubai: Gulf Research Center, 61–78.

De Boer, K., and Turner, J. M. (2007). Beyond Oil: Reappraising the Gulf States. *The McKinsey Quarterly*. Retrieved April 1, 2016, from http://www.mckinseyquarterly.com/Economic_Studies/Country_Reports/Beyond_oil_Reappraising_the_Gulf_States_1902.

Deghady, S. (2008, May 29). Higher Education Sector Sees Major Expansion in the Gulf. *The Gulf Time*. Goha, Qatar.

Denison, E.F. (1962). *The Source of Economic Growth in the United State and the Alternatives before US*. New York: Committee for Economic Development.

Gleason, N.W. (2018). *Higher Education in the Era of the Fourth Industrial Revolution*. The Author(s) 2018 N. W. Gleason (ed.), https://doi.org/10.1007/978-981-13-0194-0_7.

Hussain, R.M.R., Mamat, W.H.W., Salleh, N., Saat, R.M., and Harland, T. (2007). Problem-based learning in Asian universities.

Karen, K. Inkelas. (2016). Good Practices of Living-Learning Programmes. *Asian Journal of the Scholarship Learning* 6(1), 64–76.

Karim Aly. (2020, September). Partner at Strategy & Middle East, part of the PwC network and Ahmed Mokhtar, Principal at Strategy & Middle East, part of the PwC network.

Kapiszewski, A. (2006). *Arab versus Asian Migrant Workers in the GCC Country*. Paper presented at the United Nations Expert Group Meeting on International Migration and Development in the Arab Region: Challenges and Opportunities. Beirut, Lebanon.

Kubursi. (1984). *Oil, Industrialization and Development in the Arab Gulf States*. Published January 18, 2018 by Routledge.

Luciani, G., and Beblawi, H. (1987). *The Rentier State*. New York: Croom Helm.

Marlaine, L., and Verspoor, A. (1991). *Improving Primary Education in Developing Countries*. New York: Oxford University Press.

Mofijur, M., and others. (2021). Impact of COVID-19 on the Social, Economic, Environmental and Energy Domains: Lessons Learnt from a Global Pandemic. *Sustainable Production and Consumption* 26, 343–359.

Quality Assurance Agency. (2014). Review of UK Transnational Education in United Arab Emirates: Overview, the Quality Assurance Agency (QAA) for Higher Education. Southgate House, Southgate Street, Gloucester GL1 1UB, UK.

Rajiv, N., Nitin, V., and Rick, E. (2011). *Innovation for Economic Diversification Experience from the Middle East*, Prism/2/2011, Arthur D Little.

Romer, P. M. (1987). Growth Based on Increasing Returns due to Specialization. *American Economy Review* 77(2), 56–62.

Saif, I. (2009). *The Oil Boom in the GCC Countries, Old Challenges, Changing Dynamics*. Carnegie Middle East Center.

Sameh, EL-Sahart. (2020, June). *Fostering Human Capital in the Gulf Cooperation Council Countries*. World Bank Publication. The World Bank number 33946.

Sawahel, W. (2012, July 8). More University Places and Better Quality Needed. University World News. Issue No. 229.

Shah, I., and Baporikar, N. (2011). The Suitability of Imported Curricula for Learning in the Gulf States: An Oman Perspective. In C. Gitsaki (Ed.), *Teaching and Learning in the Arab World* (pp. 275–292). New York, NY: Peter Lang.

Shediac, R. et al. (2010). *Meeting the Employment Challenge in the GCC: The Need for a Holistic Strategy*. Booz and Company Ideation Center Insight. Retrieved from http://www.booz.com/media/uploads/Meeting_the_Employment_Challenge_in_the_GCC.pdf.

Thomas, J. Cassidy, and Mathew, L. Miller. (2001). *Higher Education in the Arab States: Responding to the Challenges of Globalization*. Conference Summary

Report of Higher Education in the Arab World: Preparing for the Global Market Place, AMIDEAST, Washington, DC.
Wilkens, K. (2011). Higher Education Reform in the Arab World. *The Brookings Project on U.S. Relations with the Islamic World*, 2011 U.S.-Islamic World Forum Papers.
World Bank Group. (2020). *COVID-19 and Human Capital*. World Bank ECA Economic Update Fall 2020.
World Economic Forum [WEF]. (2017). The Future of Jobs and Skills in the Middle East and North Africa: Preparing the Region for the Fourth Industrial Revolution. Retrieved October 8, 2019, from http://www3.weforum.org/docs/WEF_EGW_FOJ_MENA.pdf. World Intellectual Property Organization (WIPO), 2021 edition.
"Why MCS?" Yale-NUS College, accessed December 28, 2017.

CHAPTER 3

Is Work Integrated Learning a Panacea to Employability of Graduates in GCC Countries?

Shazia Farooq Fazli and Ayesha Farooq

1 Introduction

Higher education institutions are intended to prepare students to enter the workforce with the necessary information, skills, attitudes, and capacities. Recent trends in higher education worldwide suggest that education should help students become more employable and send them out into

S. F. Fazli
Department of Sociology, Faculty of Social Science, Aligarh Muslim University, Aligarh, India

A. Farooq (✉)
Department of Business Administration, Faculty of Management Studies and Research, Aligarh Muslim University, Aligarh, India
e-mail: ayeshafarooq4@gmail.com

A. Mishrif et al. (eds.), *Nationalization of Gulf Labour Markets*,
The Political Economy of the Middle East,
https://doi.org/10.1007/978-981-19-8072-5_3

the workforce with the necessary skills to do their jobs well. These institutions must provide students with opportunities to gain insight into the workplace and industry experience to apply the knowledge that they have learned in the classroom. Building a future-ready workforce across industries gives institutions a long-term competitive advantage. Employers are looking for graduates who can go right into being valuable members of a company or group. Work-Integrated Learning (WIL) and experiential learning are widely acknowledged as essential contributors to graduates' transition to the workplace.

Work-Integrated Learning (WIL) is an educational activity that combines academic learning in one area with practical application in the workplace. The purpose is for students to gain the ability to integrate their learning by combining academic and work-related activities. WIL-adherent universities make it a distinct part of their undergraduate and postgraduate programmes, focusing on student-centred learning. Work Integrated Learning is a formal component of degree programmes in such colleges, and it is recognised through assessment and credit points. Students must integrate and effectively apply past learning and information to make and justify judgements in a work-related environment through learning activities. Also, students are taught and encouraged to critically evaluate themselves by reflecting on their decisions and behaviours in those work-related activities. Summer/winter internships, industry projects, work simulations, outreach programmes, alumni mentor-mentee programmes, market survey projects, and other WIL opportunities are available to students.

In light of this, the current study has provided answers to the following research questions.

RQ1: What does the extant literature present ideas regarding the WIL practices towards employability?

RQ2: What is the current status of WIL practices in higher education institutions/business schools in GCC countries?

RQ3: What is the industry perspective concerning the contribution of WIL practices adopted by higher education institutions/business schools?

2 Review of Literature

2.1 *The Strategy of Systematic Review*

In order to study the extant literature, the researchers carried out a strategy of the systematic review. Details of review questions, keyword protocol, papers retrieved, and exclusion criteria are presented in Table 1.

3 Literature Review

3.1 *Work-Integrated Learning/Training*

Work-integrated training is a broad term used to describe teaching approaches involving theoretical and professional curricula (Rook and McManus 2016). It is conceptually based on vocational education, which primarily focuses on inculcating workplace capabilities among the students (Mei 2011). Its purpose is to prepare college graduates for professional settings by developing the competencies required by employers (Spowart 2011). The essential aspect of work-integrated learning is the placement of a student in a professional environment that integrates their learning at university with the practices and culture of the workplace (Smith 2012). In many B-schools, the students must work part-time after the first year with the employer and then transiting to full-time employment at the end of the degree programme. Work-integrated learning requires the integration of disciplinary knowledge with on-the-job learning (Smith and Worsfold 2015).

It is of policy interest to increase graduates' employability or "work-readiness" in an increasingly competitive market (Small et al. 2018).

3.2 *Vocational Training Over Traditional Education*

The instructors must possess professional and vocational knowledge to implement work-integrated learning in the colleges successfully. The universities must realise the importance of professional training and enterprise exposure of faculties regularly (Mei 2011). Besides, universities implementing work-integrated learning would attract more students by fulfilling their academic and professional needs (Rook and McManus 2016).

Table 1 Strategy of systematic review

Review question	*Keyword protocol*	*Articles retrieved*	*Exclusion criterion*
Impact of work-integrated learning on students' development in higher education/business schools and employability	(TITLE-ABS-KEY ("Work-Integrated Learning" OR "Work Integrated Learning" OR "Integrated Learning") AND (TITLE-ABS-KEY ("Higher Education" AND (TITLE-ABS-KEY ("Business Colleges" OR "B-Schools" OR "Business Schools" OR "Management Institutions" OR "Private B-Schools" OR "B Schools" OR "Management Colleges" OR "Management Schools" OR "Colleges" OR "Schools")) AND (LIMIT-TO (SUBJAREA, "Higher" AND "Busi")) AND (LIMIT-TO (LANGUAGE, "English"))	Search query has produced 32 papers from the Scopus database. Out of these, twelve papers could pass through the selection process, and only ten were accessible. Apart from the Scopus database, a few articles were produced by open access	• Papers not focused on work-integrated learning • Papers not focused on college students and employability • The papers selected have focused on work-integrated learning and employability

3.3 *Importance of Work-Integrated Learning*

Employers are no longer looking for college graduates with theoretical knowledge. They seek employees with technical and management skills to handle the on-job challenges (Spowart 2011). Work-integrated learning will help prepare the students with hands-on skill development through imparting practical know-how (Mei 2011). Through vocational training, the students will develop the skills and attributes that are required in the workplace (Rook and McManus 2016). This could be implemented through internships where students could strengthen their technical and generic skills (Pusiran et al. 2020). However, to successfully implement work-integrating training in colleges, the faculty needs to be innovative and have a thorough understanding of value creation in an industrial setting (Govender and Vaaland 2020). The higher education sector seeks to increase student employability through work-integrated learning (Jackson and Collings 2018). This has moved beyond traditional placement programmes required in education, nursing, and engineering to become a regular and advertised feature in law, accounting, and other professional subjects. Skills such as networking, problem-solving, negotiating, et cetera will be needed, in addition to the functional skills (Nicolescu & Păun 2009). These changes have contributed to the significant interest in work-integrated learning (WIL) in higher education (Cooper et al. 2010).

3.4 *Advantages of Work-Integrated Learning*

Through workplace-integrated learning, the students will experience the workplace realities and capabilities (Spowart 2011). It will also help develop the technical knowledge required on the job (Mei 2011). It inculcates practical insights among the students and helps them understand the business process clearly (Pusiran et al. 2020). Besides, the work-integrated learning adds to the competitive edge for the colleges, and in the coming years, we will see more of them incorporated into their curriculum (Rook and McManus 2016). Although current research does not prove a link between employment outcomes and work-integrated learning per se, programmes integrating learning and work can improve "non-technical skills, professional networking and exposure to the expectations and requirements of students' intended career pathway" (Jackson and Collings 2018).

3.5 *Implementing Work-Integrated Learning*

The first step of the process is to evaluate the curriculum for outcomes in work-integrated learning (Spowart 2011). The faculties will have to prepare themselves for competencies (Spowart 2011). Especially the industrial competencies, which have to be the prime focus while developing a curriculum (Spowart 2011). Also, college employees need to undergo professional training to understand the sectorial requirements (Ngubane et al. 2020). For better results, the curriculum needs to incorporate employment and management capabilities (Spowart 2011). This will help impart practical experience through enterprise learning (Mei 2011). The colleges will also need to develop networks with the industrial personnel to understand their requirements (Rook and McManus 2016). The students will have to work together collectively as their peer support, and a sense of belonging will build their confidence during their transition from school to work-related learning (McBeath et al. 2018).

3.6 *Methodologies Adopted*

Previous researchers have adopted both qualitative as well as quantitative methodologies in their studies. The survey questionnaire method has been adopted by (Spowart 2011) and (de Schepper et al. 2021). While (Spowart 2011) has focused on collecting responses from final year hospital management students (de Schepper et al. 2021), have collected responses from four types of respondents, including third-year students, fourth-year students, academic students advisor, and industry supervisors. (Spowart 2011) has used collected responses from all 65 students through the census method. On the other hand (de Schepper et al. 2021), have collected 288 responses through multi-stage cluster sampling. Review methodologies have been adopted by (Mei 2011) and (Govender and Vaaland 2020). Qualitative methodologies adopted include exploratory interviews (Rook and McManus 2016; Ngubane et al. 2020); semi-structured group interviews (McBeath et al. 2018), focused groups (van der Bijl and Taylor 2016), and case study (Pusiran et al. 2020). All of the qualitative methods have opted for purposive and snowball sampling techniques. Rook and McManus (2016) have conducted exploratory interviews with academicians (12), career advisors (8), professionals (10), and student stakeholders (8), thereby making their sample size 38. A similar approach has been adopted by (Ngubane et al. 2020), who have collected responses from 21 respondents comprising campus managers (2), senior vocational lecturers (6), and work-based education champions (13). McBeath et al. (2018) have collected responses through semi-structured group interviews. Their sample size was 25 undergraduate students (Pusiran et al. 2020), who have adopted the case study approach, have interviewed hotel management students (10) and departmental heads of hotels (10). van der Bijl and Taylor (2016) have studied the responses of 65 industry teachers through the focus group method.

3.7 Understanding Graduate Attributes

As we witness a transformational change in the job market due to the pandemic COVID-19, it becomes essential that B-school graduates develop a set of capabilities to be effective at work. Job aspirants are continuously increasing; therefore, employers no longer recruit simply based on degree status. A degree has become a prerequisite only, and it has become essential that graduates develop a profile of attributes to make themselves work-ready. Such attributes are classified into two broad categories: personal attributes and interactive attributes.

3.8 Personal Attributes

Graduates are required to develop a broad range of personal attributes, which substantially add to the ability of graduates to fit into the challenging work environment.

Knowledge: Employers consider subject-based knowledge an essential attribute in their graduate employees. Usually, the employers want that graduates possess knowledge of core areas and must have the ability to acquire knowledge (Harvey et al. 1997).

Intellect: Intellect includes a wide range of attributes. Analytical thinking, critiquing, synthesis, and problem-solving are vital attributes of graduates. Intellect is a preferred attribute for many employers than a degree. Graduates have to demonstrate their intellectual ability to solve problems using "higher-level" skills such as analysis, critique, and synthesis (Harvey et al. 1997).

Willingness to learn: Willingness and the ability to learn during employment and continuous learning are considered desirable attributes. Therefore, graduates are required to learn new skills throughout their careers (Harvey et al. 1997).

Flexibility and adaptability: In essence, the focus on intellect and willingness to learn reflects the need for graduates to be flexible and adaptable. Graduates need to respond to change, pre-empt change, and ultimately lead to change (Harvey et al. 1997).

Self-skills: In many organisations, it is important that graduate-level employees take on responsibility, use initiative, and identify their work agendas (within overall parameters) to add value with minimum supervision. Self-belief and self-confidence are also necessary when pushing boundaries and motivating others to be innovative. Graduates need to develop a range of self-regulatory skills and self-assurance skills (Harvey et al. 1997).

3.9 *Interactive Attributes*

Though essential, personal attributes are not sufficient in themselves in the context of work demands. The workplace requires various interactive features, such as communication skills, teamwork, interpersonal skills, et cetera. Present-day organisations need the ability to (Harvey et al. 1997):

- communicate, formally and informally, with a wide range of people, both internal and external to the organisation;
- relate to, and feel comfortable with, people at all levels in the organisation as well as a range of external stakeholders, to be able to make and maintain relationships as circumstances change; and
- work effectively in teams, often more than one team at once, and re-adjust roles from one project situation to another in an ever-shifting work situation. Employers and graduates indicate a wide range of desirable attributes. Still, the key ones, emphasised across all sectors, are summed up by a recent graduate: "You have got to be able to get on with people and communicate - all this working in a team".

Communication skills: Communication skills emerge as one of the most important qualities employers require of graduates. It covers an enormous range of attributes, both written and oral. Various studies have noted that a small proportion of employers indicate that some graduates showed a grasp of fundamentals that fell below their expectations of graduate standards. These fundamentals are increasingly crucial in modem organisations. Employees can no longer rely on administrative support and will increasingly have to prepare their letters and reports and communicate via direct electronic links. In present-day organisations, the primary use of IT has become more of a fundamental requirement of graduates. "Oral communication" includes, among other things, the ability to undertake formal presentations, the ability to intervene effectively in meetings and participate in group discussions, informal exchange of ideas with colleagues, and the ability to persuade others (clients and colleagues). The advent of integrated job requirements means that employees are taking on increasingly complex roles and need to engage with people at various levels to be effective (Harvey et al. 1997).

Teamwork: Teamwork is an integral part of working in a modem organisation. The team situation requires a high level of mutual trust and cooperation. Several organisations refer to the importance of teamwork in terms of problem-solving and suggest this may be a more creative way of working as it draws on the strengths of a range of individuals. Effective teamworking includes leadership. However, it is vital that employees adopt a range of teamwork roles and are not always striving to lead teams. Furthermore, leading teams is not about commanding but persuading people to do things and develop ideas. It is about encouraging involvement and ideas at all levels (Harvey et al. 1997).

Interpersonal skills: Interpersonal skills are an essential attribute of prospective graduate employees. It has been identified as a vital element in relating and interacting with clients and customers. It represents an issue high on the agenda of many organisations. More often than not, interpersonal skills relate directly to fitting into the workplace culture. Interpersonal skills are somewhat less tangible than communication or teamworking skills, and some employers regard them as slightly more challenging to develop through training programmes (Harvey et al. 1997).

3.10 Interrelationship of Interactive Attributes

Communication, teamworking, and interpersonal skills are correlated in many situations. For instance, it is difficult for someone with underdeveloped interpersonal skills to engage effectively with colleagues and clients, let alone inspire a team. Employers want manpower that will be effective in a future changing world. These interrelated attributes facilitate maximum value-added by enabling people to fit into the workplace culture. Being a good communicator, with well-developed interpersonal skills, and an effective team player with an understanding of the culture enables the graduate to "fit in" to the organisation. Such attributes are also necessary for effective organisational adaptation as good team working, communication, and interpersonal skills are vital to persuade people to innovative courses of action. Developing ideas in a corporate setting is also contingent on the coming together of these skills. On another level, communication, teamwork, and interpersonal skills are fundamental to any organisation's transformation. People who have highly developed interpersonal skills and multi-layered communication abilities and can combine these with their higher-level intellectual skills are required to help transform organisations to stay ahead of their competitors (Fig. 1) (Harvey et al. 1997).

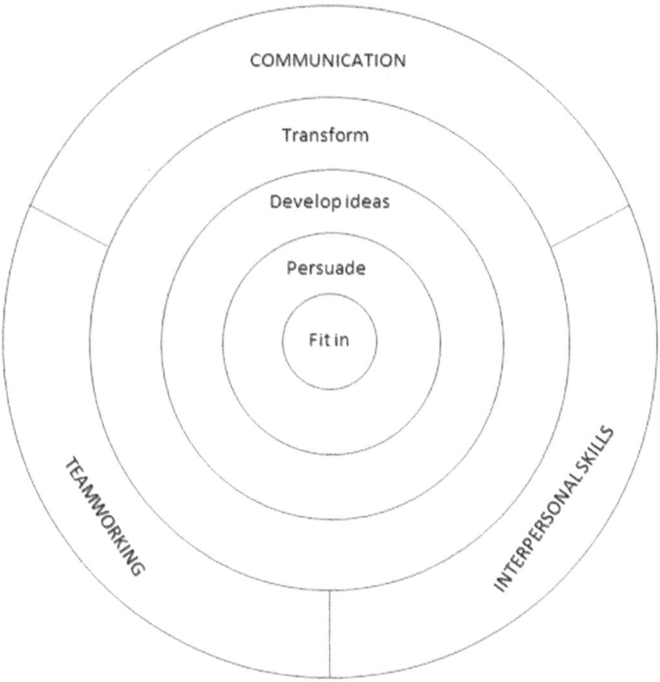

Fig. 1 Interrelationship among attributes (*Source* Harvey et al. 1997)

3.11 *Aspects of WIL at Top-Ranking UAE Higher Education Institutes*

3.11.1 *Summer Internship/Training*

Summer internship/training helps students learn skills by applying theory learnt in the classroom, being updated with the world, and using their theoretical knowledge in practice to prepare for the future. So the main goal is to level up students' skills. This is an opportunity to experience the job before students get the job. They learn about corporate life, taking on new challenges, handling clients, working on real-life projects, building networks, etc.

3.11.2 *Industry-Related Projects*

Most MBA programmes allow the students to undertake an industry project, which they complete after regular class hours. This project introduces them to an organisation and, together with nominated managers and academic support, provides an opportunity to investigate a real business problem as part of their programme of study. The Subject Coordinator offers help and support (www.sydneybusinessschool.edu.au).

3.11.3 *Interactive Business Challenges*

Students are engaged in the latest know-how, which simulates a real-world consultancy experience for an organisation, and students work as consultants. This opportunity prepares students for careers in many specialist fields and gives organisations a new perspective on their business strategies (www.sydneybusinessschool.edu.au).

3.11.4 *International Workplace Practice*

Some top business schools follow international Workplace Practice in UAE, which is designed to meet the employment aspirations of students to undertake work in global settings. This practice is a part of the curriculum and is listed as an elective subject with given credits. This subject crosses boundaries between theory and practice and maximises the students' potential to access workplace experiences leading to formal post-university employment options. Students acquire and develop work-based learning skill sets; critically examine the discourses and theories of intercultural competence; and develop cultural awareness and business communication skills that are fit for purpose regardless of students' career aspirations (www.sydneybusinessschool.edu.au).

3.11.5 Industrial Visits

B-schools arrange industrial visits to students to provide students with functional opportunities in different sectors like IT, Manufacturing and services, finance, and marketing. Industrial visits help to combine theoretical knowledge with industrial knowledge. These visits offer a great source to gain practical knowledge. Students can observe and learn how theatrical concepts are put into action, thereby aiding their practical learning. Students are exposed to the real working environment and shown how things are performed in an organisation (www.google.com/search?q=industrial+visits).

3.11.6 General Learning Outcomes

Work-integrated learning, especially where an internship or work placement is involved, is concerned with student learning in three generic areas. These are—integration and application of knowledge, development of workplace competencies, reflection on actions and decisions. Although some discipline-specific outcomes might be incorporated, it is recommended that learning outcomes reflect these areas.

- Effectively integrate and appropriately apply previous learning and knowledge to make and justify decisions in a real-world context.
- Demonstrate workplace competencies such as professionalism, confidentiality, communication, responsibility for decision-making, teamwork, et cetera.
- Reflect upon decisions, personal choices, and actions in the workplace and critically appraise their appropriateness.

4 Methodology

4.1 Problem Statement

In recent years a thought process has been developing that WIL practices in Business schools should focus upon and fulfil the needs of all the stakeholders; that is, students, employers, and business schools. The holistic approach towards WIL practices ensures that these practices have been structured as per the employability aptitudes. The different abilities and skills expected by various industries and businesses must be in line with the WIL practices adopted by the institutes. We can also argue whether

WIL practices are sufficient to solve the employability problems. Along these lines, the researchers felt the need to examine the arrangement of the abilities and skills; namely leadership, teamwork, communication, logical reasoning and analytical skills, adaptability to change, planning and organising, employee morale, ability to work under pressure, etc., expected by the industry from the higher education institutions/business schools of GCC countries. This paper attempts to study WIL practices adopted by higher education institutions/business schools of GCC countries and various stakeholders to benefit from such programmes. The critical question is whether WIL has become a panacea to employability and increases job opportunities for graduates.

4.2 *Objectives of the Study*

The following objectives are pursued, keeping in mind the research questions. Hence, the objectives of the study to be achieved are as follows:

- To identify WIL practices adopted by higher education institutions/business schools of GCC countries.
- To assess the effectiveness of WIL practices, if adopted, in developing employability skills among students of GCC countries.
- To understand the influencing factors on employers during the hiring process.

4.3 *Conceptual Model*

The proposed conceptual model of research presents the variables based on the literature review and their relationship with each other. Figure 2 illustrates the proposed model developed by the researchers for the present study.

4.4 *Research Design*

This research is a descriptive study without any experimentation. Preferably, the observations are made on the respondents' natural course of action, keeping this study a cross-sectional study. Since the observations are taken once from a single sample of respondents out of the population and do not require any similar observations from different

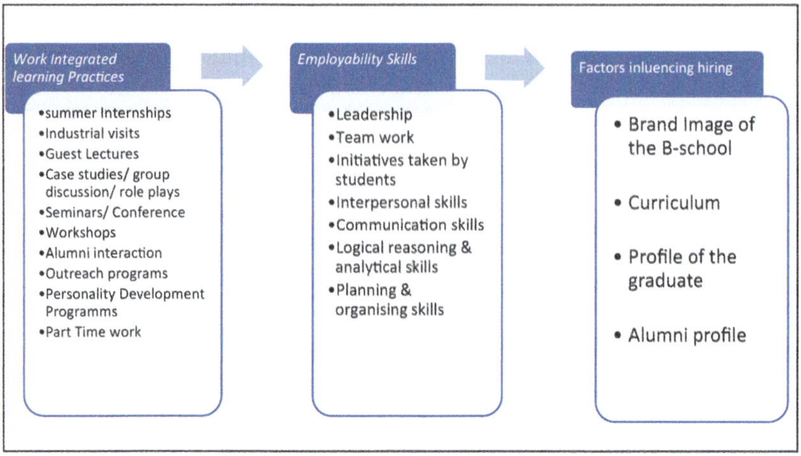

Fig. 2 Work-integrated practices and employability skills (*Source* Authors)

time-frames thus, it is called a non-experimental and single cross-sectional study (Malhotra and Dash 2011) explicitly. Based on the findings from the literature review, a set of directional hypotheses has been framed. All the possible hypotheses have been deduced based on the available literature and summarised.

4.5 *Instruments for Measurement*

At the preliminary stage, the chosen scales for research variables, i.e., WIL practices and employability, were combined with demographic variables. Two separate instruments were prepared; one for students to study WIL and another for employers to assess employability. This study used constructs with actual items adopted from previously tested and validated scales in Part A of each questionnaire.

Part B of each research questionnaire contained items related to demographics. Demographics details gather information about the name of the B-school/organisation, Course/Designation, Academic year/Experience at the present position. Considering the participants' disposition, the items used were brief, quick, and easy to comprehend. The researchers took due care to avoid ambiguous, vague, estimation based, generalisation type, leading, double-barrelled, and presumptuous questions (Boyd et al. 1981). This adapted measurement instrument was then discussed with different subject experts for their opinions and feedback. The questions were modified to suit the study's intent, and a proper format for the questions was decided. For assessing content validity, adopted items were assessed by expert opinion. This modified questionnaire was then piloted. Based on the feedback from the pilot study, the questionnaire was finalised. The quantitative data were collected on a close-ended, structured questionnaire. The research instrument consisted of statements pertaining to all the variables selected for the study. Five-point Likert scale was used for data collection.

4.6 *Sampling Frame and Technique*

To understand and suggest strategies to the stakeholders, the research was narrowed down to business schools offering various programmes in the United Arab Emirates. The literature review provided insights on how majorly WIL practices are adopted by B-schools, which are a part of higher education. Several private B-schools and public universities are imparting management education in UAE. So, firstly list of top-ranking B-schools was collected. Secondly, B-schools dealing in just one or two specialisations were not considered for the study; instead, schools offering a variety of management programmes were considered. Lastly, another criterion to filter the B-schools was based on the year of establishment/number of years of existence. B-schools existing for five years or more were considered. A purposive judgemental sampling technique has been used in the current study, which relies on the personal judgement of the researcher rather than a chance to select sample elements (Malhotra and Birks 2007).

4.7 *Sample Size*

This cross-sectional study was conducted through a direct questionnaire method. To extract the opinions of the respondents on the dimensions of WIL practices and their impact on employability, a series of questions have been formulated, keeping the study objectives in focus. During the survey, 518 questionnaires were circulated, and 294 were collected. Out of these 294 questionnaires, 37 questionnaires were either incomplete or partially filled and were not included in the data analysis as they were not suitable for use. Furthermore, five questionnaires had a high number of missing responses. After screening the number of valid responses, the total number of questionnaires used for the present study is 252.

4.8 Data Collection

Data from secondary data sources available in the private or public domain was collected. The secondary data were used to validate the primary data. These were also used to generate a holistic, contextual picture of WIL practices. The mode of primary data collection was personal. For the collection of final data, the research questionnaire reached likely respondents through personal contacts and emails. The Snowball technique for data collection was used. The B-school practices were taken through friends and relatives employed there. Some of the friends and relatives employed in the targeted universities helped carry the questionnaire personally to their present and passed out students to gather their responses. Some of the friends and relatives employed in the industry were contacted to get data on employability. The respondents were assured that the data obtained would be used only for academic research. The respondents' anonymity was also ensured.

5 Analysis

Various statistical tools were used to test the hypotheses for quantitative data analysis. Data has been analysed and presented in three categories.

5.1 Category I: Perception of Students Towards WIL Practices

It has been found that most of the B-schools understand the importance of various work-integrated learning practices and how these can be incorporated into the curriculum so that students become industry-ready at the time of job recruitment. Recently the industry has started exerting pressure on B-schools that their graduates must learn those skills which are required for effective performance on the job. Companies in almost every sector and industry tend to spend a substantial amount on new employees' induction training and orientation programmes. Companies were hiring graduates with a professional degrees but realised that these graduates are not employment-ready and lack sufficient skills pertaining to the job demands. This realisation has compelled the companies to focus on those graduates who possess the required skills and do not need extensive training. Companies demand deliverables from the side of the recruits to justify the cost associated with human resources. Therefore, to minimise the training cost and maximise the benefits, the companies influence the B-schools to revisit their professional programmes and fulfil the industry's demand. Due to this pressure, the B-schools have made visible changes and incorporated those practices, which have been named WIL practices. These practices help the students to get an idea of the work situation and the prerequisites for the job.

WIL practices have a broad-spectrum range, which can be classified into two groups: in-house practices and practices conducted outside the institute.

5.2 *Level of Attention Given to In-House WIL Practices*

Many practices such as case studies, group discussions, and role-plays have become integral to the management curriculum. Management schools also provide extension lectures, personality development programmes, career counselling, seminars and conferences, workshops, and alumni interaction (Fig. 3, Table 2).

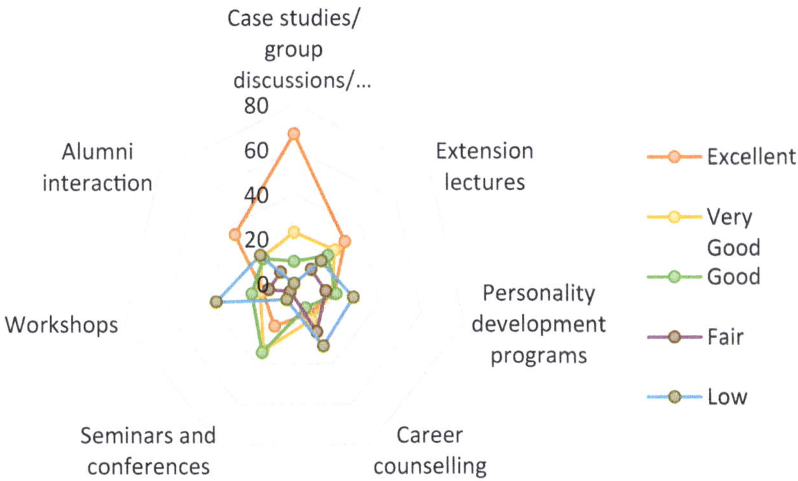

Fig. 3 In-house WIL practices

Table 2 In-house WIL practices

Values are in %

	Case study/group discussion/role play	*Extension lectures*	*Personality development programmes*	*Career counselling*	*Seminar and conferences*	*Workshop*	*Alumni interaction*
Excellent	67	30	19	15	21	15	35
Very good	23	24	18	18	33	16	19
Good	10	20	20	12	34	20	18
Fair	00	10	15	24	04	12	08
Low	00	16	28	31	08	37	20

It has been found that there is comprehensive incorporation of WIL practices in the management curriculum, and students actively participate in these activities. These practices are framed as per industry requirements and designed in consultation with industry experts and alumni of the institute. Students participate in those activities actively, which have been designed according to their level of learning. Students are aware of various practices, but their participation varies in different activities. When a wide variety of WIL practices are incorporated into the curriculum, students try to align their areas of interest with a particular activity. Though a wide variety of practices provide a broad canvas to the students, it does not guarantee that it always enhances their skills.

Most of the students feel that case studies and group discussions have become an integral part of the pedagogy in management. Management institutes also pay attention to extension lectures, and seminars and conferences attention. Alumni interaction has gained momentum recently, and alumni are often invited to their alma mater on different occasions. These interactions provide opportunities for students to learn about the challenges prevailing in the industry and to develop networks. Personality development programmes and career counselling are two grey areas requiring further attention.

5.3 *Level of Attention Given for Activities Conducted Outside the B-Schools*

It is identified that after participating in WIL practices conducted outside, such as summer internships, students encounter the opportunities which create readiness in them to transform into professionals. Faculty having industry exposure also help the students to get an insight into the opportunities and challenges posed by the industry. These activities help the students to network and develop contacts with industry professionals and potential employers (Fig. 4, Table 3).

The majority of the students are satisfied with the quality of the summer internship. B-schools have an in-house placement cell, which takes care of the summer internship requirement of the students. Students also get the opportunities to participate in management events organised by other institutes. The perception of students regarding industrial visits and outreach programmes is moderate to low.

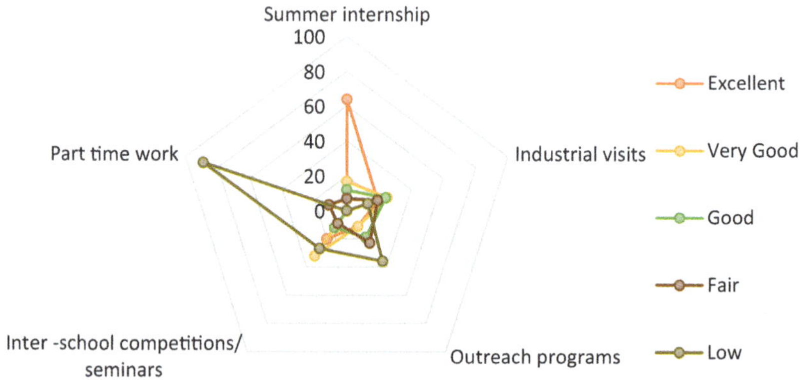

Fig. 4 Outside B-school practices

Table 3 Outside B-school practices

Values are in %

	Summer internship	*Industrial visits*	*Outreach programmes*	*Interschool competitions/seminars*	*Part-time work*
Excellent	64	19	11	20	0
Very good	17	25	11	32	0
Good	12	24	19	12	0
Fair	7	19	23	09	11
Low	0	13	36	27	89

5.4 *Category II: Comparison Between the Perception of Students vs. Employers Towards Employability Skills*

The primary purpose of incorporating various WIL practices in the curriculum is to develop the students to gain the industry skills. Business schools tend to focus on leadership development, teamwork development, developing interpersonal skills, helping them to take the initiative, developing communication skills, analytical skills, planning and organising skills, etc.

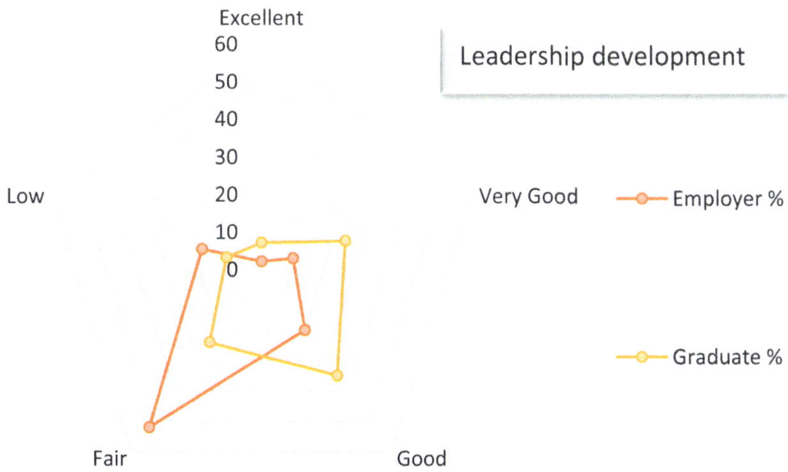

Fig. 5 Leadership development

Table 4 Leadership development

Values are in %	*Employer*	*Graduate*
Excellent	2	7
Very good	9	24
Good	20	35
Fair	52	24
Low	17	10

5.5 *Level of Attention Given to Leadership Development*

Most of the students think they have gained leadership qualities during their programme, but employers believe that most are not very good at this skill (Fig. 5, Table 4).

5.6 *Level of Attention Given for Team Work Development*

The majority of the students think that they have gained teamwork qualities during their programme, and employers also believe that most of them are pretty good when asked to work in a team (Fig. 6, Table 5).

Fig. 6 Teamwork

Table 5 Teamwork

Values are in %		
	Employer	*Graduate*
Excellent	8	7
Very good	31	20
Good	46	37
Fair	8	24
Low	7	10

5.7 *Level of Attention Given to Initiatives Taken by Students*

Students have a notion that they are pretty good at taking the initiative, but the employers feel that most graduates lack the said skill (Fig. 7, Table 6).

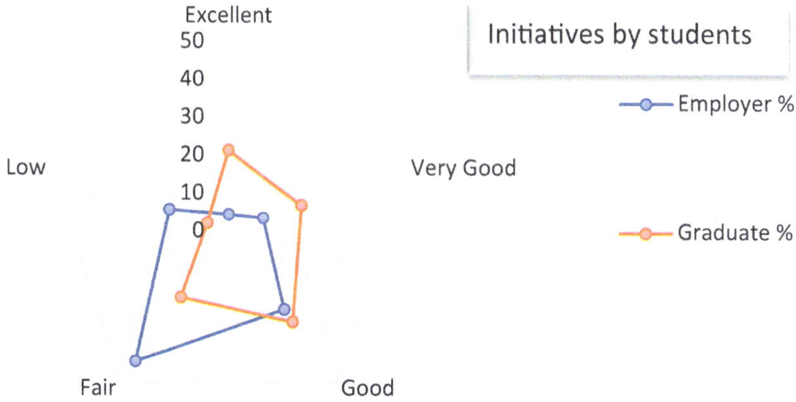

Fig. 7 Initiatives by students

Table 6 Initiatives by students

Values are in %	*Employer*	*Graduate*
Excellent	4	21
Very good	10	21
Good	26	30
Fair	43	22
Low	17	06

5.8 *Level of Attention Given to the Development of Interpersonal Skills*

The majority of the students think they have learnt interpersonal skills, but the employers disagree with this. In the real job scenario, recruits cannot manage interpersonal problems in case of conflicts (Fig. 8, Table 7).

5.9 *Level of Attention Given to the Development of Communication Skills*

The majority of the students think they have attained excellent communication skills, and employers also agree with this (Fig. 9, Table 8).

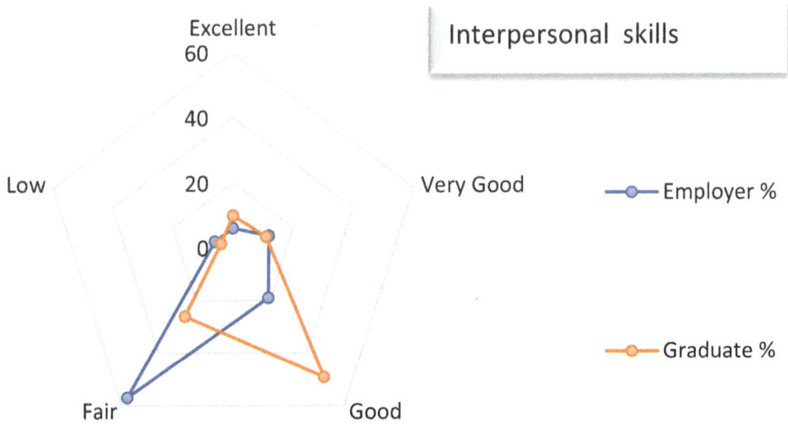

Fig. 8 Interpersonal skills

Table 7 Interpersonal skills

Values are in %		
	Employer	*Graduate*
Excellent	06	10
Very good	12	11
Good	19	49
Fair	57	26
Low	06	04

5.10 Level of Attention Given to the Development of Critical Reasoning and Analytical Skills

The majority of the students think they possess sound reasoning and analytical skills. Employers believe that management schools impart reasoning and analytical skills up to a desirable level (Fig. 10, Table 9).

5.11 Level of Attention Given to Planning and Organising Skills

The majority of the students think they are good at planning and organising, but the employers disagree with this (Fig. 11, Table 10).

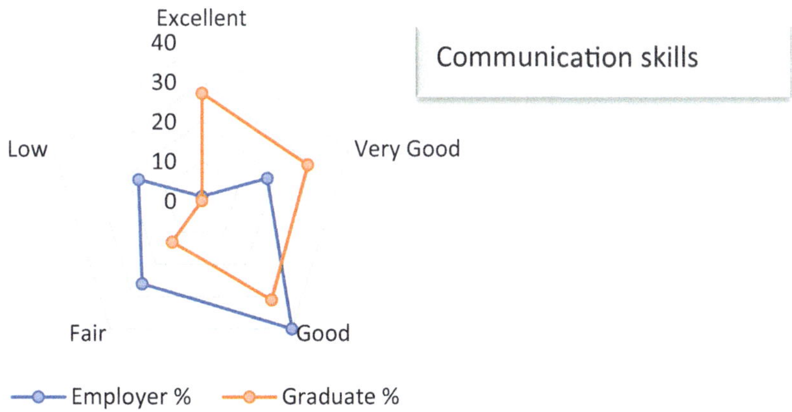

Fig. 9 Communication skills

Table 8 Communication skills

Values are in %		
	Employer	*Graduate*
Excellent	01	27
Very good	18	29
Good	40	31
Fair	26	13
Low	17	00

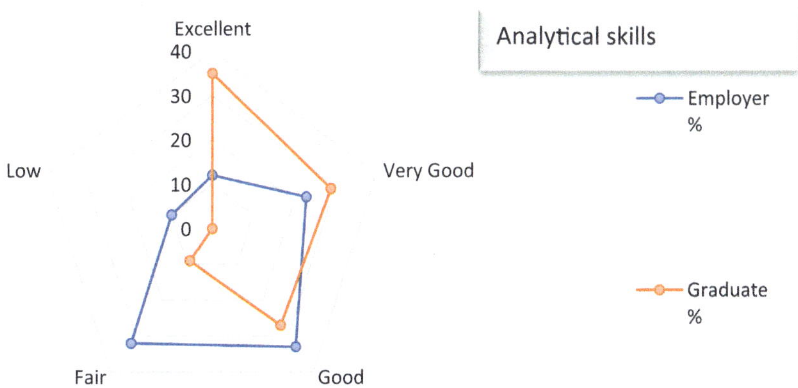

Fig. 10 Critical reasoning and analytical skills

Table 9 Critical reasoning and analytical skills

Values are in %	*Employer*	*Graduate*
Excellent	12	35
Very good	23	29
Good	33	27
Fair	32	09
Low	10	00

Fig. 11 Planning and organising skills

Table 10 Planning and organising skills

Values are in %	*Employer*	*Graduate*
Excellent	0	7
Very good	3	3
Good	18	56
Fair	64	20
Low	15	14

Table 11 Influencing factors on employers

Values are in %

Factors *Level of entry*	*Brand Image of B-schools*	*Profile of the graduate*	*Curriculum*	*Position/performance of alumni*
Entry-level hiring	36	24	29	11
Middle-level hiring	17	67	06	11

5.12 *Category III: Influencing Factors on Employers During the Hiring Process*

The employers are influenced by the brand image and curriculum of the B-school while recruiting at the entry level. The institute's credibility and quality play a significant role in entry-level hiring. Employers prefer a given B-school and tend to offer placements to the graduates of their desired institute. Often, these employers have a symbiotic relationship with a few institutes and offer assistance during curriculum development. Another factor for hiring at the entry level is the graduates' profile, including their educational background. In middle-level hiring, the most critical variable is the candidate's profile. The best predictor for any job is the candidate's past performance in a similar situation. Therefore, curriculum or WIL practices are not essential at this level of hiring (Fig. 12, Table 11).

6 Findings

The findings based on the analysis of the data are presented below.

6.1 *Category I: Perception of Students Towards WIL Practices*

- Most of the students feel that case studies and group discussions have become an integral part of the pedagogy in management.
- Management institutes also pay attention to extension lectures, seminars and conferences.
- Alumni interaction has gained momentum recently, and alumni are often invited to their alma mater on different occasions.

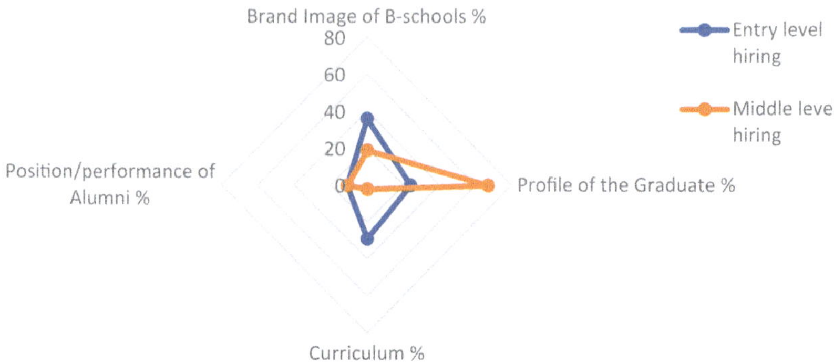

Fig. 12 Influencing factors on employers

- Personality development programmes and career counselling are two grey areas requiring further attention.
- The majority of the students are satisfied with the quality of the summer internship.
- And also get the opportunities to participate in management events organised by other institutes.
- Students feel that the institution must organise more industrial visits and outreach programmes.

6.2 *Category II: Comparison Between the Perception of Students vs. Employers Towards Employability Skills*

- The majority of the students think they have gained leadership qualities, are pretty good at taking the initiative, have learnt interpersonal skills, and are good at planning and organising, but employers believe that most are not very good at these skills.
- The majority of the students think that they have gained teamwork qualities, have attained excellent communication skills during their programme, and possess sound reasoning and analytical skills. Employers are also of the opinion that most of them are pretty good at these skills.

6.3 Category III: Influencing Factors on Employers During the Hiring Process

- The employers are influenced by the brand image and curriculum of the B-school while recruiting at the entry level.
- In middle-level hiring, the most critical variable is the profile of the candidate.

7 Managerial Implications

The findings have implications for the management institutions and other stakeholders in order to get more from work-integrated learning. Work-integrated learning can become a panacea to the employability of B-school graduates in GCC countries if the care is taken to use these practices judiciously.

- In order to make the WIL practices effective, the present research has identified that these practices should be framed according to the employers and industry requirements as well as tailored according to the student's level of learning.
- There should be wide incorporation of WIL practices in the curriculum of B-schools to develop the students' skill set and make them industry-ready.
- When students actively participate in WIL practices, there exists a readiness among the students to transform into professionals. Therefore, these practices should be designed and delivered in such a manner that the active participation of the graduates is solicited.
- B-schools should develop an industry-academia interface and assist the students in developing industrial contacts and networking. Potential employers should be contacted regularly to get their feedback, involving them in curriculum design and seeking their suggestions on the skill sets they want their future employees to possess.
- B-schools should maintain a good rapport with their alumni as they create the perception of the institute in the industry. Recognising the achievements of the alumni and involving them in B-school activities, particularly curriculum design and projects, are the key options.

8 Conclusion

An in-depth study was conducted to understand the current WIL practices adopted by various B-schools in UAE and their usefulness in employability. A growing awareness prompted this study as a gap existed between the skills and attitude imparted to the graduates in B-schools and the suitability of employable skills needed by the industry. WIL is comparatively a recent approach trying to match the demands of the industry through appropriate curriculum design and filling the gap between students' learning outcomes and their skill development. WIL programmes require great association between all stakeholders, including students, institutions, and industry. Compelling work-integrated learning exercises address the issue of industry, graduates, and B-schools in creating, conveying, and reflecting after learning encounters that advantage all stakeholders. Work-integrated learning in management schools has become an important component of the curriculum, and employers also demand employability among graduates.

References

Boyd, H. W., Westfall, R., & Stasch, S. (1981). *Marketing Research Text and Cases*. 6th ed. Chicago: Homewood.

Cooper, L., Orrell, J., & Bowden, M. (2010). *Work-integrated learning: A guide to effective practice*. Routledge, Abingdon, UK. https://www.routledge.com/Work-Integrated-Learning-A-Guide-to-Effective-Practice/Cooper-Orrell-Bowden/p/book/9780415556774.

de Schepper, J., Sotiriadou, P., & Hill, B. (2021). The role of critical reflection as an employability skill in sport management. *European Sport Management Quarterly*, 21(2), 280–301. https://doi.org/10.1080/16184742.2020.1742184.

Govender, C. M., & Vaaland, T. I. (2020). Business students and work-life: mind the gaps! *Education and Training*. https://doi.org/10.1108/ET-11-2018-0246.

Harvey, L., Moon, S., Geall, V., & Bower, R. (1997). *Graduates' work: Organisational change and students' attributes*. Centre for Research into Quality, Birmingham. https://journals.sagepub.com/doi/abs/10.1177/095042229701100504.

Jackson, D., & Collings, D. (2018). The influence of work-integrated learning and paid work during studies on graduate employment and underemployment. *Higher Education*, 76, 402–425. https://doi.org/10.1007/s10734-017-0216-z.

Malhotra, N., & Birks, D. (2007). *Marketing research: An applied approach*. Prentice Hall.
Malhotra, N. K., & Dash, S. (2011). *Marketing research an applied orientation*. Pearson Publishing.
McBeath, M., Drysdale, M. T. B., & Bohn, N. (2018). Work-integrated learning and the importance of peer support and sense of belonging. *Education and Training*, 60(1), 39–53. https://doi.org/10.1108/ET-05-2017-0070.
Mei, X. (2011). Talking about the dual-qualification teachers team construction of automation in higher vocational education under work-integrated learning. *BMEI 2011—Proceedings 2011 International Conference on Business Management and Electronic Information*, 2, 418–421. https://doi.org/10.1109/ICBMEI.2011.5917936.
Ngubane, P., Mncube, D. W., Mabusela, M. S., & Olaniran, S. O. (2020). Exploratory study of tvet stakeholders' experiences of implementing work-based education in rural ecology. *Academy of Entrepreneurship Journal*, 26(1), 1–12.
Nicolescu, L., & Pǎun, C. (2009). Relating higher education with the labour market: Graduates' expectations and employers' requirements. *Tertiary Education and Management*, *15*(1), 17–33. https://doi.org/10.1080/13583880802700024.
Pusiran, A. K., Janin, Y., Ismail, S., & Dalinting, L. J. (2020). Hospitality internship program insights. *Worldwide Hospitality and Tourism Themes*, 12(2), 155–164. https://doi.org/10.1108/WHATT-12-2019-0079.
Rook, L., & McManus, L. (2016). Viewing WIL in business schools through a new lens: Moving to the edge of chaos with complexity theory. *Emergence: Complexity and Organization*, 18(2), 1–14. https://doi.org/10.emerg/10.17357.7ac48d7ffaa06746b2a03944fcc1ee41.
Small, L., Shacklock, K., & Marchant, T. (2018). Employability: A contemporary review for higher education stakeholders. *Journal of Vocational Education and Training*, 70(1), 148–166. https://doi.org/10.1080/13636820.2017.1394355.
Smith, C. (2012). Evaluating the quality of work-integrated learning curricula: A comprehensive framework. *Higher Education Research and Development*, 31(2), 247–262. https://doi.org/10.1080/07294360.2011.558072.
Smith, C., & Worsfold, K. (2015). Unpacking the learning-work nexus: "Priming" as lever for high-quality learning outcomes in work-integrated learning curricula. *Studies in Higher Education*, 40(1), 22–42. https://doi.org/10.1080/03075079.2013.806456.
Spowart, J. (2011). Hospitality students' competencies: Are they work Ready? *Journal of Human Resources in Hospitality and Tourism*, 10(2), 169–181. https://doi.org/10.1080/15332845.2011.536940.

van der Bijl, A., & Taylor, V. (2016). Nature and dynamics of industry-based workplace learning for South African TVET lecturers. *Industry and Higher Education*, 30(2), 98–108. https://doi.org/10.5367/ihe.2016.0297.

https://find-mba.com/schools/africa/united-arab-emirates.

https://www.eduniversal-ranking.com/business-school-university-ranking-in-united-arab-emirates.html.

https://www.sydneybusinessschool.edu.au/study/work-integrated-learning/. Work-integrated learning—University of Wollongong—UOW.

https://www.google.com/search?q=industrial+visits+for+college+students&oq=industrial+visits&aqs=chrome.1.69i57j0l4j0i22i30l3j0i10i22i30j0i22i30.8452j0j7&sourceid=chrome&ie=UTF-8.

CHAPTER 4

Migrating Human Capital: A Case Study of Indian Migrants in the GCC Countries

Anisur Rahman

1 Introduction

Human resources and human capital are two concepts that are quite similar in that they both refer to current or potential human skills, abilities, and talent that are crucial to the success of any firm or organization. However, human capital refers to the skills, training, experience, education, knowledge, know-how and competencies that individuals give to businesses today. While, human resources are a pool of human abilities, knowledge and skill that may be drawn upon and extended as needed. Both human capital and resource are the key elements for the development of any nation. In simpler terms, human resources imply the entire population available to a country. It is understood to comprise not merely qualified personnel but also unskilled or semi-skilled labour force.

A. Rahman (✉)
Human Resource Development Centre, Jamia Millia Islamia, New Delhi, India
e-mail: arahman@jmi.ac.in

A. Mishrif et al. (eds.), *Nationalization of Gulf Labour Markets*,
The Political Economy of the Middle East,
https://doi.org/10.1007/978-981-19-8072-5_4

It includes, in fact, all the persons who could be put into productive activities. The development of human resources or human capital means the development of both the mental and physical aspects of the productive capacity of workers. The physical aspects of the productive capacity of workers can be developed by means of health services, nutrition, etc., and mental aspects by modern Education and proper training. Thus, human resource is "the process of increasing knowledge, skills and capabilities of all the people in a given society" (Harbison and Myers 1964: 6). Education and health care are two principal inputs for augmenting human resource development, which is also valid in the formulation of human capital. For the past few decades, it has increasingly been recognized as the primary determinant in every country's overall strategy of economic development. Economists and social scientists use the term "human capital" to describe personal characteristics that are valuable in the manufacturing process. It includes, among other things, staff knowledge, skills, know-how, excellent health and education. Governments or organizations may invest in human capital by investing in education and training, for example, to increase quality and productivity. In contemporary literature, Robert Gibbons, an economist at MIT, and Michael Waldman, an economist at Cornell University, coined the novel idea of task-specific human capital in 2004. The notion highlights that human capital is often explicitly accumulated for the nature of the activity (or the abilities necessary for the task) and that the human capital collected for the task benefits many organizations that require transferrable skills.

In the Third-World countries, the case of human resource development cannot be overstated as most of these countries do not have adequate financial resources to educate and train their requisite human resource or have a large population base or both. An alternative course of action is the import of labour force from abroad. But this is not at all a desirable solution for various reasons. It is also found that all the Gulf (Gulf Cooperation Council) countries have adopted the alternative way along with efforts to develop indigenous infrastructure for human resource development. The Gulf Cooperation Council (GCC) comprises of six countries, namely Saudi Arabia, United Arab Emirates, Kuwait, Bahrain, Oman and Qatar. The organization was formed in 1981 to bring overall development to the Gulf region. In this paper, an attempt has been made to examine the GCC's socio-demographic profiles, economic conditions, progress and development of Education and health, etc. The Gulf immigration policy has also been discussed in this paper so that the need for expatriates, especially Indian workers, can be understood in the contemporary context. Finally, how the Gulf countries will meet the challenges of human capital in their countries is being briefly examined in terms of some policy implications for these countries.

2 Socio-Demographic Profiles

Demographic change is a social reality in the twenty-first century. Fertility decline has occurred in most parts of the world. People have relished a smaller family size to maintain a reasonable quality of life, and it has now become a need of the day. People migrate from one place to another in search of jobs or education within the country and outside. The Gulf Cooperation Council (GCC) is one of the important destinations which attract a large number of expatriate labour from outside the region. It is witnessed that there is enormous diversity found within the region. Collectively, these countries accounted for four million populations in 1950, which increased to 55 million in 2017. There is about thirteen times increase in 67 years. It is projected that this population is expected to increase to about 67 million by 2030, then 77 million by 2050 and 78 million by 2100.

Further, it is noted that the share of the GCC population to the world population, which was just 0.2% in 1952, increased to 0.7% in 2017, and it is likely to remain at the same level for the next 83 years. The population of the GCC region is considered one of the highest growing populations in the world. It is mainly due to immigration as non-nationals constitute almost 50% of the total population today. To control the growth of people in the GCC region, the respective government follows strict immigration policies. Over the past few years, immigration policies have been based on approaches for localization and nationalization of their local labour force. But this region is still heavily dependent on expatriate workers.

It is evident in the Table 1 that in 1975, the percentage of nationals was more than 90% whereas foreigners were hardly 10%. There was a rapid annual growth of non-nationals of 14.5% compared to 3.2% growth in the case of the national population. Because of this, as can be seen, in 1990 the national population fell down to 63.4% from 90.3% in 1975. It is found that the composition of nationals has been declining every subsequent year whereas non-nationals have grown. The percentage of

Table 1 National and foreign populations in the GCC countries from 1975 to 2016

Year	*Absolute numbers*			*Percentage*		*Annual rate of growth*	
	Total	*National*	*Foreign*	*National (%)*	*Foreign (%)*	*National (%)*	*Foreign (%)*
1975	9,731,259	8,790,223	941,036	90.3	9.7	3.2	14.5
1990	22,522,620	14,281,239	8,241,381	63.4	36.6	3.3	5.0
2010	41,093,624	23,536,409	17,557,215	57.3	42.7		
2014–2016	51,467,147	26,253,067	25,214,080	51.0	49		

Source (Fargues and Brouwer 2012)

foreigners in the GCC countries grew from 22.9% in 1975 to 38.5% in 2002 and then to 49% of the total population of 51.4 million in the GCC.

Reliance on foreign labour has resulted in expatriates currently constituting about 88.5% in the UAE, about 90% in Qatar, about 70% in Kuwait, about 33% in Saudi Arabia, 52% in Bahrain, and about 46% in Oman. However, the composition of expatriate workers has changed periodically. If the current trend continues, the number of migrant workers is projected to grow by another 1 million. It is equally likely that the number of non-Gulf Arab workers in the GCC states will diminish, and the presence of Asian workers will likely grow further. The proportion of non-citizens in the Gulf has steadily increased during the last four decades, which is contrary to the plans and desires of the Gulf countries. The data further reveal that the proportion of non-nationals varies from country to country, ranging from 32.0% in Saudi Arabia to 88.5% in the United Arab Emirates, as shown in Table 2.

The total population in the GCC countries has increased many folds due to the influx of foreign nationals in the region. Thus, combining both the national, and non-nationals, the total GCC population is expected to reach 62 million by 2022.

3 Socio-Economic Status of GCC

As far as the case of these countries' economies is concerned, the UAE, Kuwait and Qatar fall under high-income economies whose GNP per capita income ranges from US$ 11,000 in Qatar to about US$ 17,400

Table 2 Total population and percentage of nationals and non-nationals during 2014–2016

Country/Year	*Total population*	*Nationals*	*Foreign nationals*	*Nationals*	*Foreign nationals*
Bahrain/mid-2014	1,314,562	630,744	683,818	48.0	52.0
Kuwait/March 2016	4,294,171	1,316,147	2,978,024	30.6	69.4
Oman/April 2016	4,419,193	2,412,624	2,006,569	54.6	45.4
Qatar/April 2015	2,404,776	243,019	2,161,757	10.1	89.9
UAE/mid-2010	8,264,070	947,997	7,316,073	11.5	88.5
Saudi Arabia/mid-2014	30,770,375	20,702,536	10,067,839	67.3	32.7
GCC countries	**51,467,147**	**26,253,067**	**25,214,080**	**51.0**	**49.0**

Source National Institutes of statistics, latest year or period available as of 20 April 2016. http://gulfmigration.eu/gcc-total-population-percentage-nationals-foreign-nationals-gcc-countries-national-statistics-2010-2016-numbers/

both in the UAE and Kuwait. The other three middle-income economies are Bahrain, Saudi Arabia and Oman. The GNP per capita income of these countries is US$ 7840, US$ 7040 and US$ 4820, respectively. These countries' prosperity, coupled with the oil boom, basically took place since the early 1970s. Thus, the Gulf countries have registered impressive growth in their economies. Saudi Arabia's GDP rose from US$ 3866 million in 1970 to US$ 108,640 million in 1991. The figures for Oman, the poorest among the GCC countries, were US$ 256 million and $ 10,236 million in the respective years. It is further noted that all these countries are highly urbanized except Oman, one of the least urbanized countries in the world. The average per capita income in the GCC region was estimated to be US$ 25,266 in 2016, compared to the global average of US$ 10,376. Qatar, with a high per capita income of US$ 58,247, was considered the wealthiest nation in the world in 2016. The UAE and Kuwait have a per capita income of US$ 35,384 and US$ 25,869, respectively, and stand among the top ten wealthiest nations. National citizens enjoy several benefits, such as free public education and health care and a low tax environment that leads them to the highest individual income category. This high personal income has increased the propensity of the GCC population to spend on quality education (Alpen Capital 2018).

The GCC education sector has witnessed considerable improvement in the quality of education, as shown in Table 3. Several initiatives have been taken during the past few years, such as establishing quality assurance authority, building guidelines and encouraging technology-driven education, which have combined to display improvement in the quality of education. Qatar and UAE ranked 10th and 16th on a global scale, respectively. It is interesting to note that Saudi Arabia, Oman and Kuwait are, however, ranked much lower than their regional counterparts, as shown in Table 3 (Alpen Capital 2018). Further, all the GCC countries except Oman show a high degree of urbanization which implies that a large number of populations live in urban areas. It is also noticed that urban growth in these countries is confined to large cities and country capital only, irrespective of the level of urbanization. However, the population agglomeration is found in Riyadh, Jeddah, Manama, Dubai, Abu Dhabi, Muscat and Doha. The expatriate workers were also primarily found in these cities. This urban population not only has different socio-economic requirements than its rural population but also needs a different set of facilities and services to be provided. Most of these services and requirements involve a higher level of skills and technology and, consequently, a highly skilled and trained workforce (Birks and Sinclair 1980). Hence urbanization has important implications for human resources.

4 Investment in Education

Investment in education is vital to human resource development. All GCC countries have realized the importance of investment in education that would be instrumental in creating quality human capital. It will, in turn, lead to social and human development in any country. It is interesting to note that Bahrain was the first Gulf country to introduce a modern educational system. There has been a considerable time gap in the introduction of primary education in the Gulf countries. However, a better and more planned primary education was started in the early 1960s. For instance, the enrolment in 1955 of boys and girls in primary education schools in Kuwait increased by 6.4 times and 12.9 times, respectively, in 1960. However, girls' enrolment was considerably lower than boys during the late 1950s and early 1960s. In 1980, the percentage of their enrolment in Bahrain, Kuwait and Qatar had increased to 44 and 47%, respectively (Ansari 1998: 49). Further, there has been a substantial expansion of education in the GCC countries, especially during the last two decades. It is also true in the case of secondary education, there had been 84% enrolment in the UAE, 64% in Oman and 54% in Saudi Arabia in 1993.

Table 3 Country rating—quality of education

Parameters	*Quality of primary education*	*Quality of higher education system*	*Quality of math and science education*	*Quality of management schools*	*Internet access in schools*	*Availability of specialized training services*	*Extent of staff training*
Saudi Arabia	63	41	63	52	57	67	63
UAE	16	12	13	15	13	24	15
Oman	78	75	84	116	79	113	48
Kuwait	104	89	106	111	88	121	86
Qatar	10	5	6	7	19	22	14
Bahrain	34	24	31	34	36	36	28

Source Alpen Capital, GCC Education Industry, November 13, 2018

The female enrolment at this stage is also lower compared to the male counterpart. Adult literacy rates have also been improved. These literacy rates were 85% in Oman and 63% in Saudi Arabia in 1995.

Table 4 shows that GCC countries are spending many shares of their GDP on education compared to the most advanced and developed regions of the world. In 2018, the Kingdom of Saudi Arabia and the United Arab Emirates allocated more than 20% share of their total GDP, while the expenditure of small states was as high as approximately 10% of their respective GDPs. Moreover, expenditure of Unites States, United Kingdom and Germany on education was 15.3, 12.6 and 5.2% of their GDP, respectively.

In a bid to enhance their human capital and with their sincere efforts, the GCC countries are improving their educational system to compete with upcoming challenges of the economy and human resources. Table 5 shows enrolment status in tertiary, secondary, primary and pre-primary levels. In all the GCC countries, the enrolment ratio seems to be improving. At the tertiary level, Bahrain, Kuwait, and Saudi Arabia have improved much, and their enrolment ratio was more than 60% in 2020. In contrast, the enrolment ratio was lowest in Qatar at only 21% in the same year. Likewise, Bahrain and Qatar have improved their enrolment by about 28 and 29% during 2015–2020, respectively. At the secondary level, all the GCC countries have achieved 100% enrolment except Qatar, as the data was unavailable on its enrolment. However, it is evident from historical statistics that Qatar has also achieved 100% enrolment in secondary

Table 4 Government spending on education as a % of total budget expenditure (2018)

Countries	*Percentage (%)*
Saudi Arabia	21.6
UAE	20.2
Oman	12.8
Bahrain	10.5
Kuwait	10.2
Qatar	9.4
GCC	**14.1**
US	15.3
UK	12.6
Germany	5.2

Source Alpen Capital, GCC Education Industry, November 13, 2018

Table 5 Gross Enrolment Ratio (GER) in percentage among the GCC countries

Country name	*Tertiary enrolment*			*Secondary enrolment*		
	2010	*2015*	*2020*	*2010*	*2015*	*2020*
Bahrain	NA	43.3	60.3	92.9	102.2	103.2
Kuwait	NA	55.1	61.1	97.9	97.8	98.9
Oman	23.3	39.2	45.5	NA	103.3	107.1
Qatar	9.4	14.7	20.8	105.5	NA	NA
Saudi Arabia	36.6	61.1	70.6	NA	116.5	112.6
United Arab Emirates	NA	50.1	53.7	NA	101.1	103.4
	Primary enrolment			*Pre-Primary enrolment*		
	2010	*2015*	*2020*	*2010*	*2015*	*2020*
Bahrain	NA	101.2	99.6	50.4	56.0	52.6
Kuwait	102.2	102.6	87.3	84.0	68.0	60.2
Oman	NA	108.3	104.5	NA	57.8	56.7
Qatar	102.6	102.6	103.9	NA	57.6	62.5
Saudi Arabia	106.6	110.4	100.2	11.5	21.4	21.8
United Arab Emirates	NA	111.5	115.4	85.3	80.6	94.2

Source World Bank; NA = data not available

education. Although the primary education is poor in Kuwait, as the enrolment ratio was 87% in 2020, whereas the remaining five countries have a 100% enrolment ratio in their respective primary education system. However, pre-primary enrolment is poor in most GCC countries. It is perhaps due to the building of an Islamic foundation for students by the parents at home. In terms of improvement in education, the enrolment has been improved overall and at all levels, as evident from the data available. Significantly, it is also observed that the enrolment ratio among GCC countries has improved pertinently and is comparable with developed nations such as the United States, United Kingdom, Germany, France, etc.

However, the standard of education among GCC countries is generally not very high. For example, in the case of Saudi Arabia, it was found that there was unprecedented expansion in enrolment and emphasis on Arabic and Islamic teaching. The quality of education is coupled with substandard teachers, among other factors responsible for the poor quality of school education (Wilson and Graham 1994). Moreover, vocational schools have also not been able to attract sufficient numbers of students, perhaps due to the stigma attached to manual work in Saudi society. The status of higher education in the GCC countries is also not very encouraging in quantitative and qualitative terms. Enrolment figures at the tertiary level are quite low. In 1993, the ratio of pupils' enrolment was 14% in Saudi Arabia, 10% in UAE and 5% in Oman. Comparatively, in the case of Israel, UK and USA, the enrolment figures were 35, 37 and 81%, respectively. It is further observed that only a small proportion of students opt for science, engineering and medicine disciplines where the medium of instruction is English, which makes admission difficult. Most students choose humanities and social sciences subjects where the teaching and textbooks are available in Arabic. Moreover, religious teachings were given top priority. However, these countries have attained considerable improvement in their education system after the 1990s, wherein the share of public funding and modern educational facilities has been increased.

5 Investment in the Health Care

From the healthcare perspective, the indicator of crude birth rate, crude death rate, total fertility rate, maternal mortality and infant mortality rate has shown considerable improvement due to viable and accessible health facilities among GCC countries.

5.1 Crude Birth Rate in GCC Countries

Crude birth rate denotes the total number of live births per 1000 population divided by the number of years in the period. The number of live births is often derived through a universal registration system for births, census population counts and estimation using specific demographic methodologies. Population growth is calculated using the birth rate (together with mortality and migration rates). The mid-year population can be calculated using the estimated average population. For national governments, the birth rate is a source of worry and policy. Some countries, such as Italy and Malaysia, try to boost birth rates by offering financial incentives or providing support services to new mothers. On the other hand, non-Arab countries have regulations in place to restrict the birth rate (such as China's one-child policy, which was in place from 1978 to 2015). Pro-natalist policies are those that increase the crude birth rate, whereas anti-natalist policies are those that decrease the crude birth rate. In countries like Iran and Bangladesh, non-coercive tactics like enhanced birth control information and access have yielded positive results. There has also been debate on whether putting women at the centre of development projects will result in lower birth rates. Government programs in certain nations have centred on enhancing women's rights, sexual and reproductive health, and lowering birth rates. High birth rates are typically linked to health issues, a short life expectancy, low living conditions, low social position for women and a lack of education. According to demographic transition theory, when a country develops economically and socially, its population growth slows, with birth rates serving as an indicator.

In the GCC countries, the birth rate has significantly declined due to women's participation in government activities, improved sanitization and health facilities and education. All six countries have witnessed a nearly 20–25% decline in their respective birth rate at an interval of five years. Here, Fig. 1 shows that among GCC countries, the highest birth rate of about 26.4 per 1000 people was recorded in Saudi Arabia in 2000, followed by Oman (24.1 per 1000 people) and Kuwait (22.8 per 1000 people). Since then, the birth rate is continuously declining due to improved health facilities and women's access to modern education. In 2019, the crude birth rate was highest in Oman at about 18.5 per 1000 people, followed by Saudi Arabia (17.3 per 1000 people). The lowest birth rate was recorded in Qatar (9.4 per 1000 people) and United Arab Emirates (10.2 per 1000 people). Both Bahrain and Kuwait reported moderate birth rates of about 13.3 and 13.6 per 1000 people, respectively.

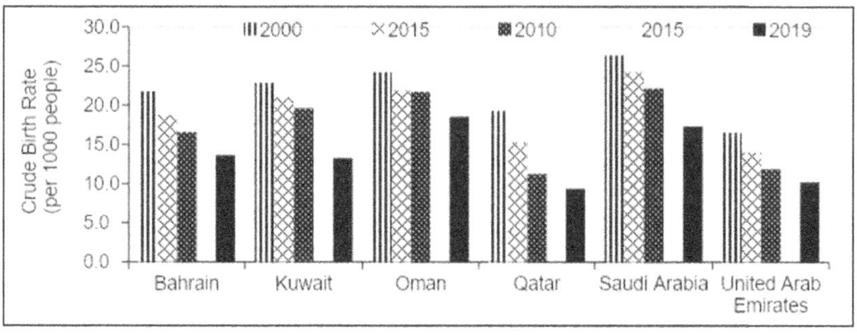

Fig. 1 Crude birth rate in GCC countries (per 1000 people) (*Source* From World Bank Data)

5.2 *Crude Death Rates in GCC Countries (Per 1000 People)*

The mortality rate, often known as the death rate, is a measure of the number of fatalities (in general or owing to a specific cause) per unit of time in a given population, scaled to the population's size. The mortality rate is usually represented in deaths per 1000 people each year. The crude death rate, which looks at mortality from all causes in a given time for a given population, is an important specific mortality rate statistic. The CIA had projected that by 2020, the global crude death rate will be 7.7 deaths per 1000 people. Moreover, according to studies, there is a link between a low standard of living caused by low income and higher death rates. Malnutrition is more likely to occur when people have a low standard of living, making them more sensitive to disease and more likely to die from it. A lower level of living can lead to poor cleanliness and sanitation, greater illness exposure and spread, and a lack of sufficient medical treatment and facilities. Poor health can lead to poor and reduced incomes, creating a vicious cycle known as the health-poverty trap. According to Amartya Sen, an Indian economist and philosopher, death rates can be used to measure economic success and failure. It is also equally applicable in GCC countries as prosperity and high economic income are proportionally related to the population's health and available infrastructure.

Qatar and the United Arab Emirates have witnessed pertinent improvement in health facilities as the death rate was lowest at about 1.2 and 1.5 per 1000 people in 2019, respectively (Fig. 2). It is one of the lowest death rates among the GCC countries and well below the world average of 7.7 per 1000 people. In the same year, all GCC countries witnessed the lowest death rate compared to the world average due to adequate health infrastructure and viable access to health centres. However, the kingdom of Saudi Arabia is the only country in GCC where the death rate was highest in 2019, at about 3.5 deaths per 1000 people. Bahrain and Oman have reported a crude death rate of about 2.4 per 1000 people. Kuwait has witnessed CDR as about 2.8 per 1000 people.

5.3 *Fertility Rates in GCC Countries (Births Per Woman)*

The total fertility rate (TFR) of a population denotes the average number of children that would be born to a woman during her lifetime if she

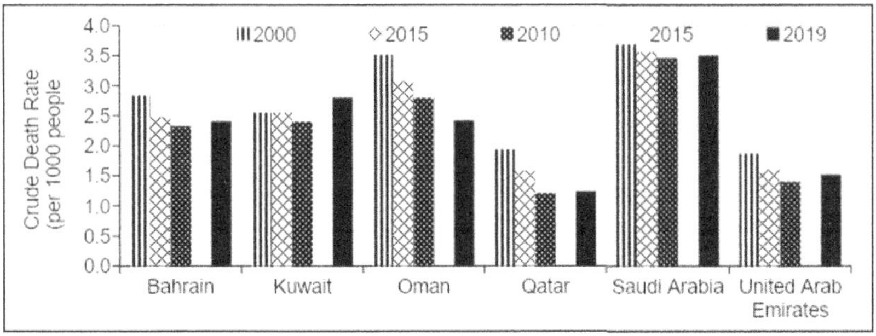

Fig. 2 Crude death rate in GCC Countries (per 1000 people) (*Source* World Bank Data)

lived from birth to the end of her reproductive life and experienced identical present age-specific fertility rates (ASFRs). It is calculated by adding single-year age-specific rates at a particular time. For example, South Korea's total fertility rate was lowest at 0.84 child per woman in 2020, whereas Niger has observed the highest fertility rate at 7.0 children per woman. Fertility is often linked to a country's degree of development. Historically, wealthy countries have had a lower fertility rate, which has been linked to wealth, education, urbanization and other factors.

On the other hand, Fertility rates are more significant in developing countries. Families desire children for their work and to care for their elderly parents. Fertility rates are also greater owing to a lack of contraception, more vital adherence to traditional religious views, lower female education and lower female employment rates. Since the 1960s, the global total fertility rate has steadily decreased. According to some analysts, the effective global fertility rate will fall below the replacement rate by the end of 2020s, which is expected to be 2.3 children per woman. It is expected that during 2050–2070, the global population will be stabilized. On the other hand, the UN predicts that some growth will continue until 2100. These forecasts suggest that the world's population will attain zero growth somewhere in the second part of this century, thus achieving a significant milestone for humanity. Important factors linked to increased fertility include the desire to have children, a high level of gender equality, religiosity, intergenerational transmission of values, marriage and cohabitation, maternal and social support, rural residence, pro-family government programs, low IQ and increased food production.

Conversely, factors linked to decrease fertility include rising income, changing values and attitudes, education, female labour engagement, population control, age, contraception, partner unwillingness to have children, a poor degree of gender equality, and infertility. Several studies suggest that "Development is the greatest contraception," which influences human progress on fertility rate. Rich countries with high per capita GDP have lower fertility rates than poor ones with low per capita GDP. Perhaps, this may appear illogical as evolutionary biology predicts that higher means should permit the generation of more kids, not fewer; the negative link between wealth and fertility has been labelled a demographic-economic conundrum. However, many of these variables are not universal and vary by area and socio-economic status. For example, religion is associated with greater fertility worldwide, but not in the West, as Scandinavian nations and France are among the least religious yet have the highest TFR, whilst Portugal, Greece, Cyprus, Poland and Spain are vice-versa. Among GCC countries, the total fertility rate in 2019 was highest at 2.8 children per woman in Oman, followed by Saudi Arabia, Kuwait and Bahrain at about 2.3, 2.1 and 2.0 children per woman, respectively. Both United Arab Emirate and Qatar have observed the lowest TFR, about 1.4 and 1.8 child per woman, respectively (Fig. 3).

As we have discussed, the Gulf region is highly dependent upon migrant workers, and thus, as the TFR represents only a small portion of population growth; it could not be assumed that the population of GCC countries is stabilized or declining. Moreover, these statistics of TFR are

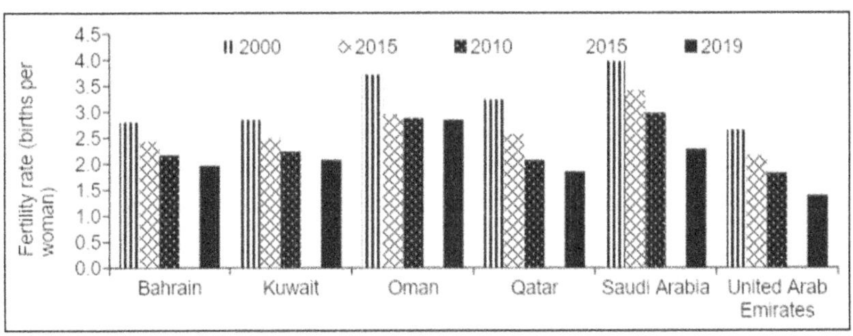

Fig. 3 Fertility rate (births per woman) in GCC countries (*Source* From World Bank Data)

used only to demonstrate the correlation with the available health facilities as developed after the oil boom due to wealth accumulation and high living standards.

5.4 *Current Healthcare Expenditure in the GCC*

The health status has also improved in the Gulf countries. The ratio of doctors and allied medical professionals' overpopulation has increased significantly. In Saudi Arabia, for example, a doctor had to take care of 7460 people in 1970, which came down to 710 people in 1993. A nurse was to take care of a burden of 2080 people in 1970, which was reduced to 460 in the same period. This indicates that health services have been improved in these countries. It was also found that people had access to health services up to the maximum level. During 1985–1995, people in Kuwait, UAE, Saudi Arabia and Oman had nearly 100% access to healthcare facilities. In terms of safe drinking water, 95% of persons in Saudi Arabia and the UAE and 63% in Oman have access to it.

Moreover, more than 77% of people have access to sanitation facilities during 1990–1995. There has been a visible sharp decline in the infant mortality rate and low-weight infants. This indicates that there have been many improvements in food quality and nutrition. Consequently, low birth weight infants declined as compared to earlier times.

In terms of capital expenditure, Table 6 shows that health expenditure has increased pertinently among the GCC countries. A good part of their respective GDP is now being spent on health infrastructure; it can be observed that the share of expenditure increased from 3.3% of GDP in 2010 to 4.6% of GDP in 2015, in five years only. Many things must be done regarding health status and for the welfare of the people at large. More infrastructure facilities are required and to be developed so that modern amenities can be provided to the needy in terms of health, nutrition and other basic requirements. By improving this kind of service, it will go in favour of human resource development in these countries.

5.5 *Labour Force and Employment*

The total number of active populations in four GCC countries was 8 million in 1980, which increased to 13 million in 1995. It is also true in the volume of the labour force that rose from 4 million in 1980 to 9 million in 1995. The average growth rate of the labour force was 5.2%

Table 6 Current healthcare expenditure in the GCC

Indicator	*2010*	*2011*	*2012*	*2013*	*2014*	*2015*
CHE by government	26.1	33.5	38.3	43.4	51.0	47.6
CHE by private	11.4	12.9	14.3	15.5	16.7	16.8
CHE as % of GDP (%)	3.3	3.2	3.3	3.6	4.1	4.6

Source Alpen Capital, GCC Healthcare Industry, March 26, 2018

during 1980–1990 and 3.4% during 1990–1995. Female participation in the workforce also increased from 8.2% in 1980 to 16.7% in 1995. Moreover, women's share of adult labour was (31%) the highest in Kuwait against the total labour (37%) as a percentage of the total population in 1995, followed by Bahrain, where women's share was 19% against 44% labour force. Saudi Arabia, UAE and Qatar had each 13% women's share as against 33, 50 and 57% labour force, respectively. In Oman, women's share was 14%, just as against 27% of cent labour force in 1995. The data indicates the share is declining in the case of agriculture, whereas in the service sector, it is just the opposite. In the industrial sector, a mixed type of composition exists. For instance, the share of the labour force declined in the case of Bahrain, Kuwait and the UAE, whereas the same rose in Qatar and Oman. As early as 1975, there were about 1.1 million expatriate workers in the GCC countries, which had increased to 5.2 million in 1990. In terms of percentage, it rose from 47 to 68. The total population of these countries was 17 million, out of which just over 10.5 million (about 60%) were nationals and 7.1 million non-nationals (Birks and Sinclair 1980). In Saudi Arabia in 1975, there was 32% expatriate labour force which increased to 40% in 1990. In the UAE, it comprised 84% of the total labour force in 1975; by 1990, its share had gone up to 89%. The corresponding figures for Kuwait were 70 and 86%, respectively. A large number of expatriates were displaced during the Gulf crisis. After a few years, except for Palestinians and Iraqis, the other expatriate workers returned to Kuwait. The composition of the foreign labour force in the GCC countries has also been changing since the 1970s. In the mid-1970s, Arabs constituted a majority (57%) of foreign workers in the region, followed by Asians (36%). During the same period, it was found that Saudi Arabia and Kuwait relied on Arab foreign workers, whereas Oman and Bahrain depended on Asian workers.

Asians have, however, been constituting a majority of the foreign workforce since the 1980s. It is because Asians are available on lower wages than their Arab counterparts. Moreover, it is noted that Asians were willing to accept lower-paid and less attractive jobs than Arabs (Amjad 1989). They were also preferred on the ground that they do not bring dependents and are perceived as the slightest threat to the existing political and social order of the host countries than communities of non-native Arabs (Omran and Roudi 1993: 25). These Asian workers are mainly from India, Pakistan, Bangladesh, Sri Lanka, South Korea, Indonesia, Thailand and the Philippines. It is, thus, noted that the Gulf countries are primarily dependent on expatriate workers. This trend would be continued till their nationals would be prepared to take the employment which is existing in these countries. All GCC countries have made concerted efforts to create jobs for the natives and at the same time to decrease the number of expatriate workers. Nevertheless, this is not feasible, at least soon. For this, GCC countries have to do a lot in the direction of their human resource development.

6 Presence of Indian Workers Since 1990s

Globalization and the economic reforms witnessed increasing developmental activities in the Arab Gulf countries. This required both skilled and unskilled foreign labour. The Gulf countries are highly known for corridors for migrants around the world. These six Gulf countries not only attract migrant workers from India but also attracts workers from south and South-East Asian countries. The Diaspora of India is influencing all the migrant communities in the Gulf countries. After China, India's population almost spread worldwide, making a significant percentage of diaspora around the world. The skilled labours or workers comprise about 30% of the Indian population of immigrants in the gulf countries. Other categories like unskilled or semi-skilled labour or workers comprise almost 70% (Khadariya 2010) of the total Indian population of immigrants. The most popular destinations for Indian immigrants within the Gulf countries are Saudi Arabia and the United Arab Emirates. The Gulf Countries have more than 60% of immigrants out of the total Indian population of migrant workers. The increased flow in the oil revenues at the time of the oil boom transformed the desert economies into one of the fastest growing regions of the world.

Indian labour migration to the Gulf countries increased dramatically after 1990. The demand for foreign workers for various infrastructural and developmental projects increased after the 1990s. The migration trend during the 1990s can be seen in increasing order. It was due to increased industrial and economic activities (Rahman 2001). Many Indian immigrants in the Gulf countries returned to their home countries during the gulf war in 1990. Between the years 1993 to 1997, the political crisis led to the decreasing immigration of Indians from the Gulf countries. It is also seen that, on average, around 384,000 Indian workers obtain contractual work permits annually, especially in the Gulf Countries. During this period, countries like Oman, Bahrain and Kuwait show a steady pattern, while countries like Saudi Arabia and the United Arab Emirates show increased growth in immigration. These two countries were the most popular destination for Indian immigrants in the Gulf countries. The total population of Indian immigrants in a specific period of the year was almost 85% in these two countries.

The first decline of Indian labour migrants can be seen from 1997 to 1999 when most of the Gulf countries adopted immigration policies to control non-native or non-Arabian populations through the policy of localization, for example, Saudization, Kuwaitization, Qatarization and Emiratization. During this period of immigration, on average, almost 323,000 workers annually obtained a contractual work permit for working in the Gulf Countries. Mainly, the local labours were recruited to control the outflow of remittances from their countries to other countries. From 2000 to 2008, Gulf countries like the United Arab Emirates undertook the requirement of semi-skilled and unskilled workers in many of their projects, and the prices of oil increased, which accelerated the revenue for growing infrastructure projects in this region. The Indian government, to accelerate migration internationally, has been setting up various emigrational posts for many regions in India. Between the periods, on average, around 471,000 workers obtained contractual work permits for the Gulf Countries. In 2009, after the global financial crisis, it was known as the declined trend for Immigrants in India. The outflow of Indian emigrants to the Gulf has been seen in a complete form. It was high as compared to the previous emigrational decade. During this financial crisis period, on an average, 626,000 annually workers obtained work permits on contractual basis for the Gulf Countries.

In recent years, a substantial change in the Gulf countries' migration policies put the migrants and the Indian government at a significant disadvantage. For Demographic and labour market reasons in the Gulf countries, these countries are now working towards controlling the number of non-native or foreign workers by restricting immigrant employment and opening working opportunities for their native workers. The big trouble for the Gulf countries lies in the rapid growth of foreign labour. If we see the migration outflow of Indians to the GCC countries, we will find a constant increase in it. For example, the number of Indian workers in the Gulf countries increased from 14,000 to 40,000 between 1948 and the 1970s.

Further, the surplus oil revenue due to rising prices of hydrocarbon energy enhanced the diversification of non-oil sectors. This paved the way for massive Indian migration to the Gulf, and their number increased to 258,000 in 1975 (Khadria 2009). Besides India, the Gulf countries have an exceptionally high inflow of international migrants from different countries. The composition of national vs. non-national population and labour force helps us to understand the justification for the restrictive policies. The foreign population has been increasing speedily in the Gulf countries for the last few decades. The number of Indians has consistently grown, as shown in Table 7. The size of Indian migrants was 1.5 million, which had risen to 8.7 million in 2017. During the last 25 years, the number of Indians has increased more than five times. It is also expected to grow the number of the Indian community in the GCC countries as the gulf employer prefers them.

7 Changing Patterns of Indian Migration

During the oil boom in the 1970s, migrant workers from India increased quite rapidly. As per the Ministry of Overseas Affairs (MIOA) report, Emigration to Gulf Countries from India is occurring mainly from these states—UP, Bihar, Kerala, Gujarat, Maharashtra, Punjab, Rajasthan and Andhra Pradesh.

Indian states like Uttar Pradesh, Andhra Pradesh, Bihar, Kerala, Punjab, West Bengal and Rajasthan were the states that sent the highest number of Indian immigrants to the Gulf countries. Uttar Pradesh sends the most significant number of labours to Gulf Countries, as shown in Table 8. In 2017, Uttar Pradesh sent 86,173 labours to the Gulf, Bihar sent 68,295, and Tamil Nadu 38,341 sent labour to Gulf countries. In

Table 7 Size of Indian workers in the Gulf countries 1991–2017

Countries	*1991*	*1999*	*2004*	*2008*	*2012*	*2017*
Bahrain	100,000	1,50,000	100,000	233,955	350,000	316,175
Kuwait	88,000	2,00,000	450,000	5,11,161	579,390	919,354
Oman	220,000	4,50,000	450,000	4,32,000	718,642	783,959
Qatar	75,000	100,000	1,00,000	239,000	5,00,000	697,500
Saudi Arabia	6,00,000	12,00,000	1,500,000	13,50,652	1,789,000	3,255,864
UAE	400,000	7,50,000	1,000,000	14,11,000	1,750,000	2,803,751
Others	22,000	1,50,000	NA	NA	NA	NA
Total	1,505,000	8,764,829	3,600,000	41,77,768	5,687,032	8,776,603

Source Anisur Rahman Indian Labour Diaspora in the Gulf: An Overview in Indian Trade Diaspora in the Arabian Peninsula by Prakash C. Jain and Kundan Kumar, New Academic Publishers, New Delhi 2012, p. 330; Annual Reports Ministry of External Affairs. https://www.mea.gov.in/Images/attach/lu6091.pdf, https://pib.gov.in/newsite/PrintRelease.aspx?relid=116414.

the January–June period of 2017, Bihar emerged as the state to have sent the maximum number of migrants to the Gulf countries. The other states of India only constitute 109,560 immigrants.

Table 8 Top ten labour sending Indian states during 2010–2017

State	*2010*	*2011*	*2012*	*2013*	*2014*	*2015*	*2016*	*2017*
Andhra Pradesh	43,131	43,052	49,782	59,789	52,121	44,644	26,574	11,138
Uttar Pradesh	136,542	156,023	189,002	214,712	226,798	234,958	141,482	86,173
Kerala	102,886	87,404	97,244	84,970	65,475	42,755	24,962	16,337
Bihar	58,746	70,932	82,759	94,609	97,359	106,719	75,480	68,295
Punjab	28,599	31,537	36,547	46,977	45,079	44,381	30,762	26,449
Rajasthan	46,844	42,745	49,935	50,617	47,767	45,925	35,029	31,914
West Bengal	26,938	28,474	34,670	39,419	49,048	62,343	51,247	33,955
Gujarat	8091	8403	6871	8418	7743	6795	4496	4194
Maharashtra	17,729	16,721	19,059	19,383	18,976	15,217	10,363	7687
Karnataka	16,955	15,582	17,819	17,670	14,953	11,867	6423	5144
Total	486,461	500,873	583,688	636,564	625,319	615,604	406,818	291,286

Source Annual Report, MOIA, GOI, 2008–2017 https://emigrate.gov.in/ext/home.action (accessed on 15/01/2018)

8 Gulf Immigration Policy

It is noteworthy that after the 1990s, the Gulf countries tried to have a tighter grip on the migration process; in that process, they have been openly endorsing anti-integration policies to prevent the permanent settlement of migrant workers in host societies. In that process, the host country tries to promote short-term contracts for migrant workers, temporary labour import from labour-sending countries, limiting the socio-economic rights of migrant workers and implementing the deportation program for irregular migrants. This set of policies and practices for international migration management is called as "Gulf model". Gulf countries have had policies that they have instituted to limit the number of non-nationals in their populations and the labour force. Such policies include ones related to maximizing the number of nationals through high fertility and participation of women in the labour force. At the same time, active efforts are being made to restrict the inflow of foreign workers. Despite the heightened efforts aimed at restricting the percentage of non-nationals, the outflows from the significant sending countries in Asia show an upward trend, as do the inflows to the six GCC countries. There are many reasons for the growth of expatriate workers.

Nevertheless, the main reasons for the increasing percentages of non-nationals are the continued need of the labour force for foreign workers and the exacerbating stock of foreign workers in the GCC countries. While data on the duration of stay of non-nationals are not available for any of the countries systematically, observation suggests that migration to the Gulf is not a "temporary" phenomenon as conceived and planned by the governments. Once in the Gulf, migrants can prolong their stay for several years. Those who are allowed to bring their families with them can produce a second generation of migrants in the host countries. A recent study from Kuwait shows that about 18% of all non-nationals were born in the country. Among high school students born in the country, about one-third of the parents were also born in Kuwait, implying that the students were, in fact, the third generation.

Factors that affect the volume and pace of migration originate in the sending countries and the Gulf. In the sending countries, the relatively low rate of socio-economic development combined with a high rate of population growth in many of the South and Southeast Asian countries ensures a continued supply of inexpensive labour that is willing and able to move to the Gulf countries to benefit from higher wages paid there, relative to those in their home countries. Labour migration continues to be encouraged by the sending countries to reduce unemployment and enhance foreign exchange earnings. Several Asian countries have developed effective regulatory mechanisms to maximize outflows and simultaneously increase the protection and welfare of their emigrating workers. In addition, vast social networks of foreign workers and their families have been established within the Gulf countries that support chain migration and the enlargement of the stock of workers.

With the rising personal income of Gulf citizens, a new dimension has been added to the lifestyle in the form of the rapid rise in demand for domestic workers. Large numbers of domestic workers from the Philippines, Indonesia, India and Sri Lanka have arrived during the last 3–4 decades to work in the Gulf. Most are sponsored by individual families and work for them. Some are sponsored by families (for a fee) but engage in freelance work, which is considered illegal. The experience of Kuwait highlights the enormity of this phenomenon. In a population of 2.2 million legal foreign residents, the country had 607,667 persons (26.4%) on a domestic service visa in 2012 (Ministry of Interior data available in the GLMM Database). The 2030 Agenda for Sustainable Development, with its commitment to leave no one behind, recognizes that international migration is of significant relevance for the development of countries of origin, transit and destination, requiring coherent and comprehensive responses. In the Agenda, Governments pledged to "facilitate orderly, safe, regular and responsible migration and mobility of people, including through the implementation of planned and well-managed migration policies" (SDG target 10.7). The 2030 Agenda also seeks to reduce remittance transfer fees, promote labour standards for migrant workers and eliminate human trafficking. To address large movements of refugees and migrants, on 19 September 2016, the General Assembly adopted the New York Declaration for Refugees and Migrants, calling for the developing of two global compacts in 2018.

The importance of the young demographic bloc is not only linked to size but also to the inherent energy of young people in working and being productive. A large number of economically productive people compared with those who are dependent constitutes a significant advantage that can help propel economic growth, resulting in a demographic dividend. Without proper investment in youth, the opportunity represented by this demographic dividend for promoting development will gradually disappear and may not recur in the Arab region. Although the slow pace of development is affecting everyone, it is especially felt by young people. Youth in the Arab region suffer to varying degrees due to the state of human development. Young people feel deeply anxious about their future and are gripped by an inherent sense of discrimination and exclusion. Many do not receive a good education, find suitable employment or have appropriate health care. Moreover, youth in Arab countries are insufficiently represented in public life and have no meaningful say in shaping policies that influence their lives. These failures are exacerbated among young women, who face additional burdens of gender inequality and the persisting gap in the empowerment of women in economic, political and social life, despite the achievements made in several countries.

9 Policy Implications for Human Capita/HRD

There have been significant implications for the prospects of human capital/human resource development in the GCC countries. One of the severe limitations of these countries is their inadequate population base. The demographic profile of these countries is predominantly characterized by the small size of their national population (Winckler 1997: 489–490). In the early 1990s, Saudi Arabia had the largest population, with over 80% of the total Gulf nationals. With about 9.5% Oman was the following largest country. Kuwait was the third largest state (4.5), followed by the UAE (3%), Bahrain (2.1%) and Qatar (1%). Thus, in a comparative sense, the Gulf nationals constitute only about a quarter of the Iranian population. It could be compared with Iraq, whose population is estimated to be a 19 million. Hence, the small population size is a significant factor in relying heavily on the expatriate labour force. The severe other weakness of the GCC countries is their low quality of available workforce which is the direct result of low quality of education and the lack of proper training. Since the late 1980s, not enough indigenous workforce has been produced in these countries despite increasing enrolment in secondary and universities owing to low levels of educational attainment. On the other hand, employers generally prefer the most cost-effective and efficiently cheap available expatriate labour force, resulting in increasing unemployment among nationals.

Like many developing countries, GCC countries have been suffering from sectarianism, favouritism, apathy, conservatism and lack of innovation and communication, which impede the path of human resource development. For instance, in Saudi Arabia and Bahrain, sectarianism hampers the process of human resource development. The Shiites who were concentrated in the eastern provinces were officially discriminated against until the 1980s concerning education, employment and social welfare measures (Abir 1993: 19). Thus, the nation was deprived of the sizeable indigenous workforce which could have been better trained and put to use for the development of the country. Thus, the prospects of human resource development in the GCC countries lie in strengthening their respective number of immigrants and absorbing them into the mainstream of society. There are two means to increase the population of the country—a high birth rate and the naturalization process. The GCC countries usually follow the pro-natalist population policy, that is, by encouraging the indigenous people to have more children. Naturalization has increasingly become only nominal, especially since the early 1980s. Thus, GCC countries have not effectively employed naturalization. It is not so even in the case of long-time resident Arab immigrants. Some countries have sought to promote pro-natalist policy. The United Arab Emirates, for instance, has established a marriage fund to induce the young to get married earlier than the average age. It has infected, not proved a practical solution because increasing the indigenous population by this method has its limits. The GCC countries need extensive regional planning in terms of the use of educational infrastructure and job training for the sake of human resource development. Although some efforts are being made in this direction, they remain piecemeal and inadequate by the reactions of individual countries. Lower rates of women's participation in the labour force have already been discussed. In the mid-1990s, women constituted only 10% or less of the labour force in Saudi Arabia, the UAE, Bahrain, Qatar and Oman. Thus, considerable scope exists for enhancing women's participation in the labour force.

Additionally, Oman and Saudi Arabia are better placed to tap another reservoir of human resources in rural areas. To sum up, all the GCC countries have only a small indigenous population and are primarily dependent on the expatriate workforce. These countries need to raise their population levels by adopting more liberal policies, at least towards those Arab immigrants who are settled and better integrated into the Gulf societies. These countries could also accommodate the non-Arab Muslims to strengthen their demographic base and defence capabilities. Moreover, modern education should be prioritized to inculcate scientific temperament and spirit among the Gulf people. We can thus think of better tomorrow in terms of human resource development in these countries.

10 Covid-19 and Its Implications for Gulf Immigrants

The COVID-19 pandemic is a global health crisis that has stopped the entire world economy. The Gulf economy and society, too, have been seriously affected due to this ongoing crisis. The impact of COVID-19 had a major effect on work, economies and education, especially the technologies and ways of working which are key to the industry 4.0 concept. Due to the pandemic, there is an increased need for medications, medical supplies and advanced information technology applications. The fourth industrial revolution, or "industry 4.0," is thought to have the capacity to satisfy customized needs amid the COVID-19 crisis. Applications of advanced manufacturing and digital information technology are where this revolution first began (Javaid et al. 2020).

Thus, Industry 4.0 refers to the expanding trend in automation, technological data sharing and manufacturing-related activities, including the internet of things (IoT) and the industrial internet of things (IIoT), Cloud computing, blockchain, artificial intelligence, and cyber-physical systems (CPS), Intelligent manufacturing and smart factories. It is under these broad themes the jobs are associated (Taneja and Nayak 2021).

Industry 4.0 is a smart system, used as a flexible production line for almost entire production processes with real-time information provided by Artificial intelligence (AI), Internet of Things (IoT) and other digital technologies. Designing and development of any medical part are done rapidly using advance designing software and further used digital manufacturing technologies like 3D printing to print the required parts (Javaid et al. 2020).

The lack of medical facilities and equipments has been a constant struggle the people and the hospitals have to face in the adverse situation like the pandemic.

The Gulf region, which has hosted many expatriate workers, especially Indians, have adversely affected by this crisis. It had impacted migrants' lives, inflow of remittances and labour-sending economies such as India, Pakistan, Bangladesh, Sri Lanka and Nepal. It is said that over 8 million strong Indian workforces, comprising of professionals, blue-collar workers and enterprising businesses, are likely to be affected adversely. The expatriate workforce, especially Indians, have been crucial to the growth story of their host countries and are preferred and acknowledged for their contributions and disciplined approach. It is also noted that they have been remitting over $40 billion back home annually. This money stays typically for extended periods in the country and constitutes over 10% of India's foreign exchange reserves. Now the COVID-19 pandemic produces unprecedented effects on the migrants' households' economy. In addition to COVID-19, the impact has gone beyond public health to social and economic issues, especially for migrant workers. Human rights groups and construction associations have rightly expressed their concerns that migrant workers are at greater risk. Migrant workers have had the hardest hit by the COVID-19 pandemic, as pointed out by the ILO Director-General, Guy Ryder. They face crowded living conditions, harsh containment measures, limited access to healthcare and essential services, poor working conditions and exploitative labour systems. Millions of migrant workers are forced to return home due to losing their jobs in the host countries. They are going to face unemployment and poverty in their home countries. Migrant workers have found themselves stranded in host countries without access to social protection and little money for food or accommodation.

11 Conclusion

We can say that the growth of the expatriate population in the Gulf countries is likely to continue. The primary reasons for this phenomenon are the demand of the Gulf countries and the supply from South Asian countries. We cannot deny that as long as the issue of national human resource development is not resolved, they would be bound to rely on exporting human capital from other countries. Localization and nationalization of the job market by the Gulf States would be simply rhetoric unless or until the national human resource is produced who can work in every sector of the economy for the country's development. The other factor may be the attitudes and perceptions of the nationals towards non-nationals as to how the expatriates feel. What kind of treatment accorded to them by nationals may also influence their decision to continue staying in a Gulf country, return home, or move to another country? No doubt, government policies relating to foreigners also matter. However, at the same time, the demand for labour in the Gulf labour market could be an essential factor in the supply of expatriate labour. Migration can introduce new foods and cultures, cause racial tensions, solve labour shortages or increase the stress on social services in the host country. Migration has thus both positive and negative effects. But as a whole, migration is considered to be beneficial to both sending and receiving countries.

References

Abir, A. (1993). *Saudi Arabia: Government, society, and the gulf crisis*. Routledge, New York.

Ahn, Pong-Sul (ed.). (2004). *Migrant workers and human rights: Out-migration from South Asia*. ILO, Subregional Office for South Asia, New Delhi, p. 7.

Alpen Capital, GCC Education Industry. (2018, November). http://www.alpencapital.com/news/2018/2018-November-13.html.

Alpen Capital, GCC Health Industry. (2018, March). http://www.alpencapital.com/news/2018/2018-March-26.html.

Amjad, R. (1989). "Economic impact of migration to the Middle East on the major Asian labour sending countries—An overview." Economics. Online at https://mpra.ub.uni-muenchen.de/38134/MPRA. Paper No. 38134, posted 17 Apr 2012 15:22 UTC.

Arab Human Development Report. (2016). *Youth and the prospects for human development in a changing reality*, UNDP.

Birks, J. S. (1980). *International migration and development in the Arab region*. ILO, Geneva.

Birks, J. S., and Sinclair, C. A. (1980). *International migration and development in the Arab region*. ILO, Geneva.

Chishti, Muzaffar. Migration Policy Institute, Washington. migrationpolicy.org.

Fargues, P., and Brouwer, I. (2012). "GCC demography and immigration: Challenges and policies." In *National employment, migration and education in the GCC*, edited by S. Hertog, Gerlach Press, Cambridge.

Gilmore, Kristin. *Convention establishes rights of all migrant workers and their families*, accessed through internet, http://www.un.org/Pubs/chronicle/2003/webArticles/070203_migrantworkers.

GLMM—Gulf Labor Market and Migration database: gulfmigration.eu.

Government of India, Ministry of Overseas Indian Affairs. (2012). *Government of India: Annual report (2015–2016)*, New Delhi.

Harbison, F., and Meyer, A. (1964). *Education manpower and economic growth*. Mac Grow Hill Book Company, New York.

Hindustan Times, November 18, 2005

Jadhav, N. (2003). Maximising developmental benefits of remittances: The Indian experience. International Conference on Migration and Remittances, DFID and World Bank, London.

Javaid, M., Haleem, A., Vaishya, R., Bahl, S., Suman, R., and Vaish, A. (2020, April 24). *Industry 4.0 technologies and their applications in fighting COVID-19 pandemic*. National Library of Medicine. Retrieved July 22, 2022, from https://www.ncbi.nlm.nih.gov/pmc/articles/PMC7180383/.

Khadria, B. (2009). *India migration report 2009: Past, present and the future outlook*.

Khadariya, B. (2010). *Paradigm shifts in India's migration policy towards the Gulf*. Middle East Institute Viewpoints.

Migration and development Brief 28 migration and remittances: Recent developments and Outlook October 2017. (2017, October). Retrieved February 24, 2018, from www.knom.org; http://www.knomad.org/sites/default/files/2017-12/Migration%20and%20Development%20Report%2012-14-17%20web.pdf (Accessed on 24 February 2018).

Migration and Remittances Factbook. (2011). 2nd Edition, World Bank, Washington.

Migration and remittances: Recent developments, outlook October 2017. (2017, October). Retrieved February 24, 2018, from www.knomad.com; http://www.knomad.org/sites/default/files/2017-12/Migration%20and%20Development%20Report%2012-14-17%20web.pdf (Accessed on 24 February 2018).

MOIA. (n.d.). Retrieved from https://emigrate.gov.in/ext/home.action.

Nangia, Parveen, and Saha, Uma. *Profile of emigrants from India: A comparative study of Kerala and Punjab*, accessed through internet, http://www.google.com/search?hl=en&ie=ISO-8859-1&q=profile+of+emigrant+from+india; Office of the Protector of Emigrants, Ministry of Labour, Government of India.

Nayyar, D. (1994). *Migration, remittances and capital flows: The Indian experience*. Oxford University Press, New Delhi.

Omran, A. R., and Roudi, F. (1993). The Middle East Population Puzzle: Population bulletin of the United Nations, vol. 48, Issue 1 of Population bulletin, Population Reference Bureau, United Nation.

Puri, Shivani. Migrant worker remittance, Micro-finance and the informal economy: Prospects issues, Working Paper no. 21, accessed through internet, http://www.gdrc.org/icm/remittance/shivani.html.

Rahman, Anisur. (2001). *Indian labour migration to the gulf: A socio-economic analysis*, Rajat Publications, New Delhi.

Rahman, Anisur. (2010). *India manpower in the Gulf strategic and economic dimensions, West Asia and the region*, edited by Rajendra M. Abhyankar, Academy Foundation, New Delhi.

Reserve Bank of India. Reserve Bank of India Bulletin (2006).

Shah, N. M. *Restrictive labour immigration policies in the oil rich Gulf: Implications for Asian countries*, accessed through internet, http://iussp2005.princeton.edu/download.aspx?submissionId=50842.

Shah, N. M. (2012). "Socio-demographic transitions among nationals of GCC countries: Implications for migration and labour force trends." *Migration and Development* 1:1.

Shah, P. F. (2011). *Socio-economic impacts of GCC migration*. Gulf Research Center Cambridge.

Taneja, S., and Nayak, S. (2021, May 11). *Must-have skills for students to stay relevant in the Industry 4.0*. Manav Rachna Vidyanatariksha. Retrieved July 22, 2022, from https://manavrachna.edu.in/blog/industry-4-0/.

Tattolo, Giovanna. *Arab labour migration to the GCC states*, accessed through internet, http://jmobservatory.eco.uniroma1.it/home.html.

UN, Population Facts, Department of Economic and Social Affairs, Population Division. http://esa.un.org/unmigration/documents/The_number_of_international_migrants.pdf.

UNDESA, World Urbanization Prospects. (2014). Retrieved January 1, 2018, from www.ese.un.org; http://ese.un.org/highlights.pdf.

Wilson, P., and Graham, D. (1994). *Saudi Arabia: The coming storm*. Routledge, New York.

Winckler, O. (1997). "The Immigration Policy of the Gulf Cooperation Council (GCC) States." Middle Eastern Studies 33 (3): 480–493. http://www.jstor.org/stable/4283889.

PART II

Higher Education and Labour Market in Selected Sectors

CHAPTER 5

Human Capital Enhancement Through International and On-Line Programs in the Universities of Qatar and the UAE

Mariam Orkodashvili

1 Introduction

The paper discusses the education sector in two Gulf states, Qatar and the UAE, and analyzes the extent to which reforms in the higher education sphere can provide models for efficient instruction in the departments of business and IT at universities. Since business and IT sectors are closely connected with knowledge-production, human capital production, and human resource management, the issue has wider implications for economic welfare and human development in the Gulf states.

M. Orkodashvili (✉)
Vanderbilt University, Tbilisi, Georgia
e-mail: morkoda@yahoo.com

A. Mishrif et al. (eds.), *Nationalization of Gulf Labour Markets*,
The Political Economy of the Middle East,
https://doi.org/10.1007/978-981-19-8072-5_5

The transformations that education systems in the GCC countries go through often incentivize the emergence of novel ideas, approaches, and the design of study programs. Oftentimes western academics claim that the challenges and transformations in the GCC countries make them think about introducing novelties in their universities as well.

The paper further analyzes the spillover effects of newly opened international universities over the local ones, and discusses the efficiency of business and IT field instruction in the higher education institutions of the Gulf states.

The pandemic period of 2020–2022 has presented both challenges and opportunities in this respect. International employment and employability have become even more widely spread throughout the COVID-19 lockdown period.

Therefore, the paper presents cases of local, international, and on-line programs from the universities of Qatar and the United Arab Emirates.

The internationalization of higher education has brought about a number of reforms to Arab universities. First and foremost, the system has become more decentralized, flexible, giving more decision-making power to individual universities to start up business relations with different companies both locally and internationally. This fact has incentivized the establishment of business departments at higher education institutions and the introduction of modern study programs in the fields of business administration, management, organizational theory, and most importantly, human capital production and human resource management. This process has led to the ability of higher education institutions to determine funding and set admission standards independently. This is a step toward autonomy and self-determination of higher education institutions.

The paper looks at the experiences of two Gulf states: Qatar and the United Arab Emirates. The process of opening up branches of prestigious western universities has been ongoing in these countries with manifold consequences. The paper attempts to investigate to what extent has the internationalization process been influencing the development of innovative and flexible business programs.

Higher education in the GCC region goes back to about 1400 years ago with the advent of Islam, beginning in Saudi Arabia, with Mecca and Medina being the centers of knowledge as well as religion. The last few decades, however, have seen tremendous growth, both in the number of institutions and number of students in the GCC region. It is surprising, therefore, that little research on internationalization of higher education either through comparative data, case studies, or institutional experiments has been conducted in this region. It is important to investigate the changing paradigm of the higher education sector in the GCC, not just for the advancement of knowledge but also for institutions and policymakers to align their strategies according to the internationalization practices and trends, especially to set up business administration departments with the emphasis on human resource management and leadership.

Putting it in a wider perspective, policies and measures by Arab governments over the last decade, and the rising demand for higher education, have led to a considerable expansion in the number of higher education institutions and considerable diversity in the features of these institutions. This diversity has taken several forms: state/private education; national/foreign universities; local programs/partnership programs with foreign universities abroad; short-term/long-term studies, etc. The number of universities active in the Arab region today stands at 398, compared to a mere 174 a decade ago; i.e. the number has more than doubled. If we add the higher institutes, community colleges, teacher-training institutes, and other higher education institutions not affiliated with universities, the total number rises to 1139.

The development of innovative and practice-oriented business programs has had multiple implications not only for business spheres but it has impacted other fields as well. For instance, such programs have been actively involved in promoting liberal, open-market-oriented economies. Over the past two decades, Gulf states have been liberalizing their economies through the ascendency of a worldwide model of neoliberal economic globalization. These neoliberal policies promoted by the World Bank (WB) and International Monetary Fund (IMF) have been pushing structural adjustment policies upon many Arab nations. At the same time, as nations worldwide attempt to transition their economies from their traditional agricultural and industrial bases to knowledge economies, the private rate of return to higher education is increasing. Therefore, the nations of Arab countries and international organizations alike are pressuring Higher Education Ministries to improve the employability of their populations through expanded higher education and higher quality instruction (Altbach and Peterson 2007). Policymakers and educators perceive expanding higher education as an important means by which the Arab world will successfully integrate its workers into the global economy. The issues of employment and employability have been reconsidered by business departments and have been tightly associated with human capital production and human resource management. The issues of human capital production and human resource management have been investigated not only in terms of local employment and employability but in terms of international job market as well.

The business departments and study programs have been most tightly associated with the internationalization process. More specifically, the internationalization of higher education has brought about a number of reforms to Arab universities. First and foremost, the system has become more entrepreneurial and flexible giving more decision-making power to individual universities. For instance, higher education institutions determine funding and set admission standards independently (Mazawi 2005. This is a step toward autonomy and self-determination of higher education institutions. The establishment of contacts with businesses and partnering of individual departments with companies have further upgraded the quality of study programs and have made them more practice-oriented that have the potential of impacting the entire population.

The present paper looks into the issue of the facilitation of knowledge-production and human capital production through business education at business departments of the universities in Qatar and UAE.

2 Theoretical Framework

Business and IT education have had an important impact on the countries' developments over the last decades. The first outstanding feature among many others that sets business education apart from most of the other university programs is its continuous emphasis on turning any theoretical knowledge and theory into a feasible and successful practice. While other fields might be still struggling to establish their practical application outside academia, business and information technologies fields have been able to transition from any theory into practice smoothly.

Another important feature of business and IT education is their incessant strife toward internationalization. International and multinational start-ups have been becoming quite common over the past decades. Looking at international cases, incorporating international issues and global trends in the study programs have become inseparable parts of business education, even more so for GCC countries which have been most active in opening up international branches and study programs of western universities on their premises. It could be even stated that they have provided the most successful examples of going global in terms of business education.

Tied on to that is the importance of intercultural understanding and human capital production with intercultural communication skills.

The literature describing trends and explaining aspects of HE internationalization has been diverse. Internationalization of HE has been defined as "The process of integrating an international, intercultural or global dimension into the purpose, functions or delivery of post-secondary education" (Knight 2004, p. 11). This definition is considered to be most comprehensive, as apart from the modalities, the definition also integrates an intercultural and international dimension into all areas of the university functioning. It particularly considers internationalization to be in response to globalization, although scholars such as Brandenburg and de Wit (2011) do not find any marked difference as they consider both concepts to be interconnected. By considering this definition of HE internationalization, the opening up of new business and IT programs should be borne in mind in the first instance.

As education institutions continue to expand beyond their flagship campuses, the trend of fast-growing international campuses likewise continues to grow. Business and IT programs have been even more entrepreneurial and innovative in this respect. Starting a new business or IT program is an exciting endeavor, especially when it is in a foreign country. However, it requires more than passion, because the process involves hard work such as finding financial support, faculty members, administrators, students, and a location to house the institution. It also involves dealing with new cultures and regulations and ensuring that the culture and the laws of the host country are respected. With the advancements in technology, today's university students have never been more connected with the world they live in, hence seeking a global education overseas might as well continue to be a widespread trend among future generations.

In the current global economy, business and IT departments at higher education institutions face numerous challenges. Factors such as the increasing international competition, achieving higher ranking among global universities, and the pursuit of creating world-class study programs have had a significant impact on business and IT education across countries. While universities respond to these challenges differently, some higher education institutions are increasingly moving toward the internationalization of their campuses. Internationalization of higher education programs includes branch campuses, cross border collaborative programs, exchange of international students, and establishment of English-medium programs and degrees. International business programs are most diverse in this respect.

The desire to "modernize" business and IT programs and overall higher education systems has not only taken the form of extensively privatizing the provision of higher education, like many neoliberal states, but also establishing extensive international partnerships with American and British universities (Mazawi 2005).

The international business and IT programs have been increasingly introducing such concepts as international outsourcing, international head hunting, teleworking for the multinationals, teleconferencing, and producing internationally employable and competitive human capital.

3 Methodology and Data Collection

The main methodology implemented by the present paper is a comparative critical analysis of education institutions in different GCC countries with the special emphasis on business and IT programs. The research mainly bases its postulates on the secondary sources obtained through the official websites of GCC countries, education institutions, and universities.

To provide illustrative examples of internationalization and on-line instruction, the present paper analyzes the cases of universities with well-branded names such as Doha's Education City, Dubai's Knowledge Village, Sharjah's University City, and other universities offering world-class business courses. Qatar's Education City has tried to brand itself as the largest concentration of universities in the world—an academic metropolis that spans 14 km, and brings prestigious institutions such as Northwestern University, Carnegie Mellon, Texas A&M, Cornell, and Georgetown to Qatar's shores. Similarly, NYU has just built a huge international campus in Abu Dhabi to the pride of the UAE. Academic standards at these international institutions are very high, and only a small percentage of students actually qualify for them. In fact, Qatar University—the only public university in Qatar—enrolls 91% of Qatari students, while the elite universities at the Education City enroll only 9% (Stasz et al. 2007). The study programs are also different at local universities and international universities. Therefore, the issues of standards, quality, and decision-making power are constantly debated in the states.

3.1 Internationalizing Business and IT Education and Research in Qatar

Being a relatively small country, Qatar puts a strong emphasis on internationalizing higher education, reinforcing business and IT education and scientific research. "*Qatar aims to build a modern world-class educational system that provides students with a first-rate education*"—Qatar National Vision 2030.

However, Qatar's National Vision 2030 goes beyond education. It also foresees the creation of a research base and innovative business and IT schools in Qatar.

Qatar's main priority in the internationalization of higher education is to build an international higher educational hub where top international universities offer international curriculum by international faculty to enrich the learning experience of the diverse international student body. To achieve this, Qatar is establishing a modern, advanced educational system designed to promote creativity, innovation, and analytical and critical thinking. Qatar is investing heavily in international best-practice education models in order to meet the requirements of a more diversified economy, while respecting Qatar's cultural values and national heritage. This system has become broader and deeper with the establishment by Qatar Foundation of international branch campuses of some of the world's leading universities, teaching some of their most highly regarded degree programs and carrying out cutting-edge research in areas in which they are world-leaders. These universities are:

- Virginia Commonwealth University in Qatar, offering four majors in design at undergraduate level as well as a master's in Fine Arts.
- Weill Cornell Medical College in Qatar, offering a pre-medical program, as well as a four-year MD degree.
- Texas A&M University at Qatar, offering four undergraduate Engineering majors and an MSc in Chemical Engineering.
- Carnegie Mellon University in Qatar, which has undergraduate programs in Business Administration, Computer Science, and Information Systems. This year it introduced the fourth program in Biological Sciences.

- Georgetown University School of Foreign Service, delivering its BSc in Foreign Service.

Northwestern University in Qatar, which teaches its undergraduate programs in Journalism and in Communication.

- HEC Paris in Qatar, offering its Executive MBA program
- UCL in Qatar (University College London) which this year will start teaching master's programs in Archeology and in Museum Studies and the homegrown Faculty of Islamic Studies, which teaches a range of undergraduate and graduate programs in both the arts and sciences.

Qatar Foundation for Education, Science and Community Development was established in 1995 and is chaired by Her Highness Sheikha Moza bint Nasser. It is leading the country's journey toward a knowledge-based society. Qatar Foundation has reached a new stage in the development of Qatar's higher education with the establishment of Hamad Bin Khalifa University, which brings together all of the higher education and related research being conducted at Qatar Foundation.

Beyond Qatar Foundation, a number of other institutions make up a full range of higher education choices for Qatar's young people. These include:

- Qatar University, established some 40 years ago after independence, which offers undergraduate and graduate programs in seven colleges
- The College of the North Atlantic in Qatar, which teaches a range of vocational programs.
- The University of Calgary in Qatar, which offers degree programs in Nursing.

Stenden University Qatar is a Dutch university. It offers four-year-bachelor degrees (BBA) in International Hospitality Management, International Business and Management Studies, and Tourism Management. There is a multi-cultural staff which includes 21 different nationalities.

College of the North Atlantic (CNA) offers a range of programs with Canadian curriculum that are designed to meet the needs of industry and the community including technician, technologist, and post-diploma programs within the Business Studies, Health Sciences, Information Technology, Engineering Technology, Industrial Trades, Banking and Financial Studies, and training through the Security Academy.

3.2 Business Education in Doha's Education City

Since 2000, the largest educational experiment in the Gulf has been taking shape in Education City on the outskirts of Doha, Qatar's capital.

Eight branches of overseas universities sit alongside think tanks, the country's top high school and the offices of al Jazeera's children's television channel in an expanding zone. Education City, established by Qatar Foundation, is arguably the defining legacy of Sheikha Moza bint Nasser al-Missned, wife of the former emir, Sheikh Hamad bin Khalifa al-Thani. The foundation funds a well-established pool of US universities in Qatar, such as Georgetown and Weill Cornell Medical College, focusing on providing undergraduate education for Qataris and other nationalities.

The gas-rich state has pledged to earmark 2.8% of gross domestic product for research and development and also plans to develop postgraduate and research capacities. University College London Qatar, for example, received its first postgraduate students in 2012. Partnering with the Qatar Museums Authority, the body charged with developing the state's cultural ambitions, UCL Qatar offers centers on archaeology, librarianship, conservation, and museum studies. "We have launched a consultative committee to be sensitive to the needs of Qatar as we develop the programme," says Anthony Smith, UCL's vice-provost for education. "The other thing is to strengthen outreach. We want to do our best to support the whole professional population working in these sectors."

Hamad Bin Khalifa University is an umbrella institution seeking to build on Education City's growing pool of academic talent to develop research. One of HBKU's first projects is a partnership with UCL Qatar on an information and library studies program, as well as preparation for recent graduates in research methods.

The next move is expected to deliver a master's program in energy and resources. "HBKU will offer advanced degrees in areas of particular relevance to Qatar and the region," says Abdulla bin Ali al-Thani, the university's president. "Graduates will be equipped with high-level skills that they may apply in various sectors, including academic and applied research."

Better Preparing Qatari youths, as well as students from around the region, remains the focus of the undergraduate universities. While insiders deny there are formal quotas, the average across the schools is a Qatari intake of about 50%, varying according to the course. "There are increasing numbers of Qatari applicants to the Education City universities," says HBKU's Dr al-Thani.

Persuading more students to attend needs a further shift in cultural perceptions and better secondary education. Most Qataris still expect cushy government jobs on graduation, but the country hopes to broaden its skills base, so that more are able to compete with expatriates for jobs in the private sector.

One student says many Qataris feel uncomfortable on the campus, where there are few signs in Arabic. But she says the zone has opened doors to better education for the many families in the Arab world who are happy for their sons, but not their daughters, to attend university in the west.

Students who fail to make the grade in academic achievement or English-language skills can attend the academic bridge program. This prepares those people to come in who are not able to stand toe to toe with the more academically prepared, says Sandra Wilkins, fashion design department chair at Virginia Commonwealth University in Qatar.

3.2.1 Structure

Education City is an educational district on the outskirts of Doha, in the city of Al-Rayyan, Qatar, opened in 2001 by the non-profit group, Qatar Foundation. It is located 6.5 miles (10.5 km) north east of Doha's city center. It covers an area of 14 square kilometers (150.7 million square feet) and houses educational institutions including schools, research centers, university campuses, and an equestrian center.

3.2.2 Universities

Education City's multi-institutional campus has branch campuses for United States universities that include Virginia Commonwealth University (VCUQ), offering a Bachelor of Fine Arts, Weill Cornell Medical College (WCMC-Q), offering 2- and 4-year medical programs, Texas A&M University (TAMUQ), offering bachelor's and master's degrees in science programs, Carnegie Mellon University (CMU-Q), offering undergraduate degrees in business and technology, Georgetown University

(SFS-Qatar), offering a bachelor's degree in foreign service, and Northwestern University (NU-Q), offering degree programs in journalism and communication.

Carnegie Mellon's undergraduate Business Administration program has earned global recognition for its approach to the study of business management as a science. More than 50 years ago, CMU developed management science, which involves analytical decision-making in complex business environments. Today, nearly all leading business schools include some form of the Carnegie Mellon model in their curricula.

The Business Administration program emphasizes a quantitative, analytical approach, training students in accounting, finance, economics, marketing, operations, management information systems, and business communications. Problem-solving is developed in a series of mathematics courses, including calculus, statistics, and forecasting. At the same time, liberal arts electives provide a balanced, well-rounded education.

Most business administration students opt for internships during their undergraduate years. Internships provide an invaluable opportunity for students to apply the skills they have learned in the classroom.

Graduates in business administration from Carnegie Mellon Qatar are highly sought after and pursue careers as analysts, strategic consultants, and managers in the fields of investment banking, corporate finance, and management consulting.

Business administration graduates from Carnegie Mellon Qatar have begun rewarding careers with some of Qatar's premier employers, including General Electric, Qatar Investment Authority, HSBC Bank, Vodafone, Microsoft, Ooredoo, and Qatar Petroleum.

As the department website of Carnegie Mellon Qatar states and explains to potential applicants as to why they should apply there, "Business administration encompasses management, leadership and teamwork. It involves organizing people, allocating resources, making decisions, and directing activities toward common goals and objectives. The Business Administration program provides the foundation for motivated students to become leaders in the business arena and have an impact on the economic growth of Qatar, the Middle East and the world."

3.2.3 Schools and Education Centers

Education City has a variety of schools with various curricula, including the Qatar Academy, K-12 school offering the International Baccalaureate programs, and The Learning Center School (TLCS), with grades 1–12 for students experiencing academic problems. The Academic Bridge Program (ABP) is a co-educational post-secondary school program founded in 2001 to help students make the transition from high school to university.

3.2.4 Research and Science Centers

- Qatar Science and Technology Park (QSTP)—a 45 thousand square meter (484 thousand square feet) office and laboratory facility that provides a supportive environment for international companies, institutes, and entrepreneurs in order to develop the latest technologies in Qatar.
- RAND-Qatar Policy Institute (RQPI)—works with decision-makers to develop and implement solutions to complex public policy issues for its clients across the Middle East, North Africa, and South Asia.
- Qatar National Research Fund (QNRF)—supports research in the fields of national interest by researchers, both students and professionals, in the private, public, and academic sectors. Currently, its funding programs are the Undergraduate Research Experience Program and the National Priorities Research Program.
- Sidra Medical and Research Center—a medical facility that provides patient care, medical education, and biomedical research, in addition to being the primary teaching venue for Weill Cornell Medical College in Qatar.

3.3 Internationalizing Business and IT Education in the United Arab Emirates

Nearly 40 years after the establishment of the United Arab Emirates, the country is moving toward becoming a competitor to countries such as China, Singapore, and the Kingdom of Saudi Arabia which have each invested considerably in establishing top-tier research universities. The efforts of the UAE in investing in its higher education system will most likely continue given its wealth and the vision of its leaders. Currently, there are 73 higher education institutions licensed by the UAE Commission for Academic Accreditation (CAA), of which 28 institutions are based in Abu Dhabi, 28 institutions are based in Dubai, and the remaining 17 institutions are located in the other emirates (Commission for Academic Accreditation 2011). It should be noted that not all institutions of higher education are accredited by the CAA; for example, in the emirate of

Dubai, 28 non-accredited institutions of higher education are in operation (The Higher Education Landscape 2010). These institutions are located in one of 5 Free Zones and are instead required to undergo the University and Quality Assurance International Board (UQAIB) quality assurance process established by the Dubai Knowledge and Human Development Authority (KHDA) which oversees the quality of higher education in institutions in the Free Zones. Many of UAE's higher education institutions are international branch campuses, such as Herriot Watt University, University of Wollongong, Middlesex University, University of Pune, and New York University, Abu Dhabi. What remains to be seen is the long-term academic and economic results of these institutions.

Some critics have suggested that the number of colleges and universities in the UAE exceeds the current demand (Moussly 2010). According to Lewin (2008), nearly two-thirds of the private institutions in the UAE were established after 2005. The speed at which universities have been established in the UAE has been referred to as ***educational gold rush***. Initially, these foreign institutions were established to cater for the Emirati students, and the children of the expatriate community who do not wish to leave the UAE and are not permitted to study in the government-financed universities that are reserved for Emirati nationals. International branch campuses in the UAE do not all share the same motives; while perhaps some establish campuses as a quick way of generating revenues, others do so to enhance research and knowledge collaboration.

Higher education system in the United Arab Emirates has evolved over generations from students migrating to far off places for learning to the present era of creation of education clusters and education hubs. Of particular interest is the transition of higher education system in the United Arab Emirates (UAE) toward internationalization with the growth of new universities, emergence of diverse programs, and international collaborations through establishment of branch campuses, making UAE the largest educational hub in the Middle Eastern region. The reforms initiated by the government and the challenges of the education system to align it with the new economy are of special interest in this respect.

Over the past five years many universities have opened their doors in the UAE, with some succeeding while others failing to deliver results either academically or economically. Government officials in the UAE continue to allow international institutions to establish campuses across the seven Emirates, with the intention to not only serve the local population, but to establish the country as a thriving regional educational hub similar to Asian countries such as Singapore and Malaysia. According to Becker (2009), between 2006 and 2009, 49 international branch campuses started their operations in the UAE, most of which were American, Australian, and British universities. A research study indicated that 62% of students in the UAE studying in UK-based institutions stated that the United Kingdom offered the best higher education in the world (Wilkins 2010). Hence, with such a positive reputation among students in the UAE, one can assume that these international campuses should not have difficulty attracting students. However, over the years, not all international universities have been successful in the UAE, as some have had to terminate their operations soon after starting.

Scotland's Heriot-Watt University is an example of a fast-growing university in the UAE. The university started with 117 students in its first year and this number increased to 500 within three years. Today, Herriot-Watts' Dubai campus student enrollment is 1400 (Mills 2010a).

New York University, Abu Dhabi started in 2010 accepting 2.1% of the 9048 applicants who applied to the university. Of those accepted, almost four out of five chose to enroll in the university. Currently, NYU Abu Dhabi has 150 students from 39 countries around the world, who speak 43 languages among them. The average SAT score of the 150 students is above 700 in the verbal and math sections. NYUAD is a project supported and funded by the government of Abu Dhabi who has invested millions of dollars into the development of the university, including a $20 million grant to support three research projects on the campus in the sciences and humanities. The total number of research money available at NYUAD has not been made public, however, according to Mills (2010a, 2010b) eight additional major research projects are under review. In order to attract students, the university contacted guidance counselors at the top 800 high schools internationally and encouraged them to nominate their two best students to apply to NYU Abu Dhabi. In 2010, the university recruited 300 students from around the world and flew them to Abu Dhabi so they could tour the city and get a glimpse of what it would be like to live in the city (Mills 2010a, 2010b).

Another internationally affiliated university that opened in the UAE is the Masdar Institute of Science and Technology, which is affiliated with the Massachusetts Institute of Technology. The assistant dean for research at Masdar states that the affiliation with MIT will provide people with the comfort that the institution is legitimate and reliable. As a postgraduate-only university, Masdar currently enrolls 92 students from 22 different countries and is planning to increase its student population to 800. Qualified students were accepted into the postgraduate program from around the world and were offered full tuition, accommodation, monthly stipend, personal computers, all text books, and travel reimbursements (Lindsey 2011).

In 2010 Abu Dhabi Education Council announced that a reform strategy is being planned to restore what it described as an ineffective and uncoordinated education system. As a part of the plan, the government plans to invest $1.3 billion in the nation's higher education by 2018. The aim of this strategic plan is to increase research and coordination among universities in the country. According to the report, due to the lack of research and coordination among the universities, the current system has been producing low-quality graduates whose skills are inadequate for the current competitive job market. According to the report, the current universities in the UAE rank poorly internationally with only one, the UAE University among the top 500 in the world.

3.4 Business and IT Education in Dubai

Dubai has emerged as a commercial, business, and IT hub in the gulf region inviting major business houses and various international companies for business and IT purposes. With the emergence of so many global firms, ample opportunities of growth and career enhancement have also been on the rise.

3.4.1 American University, Dubai

Being one of the recognized universities in Dubai, American University (AUD) aims at providing professional and practical experience for the graduates to train them professionally. Focusing on the job-oriented UAE market and the substantially growing jobs and business opportunities; the university offers a platform for the professional growth with various MBA and IT programs offered in the campus.

The American University of Dubai offers specialization in the field of Marketing and Marketing Communications, Business and Economics, Management, and Finance and Accounting. The school provides the undergraduate BBA program as well as master's in various specialized fields.

3.4.2 *University of Wollongong, Dubai*

Established in 1993, University of Wollongong is one of the oldest and is ranked as one of the best business schools in Dubai. With specialized programs for professionals, the university trains working professionals to excel in their field and achieve greater heights in their career growth. The university aims at providing world education in a multi-cultural environment.

With around 4400 students hailing from 117 nationalities, the teaching technique is designed catering to the aspirations of the young students as well as working graduates. The university provides ample opportunities for the researchers to delve and research on the related topics and fields.

3.4.3 *HULT International Business School, Dubai*

Focusing on the global business trends developing in Dubai, the HULT Business International School has emerged as one of the pioneer institutions in grooming and creating global professionals and business leaders. The highly qualified faculty members and business leaders are committed to train students with their enriching experience.

With the core value of innovating ideas and transforming education, the university provides a One Year MBA curriculum that adheres to inculcate business and leadership skills in the students. Mingling theoretical knowledge with a practical approach, the university aims to provide hands on experience to the learning graduates. A Two-Year Global Executive MBA program is designed especially for the professionals and graduates who further want to provide a cutting edge to their career potentials.

3.4.4 *London Business School, Dubai*

Ranked as one of the topmost business schools in the world, the London Business School was awarded the top position in 2012 by Bloomberg Business Week.

Launching the Dubai branch in 2006, the London Business School is set in the heart of the city in the Dubai International Financial Centre. Various MBA and IT programs are developed catering to the needs of the growing demand of education and executive professionals in the region. The school has designed a number of executive MBAs as well as other business programs leading to the elevation of knowledge in the business world. With a wide range of electives designed, the candidates can specialize in fields like HR, Finance, General Management, and Financial Analysis.

3.4.5 *Murdoch University, Dubai*

Murdoch University is one of the leading MBA universities in Dubai. Founded in 2007, the university has a reputation of excellence in education and research fields catered to the students. The graduates from the university get a practical exposure of the business and IT world and are well placed in reputable business and IT companies of Dubai.

Growing older and mature with 35 years' experience as one of Australia's leading education providers, the Murdoch University's Dubai campus provides graduates and postgraduates in various subjects like marketing, finance, IT, and various other areas of study. The university provides a cutting-edge opportunity to the graduates to get a deeper understanding in the area of specialization.

3.4.6 *SP Jain School of Management, Dubai*

SP Jain School of Management was founded in Dubai in 2004. It holds a great reputation and provides a great platform for the graduates to master their business and leadership skills. The school has an Executive MBA for the professionals who wish to sharpen their management skills while pursuing their careers as well.

Giving a comprehensive peep into the world of management, the Global MBA is a full time postgraduate program working on various areas of management and business skills like decision-making, innovative ideas with a technical knowledge of the subject.

3.4.7 *Canadian University, Dubai*

The Canadian University of Dubai is one of the popular business schools in Dubai. The school opened on the Dubai soil in the year 2006 with the Canadian curriculum. The university provides MBA programs in a number of areas like marketing, finance, Islamic Banking, Double Concentration, general management, and human resource management.

3.4.8 *University of Dubai*

The University of Dubai aims at delivering to the business some of the best global business leaders and entrepreneurs with key strategic skills and decision-making insight.

It works on sharpening the critical thinking, communication skills, and trouble-shooting technique desirable for an efficient business leader and a management professional. The university offers MBA in some of the key areas like Leadership and Human Resource Management, International Business and Marketing, Operations and Logistics, and Finance and Accounting.

3.4.9 Manchester Business School, Dubai

Reputed as one of the best business schools globally, the Manchester Business School opened up in Dubai in the year 2006. Keeping in pace with the fast changing and growing business world, the school offers some of the best MBA programs evolving the individual into a seasoned professional with sharp and critical business skills.

3.4.10 Dubai Knowledge Village (DKV)

Dubai Knowledge village is an educational campus and Free trade zone area in the City of Dubai, United Arab Emirates. Its vision is to focus and develop the region's talent and to establish the country as a knowledge-based economy. It is located about 22 kms away from City Center along the famous Sheikh Zayed Road within the Dubai Technology Free Zone—TECOM. Dubai Internet City and Dubai Media City are also in the same area.

Some of the Partner and member institutions at Dubai Knowledge Village:

- American College of the Emirates
- University of Wollongong in Dubai
- Birla Institute of Technology & Science, Pilani—Dubai
- European University College Brussels
- Heriot-Watt University Dubai
- Islamic Azad University
- Mahatma Gandhi University
- Middlesex University, Dubai
- University of New Brunswick in Dubai
- Saint-Petersburg State University of Engineering and Economics
- British University in Dubai
- Eton Educational Institute.

Dubai Knowledge Village (DKV), launched in 2003, places the Middle East on the map as a destination for learning excellence. Its picturesque campus sets the right environment for a knowledge-based sector with many professional training centers and learning support entities. This thriving knowledge community was founded as part of a long-term economic strategy to develop the region's talents, in an effort to introduce new skills and the latest learning methods and tools following international standards of upgrading individual skill and professionalism.

3.4.11 DKV's Business Partners

The benefits for Dubai Knowledge Village partners are immense and include 100% foreign ownership, 100% freedom from taxes, 100% repatriation of assets and profits, and effortless visa issuance procedures. DKV also offers first-rate facilities for the use of its knowledge partners and their students including serene landscapes, a food court, sports grounds, and a gym.

DKV has over 300 partners originating from different countries of the five continents. They have crossed the world to set up training and professional centers, institutes, and HR companies. DKV is totally focused on professional training and learning support services.

3.4.12 Dubai International Academic City (DIAC)

Dubai International Academic City (DIAC) located in the Dubai Academic City is the world's only Free Zone dedicated to higher education. A regional base for premier international higher education institutions, DIAC is the world's first dedicated tertiary cluster development. Spread across an area of 25 million square feet, the DIAC campus provides an environment of vitality and inspiration for students and faculty.

There are currently over 20 international universities of higher learning from diverse regions including Australia, India, Pakistan, Iran, Russia, Belgium, the United Kingdom, and Ireland operating out of DIAC, catering to over 9000 students. These include The University of Wollongong in Dubai, from Australia, Middlesex University Dubai Campus, from the United Kingdom, and SP Jain Centre of Management Dubai, from India, among others. These institutions offer programs that range in duration from one year to four years.

Major academic programs include engineering, computer science, fashion and design, biotechnology, environmental studies, quality management, and business management programs.

3.4.13 University City of Sharjah

Over the past years, Sharjah has become one of the most important learning centers in the Middle East. A multi-dimensional education system with a wide and varied network of schools and institutions has played a pivotal role in the development of Sharjah. Sharjah's University City, a huge six-campus development near the airport, was founded in 1997 and consists of the American University of Sharjah (AUS), Sharjah Men's University, Sharjah Women's University, the Higher College of Technology for Men, the Higher College of Technology for Women a pioneering project in the country providing students with professional training. It also includes Sharjah Police Academy and the Sharjah Library. The colleges are affiliated to a number of universities from the United States and Great Britain. Several new schools have been established here in the past year among them the first Australian International School in the UAE. The University City is located to the east of the city and comprises several magnificent buildings.

University City is an educational complex in the Al Juraina district of the city of Sharjah, United Arab Emirates (UAE), founded in 1997. It covers an area of over 1600 acres (6.5 square kilometers), with landscaped terrain and contains campuses for the American University of Sharjah (AUS), University of Sharjah (a.k.a. Sharjah University), the Sharjah Higher College of Technology (HCT) for Men (a.k.a. Sharjah Men's College), and the Sharjah Higher College of Technology (HCT) for Women (a.k.a. Sharjah Women's College).

University City Sharjah also encompasses the Skyline College, Sharjah Teaching Hospital, Sharjah Police Academy, Research and Studies Center, University City Hall, and Sharjah Library.

The Business Education Program at the University City of Sharjah aims at providing conceptual background to the students in core business and management areas. Program contents have been designed to expose students to the functions of business, organization structure and design, finance, and legal aspects of business toward developing an attitude for conducting and leading business enterprises effectively and innovatively.

The UAE by virtue of its location between Asia major and African continents provides crucial advantage for exports and re-exports from this region. In addition to the location advantage, the economic policies on imports and exports and free zone facilities extended to manufacturing, trading, and logistics for products and service sector has led to an exponential growth in foreign direct investments and foreign trading activities. To understand and operate international business transactions and to participate in the strategic management decision process, qualified manpower in this field is required. BBA in International Business provides the details of operations and management of international business in its various dimensions and contexts and equips the students to execute their responsibilities. BBA in International Business gives students an opportunity to focus and understand how business is conducted on a global scale, and how it is different from a domestic enterprise.

Information Systems form the backbone of Business Enterprises. Organizations, irrespective, of their business paradigms rely heavily on functional, cross-functional, and industry information. The growth in Secured Information Technology has fueled the information revolution, providing access anytime, anywhere to corporate information, thus enabling rational decision-making.

BBA in Information Systems is designed to develop Technologically Expert Knowledge workers who are well versed with technological aspects of information, and understand the business functions and is intended to utilize the emerging concepts in Information System.

Since its inception, Skyline University College has been training professionals in the field of Management Education, Travel & Tourism, Marketing, Human Resource, Information Systems, Strategic Management, and Finance. The institution has identified Retail Marketing, Public Administration, and e-Governance as new areas for training the manpower required of these industries. SUC has carved out a name for itself in the local and international markets as a quality business education provider at a reasonable cost.

Over a period of time, the University has carved a niche for itself in Business Management Education and training required for the industry.

SUC offers Bachelor of Business Administration (BBA) in Travel & Tourism Management, Information Systems, International Business, Marketing and Retail Management, Finance and Public Administration, and also Weekend BBA in International Business. SUC offers Master of Business Administration (MBA) Program, with emphasis in Marketing, Finance, Human Resource Management, Strategic Management & Leadership, and e-Governance during weekdays and weekends.

4 Findings and Discussion

The provided examples from Qatar and the UAE illustrate the point that human capital production has been closely intertwined with internationalization of the programs. In addition, the on-line provision of programs has made the education even more accessible and more international in nature.

The research has analyzed the importance of developing and incentivizing higher cognitive capabilities, IT proficiency, and leadership skills in individuals for the purposes of their wider inclusion in the human capital production process. The three important aspects are emphasized in this respect.

Firstly, the identification, enhancement, and facilitation of the appropriate human cognitive capabilities, leadership skills, technological proficiency, and empowerment of individuals to utilize those potentials to the full extent will contribute to both raising public awareness and to engendering positive socioeconomic change.

Secondly, the development of trust and intercultural awareness in international relations are yet further key issues in human capital production and human resource management process.

Thirdly, empowering employees' decision-making and creative innovating potentials are essential elements of human capital and resource facilitation.

And, finally, the increased internationalization and on-line mode of education has added further assets and opportunities to business and IT fields.

The tables present the general trends and student perceptions of education preferences throughout the 2019–2022 period. The data were collected through on-line surveys and questionnaires.

Table 1 presents the survey findings regarding business directions. The surveys were conducted among students on-line in Qatar and UAE throughout 2019–2022. The surveys clearly indicate the preference for international programs, IT competence, and leadership skills among the majority of students.

Table 2 presents the survey findings on the priorities that the students have when considering business education. As it can be seen from the table, engagement in international programs, sense of trust with business partners, goal achievement, and innovating and creativity are among the top priorities that students wish to attain while taking business courses.

Table 1 Predominant business directions across universities in Qatar and UAE

International programs	30%
IT orientation	25%
Leadership	20%
Decision-making	10%
Human resource management	10%
Financial knowledge	5%

Table 2 Student perceptions of business education priorities

International engagement	35%
Trust	25%
Goal achievement	20%
Innovation, creativity	20%

Table 3 presents the survey findings regarding IT directions. The surveys clearly indicate the preference for international programs and IT mastery among the majority of students.

Table 4 presents the survey findings on the priorities that the students have when considering the IT field. As it can be seen from the table, engagement in international programs and innovating and creativity are among the top priorities that students wish to attain while taking IT courses.

Table 3 Predominant IT directions across universities in Qatar and UAE

International programs	45%
IT mastery	35%
Programming	20%

Table 4 Student perceptions of IT education priorities

International engagement	55%
Innovation, creativity	35%
Goal achievement	10%

5 Concluding Remarks

Although the growing importance of internationalization of business and IT education and its impacts on higher education systems is dynamic in evolution, it is becoming more evident that the rationales that drive the process vary from region to region, country to country, or even between institutions that are themselves also evolving. The main outcome of the internationalization process seems to be at the national level, as countries would be interested in developing their human capital, or developing knowledge workers for contributing to their economy. Thus, four rationales for internationalization can be listed in the following order: the academic, the business oriented, the cultural/social, and the economic. All the rationales are significant for GCC countries, their higher education institutions, and human capital production.

References

Altbach, Philip G., and Patti McGill Peterson. (2007). Higher Education in the New Century: Global Challenges and Innovative Ideas. Rotterdam, The Netherlands: Sense Publishers.

Becker, R.F.J. (2009). International Branch Campuses: Markets and Strategies. London: The Observatory on Borderless Higher Education.

Commission for Academic Accreditation. (2011). Retrieved from http://www.caa.ae.

Lewin, T. (2008, February 10). U.S. Universities Rush to Set Up Outposts Abroad. The New York Times. Retrieved from http://www.nytimes.com/2008/02/10/education/10global.html.

Lindsey, U. (2011, January 30). A Future Minus Oil: Anticipating the End of Their Source of Wealth, Persian Gulf Universities Study Alternative Energy. The Chronicle of Higher Education. Retrieved from http://chronicle.com/article/At-Persian-Gulf-Universities/126092/.

Mazawi, Andre Elias. (2005). "Contrasting Perspectives on Higher Education in the Arab States." In Higher Education: Handbook of Theory and Research, vol. XX, ed. John Smart (pp. 133–189). London: Springer.

Mills, A. (2010a, June 10). Abu Dhabi Proposes Ways to Improve a Higher-Education System That Falls Short. The Chronicle of Higher Education. Retrieved from http://chronicle.com/article/Abu-Dhabi-Proposes-Ways-to/65851/.

Mills, A. (2010b, July 19). Why Some Branch Campuses Thrive in the Persian Gulf While Michigan State Pulls Back. The Chronicle of Higher Education.

Retrieved from http://chronicle.com/article/Why-Some-Branch-Campuses/123612/.

Moussly, R. (2010, January 3). Universities Face Shrinking Classes. The Gulf News. Retrieved from http://gulfnews.com/news/gulf/uae/education/universities-face-shrinking-classes-1.561224.

Stasz, Cathleen, Eric Eide, and Francisco Martorell. (2007). "Post-Secondary Education in Qatar: Employer Demand, Student Choice and Options for Policy." Arlington, VA: RAND Corporation.

The Higher Education Landscape in Dubai 2010. (2010). Knowledge and Human Development Authority, Dubai, United Arab Emirates. Retrieved from http://www.khda.gov.ae.

Wilkins, S. (2010). "Higher Education in the United Arab Emirates: An Analysis of the Outcomes of Significant Increases in Supply and Competition." Journal of Higher Education Policy & Management 32 (4): 389–400.

CHAPTER 6

Formulating Digital Right-Skilling in the Gulf's Healthcare 4.0 Ecosystem to Enhance Professional Capabilities

Náder Alyani

1 Introduction and Orienting Remarks

Progressive technology-mediated developments in digital health sector have caused digital skills mismatches in healthcare professionals: digital upskilling is an emerging global phenomenon, the practical mechanisms of which are understudied at the specific sectoral level of many countries. We firstly provide a circumscribed overview of selected recent studies

The author is responsible for any errors or omissions on a personal capacity: comments and suggestions are welcomed and appreciated.

N. Alyani (✉)
Bloomsbert Associates, Aachen, Germany
e-mail: n.alyani@gmail.com

A. Mishrif et al. (eds.), *Nationalization of Gulf Labour Markets*,
The Political Economy of the Middle East,
https://doi.org/10.1007/978-981-19-8072-5_6

and reports, initiated globally and expanded regionally, that highlight the challenges and opportunities of Industry 4.0 (I4.0) and Artificial Intelligence (AI), facilitating a move towards an Enterprise 4.0 model applied in healthcare operations. We observe that as the volume of the digital upskilling literature continues to increase in the recent decade, the conceptual terms such as 'reskilling' and 'upskilling' (often loosely defined and indirectly referring to 'right-skilling' as increasing, reorienting and improving performance-linked professional and lifelong competencies, based on contemporary demands of sector-specific organisations and business cycles) and particularly the practical means to operationalise the terms, via grounded pedagogical interventions, have become ambiguous. We therefore utilise 'right-skilling' to refer to how the new demands of the healthcare sector requires retraining the professional workforce and when needed, acquiring and developing people's capabilities with the right (i.e. appropriate) skills to fill the gaps in adding value to the digital activities of the enterprise.

Secondly, after drilling further into the unique strands in the human capital situation of the regional healthcare sector, we outline the region's increasing challenges of dealing with prevalent non-communicable diseases (NCDs) in brief. We then expand on how digital learning and right-skilling tools, such as digitally enhanced learning (e.g. blended learning within a hybrid corporate academy) design, can assist in addressing the gap in professional performance, considering the evolving trajectory of digital skill mismatch within the Gulf region's healthcare, anchoring on United Arab Emirates (and with a passing glance at the trends demonstrated via the recent cited studies in Oman, as well as Saudi Arabia and Iran).

Whilst acknowledging the previous work on the healthcare education, training systems and capabilities development regionally, and the increased emphasis on promotion of health-related subjects for 'local nationals', we highlight the tension in the policy intentions and challenges of implementation for the healthcare professionals as required for fully engaging in, and developing the capabilities to deal with the full consequences of the digitalisation in the healthcare.

In the final part of the chapter, we conclude by glancing at the possibilities offered by exploring and developing the digitally enhanced learning models for organisations and individuals within the Gulf's healthcare sector to build capability and capacity so as to significantly and sustainably participate in the current wave of healthcare enterprise 4.0 level and tentatively offer remedial scenarios and actions to take to avoid potential unintended consequences.

1.1 The Current State of Play on I4.0 Skills

We start by considering the state of play globally and then rapidly converge on the regional context of the Gulf and specifically within the healthcare sector. There is much written during the recent years in academia, government policy circles, think tanks and business consultancy (e.g. 'grey') literature about, firstly, the capabilities of the new evolutionary wave of digital technology sector, specifically Industry 4.0 (Kagermann et al. 2011; Schwab 2015) and Artificial Intelligence (encompassing Machine- and Deep-Learning) and an emerging set of related technologies and digital solutions, with multiple potentials for use cases, such as in Internet of Things (IoT, including combined labels like *Medical IoT*) and new generation of advanced robotics, smart devices (e.g. in smart-cities, -mobility and -buildings) and 'expert' analytical and diagnostic systems. In addition to Industry 4.0, Enterprise 4.0, a term recently promoted by Goldman Sachs research acknowledging the emerging software capabilities, and is

> Defined by technology that is very lightly penetrated at the moment or in some cases in its infancy. [... however, it is expected that] these emerging technologies will have profound impacts on the future of work and the way we interact with both the digital and physical worlds. (Goldman Sachs 2020: 5)

For the purpose of our studies and considering the broadening of the definition and the current state of post-pandemic digitalisation momentum, we include the following 4 broad categories in I4.0:

1. Enhanced *Connectivity and Communication* (e.g. Industry/Medical Internet of Things and Cloud and Cyber Security)
2. Coherent *Data, Intelligence and Analytics* (e.g. applied Artificial Intelligence and Big Data and Analytics tools)

3. Systematic *Advanced Production* (e.g. Additive Manufacturing Technologies, and Advanced Automation and Robotics); and thus all factors above leading to
4. Amplified *Human–Machine Interactions* (e.g. Simulations of Products and Scenarios, and Virtual/Augmented Reality).

At the enterprise level of the industry (E4.0), other technologies (from existing and emerging technology companies) that will define Enterprise 4.0 era, as a contributing building block of Industry 4.0, include SaaS and DaaS (Software/Desktop as a Service), Zero Trust Security, 'Work from Anywhere' and digital engagement and collaboration tools, video communication, public cloud services, 'Low Code/No Code' platforms, DevOps, Robotic Process Automation, AI (& ML), Edge Computing, Extended Reality and IoT (Goldman Sachs 2020: 4).

As a consequence of the widespread diffusion of new digital technologies, there are also multiple debates and at times contrasting views on the impact of these on the workplaces, including automation and robotics at the healthcare settings, and reskilling, upskilling and in our preferred terminology, *right-skilling* in the sectoral labour markets to tackle the engrained skill mismatches. These extend to the daily realities of life and nation's prosperity and welfare, including opportunities in reforming regional higher and medical education institutions (HEIs/MEIs) and ultimately, building potential for economic and technological 'leapfrogging' (Deloitte and Huawei 2017; McKinsey Global Institute 2018; for critiques, see Morgan 2019; Pfeiffer 2017; Ross et al. 2018; The Economist 2019, 2022a; WEF 2017).

A significant proportion of the debate and scenarios (particularly as asserted before the global Covid-19 pandemic effects) swings between the utopian and dystopian tendencies of the possibilities in the advanced industrial economies and generally misses out the regional intricacies such as the nuances of the contextual characteristics, including the unique labour market features of the GCC countries (and Iran). In contrast, as part of our circumscribed policy review, we foreground the multi-layered regional contextual factors (El-Saharty et al. 2020; Hertog et al. 2020; World Bank 2012, 2018) and look cautiously for capturing 'lessons-learned' at the overview of global policy lessons (DBEI 2019; Industrial Strategy Council 2019; Kispeter 2018; MITI 2018; OECD 2005, 2019; PwC 2020; The Asia Foundation and Microsoft 2020). In our analysis, we consistently forego the 'science fiction' scenarios so as to offer a more grounded exploration of the debates, with particular reference to enhancing the local labour market's capacity and capabilities, and the skills required, be it via sectoral reskilling, upskilling, and ultimately right-skilling interventions. In so doing, the local labour, be it Gulf nationals or expatriate can more fully engage with, participate in, and in time excel at (as a minimum, in a narrow strand of) the activities of the existing and the newly emerging healthcare spheres.

Drawing on the global policy agenda, it is apparent that a number of countries have identified, albeit implicitly that digital skill mismatches will need to be further attended to and unpacked. As a recent well-structured and insightful policy-design report from Malaysian government, drawing on global practices on I4.0 and its implications on skills and talent, summarises:

> Industry 4.0 is fundamentally reshaping the jobs landscape and will foster significant changes... [in performing jobs]. Entirely new jobs with very different skill requirements will be created, while some tasks will become obsolete. The shifting employment landscape has significant implications for industry, education systems and the government. A qualified and skilled workforce is indispensable for the introduction and adoption of industry 4.0. The technical knowledge required is high, and will be primarily recruited from the STEM (science, technology, engineering and mathematics) subjects. [...] Particular attention also needs to be given to reskilling and upskilling... (MITI 2018: 45)

In another recent and proactive policy report, from the government of Ireland, the issue of skill development is embedded primarily within the multifaceted support for the implementation of firm-level industry 4.0 strategies. Ireland intends to continue building knowledge across sectors and promote process innovation, economies of scale, encouraging mutual learning (via I4.0 firm consortia) and spillovers between firms, so that her companies can compete internationally (DBEI 2019: 26–30).

The report further highlights that

> Industry 4.0 will have a significant impact on existing roles... [and thus will] require a hybrid set of competencies in future graduates, combining mechanics, electronics and software. [...] skills [on technologies, systems and standards] related to leadership and strategic management in industry 4.0 will be essential in the future workforce. [...] the appropriate hybrid mix of ICT and engineering skills as required for Industry 4.0... [is a

> necessity to] understand the skills requirements for enterprises engaging in Industry 4.0. [...] better alignment of [HEIs'] funding to the skills needs of the economy, will ensure continuing responsiveness of the system to identified skills needs including those relating to Industry 4.0. (ibid. 2019: 29)

On a tangential note, it is worth highlighting that the new generation of AI (including emerging AI in the healthcare solutions) will share a set of common characteristics as a unique form of technological disruption where a tested algorithm is globally disseminated with relative ease of mobility. It has thus been highlighted that AI processes and products share three key features: (1) they can be "infinitely replicable and instantly distributable," low cost and updatable; (2) they are seemingly supported by an extensive venture capital industry; and (3) China is an emerging significant player in AI innovation, redirecting technology flows from earlier eras (Lee 2018: 152).

The UK government agencies, in partnership with industry and academia, have also raised concerns in multiple reports, including the likely scenarios for digital skills mismatches, skills which are '*important today, critical tomorrow*' and the sectors most at risk, highlighting that:

> Existing evidence suggests the UK's demand for skills – particularly technology and interpersonal/people skills – will increase considerably over the next decade, while the supply of those skills will be constrained. [...] The scale and type of skills shortfall anticipated, cannot be addressed through formal education outside of the workplace alone. An urgent shift to a new norm of lifelong learning in the UK workforce is required. Employers, government and individuals will all have a role to play in reskilling and upskilling the existing workforce. (Industrial Strategy Council 2019: 3–4)

Elsewhere, another UK review, which as well as broad definitional terms, looked specifically at digital skills in three UK sectors (i.e. health and social care; culture and creative industries; and financial services) points out an important conceptual and methodological conundrum in the policy and research literature, as:

> ... it is difficult to establish the boundary between essential and more specialised digital skills for the general workforce and identify a list of digital skills beyond the essential level. Descriptions of digital competence as a 'T-shaped skill set', in which individuals possess in depth knowledge

in one area and good knowledge across many other areas may be useful here. (Kispeter 2018: 7)

Following on from the above themes and acknowledging that skill, particularly at workplaces and sectoral levels, can be a complex concept which is challenging to measure and accredit, we follow the definitions of skill mismatch offered at macro, meso (sectoral) and micro levels. This is defined, based on and in line with previous overviews (Brunello and Wruuck 2019: 4) on a macro level as "the gap between the (aggregate) supply and demand for skills, typically with reference to a specific geographical unit (region, country or country group)" and on a micro (firm) level as "when workers have a level of skills that is different from what is required for [their optimal performance in] their jobs."

We therefore define competence in digital skills (particularly based on significant uptake of digital transformation) as the ability to be an optimally performative *user* and/or *creator and editor* of digital tools and technologies, broadly acting as 'users and/or producers' at the different *operational* and *advanced* levels, in sector-specific applications and functions.

Before concluding this section and turning to the context of the Gulf as our case vignette, we should highlight the healthcare sector's global challenges with digital upskilling, which have been captured by a number of recent national, regional and internationally inspired policies as well as local studies and technical reports (Australian Digital Health Agency 2020; Deloitte 2019; Department of Health and Social Care 2018; for an overview, cf. Loizou and Xu 2020; NHSx 2021; OECD 2021; World Economic Forum 2019).

As a summary research in the United Kingdom concludes (ibid. 2020: 14)

> Overall, ... there is still a long way to go in order to close the digital skills gaps and bring about a successful digital transformation. Generally, skills gaps exist on various aspects and within different stakeholder groups: front-line healthcare practitioners need to become more confident in recommending and using digital technologies; senior management needs to acquire a wider and deeper understanding on what digital transformation means for effectively guiding the process; patients' skills and competencies also need to be taken into consideration when implementing digital technologies. To address such skills shortages, it is necessary to

> adopt a systematic and holistic approach that addresses all aspects of the transformation process including creating a supportive culture, upgrading the infrastructure, and providing training for general and specific digital skills. [... by utilising streamlined and targeted learning using delivery modes such as scenario-based learning, online and/or blended learning courses as CPD programmes]

It is with the above full considerations of the global debates in mind that we turn our attention to the situation in the Gulf region's healthcare digital skills. From a human capital supply perspective, whilst we acknowledge the need for educational reforms, particularly in the elementary levels to ignite interest in STEM and in higher education landscape seeking a better alignment with the local labour market and national industrial policy priorities (and the fledgling R&D capabilities), plus the much debated increasing motivational factors for 'national students' (in the GCC), our starting position is to look at the healthcare workplace and related requirements and demands.

In line with the technology path-dependency argument, the manner in which digital skills are deployed with practical solutions today will shape the path that the enterprises will take in it for tomorrow. Zooming out, from an evidence-based policy-design perspective, the mainstream macroeconomic and longitudinal studies on education in the region, spanning a number of decades are essentially inconclusive on causality and replication (EIU 2017b; Galal 2008; WEF 2017) with reference to digital technology specialist or advanced skills for the labour market. The context, institutional history and the dominant structure of each country matter immensely and based on our analysis of the skill mismatches and future requirements, ***path dependence*** rather than ***new path creation*** is widely witnessed.

Our core message is therefore relatively sanguine and practical compared to the futuristic hyperbole circulated about I4.0 and AI, particularly on the regional labour market transitions, namely that regionally we are not facing a sudden labour market ***revolution*** but most likely a gradual and potentially bifurcated ***evolution***. As will be expanded upon later, that general position and path-dependency is highly likely to be applicable to the healthcare sector too.

As articulated elsewhere, the broader argument is that whilst the technology is fundamentally changing the way businesses operate, we need to further explore the opportunities to 'rehumanise work', developing 'human^{+}' machine collaboration to boost capabilities and productivity, bringing new opportunities and more satisfying work (Daugherty and Wilson 2018) whilst sustainably utilising advanced digital tools.

In exploring the regional challenges with a case vignette of the increasing trends of non-communicable diseases (NCDs) and the digital skills development of the healthcare staff to adequately deal with the new trends, we draw our material from a range of macro and meso (sectoral) levels regionally, for example from Dubai (and at times, Abu Dhabi), and UAE's policy perspectives (Bohsali et al. 2017; EIU 2017a; KPMG 2020; Oman MoE & MoHE 2021; PwC 2021; Strategy& 2021; UAE Government 2017, 2019; AlBasri et al. 2022), as well as a circumscribed academic research literature both from UAE (both Abu Dhabi and Dubai) and Oman, as well as glancing at similar themes in Saudi Arabia and Iran (Albejaidi and Nair 2021; Al-Mawali et al. 2021; Alnakhi et al. 2021; Alnowibet et al. 2021; Alqunaibet et al. 2021; Asadi et al. 2018; Azadnajafabad et al. 2021; Cheema et al. 2021; Hannawi and Salmi 2014; Lin et al. 2021; Mohamed and Al-Lawati 2022; Paulo et al. 2019; Qureshi 2020).

As a brief socio-epidemiological observation and synopsis, NCDs in the region has developed as a by-product condition of the living experience of *compressed-modernity* where within three to four decades, based on societal changes quietly effecting cultural practices, Western-inspired dietary additions rich in sugar have been combined with an increasingly sedentary lifestyle and work patterns. Relatedly, the high temperatures of the average climate of the Gulf region for about 6 months of the year and in Iran's case (including in northern regions away from the Gulf's extreme seasonal heat), the serious chronic air pollution in larger cities and urban areas, have regularly acted as a prohibiting factor in regular physical activity and total daily energy/caloric expenditure. NCDs then, as the leading cause of death and disability globally, have entered the Gulf region rapidly and yet initially in stealth.

NCDs, in particular obesity-related conditions, diabetes, heart disease and cancer have made a significant impact on the future demands on the healthcare, where curative analysis and action have been superseded by preventative measures. Sociocultural factors confound the situation particularly for women (The Economist 2022b). Providing public health awareness and education programmes, at times as part of national policy visions, early diagnosis and preventative measures (such as an emerging punitive taxation on sugary drink and tobacco), has attempted to better inform and empower the at-risk population and potential patients with alternative choices, and better equip the healthcare professionals in anticipating and dealing with the potential "perfect storm".

Global and regional lessons-learnt from the taming of the recent pandemic has also highlighted the greater role of telehealth adoption and healthcare digitalisation, such as extensive use of remote sensors and diagnosis, and where applicable treatment. As the acuteness of the recent Covid-19 pandemic justifiably shifted the focus from NCDs to communicable disease prevention and management, the risk of infection and transmission were successfully controlled and mediated in the Gulf States (and with mixed outcomes in Iran). This has also turned the spotlight on healthcare professionals' digital skills in order to offer healthcare practice innovation and generate workflow efficiencies with policy lessons learned.

We acknowledge the increasing utilisation of the digital healthcare 4.0 lexicon and digital healthcare ecosystem approach (HIMSS 2021; NHS 2022; Siemens Healthineers 2019; Singhal et al. 2020) in order to offer a conceptual framework on how the multiple stakeholders can both act upon, and benefit from a more *unified ecosystem approach*, inter alia, to workforce skill development and digital technology-enhanced decision-making and digital-twinning for precision-medicine (Siemens Healthineers 2020), particularly around enhancing the combination of value-adding 'high-tech' and 'high-touch' skills of healthcare professionals (OECD 2021: 54–56) (Fig. 1).

The synopsis of the above-mentioned recent OECD research and recommendations (ibid.), drawing conceptual lessons based on a myriad of national case studies (e.g. on Canada, Denmark, England, Estonia, New Zealand, Norway and European Commission's AI efforts) is worthy of a closer examination. Prepared by the OECD Directorate of Employment, Labour and Social Affairs (ELS), Health Division, for the 2020 German Presidency of the Council of the European Union and with the support from the German Federal Ministry of Health, it reviews various challenges of the current healthcare era, highlighting that:

> Successful digital transformation in the health sector is not a simple matter of technical change but requires a complex adaptive change in human attitudes and skills as well as in the organisation of work... Digital technologies only provide the tools and cannot transform the health sector on its own but need to be put to productive use by the health workers and patients. Many health workers already use some digital tools and solution

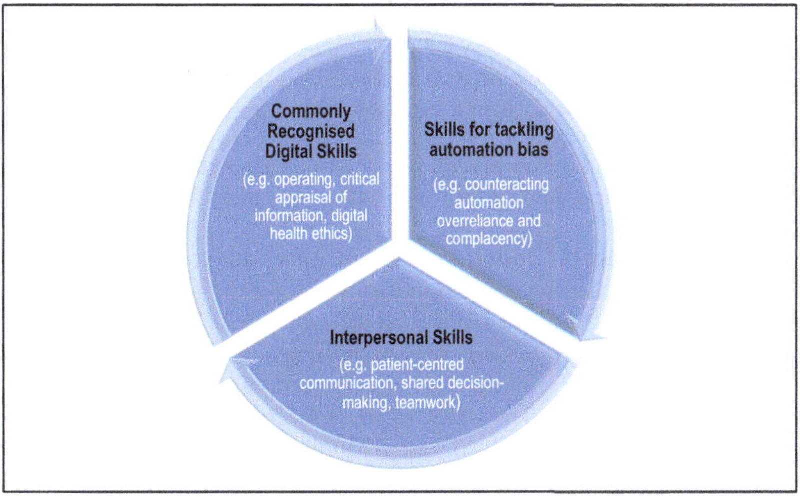

Fig. 1 Combining 'high-tech' and 'high-touch' skills as required by current healthcare era (OECD 2021: 55)

> [perceiving their full benefits] ... many also question the value digital technologies produce in health care or complain about technology getting in the way of their work. Moreover, health workers often report not having opportunities for the upskilling required to put the technology to full use or that the legal, financial, and organisational aspects of work – designed in the pre-digital era – are not adequately reformed to enable the technology to add value. (ibid.: 7)

> On average today, the health systems consume a tenth of the respective national incomes, with the growth of health expenditure outpacing economic growth for most of the past half century... – a trend that is likely to persist in the future... More efficient spending, whilst still improving the access to and the quality of health services, is a key policy challenge. In this context, digital transformation offers unique opportunities to strengthen health systems and meet the challenges of responding to the changing health needs of the public and health workforce shortages. (ibid.: 11)

On the systematic effort to combine 'high-tech' and 'high-touch' skills, it is worth recalling that this endeavour (despite pilot research on the EU and EU-US level) has been challenging, as:

> "progress in building or modernising the digital health curricula has been slow and uneven." (ibid.: 54) [...] "The clinician-leaders and managers increasingly need to combine their understanding of clinical practice with that of technology and change management to ensure the digital technology fits into the realities of health care practice, to secure the buy-in from the frontline health workers, as well as to manage the culture change needed to drive learning across health care organisations." (ibid.: 58–59)

With those valuable insights borne in mind and held in the background, we now turn to foreground some of the details of the regional context. Promoting the dual priorities of ***value-based healthcare reforms*** and ***rising patient expectations***, we rapidly mark out the similarities and the distinct differences in the challenges faced by the regional healthcare services. The smaller states with a large number of expatriate healthcare staff, such as the UAE, are undoubtedly facing different 'right-skilling' learning and development challenges, compared to the larger national healthcare services (e.g. of Saudi Arabia and Iran). Metaphorically outlined, the Gulf's regional healthcare systems are ***all likely to be in the same storm but are not in the same boat***. That said, our concluding suggested pathway, offered later, for the systematic use of hybrid corporate academies as a viable route to right-skilling is likely to be applicable, with some minor adjustments, in addressing many of the regionally shared learning and development needs.

As the diffusion of new digital healthcare technologies reshape the regional activities unevenly, a smart and where necessary, specialised and bespoke digital skill policy becomes critical to ensure growth and relevance. The Gulf States and Iran therefore, tackling their own unique challenges, have to (re-)design, develop and deliver smart and modularly built and delivered policies to raise their healthcare human resources performance capacity, ensuring societal well-being. Demographic pressure and NCDs trends will present multifaceted digital skill needs which cannot be ignored: in short, increasing healthcare staff's skills can help drive the next phase of the Gulf's development within this sector, which has experienced robust growth in the last decade. The next phases will increasingly demand people to upgrade their skills to perform new and emerging tasks in their existing jobs or acquire new skills in order to fit into new jobs.

Drawing selectively on both academic and practice-based professional and consultancy literature, the objective of the next section of this chapter is to provide a space to explore and examine the recent trends within the regional healthcare sector, with a particular focus on implementation challenges of digital right-skilling.

1.2 Digital Right-Skilling of Healthcare Professionals in the Gulf

The multifaceted aspects of the digital skills development of the regional healthcare professionals have recently received some tangential yet timely attention, as part of the broader topics of developing capabilities in regional events (e.g. the GCC Taskforce on Workforce Development in Digital Healthcare based in the UAE and affiliated to HIMSS) and specialist publications (KPMG 2020; Qureshi 2020; Sheikh et al. 2019).

In line with other consultancy report's tonality, at times bordering on becoming unduly congratulatory, the KPMG 2020 report highlights several interesting challenges. It pinpoints for example that the effects of digital technology on healthcare will be significant and takes a sober look at the imbalance in healthcare workforce demand and supply (latter being via international recruitment of already trained staff or local training of both local and non-local medical students) discussing the merits of incentive programmes, such as longer and more attractive visa terms and schemes for, inter alia, healthcare professionals.

Whilst on the recent consultancy reports, we should reiterate three ongoing skill policy dilemmas too. Firstly, as highlighted widely, there is a global shortage of trained healthcare professionals and the situation is exacerbated in the entire Gulf region with differing levels of impact, based on the size of the local (i.e. national) healthcare workforce. In UAE for example, whilst the Emiratis form about 12% of the country's population, over 80% of all physicians and over 95% of all nursing staff are currently expatriate. There is therefore a long-term critical high dependency on foreign workforce with the associated high elements of churn (at times labelled as cyclical sectoral 'brain-drain'), based on the motivation of seeking better life prospects upon gaining some experience within UAE and/or GCC and then migrating out of the country and region, heading for greener pastures. Healthcare professionals' migration is also significant issue in Iran, with similar underlying aspirations.

Secondly, the level of opportunities for training, learning and development is significantly different between the public and private sector providers, the latter which are where a large majority of expatriate workforce are employed. The uniformity of the professional skill levels (at the lowest common denominator) is therefore maintained by local compulsory licensing and accreditation, which is a suitable entry mechanism into the profession but may be broadly questionable at the enforcement level or deemed unsuitable or inadequate for staff retention and retaining ongoing specialisation skills and as importantly, developing new higher clinical standards at existing workplaces. The private sector healthcare providers in particular employing large expatriate workforce therefore will need a longer-term motivational remedy for this situation, to promote lifelong learning and developing emerging specialisations.

Third and lastly, beyond the short-term effects of the recent pandemic as a healthcare system's stress-test, there is a clear potential of a 'perfect storm' brewing with reference to the region's NCDs and the previous vacuum of a coherent multi-faceted policy promoting healthy lifestyle reorientation. As the Gulf States and Iran are seriously at risk of a significant increase in epidemiological and pathological trends of NCDs, there will continue to be a rising demand in specialised and chronic treatment, in areas such as cardiovascular, diabetes and oncological care. This will then place a higher demand on the State and the providers to offer leading edge care options as to reduce the burden of the local patients having to travel out of the national region and country for advanced treatment and offer the full 4 points cycle of *prevention and screening*; *diagnosis*; *treatment*; and *long-term disease management* (cf. Broadband Commission 2018: 22) with reasonable ease of access.

The three points above, taken together on a practice level of delivering the services, further outline the case that highly curated digital learning could play a more central role in equalising and standardising right-skilling of healthcare professionals in the Gulf.

Returning to the context of the region, Qureshi's account, as a trained medical professional herself, avoids embellishments and makes a convincing case for the necessary staffing platform rearrangements and better HRD policies to implement innovations in the UAE's healthcare sector. Whilst her reported study cannot be easily generalised as is based on a small-scale exploratory investigation, it successfully endeavours to draw attention to some of the less transparent issues that recent consultancy reports often miss out (or choose to side-line). Revisiting and reframing the core themes of Hannawi and Salmi's work (2014), she highlights a number of ongoing system-wide structural factors such as '*high turnover rates and low retention*' and '*skill mix imbalance and weak knowledge*' (Qureshi 2020: 294) of the UAE's healthcare professionals.

As stated, as 'an under-researched topic' before the onset of the global pandemic, in this context:

> Upon close observation... UAE healthcare has shown minimal progress toward the adoption and implementation of healthcare innovation since 2014. Although many conferences and seminars have taken place in the region [and despite the best policy intentions], the practical implication of healthcare innovation strategies has moved at a slow pace. (ibid.: 276)

She further argues that whilst much cutting-edge technology from international medical technology companies as well as 'best-practice' ideas from regulatory authorities are already present and utilised in the UAE's healthcare; readiness and preparedness of healthcare professionals to fully 'adopt and adapt' to manage the change and innovation, with a view to continuous improvement, is an ongoing challenge of the actual practice. Nonetheless, she concludes positively by differentiating on the macro, meso and micro levels; highlighting that UAE (with Dubai and Abu Dhabi as leading the effort) is poised to do well on the macro and meso level based on supportive strategies and resources, the healthcare system is viewed as progressing in the right direction. More detailed and nuanced attention however, such as more coherent career development activities and systematic performance appraisals may well be needed in parallel, as at

> the micro level, especially physicians and nurses seem to be in need of developing skills to effectively and efficiently participate in this wave of health innovation in the UAE. (ibid.: 295)

Moving on from the UAE, another recent debate with a broader scope and covering the entire GCC States with policy and practical examples of capability development and capability retention pathways is worth examining. Sheikh et al. (2019) explore a number of factors, outlining significant progress in some areas as well as identifying ongoing challenges in the Gulf's CPD/CME (Continuing Professional Development/Continuing Medical Education) programmes, including international education and training cooperation schemes and conclude that

> health care professionals from multiple disciplines (physicians, nurses, pharmacists, dentists, midwives, others) in the GCC's health care workforce and increasing the number of locally-trained graduates are important steps

> to address challenges with the type and supply of health care professionals. Along those lines, establishing models of team-based training and diversifying health care curricula and CME/CPD programs are vital for capacity building endeavors. [...] To increase the professional competence (skills and knowledge), culturally-sensitive capacity building efforts should be based on country-specific needs assessments that include an educational approach focused on problem-based and competence-based learning. Capacity building can play a vital role in addressing the major health challenges of this region, which include: an aging population, the increase of chronic non-communicable diseases, the continuing threat of infectious disease, the rising concern of mental health issues, and inequity in women's health. (Sheikh et al. 2019: 7–8)

Drawing on ongoing global debates, they also usefully highlight that

> Capacity building education programs, which include task shifting from physicians to other health professionals, can lower cost and expand capacity in resource-short areas. Task shifting in the GCC countries will strengthen interdisciplinary and interprofessional collaboration, leading to improved health outcomes for individuals, communities, and the wider population. (ibid.: 5)
>
> Along with health care reform, there is therefore a need for a broad curricular reform to upgrade the existing health education programs within the GCC countries. Challenges associated with reforming education programs include a) the rapidly expanding base of medical knowledge, b) the conflict between 'top down' lecture systems and more flexible and innovative 'flipped' classroom teaching, and c) the growing disconnect between the traditional curricula with reductive biological basis and the increasing prevalence of chronic diseases, which have strong social determinants. Even when such challenges are identified, the cost, time, and effort required to upgrade the educational systems can present significant hurdle. (ibid.: 2)

As outlined in the long quotations form the above-mentioned recent studies then, there are several recurring issues with reference to the digital competencies, requiring right-skilling of the healthcare professional in the Gulf. Offering a formulation and pathway for a comprehensive solution will not only require time, but also active policy and practice experimentation and prototyping, the scope of which is outside the focus of this chapter.

Having outlined the plethora of contributing factors from a global, regional and healthcare sector-specific lens, the remaining third part of this chapter will turn to draw attention on the possibilities offered by digital learning scenarios, specifically the design of blended learning programmes within a hybrid corporate academy structure within healthcare organisations, to address some of the challenges. Digitally enhanced quality healthcare service delivery requires the close cooperation of multiple audiences, particularly healthcare professionals and patients. Drawing a hard distinction between *high-touch* or *high-tech* is a false dichotomy as we need to develop appropriate skills to be able offer both by attempting to *co-create* services, based on the circumstances and priorities.

1.3 Enhancing Capacity Building via Digital Right-Skilling and Improving Competencies

Under the emerging regional circumstances of a market-driven and competitively priced sector, the Gulf healthcare organisations may not possess many influential levers to reduce the *churn* and turnover in the supply of professionals. Tangentially, the reorientation of visa incentive schemes (in UAE's healthcare, for example) will require some time to demonstrate a clear impact. Improving quality and enhancing service outcomes can therefore be initiated by pragmatic and practical steps in terms of specific programmes, many of which can now be delivered by blended learning, partially remotely at existing healthcare workplaces, within a hybrid corporate academy model.

Considering the remits of managing chronic NCDs, digital right-skilling can result in a 'multiplier effect' when designed in smart ways that engage both the professionals involved as well as increase patient's motivation for engagement and self-efficacy. Digital tools, co-creatively implemented, can significantly assist in managing remote patients monitoring, managing multimorbidity, designing and delivering precision care and medicine, and increasing medication adherence.

It is noteworthy to highlight that UAE public organisations including the healthcare agencies already offer an impressive array of online and blended courses. In the recent years, programmes such as *TDRA Virtual Academy*, *Al Mawrid eLearning Portal* and more specifically *Maharati Healthcare eTraining System* have attempted to increase capabilities of the public sector professionals. More specifically for NCDs issues, a number of CPD/CME training opportunities have also been formulated and offered via BMJ Learning; and post-pandemic, via the Dubai Health Authority in collaboration with external providers such as *iheed* (officially launching *DARB* and *MANAAR* as part of the 2020 Gitex event) accredited by Warwick University (UK) and the Irish College of General Practitioners.

Based on anecdotal evidence, the above programmes have generally been well-received. In time however, a more coherent and externally validated evaluation system may well be useful in assessing their value-add and professional impact. At the time of writing, we were unable to access such evaluations in the public sphere which may indicate the recency of some of the mentioned programmes.

1.4 Digitally Enhanced Learning with Co-creation and Hybrid Models

> Making improvement happen... requires leadership that enables connections between the aims of changes and the design and testing of those changes; that pays serious attention to the policies and practices of reward and accountability; and unshakeable belief in the idea that everyone in healthcare really has two jobs when they come to work every day: to do their work and to improve it. (Batalden and Davidoff 2007: 3)

Our review so far has argued that the effective utilisation of digital healthcare, and the related skills development to undertake this, should be viewed as a key enabler in delivering healthcare now and in the future. Building the professionals' digital capabilities is a system-wide transformation strategy positively influencing service and care delivery, clinical practice and decision making, as well as medical education (CME/CPD) and research, offering tangible benefits to patients and enhancing the role of professionals.

Within the outlined example of the UAE, health regulators have continuously considered and prototyped the adoption of innovative and smart medical and educational technologies (*MedTech & EdTech*) including the exploratory use of AI within the sector, in a dedicated drive to modernise the country's healthcare ecosystem. It is probably too soon to judge but the current results as demonstrated by glances at practice have been encouraging. UAE and the other Gulf states, including Iran, already possess a few islands of clinical and medical excellence and a wide-ranging, albeit fledgling, programme of implementing research and evidence-based practices. The core challenge is in harmonisation and standardisation of optimal care and scaling up the productive and value-added use of digital tools, and digitally enhanced learning for professionals in a people-centred and continuous manner.

Within the broader literature of *technology enhanced learning* (TEL) and the newer and more current term of *digitally enhanced learning* (DEL), there are already numerous reviews spanning years of debates, assessment reviews and good practice, contingent on the context of healthcare applications. These can offer valuable insights for future research in charting a new course for the region's professional capacity building effort based on the '*here and now*' of digital learning affordances. Instead of revisiting the multi-strands of issues, covered elsewhere in academic and consultancy reviews, and/or marketed as learning platform solutions by information technology system vendors, we draw attention to just two conceptual issues for consideration in the Gulf's healthcare, in the remaining space of this section; firstly, the importance of designing opportunities for *co-creation* to increase the impact of digitally enhanced learning; and secondly, exploring the blended learning approaches in the form of a new generation of *hybrid corporate academy* (HCA) as a design and delivery model.

The concept of co-creation of learning opportunities, particularly as a reflective healthcare practitioner, argues for inclusive innovation processes in order to ensure equitable access to new professional learning opportunities. The design of pedagogical interventions should therefore allow the professionals to actively participate in the development of digital learning rather than framing and then imposing innovation top-down without gaining an in-depth understanding of the daily practices and workload demand.

This is where the diagnostic process of *Training Needs Analysis* (TNAs—also at times referred to as *Learning Needs Analysis*—LNAs) linked to occupational roles and skill profiles must be explored in a more nuanced way. The pathway of the learning journey should be bidirectional—healthcare institutions and organisations need to offer right-skilling and education to the professionals, and in parallel, healthcare professionals need to distil their exposures with patient's needs to inform and influence healthcare organisations on the context of their routine experience. This can then significantly assist in taking ownership and empowering the professionals for improving the processes to 'adopt and adapt'.

Let us recall that

> "co-creation can also be considered a learning process, in which actors learn how to use each other's competences to develop new ways to confront… challenges…" (Voorberg et al. 2017: 178) and "learning in co-creation is a social process, in which shared convictions about problems and solutions are the result of a dialog between actors." (ibid.: 180)

Co-creation opportunities also offer more engagement and entail the healthcare professional to play an active role in redesigning the associated sociotechnical systems, and mitigating the psychosocial risks embedded within the hierarchy of healthcare organisations. Healthcare organisation within the Gulf may need to be regularly reminded that the design and performance of any organisational system can be better understood and improved upon when the 'psychological', 'social' and 'technical' aspects are brought together and treated as interdependent parts of a dynamic system: this delicate balancing act is at the core of an agile implementation.

With co-creation in mind, a new generation of blended learning strategies, with the use of hybrid corporate academy model is worth exploring, as it can be tailored to offer specificity, impact and flexibility, as a right-skilling intervention. Pedagogy (and not the latest digital tool) is paramount in the hybrid corporate academy model. Relatedly, the ADE^2 heuristic model outlined below (taking the first letters of the action verbs used to describe the focal activities, squared—i.e. to the power of 2—as abbreviation) is intended to highlight, in brief, the interconnected processes that need to be attended and attuned to in designing the healthcare professional personalised (albeit role-based and performance-driven) learning and development journeys. Intentionally kept lean, the aim of ADE^2 heuristic model is to connect, engage and inform the healthcare professionals in their occupational pathway and lifelong learning (Fig. 2).

Following the practical lessons learnt as part of dealing with Covid-19 pandemic and then moving to an endemic state within the health sector, the use of hybrid corporate academy model for the health sector organisations is timely and already in practice, under different guises. The renewed ideas behind *hybrid corporate academy* (HCA) are an evolving manifestation of a leaner *corporate university* model (Rademakers 2014), with a greater focus on hybridity as a result of the new virtual orientation to learning and development at work following the pandemic-induced work

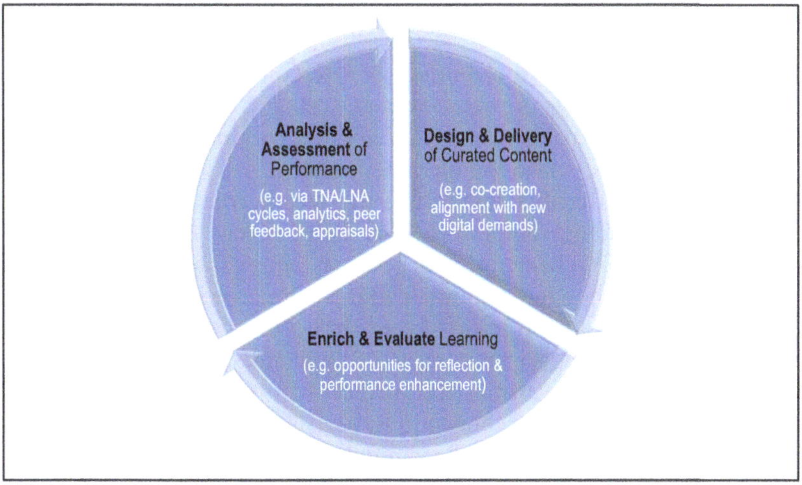

Fig. 2 ADE^2 Heuristic Model: Combining three interconnected processes in healthcare professionals' L&D

reorganisation; and the requirement for a much closer link to performance and more transparent and meaningful return on investment (RoI) on learning programmes within the organisation, whilst simultaneously (and at times, implicitly) promoting a *self-directed learning* (SDL) approach as part of an intervention mode to increase competencies. As witnessed in recent post-pandemic empirical work on other education-allied domains (Alyani 2022), the incentives for nurturing self-directed learning will need a careful examination of the motivational impulses of the Gulf's healthcare professionals' context. These can then promote ***interprofessional learning and judgement*** (Alyani 2018) as an essential ingredient for enhancing innovation in the regional healthcare.

Ending on an optimistic note, as a result of mass uptake of digitally enhanced learning during the pandemic, blended learning models when inbuilt with requisite quality in the curriculum and pedagogy, are perceived more positively and accepted favourably. Previous major challenges and (negative) perceptions within the Gulf region with professional blended learning models concerning the national legislation, quality assurance and reputation (of CME/CPD), whilst still lingering, are now unlikely to be as highly entrenched as before.

2 Concluding Remarks

This chapter has explored a number of interconnected arguments scanning through various previous studies, using a combinational rapid review research approach, at times attempting to move beyond the hype and where possible, 'make the invisible, visible'.

The effects of the digitalisation in the healthcare and the associated digital skill upgrading requirements are here to stay. Also 'Black Swan' events and VUCA characteristics need to be met and bridged. The current effort of the Gulf region to address the growing needs for digitally skilled healthcare professionals, in the form of strategic plans on a policy level, and practical brokerage on a practice-at-organisation and -sector level and via universities and medical schools, are welcome moves. Healthcare ecosystem interconnections, globally and locally, in pursuit of quality and specificity, need to be carefully thought-through with potential unintended consequences and implementation challenges identified and addressed. Policy design in healthcare therefore is much more than (globally oriented) policy-borrowing, and is contingent upon building critical ecosystem mechanisms for right-skilling the existing in-service healthcare professionals as the engine of the health system.

In preparation for I4.0 skill developments, a number of broader recommendations have already been identified within the policy literature, so as to endeavour to 'mind the gaps'. These are applicable to healthcare too and we have drawn together the following three recommendations in brief (originally developed by *Asian Development Bank*), which can be equally applied to GCC States and Iran's circumstances, by utilising a multi-stakeholder 'quadruple helix' engagement approach.

- Developing I4.0 and digital healthcare skills transformation road maps for key growth areas: Similar to Singapore's practical effort, GCC and Iran could consider the development of 'Health Sector Transformation Maps' which endeavours to provide information on digital technology impacts, career pathways, skills required for different in-sector occupations, and reskilling options. As a starting point, healthcare roles- and specialty-specific road maps for priority or growth areas (such as NCDs) can be drawn up first;
- Strengthening the market-relevance and quality assurance mechanisms for local HEIs and Training Institutions providers with reference to digital skills;

- Designing and implementing new and smart incentive schemes for healthcare organisations to train employees for digital skills (potentially linked to tax rebates and other financial or administrative incentives).

In addition to above, in crafting a smart digital right-skilling policy in the region, it would be of immense value to take account of the overlapping layers of existing policies and the logic of ***strategic incrementalism***, referring to developing and facilitating methods of gradual change by which many small policy changes are enacted over time in order to create and facilitate a larger broad-based policy change, increasing confidence in the implementation and realisation stages. Prototyping small digital right-skilling programmes and schemes, with qualified partners, can lead the way. These could then help to clarify the nature of the emerging healthcare digital skill levels and co-create ecosystems, and inform policy-makers and organisations of the specific remedial measures to pursue in order to better formulate and optimise their capabilities.

References

AlBasri, Mahdi, Hani Elwan, Panco Georgiev, and Ali Ustun. 2022. Growth Opportunities for Digital Health in KSA and UAE. Dubai, Riyadh & Doha: McKinsey & Company.

Albejaidi, Fahad, and Kesavan Sreekantan Nair. 2021. "Nationalisation of Health Workforce in Saudi Arabia's Public and Private Sectors: A Review of Issues and Challenges." Journal of Health Management 23(3):482–97. doi: https://doi.org/10.1177/09720634211035204.

Al-Mawali, Adhra, Sathish Kumar Jayapal, Magdi Morsi, Waleed Al-Shekaili, Avinash Daniel Pinto, Hilal Al-Kharusi, Ayaman Al-Harrasi, Zainab Al-Balushi, and John Idikula. 2021. "Prevalence of Risk Factors of Non-Communicable Diseases in the Sultanate of Oman: STEPS Survey 2017." PloS One 16(10):e0259239. doi: https://doi.org/10.1371/journal.pone.0259239.

Alnakhi, Wafa K., Heba Mamdouh, Hamid Y. Hussain, Gamal M. Ibrahim, Amar Sabri Ahmad, Raghib Ali, and Abdishakur Abdulle. 2021. "The Socio-Demographic Characteristics Associated with Non-Communicable Diseases among the Adult Population of Dubai: Results from Dubai Household Survey 2019." Healthcare 9(9):1139. doi: https://doi.org/10.3390/healthcare9091139.

Alnowibet, Khalid, Adel Abduljabbar, Shafiq Ahmad, Latifah Alqasem, Nabil Alrajeh, Luigi Guiso, Mazin Zaindin, and Madhusudhan Varanasi. 2021. "Healthcare Human Resources: Trends and Demand in Saudi Arabia." Healthcare 9(8):955-. doi: https://doi.org/10.3390/healthcare9080955.

Alqunaibet, Ada, Christopher H. Herbst, Sameh El Saharty, and Abdullah Algwaizini. 2021. Noncommunicable Diseases in Saudi Arabia: Toward Effective Interventions for Prevention. Washington, DC: World Bank.

Alyani, Náder. 2018. "Learning to Innovate Collaboratively with Technology: Exploring Strategic Workplace Skill Webs in a Telecoms Services Firm in Tehran." PhD Thesis, University College London, London.

Alyani, Natallia. 2022. "Exploring Self-Directed Learning and Professional Development of EFL Teachers in Online Learning Contexts." Master's thesis in Education, University of Warsaw, Warsaw, Poland.

Asadi, Heshmatollah, Batoul Ahmadi, Saharnaz Nejat, Ali Akbari Sari, Ali Garavand, Abdollah Almasian Kia, and Mojtaba Hasoumi. 2018. "Factors Influencing the Migration of Iranian Healthcare Professionals: A Qualitative Study." PLOS ONE 13(6):e0199613. doi: https://doi.org/10.1371/journal.pone.0199613.

Australian Digital Health Agency. 2020. National Digital Health Workforce and Education Roadmap. Sydney, NSW: Australian Government.

Azadnajafabad, Sina, Esmaeil Mohammadi, Arya Aminorroaya, Nima Fattahi, Shahabeddin Rezaei, Rosa Haghshenas, Negar Rezaei, Shohreh Naderimagham, Bagher Larijani, and Farshad Farzadfar. 2021. "Non-Communicable Diseases' Risk Factors in Iran; a Review of the Present Status and Action Plans." Journal of Diabetes and Metabolic Disorders 1–9. doi: https://doi.org/10.1007/s40200-020-00709-8.

Batalden, Paul B., and Frank Davidoff. 2007. "What Is 'Quality Improvement' and How Can It Transform Healthcare?" Quality & Safety in Health Care 16(1):2–3. doi: https://doi.org/10.1136/qshc.2006.022046.

Bohsali, Samer, Sevag Papazian, Melissa Rizk, and Ali Matar. 2017. Empowering the GCC Digital Workforce: Building Adaptable Skills in the Digital Era. Dubai, UAE: Strategy&, PwC & Linkedin.

Broadband Commission. 2018. The Promise of Digital Health: Addressing Non-Communicable Diseases to Accelerate Universal Health Coverage in LMICs. Geneva and New York: Broadband Commission for Sustainable Development, ITU, UNESCO.

Brunello, Giorgio, and Patricia Wruuck. 2019. Skill Shortages and Skill Mismatch in Europe: A Review of the Literature. EIB WP 2019/05. Luxembourg: European Investment Bank.

Cheema, Sohaila, Patrick Maisonneuve, Albert B. Lowenfels, Amit Abraham, Sathyanarayanan Doraiswamy, and Ravinder Mamtani. 2021. "Influence of

Age on 2040 Cancer Burden in the Older Population of the Gulf Cooperation Council (GCC) Countries: Public Health Implications." Cancer Control 28:1–7. doi: https://doi.org/10.1177/10732748211027158.

Daugherty, Paul R., and H. James Wilson. 2018. Human + Machine: Reimagining Work in the Age of AI. Boston, MA: Harvard Business Review Press.

DBEI. 2019. Ireland's Industry 4.0 Strategy 2020–2025: Supporting the Digital Transformation of the Manufacturing Sector and Its Supply Chain. Dublin: Department of Business, Enterprise and Innovation (DBEI, renamed DETE after 2020), Government of Ireland.

Deloitte. 2019. Closing the Digital Gap: Shaping the Future of UK Healthcare. London: Deloitte Centre for Health Solutions.

Deloitte, and Huawei. 2017. National Transformation in the Middle East: A Digital Journey. Dubai, UAE: Deloitte Touche (M.E.) & Huawei Technologies.

Department of Health and Social Care. 2018. The Future of Healthcare: Our Vision for Digital, Data and Technology in Health and Care. London: UK's Department of Health and Social Care.

EIU. 2017a. GCC Health 2.0: Tackling Diabetes and Obesity in an Age of Technological Acceleration. London and Dubai: Economist Intelligence Unit [sponsored by EY].

EIU. 2017b. Powering the UAE Digital Economy: Developing the UAE's Computer Science Talent (Commissioned by Google). London and Dubai: Economist Intelligence Unit.

El-Saharty, Sameh, Igor Kheyfets, Christopher H. Herbst, and Mohamed Ihsan Ajwad. 2020. Fostering Human Capital in the Gulf Cooperation Council Countries. Washington, D.C.: World Bank Publications.

Galal, Ahmed. 2008. The Road Not Traveled: Education Reform in the Middle East and North Africa (MENA Development Report). Washington, D.C.: World Bank Publications.

Goldman Sachs. 2020. Future of Work: Accelerating the Transition to Enterprise 4.0, the next Evolution of the Digital Workplace [Equity Research: Software]. New York: Goldman Sachs Group.

Hannawi, Suad, and Issa Al Salmi. 2014. "Health Workforce in the United Arab Emirates: Analytic Point of View." The International Journal of Health Planning and Management 29(4):332–41. doi: https://doi.org/10.1002/hpm.2198.

Hertog, Steffen, Tariq Anwar-Al Haq, Alhussein Eman, and Afshin Molavi. 2020."Citizens, Expatriates, and the Future of Gulf Labor Markets: AGSIW's Virtual Panel Discussion Examining the Effects of the Coronavirus Pandemic on the Long-Standing Issues Confronting Gulf Labor Markets," May 20, Washington, D.C.

HIMSS. 2021. "Building a Digital Health Ecosystem." Healthcare Information and Management Systems Society (HIMSS). Retrieved December 31, 2021 (https://www.himss.org/resources/building-digital-health-ecosystem).

Industrial Strategy Council. 2019. UK Skills Mismatch in 2030 - Research Paper (with MGI & DBIS). London: UK's Industrial Strategy Council, Department for Business, Energy & Industrial Strategy.

Kagermann, Henning, Wolf-Dieter Lukas, and Wolfgang Wahlster. 2011. "Industrie 4.0: Mit Dem Internet Der Dinge Auf Dem Weg Zur 4. Industriellen Revolution." VDI Nachrichten, 3–4.

Kispeter, Erika. 2018. What Digital Skills Do Adults Need to Succeed in the Workplace Now and in the next 10 Years? Coventry: Warwick Institute for Employment Research, University of Warwick.

KPMG. 2020. Who Cares, Wins: UAE Healthcare Perspectives. Dubai, UAE: KPMG (Lower Gulf).

Lee, Kai-Fu. 2018. AI Superpowers: China, Silicon Valley, and the New World Order. Boston, MA: Houghton Mifflin Harcourt.

Lin, Tracy Kuo, Tim A. Bruckner, Taghred Alghaith, Mariam M. Hamza, Mohammed Alluhidan, Christopher H. Herbst, Hussah Alghodaier, Adwa Alamri, Rana Saber, Nahar Alazemi, and Jenny X. Liu. 2021. "Projecting Health Labor Market Dynamics for a Health System in Transition: Planning for a Resilient Health Workforce in Saudi Arabia." Globalization and Health 17(1):105. doi: https://doi.org/10.1186/s12992-021-00747-8.

Loizou, Michael, and Zimu Xu. 2020. Digital Skills Gap in the Healthcare Sector: Technical Report. Coventry: Institute of Coding, Coventry University.

McKinsey Global Institute. 2018. Skill Shift: Automation and the Future of the Workforce [MGI Discussion Paper]. Global offices [Principal offices in North America, Europe and Asia/Pacific]: McKinsey Global Institute, McKinsey & Company.

MITI. 2018. Industry4WRD: National Policy on Industry 4.0. Kuala Lumpur, Malaysia: Ministry of International Trade and Industry.

Mohamed, Nazar, and Nahida Al-Lawati. 2022. "How to Make the Best Use of the Workload Indicators of Staffing Needs Method in Determining the Proportion of Time Spent in Each of the Workload Components and Its Implication in Decision Making: The Experience of the Sultanate of Oman." Human Resources for Health 19(1):113. doi: https://doi.org/10.1186/s12960-021-00656-2.

Morgan, Jamie. 2019. "Will We Work in Twenty-First Century Capitalism? A Critique of the Fourth Industrial Revolution Literature." Economy and Society 48(3):371–98. doi: https://doi.org/10.1080/03085147.2019.1620027.

NHS. 2022. "The Healthcare Tech Ecosystem [Part of Introduction to Healthcare Technology in the NHS in England]." NHS England. Retrieved February

18, 2022 (https://digital.nhs.uk/developer/guides-and-documentation/introduction-to-healthcare-technology/the-healthcare-tech-ecosystem).

NHSx. 2021. Listening to Digital Health Innovators Report 2021 [Second Report from NHSx (User Experience) on Technology, Digital and Data, to Be Merged with NHS England in 20222]. London: National Health Service (NHS), UK.

OECD. 2005. The Definition and Selection of Key Competencies: Executive Summary (the DeSeCo Project). Paris, France: Organisation for Economic Co-operation and Development.

OECD. 2019. OECD Skills Strategy 2019: Skills to Shape a Better Future. Paris: OECD Publishing.

OECD. 2021. Empowering the Health Workforce: Strategies to Make the Most of the Digital Revolution [Authored by Karolina Socha-Dietrich]. Paris, France: Organisation for Economic Co-operation and Development.

Oman MoE & MoHE. 2021. Oman National Framework for Future Skills. Muscat, Oman: Ministry of Education and Ministry of Higher Education (Research and Innovation).

Paulo, Marília Silva, Tom Loney, and Luís Velez Lapão. 2019. "How Do We Strengthen the Health Workforce in a Rapidly Developing High-Income Country? A Case Study of Abu Dhabi's Health System in the United Arab Emirates." Human Resources for Health 17(1):9. doi: https://doi.org/10.1186/s12960-019-0345-9.

Pfeiffer, Sabine. 2017. "The Vision of 'Industrie 4.0' in the Making—a Case of Future Told, Tamed, and Traded." NanoEthics 11(1):107–21. doi: https://doi.org/10.1007/s11569-016-0280-3.

PwC. 2020. Curriculum Guidelines 4.0 [Skills for Industry]: Future-Proof Education and Training for Manufacturing in Europe - Final Report [PwC for EASME as Curriculum Guidelines for Key Enabling Technologies (KETs) and Advanced Manufacturing Technologies (AMT)]. Brussels: European Commission.

PwC. 2021. Value Based Healthcare [Note on the GCC]. Dubai, UAE: PricewaterhouseCoopers.

Qureshi, Wardah. 2020. "The Role of Human Capital in the Implementation of Healthcare Innovation in the UAE." Pp. 275–310 in Human Capital in the Middle East: a UAE perspective, Palgrave Studies in Global Human Capital Management, edited by V. Pereira, M. Neal, Y. Temouri, and W. Qureshi. Cham, Switzerland: Palgrave Macmillan/Springer.

Rademakers, Martijn F. 2014. Corporate Universities: Drivers of the Learning Organization. Abingdon, Oxon and New York: Routledge.

Ross, Emily, Bill Schaninger, and Emily Seng Yue. 2018. "Right-Skilling for Your Future Workforce: Building a Competitive Workforce of the Future Requires 'Right-Skilling' - Organizations Need to Have a Strategic Plan for

Talent to Make the Shift." McKinsey Organization Blog. Retrieved May 31, 2021 (https://www.mckinsey.com/business-functions/people-and-organizational-performance/our-insights/the-organization-blog/right-skilling-for-your-future-workforce).

Schwab, Klaus. 2015. "The Fourth Industrial Revolution: What It Means and How to Respond." Foreign Affairs, December 12.

Sheikh, Javaid I., Sohaila Cheema, Karima Chaabna, Albert B. Lowenfels, and Ravinder Mamtani. 2019. "Capacity Building in Health Care Professions within the Gulf Cooperation Council Countries: Paving the Way Forward." BMC Medical Education 19(1):83. doi: https://doi.org/10.1186/s12909-019-1513-2.

Siemens Healthineers. 2019. Embracing Healthcare 4.0: Digitalizing Healthcare as a Key Enabler for High Value Care. Erlangen, Germany: Siemens Healthcare.

Siemens Healthineers. 2020. Holistic Decision-Making in a Digital World: Smart Data Integration and Decision Support along the Patient Pathway. Erlangen, Germany: Siemens Healthcare.

Singhal, Shubham, Basel Kayyali, Rob Levin, and Zachary Greenberg. 2020. The next Wave of Healthcare Innovation: The Evolution of Ecosystems (McKinsey on Healthcare [Pre-Pandemic Material]). Detroit, MI, USA: McKinsey's Healthcare and Public & Social Sector Practices, McKinsey & Company.

Strategy&. 2021. The Future of Healthcare Has Arrived: How Middle East Healthcare Players Can Respond. Dubai, UAE: Strategy&, PwC.

The Asia Foundation, and Microsoft. 2020. The Future of Work across ASEAN: Policy Prerequisites for the Fourth Industrial Revolution - Recommendations and Country Studies [for Cambodia, Indonesia, Malaysia, Philippines, Singapore, Thailand and Vietnam). San Francisco: The Asia Foundation.

The Economist. 2019. "An Accidental Doom-Monger [Schumpeter]: A Notorious Forecast about the Automation of Jobs Has Been Hugely Misunderstood, Says One of Its Authors." Economist, June 29.

The Economist. 2022a. "The World Should Welcome the Rise of the Robots [Automation]: Concerns over Mass Unemployment Are Unfounded." Economist, February 26.

The Economist. 2022b. "Why Women Are Fatter than Men in the Arab World [the Obesity Gap]: Society Does Not Make It Easy to Shed Pounds." Economist, July 28.

UAE Government. 2017. UAE's Fourth Industrial Revolution Strategy [Summary Report]. Government. Dubai, UAE: The Prime Minister's Office at the UAE Ministry of Cabinet Affairs and the Future.

UAE Government. 2019. "Future Skills [Overview on Future Skills, Promising Sectors and Special Programmes]." The Official Portal of the UAE Government. Retrieved May 1, 2019 (https://government.ae/en/information-and-services/jobs/future-skills).

Voorberg, William, Victor Bekkers, Krista Timeus, Piret Tonurist, and Lars Tummers. 2017. "Changing Public Service Delivery: Learning in Co-Creation." Policy and Society 36(2):178–94. doi: https://doi.org/10.1080/14494035.2017.1323711.

WEF. 2017. The Future of Jobs and Skills in the Middle East and North Africa: Preparing the Region for the Fourth Industrial Revolution [Executive Briefing]. Geneva: World Economic Forum.

World Bank. 2012. "Skills or Jobs - Which Comes First?" Pp. 174–78 in World Development Report 2013: Jobs. Washington, D.C.: World Bank Group.

World Bank. 2018. The Jobs Agenda for the Gulf Cooperation Council Countries. 125505. Washington, D.C.: World Bank Publications.

World Economic Forum. 2019. Health and Healthcare in the Fourth Industrial Revolution [Global Future Council on the Future of Health and Healthcare 2016-2018 - WEF Insight Report]. Geneva: World Economic Forum.

CHAPTER 7

A Hospitable Kingdom? Building New Employment Opportunities for Saudi Youth in the Culture, Tourism and Hospitality Sectors

Annalisa Pavan

1 Introduction: Readjusted Plans, Ambitions on Hold

In the wake of the international outcry caused by the brutal Khashoggi murder and under the markedly controversial leadership of the de facto ruler, Crown Prince Mohammed bin Salman, popularly known as MbS, January 2020 saw Saudi Arabia assume the G20 Presidency. The Kingdom had high hopes of benefiting from this role on the international scene, but

A. Pavan (✉)
University of Padova, Padova, Italy
e-mail: annalisa.pavan@unipd.it

A. Mishrif et al. (eds.), *Nationalization of Gulf Labour Markets*,
The Political Economy of the Middle East,
https://doi.org/10.1007/978-981-19-8072-5_7

with the outbreak of the COVID-19 pandemic, 2020 turned into a nightmare year for Saudi Arabia, and for the whole world. As for the Crown Prince, "His reputation ebbed globally, his purchasing power declined, and his dreams to open Saudi Arabia to the world financially and through tourism are on hold" (Al Rasheed 2020).

The Kingdom's global positioning as a world-class tourist hub had officially started in September 2019, with the launch of the tourist e-visa for 49 countries. But suddenly, in March 2020, the world was driven online by the health emergency and all travel was halted, in a global attempt to contain the deadly spread of SarsCov2. Saudi Arabia had to scale down its plans and ambitions. At the time of writing this paper (Fall 2021), the evolution of the pandemic is still largely unpredictable, with global economies and individuals alike struggling to envision and transition to a "new normal".

It is against this very uncertain scenario that the author will seek to address the following questions: what are the economic, social and political goals behind investments to build from scratch and develop the *leisure* tourism industry in Saudi Arabia (Sect. 1)? What plans and actions are being adopted by the Saudi leadership to create new employment opportunities for Saudi youth (Sects. 2, 3, and 4)? How are Saudi higher education policies being adjusted, as concerning education and training for the tourism sector, to comply with the Saudi Vision 2030 mandate "to close the gap between the outputs of higher education and the requirements of the job market" (Sect. 5)? Does the nascent Saudi leisure tourism industry—now reliant on the PIF (Public Investment Fund, the Saudi sovereign wealth fund chaired by MbS)—have the capability to build the skills (Sect. 6) and, over time, to nurture and sustain the motivations and aspirations of Saudi youth in the quest for stable and well-paid employment (Sect. 7)?

The development of the leisure tourism industry in Saudi Arabia is currently a work in progress, and as such, a subject of anecdotal propaganda inside and outside Saudi Arabia, but it has been under-researched thus far at academic level. This paper will rely on existing—albeit scarce—academic literature, as well as on Saudi and international press reports, official documents, and extensive web searches.

2 Re-Defining Tourism and Hospitality in Saudi Arabia

According to the World Tourism Definition, a tourist is a person travelling for holiday, leisure, business and religious purposes (Burns 2007). A "virgin sector" in Saudi Arabia (Royal Embassy of Saudi Arabia in Rome 2021, 49), tourism has traditionally relied almost exclusively on the pilgrimage to Mecca and Medina, the two holiest Muslim sites. Before the outbreak of the COVID-19 pandemic forced Saudi authorities first to halt and then to restrict religious tourism, the pilgrimage had been the major tourism resource of the Kingdom. In 2019, Hajj pilgrims to Saudi Arabia numbered 7,457,663, and the previous five years had recorded an impressive growth of around 1.7 million (Parveen 2020). Until very recently (see General Authority for Statistics 2018; Castlereagh Associates 2019), the development of tourism in Saudi Arabia has tended to be one-dimensional in nature (Ekiz et al. 2017), i.e. evolving almost exclusively as religious tourism.

Burns (2007) affirms that there has been no international leisure tourism in Saudi Arabia as defined by most academic observers, citing Smith (1989) and Burns and Holden (1995). According to Henderson (2017), it is precisely because Saudi Arabia is a leading religious tourist destination that it cannot simultaneously host inbound leisure tourist flows. Moreover, researchers who focus on the GCC tourism and hospitality sectors usually ignore Saudi Arabia and prefer to highlight the potential, challenges and achievements of neighbouring countries instead (see for example the recent works of Karolak 2015, 2018; Burns and Bibbings 2017; Hilal, 2020; Scharfenort 2020, among others).

It is generally agreed that Saudi Arabia finally committed to open up to global *leisure t*ourism in April 2016 with the launch of Saudi Vision 2030, a set of social and economic reforms—largely inspired, it is thought, by the McKinsey Consulting Group (Pavan 2021)—aimed at diversifying the Saudi economy, with the young Crown Prince MbS providing the public face of the diversification plan (Moshashai et al. 2020). In their efforts to implement Saudi Vision 2030, "the Kingdom's rulers seek to rewrite the Saudi social contract by retrenching the state's largess to its citizens while granting a modicum of social liberalization", but "retaining absolute political control in the hands of an unelected monarchy" (Moshashai et al. 2020, 382). Quilliam (2019) affirms that "while the broader goal of the Vision is to transform the economy and, in doing so, some social change is essential, the project is ultimately intended to sustain the rule of the leading family". In Saudi Arabia, the regime's propaganda describes Saudi Vision 2030 as "an ambitious and wide-ranging plan to diversify Saudi Arabia's economy, reduce its reliance on oil, and increase foreign investment, transforming the Kingdom's economic model by establishing the private sector as an engine for growth and jobs" (Al Sarhan 2021). Foreign propagandists insist that "Vision 2030 aspired to modernize the country where it mattered most—among the able-bodied and creative youths" (Kéchichian 2019, 50–51), but it is unfortunate that among the sectors covered by the Vision, specific direct reference to *the youth* is nowhere to be found. The Vision depicts the "vibrant society", the "real wealth" of the country; it mentions families, children, the academic and educational system, but it does not explicitly mention youth.

Since 2016, a string of economic and social initiatives, relentlessly trumpeted and amplified by the Saudi media, have bolstered strenuous efforts to polish the Saudi image abroad and reinforce vital domestic support for MbS, "the boy king" (Hearst 2018). Before the outbreak of the pandemic, American influencers were employed (Khalife 2019) to promote the Saudi social and natural environment, and to counterbalance caution, suspicion and open criticism towards actual change, openness and progress in the conservative Kingdom (Bayoumi 2018; Sheline 2019).

Youth unemployment is still a very troubling problem for Saudi rulers. The age group 15–34 is the largest (36.7%) of the overall population, and 67% of all Saudis are under the age of 34 (General Authority for Statistics 2020a). 60.7% of unemployed Saudis belong to the age group 20–29 (in Q3 2020), with male unemployment accounting for 7.2% and female unemployment accounting for 21.2% (General Authority for Statistics, 2021). 53.5% of unemployed Saudis hold a bachelor's degree, 24.9% hold a diploma or higher degree, and are specialized in humanity studies (General Authority for Statistics 2020b). The aim of Saudi Vision 2030 is to reduce the overall unemployment rate to 7% by 2030.

Saudi Vision 2030 states that tourism and leisure are among the promising sectors due to become new pillars of the Saudi economy: "We will create attractions that are of the highest international standards, improve visa issuance procedures for visitors, and prepare and develop our historical and heritage sites" (2016, 44). It also sets the broad goal "to close the gap between the outputs of higher education and the requirements of the job market" (2016, 40), which implies that the needs of the labour market must be carefully assessed when reforming higher education curricula and funding tertiary education.

As will be explained in the headings that follow, Saudi rulers have realized that the development of leisure tourism could achieve two equally important economic and social goals: economic diversification and job creation, especially for qualified youth, although it is obvious that for this to be possible, the image of the country must first be revamped. In addition, young Saudis who have jobs will be much more faithful supporters of the establishment, signifying that youth employment strategies can also be seen as having political benefits.

Following the launch of Saudi Vision 2030 in the pre-pandemic era, Saudi Arabia stated the ambitious goal of receiving 100 million foreign tourists (10% GDP) in 2030—a giant leap forward from the 15 million (3.8% GDP) recorded in 2018 (Castlereagh Associates 2019). Prior to September 2019, the very strict Saudi visa policies had been a key factor in inhibiting the development of leisure tourism (Ekiz et al. 2017). But in February 2020, Saudi officials announced that over 400,000 tourist visas had been issued since the borders of the secretive Kingdom finally opened to foreign vacationers of 49 countries, thanks to the tourist visa scheme launched in September 2019. At the same time, officials made it clear that more substantial investments were needed in order to build suitable infrastructures that would transform the Kingdom into a world-class tourist hub (Nereim 2020a).

But developing domestic tourism too is a key ambition of the Crown Prince, with staycations boosting Saudi economy in Summer 2021 (Jalabi and Rashad 2021).

Saudi Arabia needs to diversify its economy, to attract foreign investments, to expand the private sector, to tackle youth unemployment and to secure the continued support of its citizens for the ruling family. And the tourism, hospitality and culture sectors afford optimum tools for pursuing and achieving all of these goals.

In particular, with the aim of building new employment opportunities for Saudi youth in the nascent leisure tourism industry, the Saudi establishment, relying on an orchestrated propaganda campaign designed and conducted by overpaid foreign (usually American) consultancies, has been moving in three directions: *the giga-projects* (Red Sea Project, Ad Diriyah, Qiddiya, Neom); *initiatives sponsored by the Ministry of Culture* (including a renewed commitment to UNESCO); and the *marketing of Al Ula*.

3 Thinking Big: The Giga-Projects

As Ekiz et al. (2017) observe, "There are opportunities for Saudi Arabia to promote a range of destinations, attributes and local assets. Accordingly, there is considerable scope for marine diving tourism, nature/wellness tourism, activity tourism, eco-tourism and cultural heritage tourism—all positioned under the wider leisure market".

The Red Sea Project (theredsea.sa/en), "the world's most ambitious luxury tourism development", a sand and sun sports heaven, is being developed on an archipelago of more than ninety pristine islands. In February 2021, MbS, the Crown Prince and Chairman of the Red Sea Development Company, unveiled a new luxury experience, in addition to the already exclusive luxury of the overall Red Sea Project, to be built by Foster & Partners on Shurayrah Island: The Coral Bloom (Saudi Gazette, February 10, 2021). The whole project will be compliant with the highest standards of eco-sustainability (Pagano 2021).

Ad Diriyah (dgda.gov.sa/our-destinations/diriyah.aspx), "the cradle of the Saudi state", the ancestral home of the Al Saud family, is to become a global tourism destination inspired by the principles of new urbanism and historic Najdi architecture. The Board of Directors, chaired by MbS, is in charge of developing the "ultra-luxury" hospitality venues. The project will include hotels, restaurants, museums and recreational spaces.

Qiddiya (qiddiya.com), an ancient village near Riyadh, is being transformed into Saudi Arabia's "capital of entertainment, sports and the arts", scheduled to open in 2023. The Board of Directors, chaired by MbS, will seek to attract and retain a portion of the 23 billion dollars Saudis spend abroad annually.

Neom (neom.com), the most celebrated of the giga-projects, located in the Tabuk province—now also including new plans for a city called "The Line", and Amaala, an ultra-luxury destination in the Prince Mohammed bin Salman Nature Reserve, consisting of three most exclusive communities, Triple Bay, The Island and The Coastal Development—is MbS' flagship venture (Royal Embassy of Saudi Arabia in Rome 2020) and it is aimed at a cosmopolitan elite (Surkes 2021). The Crown Prince's 500 billion dollar "desert dream" incorporating flying cars, robot dinosaurs and a giant artificial moon (Scheck et al. 2019), and powered entirely by renewable energy sources, has been challenged and slowed down by at least three factors: the murder of Jamal Khashoggi (2018) and the subsequent distancing/disengagement of several foreign financing entities out of moral unease; reports that surfaced in the international media about attempts by Saudi security forces to evict 20,000 members of the ancient Huwaitat tribe from their historic homeland—one of whom was killed—to make way for the development of Neom (Michaelson 2020; Nereim 2020b); the falling price of oil, and the global recession caused by the outbreak of the COVID-19 pandemic.

At the time of writing (Fall 2021), no official figures are available on the actual impact of the four giga-projects on the Saudi unemployment rate. On the other hand, there have been repeated indications that Neom will be financed by the PIF ($500 billion), and it is also known that US companies have won some of the major contracts for the development of these projects (King Faisal Center for Research and Islamic Studies 2021).

4 The Ministry of Culture: Initiatives

The new Saudi Ministry of Culture, created in 2018 and currently led by Prince Badr bin Abdullah, has been working relentlessly to establish the Kingdom as a world-class culture hub through various initiatives that can be divided into three groups: (a) an expanded vision of culture and arts to be incorporated into school and university curricula; (b) the launch of new scholarship programmes to support the education and training of young Saudis who will be employed in the culture, tourism and hospitality sectors; and (c) a stronger partnership with UNESCO.

(a) In 2020, the Ministry signed an agreement with the Ministry of Education to favour cooperation in facilitating licensing and permitting procedures for educational programmes and activities related to 16 cultural sectors in school and university curricula. With the stated aim of creating "an educational environment incubating national talents in various creative fields" (Saudi Gazette, January 2, 2020), the Ministry's basic task—despite the existing and often brutally enforced red lines barring individual freedom of expression, which could raise serious doubts as to the possibility of developing an authentically creative environment (Pavan 2021), given that no amount of financial support can take the place of freedom—is to address the problem of unemployment among young Saudis, in line with the goals of Saudi Vision 2030.

In June 2020, Prince Badr announced that for the first time in the Kingdom's history, official occupational status would be given to more than 80 jobs in the arts and culture sector (i.e. heritage, language, books, fashion, movies, visual arts, theatres, among others). And in March 2021 the newly launched "Your future is tourism" campaign, sponsored by the Ministry of Tourism, promised to create 100,000 jobs by the end of the year (Saudi Gazette, March 30, 2021).

(b) On 30 December 2019, in an educational "first", Prince Badr announced the launch of a cultural scholarship programme aimed at "developing Saudi culture" (Saudi Gazette, December 30, 2019); this would allow Saudi students to study archaeology, design, museums, music, theatre, film-making, literature, visual and culinary arts, and much more, at leading international institutions, with bachelor's, master's and Ph.D. degrees available. The programme is aimed at empowering national talent, fostering creativity and innovation and, above all, maximizing the employability of young Saudis in the new tourism and hospitality sectors. Although in July 2021 the Ministry announced that 149 additional scholarships would be awarded (Arab News, July 28, 2021), it is unfortunate that, to date, the pandemic has hindered the full implementation of the programme.

Earlier in the year, July 2019, the Saudi General Entertainment Authority and the Qiddiya Investment Co. had also jointly launched an international scholarship programme for young Saudis to pursue bachelor's and master's degrees in entertainment-related disciplines at selected prestigious universities around the world (Arab News, July 4, 2019). And in May 2020 it was Neom's turn to promise the provision of technical skills—and the prospect of a job—in the tourism and hospitality sectors for to up to 6000 trainees over five years through the "Neom Vocational Diploma Ending with Employment" scheme (Saudi Gazette, May 5, 2020).

In January 2021 the Saudi Cabinet approved the establishment of the Cultural Development Fund (CDF). It will support the objectives of the National Culture Strategy announced by Prince Badr in March 2019 (Pavan 2021). The CDF will have the authority to provide financial, technological and non-financial advisory services to all bodies and individuals operating in various cultural fields (Arab News, January 7, 2021). The aim is to create a highly ambitious 70,000 jobs by 2030 (About Her 2021).

(c) A UNESCO co-founder, and a member of the Organization since November 4, 1946, in 2015 Saudi Arabia became one of the 21 elected members of the UNESCO World Heritage Committee, on a six-year mandate, and in 2019 assumed membership of the UNESCO Executive

Council until 2023. A female Saudi royal was appointed to be the Kingdom's Permanent Representative to UNESCO (Arab News, January 14, 2020). At present, Saudi Arabia hosts six UNESCO World Heritage List sites: Mada'in Salih (2008), At-Turaif (2010), Historic Jeddah (2014), Rock Art in the Hail Region (2015), Al-Ahsa Oasis (2018) and Hima Cultural Area (2021).

Following the establishment of the UNESCO Emergency Fund in July 2012, Saudi Arabia made at least two donations to the Organization, in October 2012 ($20 million) and in July 2019 ($25 million, "for the protection of heritage": UNESCO 2019). The Kingdom currently has ten sites on its tentative list of properties that the government intends to consider for nomination. After centuries of well-documented history recording Wahhabi-inspired, systematic destruction of early Islamic heritage sites, Saudi cultural heritage policies now focus on preserving Arab culture and heritage, and on the protection and enhancement of biodiversity and regenerative tourism. This U-turn has at least two goals: to build new employment opportunities in the tourism sector—so as to comply with the triple mantra of Saudi Vision 2030: vibrancy, prosperity and ambition—and to present a modern, open and dynamic image of the country to international tourists and to the world.

5 The Marketing of Al Ula, a Place like no Other

Al Ula (experiencealula.com) has recently become *the* Saudi destination, the place to be. Marketed as Saudi Arabia's most romantic hidden gem, the country's gift to the world, an untold story, a breath-taking jewel, a boutique haven... the management of its image and development as a tourist destination has been entrusted to the Royal Commission for Al Ula (RCU), created in 2017, chaired by MbS and overseen by Prince Badr.

Located in the Medina region, Al Ula is a living museum covering an area of 22,561 km^2 and dating back more than 2000 years. It includes the ancient city of Hegra—nowadays known as Mada'in Salih—the main city of the southern part of the Kingdom of Nabataeans; Dadan, the ancient capital of the Kingdoms of Dadan and Lihyan; rock art sites; and the Old Town of Al Ula.

As RCU officials explained in 2019, the idea behind the great efforts to turn Al Ula into a major tourist destination is underpinned by economic goals: "Our priority is the local community and to provide them with jobs. We want these jobs that we'll create to be filled by the locals first" (Arab News, February 19, 2019).

According to the Al Ula website, besides the Hammaya programme—a community advocacy initiative that will provide 2500 employment opportunities encouraging locals to become stewards of Al Ula's cultural and natural heritage—the RCU set up a scholarship programme for young unemployed locals. The scholarship programme will have a five-year span (phase 2 started in September 2019 with 300 places) and is aimed at building up human capabilities and opportunities for practical training. It is open to 1000 Saudi male and female students "of exceptional potential" from Al Ula, who will be able to study abroad (US, UK, France and Australia) at different levels (diplomas, bachelor's and master's degrees) in a range of fields related to Al Ula's development needs, i.e. tourism and hospitality, history, archaeology, agriculture. However, it is stated that "participation in the program does not ensure long-term employment for students, rather it builds their capabilities to make them competitive candidates for future opportunities". To date, details on the achievements of the scholarship programme are not available, and only sporadic news emerges from the media (see, for example, Saudi Gazette, June 17, 2020). The opening in October 2021 of two Michelin-starred restaurants in Al Ula and the resumption of domestic tourism, with the prospect of international tourists arriving later on, will be the prelude to future developments of the scholarship programme and employment opportunities.

Moreover, beyond the fight against youth unemployment, it appears there is another, different goal in the pervasive marketing of Al Ula. Many scholars highlight that updated Saudi schools' textbooks, contrary to past editions that did not portray the pre-Islamic era in a positive light, now tend to celebrate sites like Al Ula, the most prominent example of the pre-Islamic Nabataean civilization in Saudi Arabia. At the same time, textbooks describe the role of the royal family as going back 200 years before the birth of Islam, with the implicit aim of justifying the legitimacy of the Al Saud rule based on continuity (Alhussein 2019) and tribal allegiances (Feighery 2017).

6 Scholarships and More Scholarships

As reported in the National Budget Statement for the Fiscal Year 2021, with total projected expenditure set at SAR1068 billion ($285 billion), spending on the education sector (SAR205 billion, $55 billion) takes priority among the 9 key sectors covered by the budget, followed by the military (SAR195 billion, $52 billion).

The education sector general mandate includes "setting up of schools, colleges and university cities; managing external scholarship programs of the Custodian of the Two Holy Mosques; support of research, development and innovation; setting up university hospitals; supporting knowledge sources". In particular, among the key projects planned for 2021, three are relevant to this paper: "attracting distinguished foreign universities to open branches within the Kingdom (1); launching the fourth phase of the external scholarship program of the Custodian of the Two Holy Mosques—continuation of the scholarship program (2); launching the cultural scholarship program for undergraduate level and above in the most influential educational institutions around the world—awarding scholarships and trainings to 10,000 students (3)" (Ministry of Finance 2020, 34–44).

Key project (3) was discussed in Sect. 3; this heading will focus on key project (1) and key project (2).

Key project (1). To date (Fall 2021), amid the global uncertainty surrounding the COVID-19 pandemic, Saudi decision-makers have not as yet provided further clarifications about the project that would see foreign universities granted permission to open branches in the Kingdom. Since the very first announcement in 2019 (Arab News, October 29, 2019), following years of shifts and disclaimers (Pavan 2017b), the publication of the 2021 Budget Statement mentioning key project (1), and news of ongoing plans at the Ministry of Education to attract prestigious foreign universities to open their branches in Saudi Arabia as part of the issuance of the new University Law in November 2019 (Saudi Gazette, February 17, 2021), no more details have been released by the competent authorities so far.

As far as key project (2) is concerned—despite the current pandemic crisis and all the related challenges, and especially the difficulties for students to attend in-person classes—in December 2020 the Minister of Education reassured all scholarship students that in view of the prolonged COVID-19 global emergency, government support would continue, as it had since the onset of the pandemic in March 2020 (Saudi Gazette, March 29, 2020), for those attending online courses delivered by foreign universities during the Spring semester 2021, thereby confirming the long-established commitment of Saudi rulers to scholarship-oriented policies (Pavan 2013, 2017a).

The King Abdullah Scholarship Program (KASP) was launched in May 2005, extended twice, and after a turbulent transition following the death of King Abdullah, entered a third stage in 2015 under the new name Custodian of the Two Holy Mosques' Overseas Scholarship Program. The third stage came with a new scheme—Your Job and Your Scholarship—under which specialties sponsored by the foreign scholarship programme would be designed to meet the needs of the Saudi labour market. The new scheme would be open to Saudi male and female students who wished to study abroad and were eligible to take up the jobs assigned by the government. On their return, graduates would be recruited immediately by the employers who had covered their scholarships. The Ministry of Education signed dozens of cooperation agreements with various government agencies to provide work opportunities for graduates after completing their studies abroad (Pavan 2017b). This new shift towards a more quality-oriented approach in the scholarship programme was intended to implement the Saudi Vision 2030 statement that: "Scholarship opportunities will be steered towards prestigious international universities and be awarded in the fields that serve our national priorities".

The third stage of the scholarship programme ran until 2019, its conclusion coinciding with the outbreak of the pandemic, whereupon the Ministry of Education began to plan the fourth phase, which was announced in October 2020 (Saudi Gazette, October 26, 2020): the "Path of Excellence for Scholarships". According to the Ministry's website, the new phase intends to keep working towards the implementation of the Saudi Vision 2030 goals, namely, diversifying the Saudi economy and enabling Saudi graduates to specialize and compete at global level. The programme includes 32 specializations that reflect the Government's goals for national sustainable development. Selected fields of study now include Sports and Sports Administration, Hospitality Management, Tourism and Tourism Management, Media and Communication Sciences, Maritime Sciences, Environmental Sciences, and Environmental Management, as the country seeks to become part of the global tourism market. Path Conditions for Saudi students to apply to 70 universities worldwide no longer include the age requirement, and online submissions are accepted throughout the year (Ministry of Education 2021).

Tourism and hospitality have been part of the public and private educational offering at Saudi tertiary education institutions for over a decade (Aljubaili 2015). In addition, the Saudi Technical and Vocational Training Corporation (TVTC), operating under the umbrella of the Ministry of Education, has established lots of tourism and hospitality training programmes in cooperation with Saudi (Saudi Aramco, the Ministry of Tourism, the Ministry of Labour) and international entities: FHM (fhm.edu.sa), HTMI (htmi.menadev.edu.sa), AHLEISA (ahleisa.org), among others.

It is noteworthy that in Summer 2021 the Human Capital Development Agency, sponsored by the Ministry of Tourism, launched a new strategy, targeting recent graduates, job seekers and workers in the tourism sector. It consists of 15 qualifying programmes, including a Tourism Scholarship programme, and applicants to all programmes must be Saudi males and female citizens (Government of Saudi Arabia 2021).

The efforts made to link both external and national scholarship programmes to the demands of the Saudi labour market clearly indicate the Saudi leadership's acute awareness of the challenges posed by youth unemployment and the need to move the Saudi economy away from oil dependence. It remains to be seen, once the world gets back to a "new normal", whether or not these efforts produce the expected outcomes in terms of stabilizing a rise in employment rates sustainably. In addition, there are many expectations that the scholarship programmes will support the pro-women social liberalization that has become one of the signature aspects of the MbS era, and part of the massive socioeconomic modernization taking place in the Kingdom.

It is undeniable that Saudi Vision 2030—with its stated goal of increasing women's participation in the workforce from 22 to 30% by 2030—is the key driver for the "spectacular surge of the Saudi female labour force". Between 2018 and 2020, the employment rate of Saudi women increased from 68 to 76%, while female unemployment decreased from 32 to 24%. In particular, the number of women with secondary education employed in the labour market increased almost threefold, from 9 to 25%; this surge was not driven by the public sector but was "genuine private-sector-led" employment growth. So, this particular goal of Saudi

Vision 2030 seems to have been achieved 10 years early (Gomez Tamayo et al. 2021).

It remains to be seen how future statistics will record data regarding graduate Saudi females entering the labour market. In Saudi Arabia the participation rate in the labour market for females with bachelor's degrees stands at 62%, far below that of males with bachelor's degrees (89%). In addition, it is a feature of Saudi tertiary education that while males concentrate on engineering studies, females opt for humanities. Consequently, male graduates emerge with transferrable skills that are useful in many professions, whereas female graduates may miss out on effective opportunities to acquire the skills they need to find a job in the era of the Fourth Industrial Revolution (Deloitte 2018). Like other countries worldwide, Saudi Arabia has begun setting up policies to increase the numbers of female students in STEM subjects (KAPSARC 2019).

However, as it cannot be expected that the persistent trend of female gravitation towards the humanities will be reversed any time soon, the initiatives described to bring young Saudi graduates of both sexes into the culture, tourism and hospitality sectors may have the effect of boosting Saudi female employment rates overall.

7 Sectors and Skills

At the time of writing this paper, the global decline in the hospitality and tourism sectors caused by the COVID-19 pandemic is still under scrutiny, and attention is being focused on how leisure tourism can be resumed safely. It is generally agreed that it will not be possible to establish a "new normal" in global travel before 2023 or even 2024. It is in this extremely complicated and uncertain scenario that Saudi Arabia seeks to develop its tourism industry. The Ministry of Tourism declared that the impact of the disruption caused by the pandemic to the leisure tourism and hospitality sectors in the Kingdom could result in a 35–45% decline [in profits] (Reuters 2020), although new expectations and hopes for tourism growth were raised by the vaccination campaign in the first quarter of 2021. It was also announced that new projects and overall development of the tourism sector would create around one million jobs and increase the sector's contribution to GDP from 3.8 to 10% by 2030 (Asharq Al-Awsat, January 5, 2021).

In order to successfully expand its tourism sector, Saudi Arabia needs to focus on the different sectors of the hospitality industry, on the skills required for hospitality management and on the ability of the country to equip its youth with these skills.

It is generally agreed that the hospitality industry includes four sectors: entertainment/recreation; the food and beverage industry; the hotel industry (accommodation); and travel & tourism (Andrews 2007). How has Saudi Arabia been developing these sectors?

In general, Saudi decision-makers have spared no efforts to develop all of the four sectors equally since 2016. On closer inspection of the giga-project masterplans, one can see how promising and attractive for international leisure travellers they should be once they become fully operational, in the hopefully near future. As for the entertainment sector, the Kingdom has spared no expense in serving up a veritable bonanza of West-inspired, top-down entertainment (Pavan 2021) that has been one of the trademark enterprises of the MbS era. But critics point out that entertainment and tourism projects have catered mostly to a specific target group due to the costs and types of events promoted (Al Hussein 2021, among others).

Besides the local colleges and academies delivering tourism and hospitality management courses, the scholarship programme sponsored by the Ministry of Culture is expected before long to provide thousands of skilled young Saudis ready for recruitment to the culture, tourism and hospitality sectors.

According to a recent Deloitte report on opportunities for the business community to contribute to the growth of the future workforce for the Fourth Industrial Revolution (2018, 17) besides workforce readiness, technical skills and entrepreneurship, soft skills also play a central role as "essential human skills": "There is a growing emphasis on 'global competence': the ability to apply acquired soft skills in cross-cultural, multicultural, and global contexts". Soft skills and global competencies "are decidedly 'human' traits that, for now, are irreplaceable by machines".

What are the skills required for hospitality management? The job of hospitality management staff is to make people relax and enjoy the host country and its culture. More specifically, when direct interaction with customers is involved, staff need first and foremost to master a set of soft skills: customer service, communication, flexibility, language, problem-solving, teamwork and multitasking skills, and cultural awareness are the most important.

It seems that the Saudi establishment's "cultural diplomacy" (Pavan 2021, 6–7) will have to rely on a generation of young Saudis who can acquire crucially important hospitality-oriented soft skills in three different settings: home training in local colleges and academies; scholarship programmes to study abroad at leading institutions (Pavan 2020); and in the near future, international campuses on Saudi soil. This could be seen as a *multi-option training model.*

Exploring recent developments in the Saudi tourism industry, any attempt to define the nature of the model adopted by Saudi Arabia can present a challenge: is it a public model, a private model, or both?

8 Public or Private?

Tourism is defined as a mixed industry (World Tourism Organization 1997; Andersson and Getz 2009). Sustainable development of tourism and its economic, social and ecological aspects are based on dialogue and partnership between public and private sector. Some typical public–private partnership ventures in tourism include: products – marketing and sales—research and technology—infrastructure—human resources—financing (Cetinski and Peric 2008). In 2000 the World Tourism Organization identified four main areas of possible public–private cooperation in tourism: improving attractiveness of destination—improving marketing efficiency—improving productivity—improving overall management of the tourism system.

At present, the Public Investment Fund (PIF)—the sovereign wealth fund of Saudi Arabia, chaired by the Crown Prince—as stated in its 2021–2025 Program, directly or indirectly controls all the strategic sectors in the country: aerospace and defence, food and agriculture, construction and building, health care, real estate, financial services, transport and logistics, telecom-media & technology, to name just a few. The PIF also controls the entertainment, leisure and sports sectors, as already mentioned in reference to the giga-projects. The expected impact of PIF investments on employment by the end of 2025 is to create 1.8 million direct, indirect and ancillary jobs (PIF Program 2021, 50).

In the current state of affairs, it is controversial to state that the tourism and hospitality sectors in Saudi Arabia are developing as a mixed industry according to international standards. Although in principle Saudi rulers seem to acknowledge the strategic role of the private sector in developing the culture and tourism industry (see for example Arab News, August

1, 2021), where the existing Saudi private sector is involved (healthcare, financial services...), apparently it has to be in line with PIF terms and conditions, or at any rate under the PIF umbrella, because PIF is now the de facto public sector in Saudi Arabia.

It is too early, especially with the pandemic still causing disruption worldwide, to predict whether or not the PIF strategy will be successful in establishing Saudi Arabia as an attractive world-class tourist hub. For the enterprise to succeed, there must be a diversity of stakeholders, views and financial sources involved in the development of the tourism industry (Cetinski and Peric 2008). When this diversity is missing, the outcomes will be uncertain.

Moreover, the successful development of the tourism industry in the Kingdom may be hampered by the well-known preference among Saudi youth for permanent public sector employment, where salaries are higher, working hours are more flexible and jobs are secured for life (see, for example, Fakhreddine and Owen 2015, among many others). On the other hand, there are signs of changing preferences and mindsets among young Saudis, who have started to lower their expectations, and this is a trend that will merit careful analysis.

Notwithstanding the plan of Saudi Vision 2030 to expand the private sector, will the PIF-led development of the tourism industry be able to attract, employ and retain the skilled unemployed youth? Will it be perceived as a stable alternative to public sector employment? Will the PIF's role and strategy win the trust of Saudi youth in the medium-long term?

9 Concluding Remarks

In January 2021 MbS unveiled a plan for Riyadh to become one of the ten largest urban economies in the world in terms of population, industry, innovation, services, quality of life, education, amenities and tourism. This ambitious vision for the future of the Saudi capital has been dubbed the "Riyadh Renaissance" by the Saudi media (Al Arabiya English, January 28, 2021).

In the midst of the COVID-19 pandemic, Saudi rulers are struggling to plan the post-pandemic Kingdom at economic, social and cultural level. The next few years will witness the implementation of Saudi Vision 2030 with MbS at the helm. Being the majority of the population, the youth play a strategic role in providing economic and political support to the future king. However, several issues need to be addressed by Saudi decision-makers if they are to transform their country into a hospitable and attractive global tourist hub and, equally important, to reduce youth unemployment through the creation of jobs in the nascent tourism industry.

The first overall challenge for Saudi Arabia is to bring about a serious improvement of its actions and image, in keeping with international standards: respect for human rights, moderation, openness in civil and religious life, and transparency at all levels. Saudi Arabia needs to come to terms with the not-so-covert Saudiphobia permeating the international community.

Secondly, the Saudi Cultural Offices at Saudi Embassies could play an important role in promoting a more open and proactive role for Saudi Arabia in the global world. At present, many of these offices at Saudi embassies around the world seem to be in a dormant state, and it remains unclear what task they are supposed to perform, beyond exerting tight control—as mandated by the Ministry of Education—over Saudi students on scholarship programmes.

Thirdly, it is hoped that the Saudi establishment will make a final decision on the opening of foreign university campuses in the Kingdom. Along with continuation of the various scholarship programmes, foreign universities operating on Saudi soil would offer world-class courses to build skills in line with the needs of the labour market.

In conclusion, while the current cultural openness (cultural diplomacy) in Saudi Arabia, inspired and managed by foreign consultancies for the most part, is attractive and helps to appease the young, the reality is that basic red lines are still firmly in place and fully enforced, and Saudi youth, like the rest of the population, are not entitled to express themselves freely. Cultural and economic renaissance will be neither achievable nor sustainable without promoting the social progress of the country.

References

About Her. 2021. Saudi Arabia's cultural development fund to create 70,000 new jobs by 2030. Accessed 30 March 2021. https://www.abouther.com/node/35126/people

Al Arabiya English. January 28, 2021. Saudi Crown Prince reveals plan for Riyadh to be top largest city economy in world. Accessed 30 March 2021. https://english.alarabiya.net/News/gulf/2021/01/28/Vision-2030-Saudi-Arabia-s-Riyadh-will-be-one-of-largest-city-economies-Crown-Prince

Al Rasheed, Madawi. December 23, 2020. Saudi Arabia: 2021 promises to be another grim year. Accessed 20 March 2021. https://www.middleeasteye.net/opinion/saudi-arabia-2021-promises-be-another-grim-year

Al Sarhan, Saud. 2021. Foreword. In King Faisal Center for Research and Islamic Studies. Vision 2030 and reform in Saudi Arabia: Facts and figures. April 2015–April 2021. Special Report.

Alhussein, Eman. October 17, 2019. New Saudi textbooks put nation first. Accessed 1 January 2020. https://agsiw.org/new-saudi-textbooks-put-nation-first/

Alhussein, Eman. June 17, 2021. Keeping the spirit alive: Vision 2030 five years on. https://agsiw.org/keeping-the-spirit-alive-vision-2030-five-years-on/

Aljubaili, Saleh. 2015. Graduate student profile of Saudi Arabian students enrolled in the hospitality and tourism management program at RIT. Unpublished thesis. Rochester Institute of Technology.

Andersson, Tommy D., and Getz, Donald. 2009. Tourism as a mixed industry: Differences between private, public and not-for-profit festivals. Tourism Management 30(6): 847–856.

Andrews, Sudhir. 2007. Introduction to tourism and hospitality industry. India: McGraw-Hill Education.

Arab News. February 19, 2019. Al-Ula Royal Commission launches second phase of university scholarship program. Accessed 1 April 2019. www.arabnews.com/node/1455051/saudi-arabia

Arab News. July 4, 2019. Saudi GEA inaugurates international scholarship program for Saudi youth. Accessed 1 January 2020. https://www.arabnews.com/node/1520346/saudi-arabia

Arab News. October 29, 2019. Foreign universities to open branch campuses in Saudi Arabia. Accessed 1 January 2020. https://www.arabnews.com/node/1576231/saudi-arabia

Arab News. January 14, 2020. Princess Haifa named Saudi Arabia's permanent representative to UNESCO. Accessed 11 March 2020. https://www.arabnews.com/node/1612986/saudi-arabia

Arab News. January 7, 2021. Saudi culture minister lauds Cabinet approval of Cultural Development Fund. Accessed 30 March 2021. https://www.arabnews.com/node/1788386/saudi-arabia

Arab News. July 28, 2021. Saudi Culture Ministry issues 149 more scholarships. Accessed 9 September 2021. https://www.arabnews.com/node/1901266/saudi-arabia

Arab News. August 1, 2021. Saudi Arabia eyes global tie-ups to tap 20$bn in cultural opportunities. Accessed 12 September 2021. https://www.arabnews.com/node/1903806/business-economy

Asharq Al-Awsat. January 5, 2021. COVID-19 vaccine spurs expectations for Saudi tourism growth. Accessed 30 March 2021. https://english.aawsat.com/home/article/2723101/covid-19-vaccine-spurs-expectations-saudi-tourism-growth

Bayoumi, Moustafa. March 22, 2018. Mohammed bin Salman's talk of reform is a smokescreen. Accessed 15 August 2018. https://www.theguardian.com/commentisfree/2018/mar/22/mohammed-bin-salmans-talk-reform-smokescreen

Burns, Peter. 2007. From Hajj to hedonism? Paradoxes of developing tourism in Saudi Arabia. In Tourism in the Middle East. Continuity, change and transformation, edited by Rami F. Daher, 215–236. Clevedon: Channel View Publications.

Burns, Peter, and Bibbings, Lyn. 2017. Kuwait. Why tourism? In International tourism development and the Gulf Cooperation Council states. Challenges and opportunities, edited by Marcus L. Stephenson and Ala Hamarneh. ebook. Oxon: Routledge.

Burns, Peter, and Holden, Andrew. 1995. Tourism: A new perspective. Hemel Hempstead: Prentice Hall.

Castlereagh Associates. 2019. Tourism as a pillar of the new Saudi Arabia? www.castlereagh.net

Cetinski, Vinka and Peric, Marko. 2008. Public and private sector sinergy in tourism and partnership models. Conference paper. https://www.researchgate.net/publication/337111065_PUBLIC_AND_PRIVATE_SECTOR_SYNERGY_IN_TOURISM_AND_PARTNERSHIP_MODELS

Deloitte. 2018. Preparing tomorrow's workforce for the Fourth Industrial Revolution.

Ekiz, Erdogan, Öter Zafer, and Stephenson, Marcus L. 2017. Tourism development in the Kingdom of Saudi Arabia. Determining the problems and resolving the challenges. In International tourism development and the Gulf Cooperation Council states. Challenges and opportunities, edited by Marcus L. Stephenson and Ala Hamarneh. ebook. Oxon: Routledge.

Fakhreddine, Jihad and Owen, Trevis. August 19, 2015. Given a choice, Saudis prefer government jobs. Accessed 26 May 2021. https://news.gallup.com/businessjournal/184745/given-choice-saudis-prefer-government-jobs.aspx

Feighery, William. G. 2017. Discourses of tourism and identity in the Arabian Peninsula. In International tourism development and the Gulf Cooperation Council states. Challenges and opportunities, edited by Marcus L. Stephenson and Ala Hamarneh. ebook. Oxon: Routledge.

General Authority for Statistics, Kingdom of Saudi Arabia. 2018. Tourism Establishments Survey.

General Authority for Statistics, Kingdom of Saudi Arabia. 2020a. Saudi youth in numbers. A report for International Youth Day 2020a.

General Authority for Statistics, Kingdom of Saudi Arabia. 2020b. Labor market statistics Q3 2020b. http://www.stats.gov.sa

General Authority for Statistics, Kingdom of Saudi Arabia. 2021. Labor market statistics Q1 2021. http://www.stats.gov.sa

Gomez Tamayo Sofia, Koettl Johannes, and Rivera, Nayib. April 21, 2021. The spectacular surge of the Saudi female labor force. Accessed 7 May 2021. https://www.brookings.edu/blog/future-development/2021/04/21/the-spectacular-surge-of-the-saudi-female-labor-force/

Government of Saudi Arabia. 2021. Unified national program. Visa & tourism. Accessed 9 September 2021. https://www.my.gov.sa/wps/portal/snp/aboutksa/tourism#header2_6

Hearst, David. October 16, 2018. Trump and the boy king: Mohammed bin Salman's reign is over before it even began. Accessed 1 February 2020. https://www.middleeasteye.net/opinion/trump-and-boy-king-mohammed-bin-salmans-reign-over-it-even-began

Henderson, Joan C. 2017. Pilgrimage and tourism development in Saudi Arabia. Understanding the challenges and opportunities. In International tourism development and the Gulf Cooperation Council states. Challenges and opportunities, edited by Marcus L. Stephenson and Ala Hamarneh. ebook. Oxon: Routledge.

Hilal, Nazar. 2020. Tourism in the Gulf Cooperation Council countries as a priority for economic prospects and diversification. Journal of Tourism and Hospitality 9(7) https://doi.org/10.35248/2167-0269.20.9.451

Jalabi, Raya, and Rashad, Marwa. August 26, 2021. Arabian nights buzz: Staycations boost Saudi economy. Accessed 1 September 2021. https://www.reuters.com/world/the-great-reboot/arabian-nights-buzz-staycations-boost-saudi-economy-2021-08-26/

Karolak, Magdalena. 2015. The cruise industry in the Arabian Gulf: The emergence of a new destination. Journal of Tourism Challenges and Trends VIII(1): 61–78.

Karolak, Magdalena. 2018. Destination place identity, touristic diversity and diversification in the Arabia Gulf. In Economic diversification in the Gulf Region, Volume I. The political economy of the Middle East, edited by Ashraf Mishrif and Yousuf Al Balushi Singapore: Palgrave Macmillan. https://doi.org/10.1007/978-981-10-5783-0_9

Kéchichian, Joseph A. 2019. Saudi Arabia in 2030. The emergence of a new leadership. ASAN Report.

Khalife, Leyal. September 13, 2019. A 'Pictoresque' Kingdom: Influencers have been exploring Saudi Arabia. Gateway KSA has been inviting influencers to Saudi Arabia. Accessed 1 January 2020. https://stepfeed.com/a-picturesque-kingdom-influencers-have-been-exploring-saudi-arabia-6212

King Abdullah Petroleum Studies and Research Center—KAPSARC. 2019. How to empower Saudi women in the labor force?

King Faisal Center for Research and Islamic Studies. 2021. The US–Saudi economic relationship: More than arms and oil. Special report by David Kenner and Kameal Al-Ahmad.

Kingdom of Saudi Arabia. (2022). Saudi Vision 2030. https://www.vision2030.gov.sa/v2030/overview/

Michaelson, Ruth. May 4, 2020. 'It's being built on our blood': The true cost of Saudi Arabia's $500bn megacity. Retrieved 20 March 2021. https://www.theguardian.com/global-development/2020/may/04/its-being-built-on-our-blood-the-true-cost-of-saudi-arabia-5bn-mega-city-neom

Ministry of Education, Kingdom of Saudi Arabia. 2021. The custodian of the two holy mosques' External scholarship program: Qualifying competencies to compete in the labor market and scientific research globally and locally. Accessed 6 May 2021. https://www.moe.gov.sa/en/education/highereducation/Pages/Scholarship.aspx

Ministry of Finance, Kingdom of Saudi Arabia. 2020. Budget statement. Fiscal year 2021.

Moshashai, Daniel, Leber, Andrew M., and Savage, James D. 2020. Saudi Arabia plans for its economic future: Vision 2030, the National Transformation Plan and Saudi fiscal reform. British Journal of Middle Eastern Studies 47(3): 381–401.

Nereim, Vivian. 2020a. Saudi Arabia has granted 400,000 visas since opening to tourism. Accessed 24 February 2020a. https://www.bloomberg.com/news/articles/2020a-02-24/saudi-arabia-s-granted-400-000-visas-since-opening-to-tourism

Nereim, Vivian. 2020b. Hope turns to doubt, then gunfire, as Saudi megacity emerges. Accessed 24 April 2020b. https://www.bloomberg.com/news/articles/2020b-04-24/hope-turns-to-doubt-then-gunfire-as-new-saudi-megacity-emerges

Pagano, John. April 23, 2021. Five years into Saudi Vision 2030: Long-term plan means we are well placed for future of travel. Accessed 6 May 2021. https://www.arabnews.com/node/1847386

Parveen, Musrrat. 2020. Challenges faced by pandemic COVID19 crisis: A case study in Saudi Arabia. Challenge 63(6): 349–364.

Pavan, Annalisa. 2013. A new perspective on the quest for education: The Saudi Arabian way to knowledge society. Higher Education Studies 3(6): 25–34 (Also published by the Ministry of Higher Education, Kingdom of Saudi Arabia, Observatory on Higher Education, under the title: 38 Saudi Universities to produce and share knowledge, in The Chronicle of Saudi Higher Education, Issue 7, April 2014).

Pavan, Annalisa. 2017a. Saudi Arabia approaching 2030: The shift from quantitative to qualitative ambitions in education, enhancing human development. International Research in Higher Education 2(2): 8–14.

Pavan, Annalisa. 2017b. The custodian of the two holy mosques' Overseas scholarship program: Targeting quality and employment. World Journal of Education 7(4): 32–39.

Pavan, Annalisa. 2020. Higher education abroad in the new millennium: GCC scholarship programs as GCC culture and identities boosters. Saudi Arabia in the spotlight. In Gulf Cooperation Council culture and identities in the new millennium: Resilience, transformation, (re)creation and diffusion, edited by Magdalena Karolak and Nermin Allam, 221–243. New York: Palgrave Macmillan.

Pavan, Annalisa. 2021. "The sky is the limit": Saudi youth in a changing kingdom, beyond narratives, interpretations and misperceptions. World Journal of Social Science 8(2): 1–12.

Public Investment Fund Program 2021–2025. 2021. https://www.pif.gov.sa/en/Pages/publicinvestmentfundprogram.aspx#1

Quilliam, Neil. September 13, 2019. Delivering Vision 2030: Empowering youth and re-engineering the economy. Accessed 1 January 2020. https://www.lesclesdumoyenorient.com/Delivering-Vision-2030-Empowering-youth-and-re-engineering-the-economy-3003.html

Reuters. April 24, 2020. Saudi tourism sector could see 35%–45% decline this year on coronavirus. Accessed 30 March 2021. https://www.reuters.com/article/health-coronavirus-saudi-tourism/saudi-tourism-sector-could-see-35-45-decline-this-year-on-coronavirus-idUSL5N2CC70A

Saudi Gazette. December 30, 2019. Foreign scholarship program for culture launched. Accessed 2 January 2020. https://saudigazette.com.sa/article/585972

Saudi Gazette. January 2, 2020. 16 cultural sectors set to be part of school, university curricula. Accessed 1 February 2020. https://saudigazette.com.sa/article/586167

Saudi Gazette. March 29, 2020. Kingdom to continue disbursing financial allocation for scholarship students. Accessed 30 March 2020. https://saudigazette.com.sa/article/591324/SAUDI-ARABIA/Kingdom-to-continue-disbursing-financial-allocation-for-scholarship-students

Saudi Gazette. May 5, 2020. NEOM Academy opens its doors to train 1,000 students in its first year. Accessed 20 March 2021. https://saudigazette.com.sa/article/592713

Saudi Gazette. June 17, 2020. Business as usual for young Saudi chefs in Al Ula. Accessed 20 March 202. https://www.saudigazette.com.sa/article/594398

Saudi Gazette. October 26, 2020. Al-Sheikh launches path of excellence for scholarship. Accessed 6 May 2021. https://saudigazette.com.sa/article/599574/SAUDI-ARABIA/Al-Sheikh-launches-Path-of-Excellence-for-Scholarship
Saudi Gazette. February 10, 2021. Crown Prince unveils 'Coral Bloom', stunning nature-inspired designs for Red Sea Project. Accessed 30 March 2021. https://saudigazette.com.sa/article/603413
Saudi Gazette. February 17, 2021. Saudi Arabia soon to have branches of prestigious foreign universities. Accessed 30 March 2021. https://saudigazette.com.sa/article/603619
Saudi Gazette. March 30, 2021. Ministry of Tourism paves the way for young Saudis. Accessed 31 March 2021. https://saudigazette.com.sa/article/604991/SAUDI-ARABIA/Ministry-of-Tourism-paves-the-way-for-young-Saudis
Scharfenort, Nadine. 2020. Generating jobs for youth GCC nationals? Tourism development, demographic change, and labour market situation in GCC countries. ZfTW 12(2): 274–298.
Scheck, Justin, Jones, Rory, and Said, Summer. July 25, 2019. A Prince's $500 billion desert dream: Flying cars, robot dinosaurs and a giant artificial moon. Accessed 1 January 2020. https://www.wsj.com/articles/a-princes-500-billion-desert-dream-flying-cars-robot-dinosaurs-and-a-giant-artificial-moon-11564097568
Sheline, Annelle R. June 10, 2019. Saudi Arabia is changing, but don't give MbS all the credit. Accessed 16 June 2019. https://lobelog.com/saudi-arabia-is-changing-but-dont-give-mbs-all-the-credit/
Smith, Valene L., ed. 1989. Hosts and guests. The anthropology of tourism. Philadelphia: University of Pennsylvania Press.
Surkes, Sue. June 12, 2021. As Saudis sell city of the future, investors and critics see a desert mirage. Accessed 9 September 2021. https://www.timesofisrael.com/as-saudis-sell-city-of-the-future-investors-and-critics-see-a-desert-mirage/
The Royal Embassy of Saudi Arabia in Rome. 2020. Saudi National Day. Special Edition.
The Royal Embassy of Saudi Arabia in Rome. 2021. Saudi Arabia in focus. Periodic report. January–February 2021.
UNESCO. July 12, 2019. Saudi Arabia commits US$25 million to UNESCO for the protection of heritage. Accessed 1 January 2020. https://en.unesco.org/news/saudi-arabia-commits-us25-million-unesco-protection-heritage
World Tourism Organization—WTO. 1997. Towards new forms of public private partnership.
World Tourism Organization—WTO. 2000. Public-private sector co-operation: Enhancing competitiveness.

CHAPTER 8

Workforce Nationalization in the UAE: Creating a Framework for Training Emirati Nationals for the Banking Sector

Sowmya Vivek and Allen Baby

1 Background

Banking and financial services industry plays a strategic and developmental role in the UAE economy and is an important employer of UAE nationals. As a testament of the importance that the government places on the industry with respect to national human resource development, as early as 1999, an aggressive employment quota system was applied to all banks in the UAE. A Cabinet Decree was issued in 1999 making it mandatory

S. Vivek (✉)
EM Normandie, Dubai, UAE
e-mail: sowmya_viv@yahoo.com

A. Baby
Emirates Institute for Banking and Financial Studies, Sharjah, UAE
e-mail: allenbaby1@gmail.com

A. Mishrif et al. (eds.), *Nationalization of Gulf Labour Markets*,
The Political Economy of the Middle East,
https://doi.org/10.1007/978-981-19-8072-5_8

for all banks in the country to increase the UAE nationals in their workforce by 4% every year. These initiatives helped in increasing the overall number of UAE nationals in the banking industry over the past decade.

However, most UAE nationals working in the banking sector are employed in functions like Retail banking, Human Resources (HR), Marketing and other support functions. As of 2018, out of the total workforce employed in UAE banking sector, approximately 25% were UAE nationals. As a percentage of the banking workforce, 15% of the UAE nationals are employed in mid and senior management levels. Also, only 5.96% of them are in critical positions in banking sector, with vast majority in retail banking. Training and development, transfer of knowledge from expatriate to nationals and getting more women in the workforce have been identified as critical drivers to attain the objective of nationalization in the banking sector.

In 2019 the UAE Cabinet introduced new Emiratization targets which involve employing 7500 more UAE nationals in banking sector by 2022. Attaining these targets requires significant reskilling and upskilling of UAE nationals to meet the current needs of the banking sector. Banking sector in UAE has undergone massive change in the recent times with movement from traditional banking to digital and customized banking. The basic reason behind this transformation is the change in needs and preferences of customers and percolation of technology in all facets of life.

With the change in banking sector there has also been a change in the requirement in terms of skill set of bankers. Traditionally the required skill set for banking included technical skills, inter-personal and communication skills, and management skills. However, with the advent of fintech there is now a huge focus on future skills which is mainly techno-functional skills which involve understanding application of current and emerging technology in the day-to-day business functions.

As vast majority of UAE nationals in the banking sector work in retail banking roles, especially in branches, where jobs and career opportunities are fast declining, it is imperative to upskill and reskill them for specialized roles and management roles.

Given this background the paper attempts to quantify the current competency of UAE nationals in banking sector and develop a framework for developing the skills of UAE nationals for banking sector in UAE. Training and development have been identified as a key focus area that will enable the banking sector to reach the Emiratization targets.

Hence this research is critical as it will help to identify a holistic multi-dimensional skills framework that will be required for UAE nationals to succeed in the banking industry and help them occupy key critical positions in banking sector.

2 Research Objectives and Key Research Questions

The objective of this research is to identify the skill gap of UAE nationals working in banking sector in UAE. The key research questions that the study looks to answer are as below:

- What are the skills required to succeed in banking sector in twenty-first century?
- What is the current level of UAE nationals wrt key skills required to succeed in banking sector in twenty-first century?
- What are the specific skill gaps and hence what are the training requirements for UAE nationals?

3 Research Scope

The research is focused on UAE nationals currently working in different management levels in banking sector in UAE. The study can in future be extended to study the skill gap and training requirements in allied areas like insurance.

4 Literature Review

4.1 Disruption in the Banking Sector

Banking and the financial services sector per se are just as challenged by the swift velocity of change as any other industry in the VUCA world. Even a passing assessment of the industry literature reveals that this sector is being severely disturbed (Gomber et al., 2018).

A broader viewpoint of banking is becoming the need of the hour, considering that the future is mutual, and that banks must be much more customer-focused, and need to keep pace with the technology-enabled innovation that appears to be the catalyst of major disruption in this sector.

4.1.1 Technology

The December 2017 edition of one of the industry's leading professional magazines, The American Banker, published an article identifying the following sources of disruption in banking:

AI and data analytics
App experimentation
Cyber security
Chat bots
Commercial banking innovation—technology vs footprint
Non-traditional competitors
Data sharing
FinTech's (here referring to companies)
Crypto currency.

All the above-mentioned 'Fintech' technological innovations are considered as 'disruptive', 'revolutionary' and armed with 'digital weapons', that will 'tear down' obstacles and conventional financial establishments (World Economic Forum, 2017), and are expected to alter the banking practices quite drastically. Financial services institutions will be forced to reinvent to be much more responsive, inventive and customer-centric in their approach.

Technology is certainly not the only disruptor of financial services. It is the most omnipotent dynamic influence. There is no feature of banking that is invulnerable to the 4th IR. To support these and other novel diktats of innovation amidst a radically evolving market and a disrupted business model—banking will require an improved and embryonic skill sets.

4.1.2 Innovation and Agility

It is evident that two ground rules of success in the VUCA world are organizational originality and dexterity. Developing vital levels of these two prerequisites will exhort banks to transform their way of functioning, their direction team, and the talent pool that enable them to prosper.

However, this is not adequate. Apart from being customer-centric, as foretold by VUCA authors, banks are faced with the need to promote agility. Deloitte (2018) mentions:

The core objective for most banks is to achieve organizational agility, and to do so they should consider embracing innovation, managing talent differently, and pursuing key partnerships within a broader ecosystem to manufacture and deliver solutions for customers.

4.1.3 Client-Centricity

In 2014, prominent banking industry analyst and Senior Partner, Global Leader Digital McKinsey (Financial Services) at McKinsey & Company Inc., Somesh Khanna spoke about the relationship of digital technologies to client experience:

> As digitization takes hold, customers will have a greater range of alternatives to meet the needs traditionally met by banks. Where the historical banking brands focused on stability and trustworthiness, these are no longer enough to retain customers and grow sustainably.

The following year, the McKinsey Global Banking Annual Review pointed out that as digitization would speed up; banks would be locked in a 'battle for the customer' that would characterize the industry trend for the coming 10 years. Deloitte (2018), another major international consultancy and respected source of banking industry, echoes similar thought as it claims long-term sustainable growth in the banking industry possible only with a radical exodus from a fanatical sales and product mindset to one of legitimate customer centricity. Thus, customer experience of the future will materialize from the joint effort of players of a whole commerce network rather than solely from a service ethos of frontline staff.

Client-centricity can thus be obscure. It is the upshot of mindsets and problem-solving skills, sustained by partnerships in a bank ecosystem (Chopra & Rajendran, 2017). While considering the relationship of client-centricity and technology, PwC (2014) finds that there are certain inconsistencies and incongruities to be navigated. The report stresses that in the emerging world intelligence quotient will be necessary to:

> Balance automation with the human touch... sixty percent of great experiences are due to great staff... twenty-five percent of customers rely on staff to do research, 46% to select products and 63% to resolve their problems...

> create a multi-channel strategy that balances cost and service.... encourage self-service for routine matters and refocus branch and contact centre.

As the industry revolutionizes, the nature of work done in banks will inexorably transform. Customer centricity will be as all-encompassing as innovation and agility. The work done by bankers in coming days will be an outcome of both the crucial client-centricity and work as wrought by technology.

4.1.4 Regulation and Compliance

The triumph of all economies depends upon the effectiveness and liquidity of its financial souks. The root of Global Financial Crisis can be traced to banking failures and pragmatic findings support the view that strong financial liaison balance sheets are keys for the resurgence of credit and economic feat after large financial sector alarms (Blundell-Wignall et al., 2018). Bank strength was important for recovery from the GFC and regulatory measures and following that event wanted to adjust the performance of banks (Kapan & Minoiu, 2018).

Worldwide monitors are focused on safeguarding customer and product fitness, and while they are reluctant to endorse individual products before their introduction, they do not waver from reprimanding banks with hindsight. Banking plays a key role as a go-between investors and borrowers, in providing operational platforms, and in providing admission to risk-management preparations.

4.1.5 Risk Management

Risk in finance is defined as the 'randomness of the return of investments, including both positive and negative outcomes' Bessis (2015). Risk in the financial industry is defined by the ambiguity that has unfavorable consequences on income or capital, or the uncertainty associated with negative effect only. Superior values of risk management are always imperative (Bessis, 2015).

The above five disruptors, namely technology, innovation and agility, client-centricity, regulation and compliance, and risk management, impinge on not just the world of banking, but the way erudition takes place, and the nature of the information and talent required to function in the VUCA banking world.

4.2 Learning and Working in Banking and Financial Services

It is evident in the context of VUCA banking that banking should develop radically in the coming years. Solomon (2018) points out that, even though the bulk of retail banking customers visit a bank branch at least once in six months over 80% of the regular retail banking customer's exchanges take place through self-service channels.

Thereby this corroborates the prophecy that the future bank branch will play varied roles, and rather than merely serving customers in a formal manner, will soon become a 'destination for complex advice and problem resolution' which entails 'from a talent standpoint, some reshuffling required at a pretty rapid pace'.

Deloitte (2018) further expects the future workforce as likely to include freelancers working with several banks (along with permanent employees and contractors), fintech hackathon-ers to produce fresh results, and even robots working in conjunction with humans.

Bank workforces need to be more mutual and comprehensive, while banks will be expected to supply them with more inclusive employee experiences to reflect the richer customer experience that the workforce is enabling (Deloitte).

4.2.1 The Learner of the Twenty-First Century

Anderson et al. (2017) point out that right from the beginning of 2015, the majority of workforce started comprising of millennials—referring to those born between 1982 and 1999 (also called GenY, nGen, GenMe or 'digital natives'). Literature seems to concur that these millennials differ greatly from previous generation of workers (Anderson et al., 2017).

The main differences between Millennials and previous generations include their prospects regarding the position of work in their lives, a desire for relaxation and work-life balance (Lyons & Kuron, 2014). Millennials require regular pointers and praise, and are generally not team-focused, but rather seem to be focused strongly on independence. In a group, they tend to be more ecologically conscious. They also possess some of the typical adult learner traits, including the need for propinquity (Everett, 2017).

Additionally, Millennials are the technologically advanced generation as they are raised with digital technology competencies (Madara et al., 2018). As Millennials habitually use technological devices in their daily milieu, they expect to have the same application in the learning surroundings (Everett, 2017). Hence Twenge (2013) suggests that instructors of millennials engage them in technology-based empirical strategies such as blogs and social bookmarking.

While the workplace must consider how to manage this new breed of employee, this nuance of the 'learning style' of the typical Millennial, should influence the way in which curricula are designed and education is presented.

4.2.2 Changing Knowledge and Skills in Banking

Houghton and Sheehan (2000) study the nature of work in an information economy and predict that the future human skills that will be required will be progressively more balancing with information and communication technology instead of replacing them. They predict that Information Technology will contain codified knowledge and work will demand unique human (tacit) skills such as intangible and inter-personal management and communication skills (Houghton & Sheehan, 2000).

Brown et al. (2003) emphasize that it will be crucial to get 'great talent' since the gap value created by the most talented knowledge workers is 'huge'. They uphold that, as the economy becomes more knowledge-based, 'the differential value of highly talented people continues to mount' (Brown et al., 2003).

To map a path through complexity in VUCA, professionals can assume the principles of 'VUCA Prime' which holds that there are features that can help to counterbalance the disturbing and arresting effect of VUCA. According to Glowania (2018) these are:

- Vision provides the steady path that can compensate the impact of instability.
- Understanding—arising from deep insight into the divisions and relations of a complex system—offsets ambiguity to a degree.
- Clarity that emerges from accurate acceptance enables action to be taken with a greater degree of conviction.
- Agility—the ability to decide on a course of action and modify stratagem rapidly—helps to offset vagueness.

The authors would however like to propose that the term 'Clarity' can be replaced with the term 'Cooperation' as it is becoming clearer that ‘twenty-first-century skills’ include teamwork, communication (in addition to digital literacy, citizenship, problem-solving, critical thinking, creativity and productivity) (Van Laar et al., 2017). Binkley et al. (2010) identified a set of ten twenty-first century skills in four main consortiums, namely ways of thinking, ways of working, tools for working and living in the world.

5 Research Framework

The literature review has clearly established the major themes in terms of skills required for the banking sector of the twenty-first century. The literature review has also helped in identifying the skills within these themes. The proposed research framework for the study is as given below (Fig. 1).

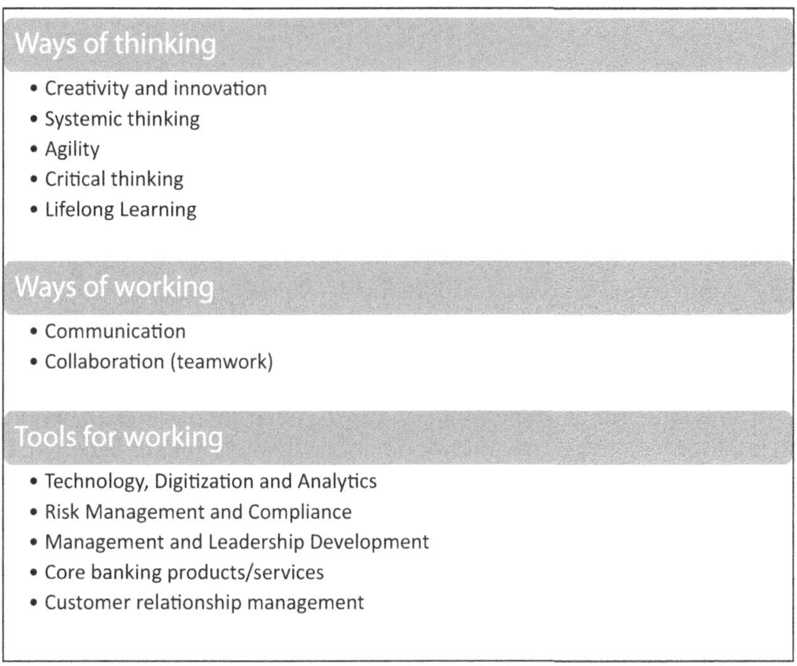

Fig. 1 Research framework

6 Discussion and Analysis

6.1 *Research Methodology*

The research methodology uses both 'quantitative and qualitative methods'. 'Qualitative' methods involve a detailed survey of the existing literature on the subject to identify research gaps and build a research framework. The quantitative method focuses on a survey to specifically understand the skill gaps for UAE nationals working in the banking sector in UAE.

The survey was conducted using a questionnaire which was electronically shared with the banks in UAE. The questionnaire was filled by 100 UAE National bankers in UAE with demographics as shown below (Fig. 2).

6.2 *Survey Findings*

6.2.1 *Key Findings*

Tools for working have emerged as the top training requirement for UAE nationals. This can be attributed to the fact that many are fresh graduates and require training in technical aspects of banking something which is not taught much at university level.

According to the WEF (2017), current education systems seem to be distant from the skills needed at the workplace and the exponential growth in technology is only adding fuel to this fire. It will be too ambitious to expect ready-made cross-functional and technical skills from new entrants into the workplace and these skills must be developed at the workplace with constant training efforts (Fig. 3).

In line with the current trend as can be seen in the VUCA world, Technology, creativity and innovation and systemic thinking emerged as the top three skills that require extensive training. It is no surprise that technology, digitization and analytics has emerged as the top skill that requires training among UAE nationals. Banking is undergoing unprecedented changes in terms of digitization and the COVID pandemic has only accelerated the process.

Ways of working skills communication and collaboration have emerged as skills that UAE nationals are comfortable with and don't need extensive training (Fig. 4).

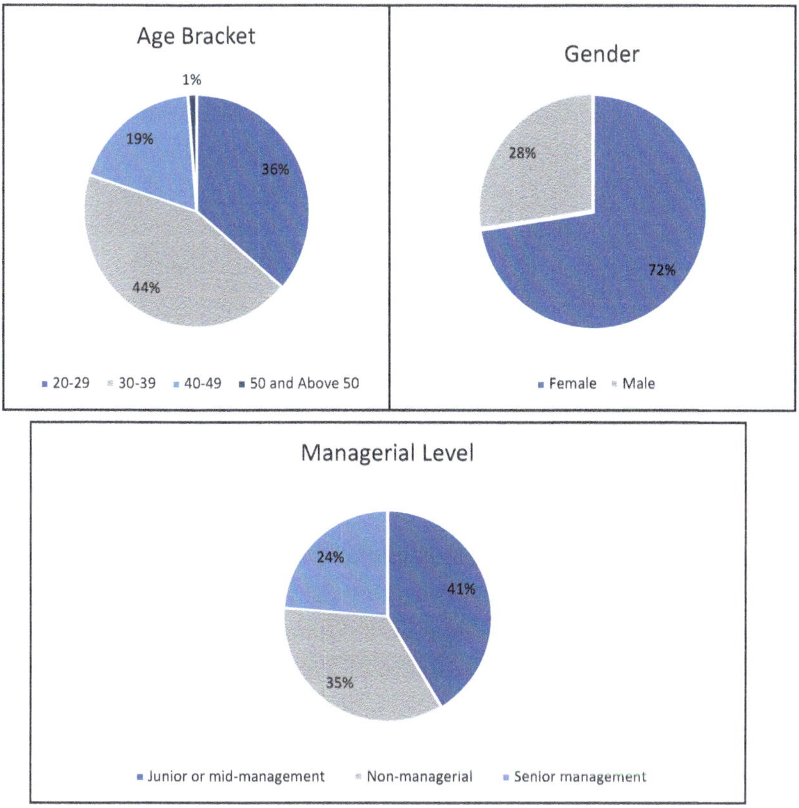

Fig. 2 Demographics of the participants

Ways of Thinking

Creativity and Innovation

Figure 5 provides the response received from UAE nationals on the level of training required WRT creativity and innovation.

Systemic Thinking

This skill is recognized to be critical in handling complex situation and is considered to be complimentary to critical thinking and problem-solving abilities

Fig. 3 The top training requirement for UAE nationals

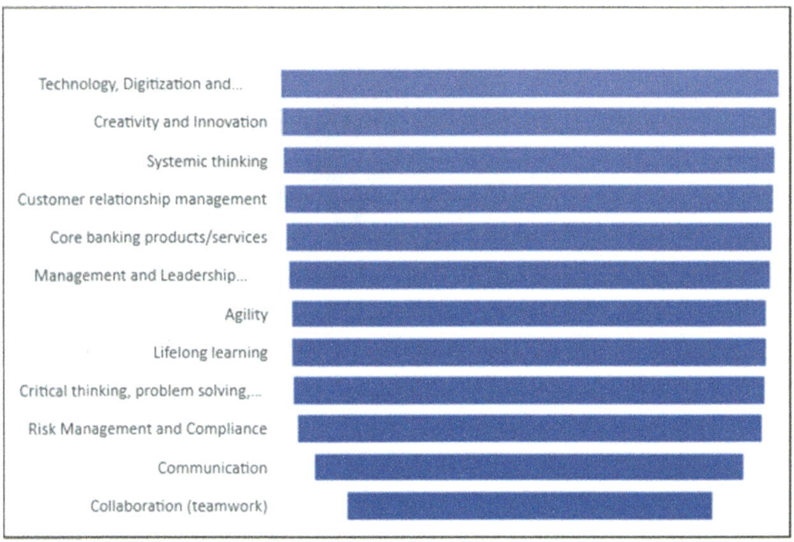

Fig. 4 Ranking in terms of skills

Figure 6 provides the response received from UAE nationals on the level of training required WRT Systemic thinking.

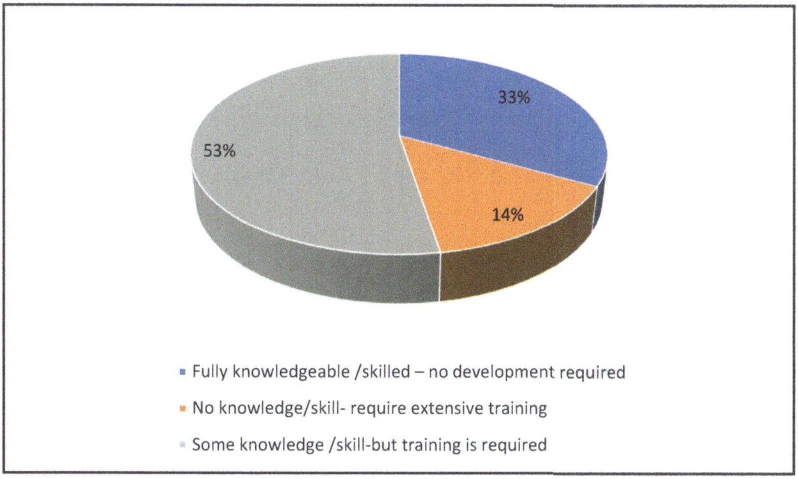

Fig. 5 UAE nationals' response on the level of training required WRT creativity and innovation

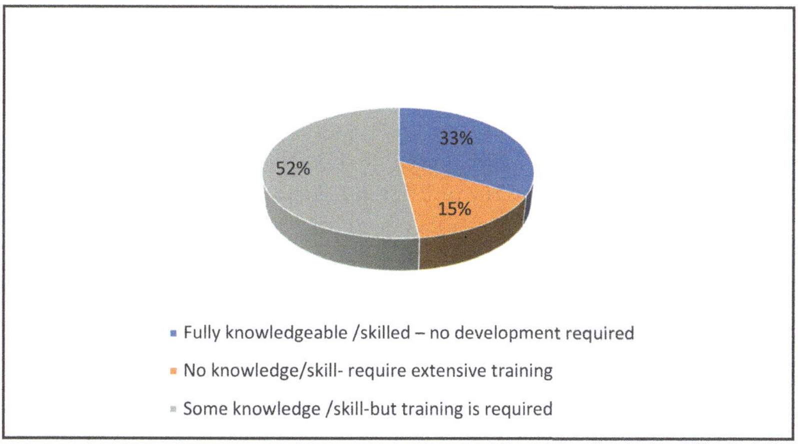

Fig. 6 UAE nationals' response on the level of training required WRT Systemic thinking

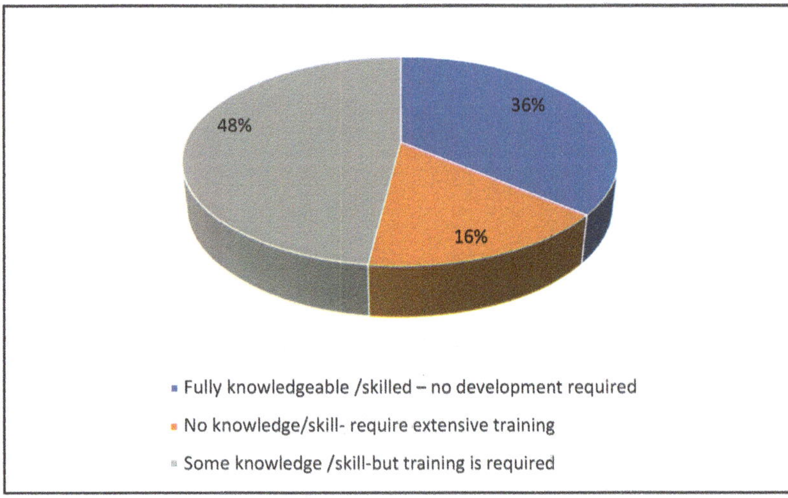

Fig. 7 UAE nationals' response on the level of training required WRT critical thinking

Critical Thinking
Critical thinking skills broadly encompass skills like understanding assumptions, evaluating evidence and based on analysis coming up to a rational conclusion. Experts agree that success in the VUCA world will depend upon ability to understand ever-changing environments, analyzing and short-listing possible course of action, taking decisions and action while maintaining the ability to adapt. All this requires advanced thinking skills, that can be communicated and applied in an agile manner to a rapidly changing and uncertain world.

Figure 7 provides the response received from UAE nationals on the level of training required WRT critical thinking.

Agility and Learning to Learn
Agility is also an important skill in the VUCA world together with critical thinking and problem-solving skills. With new situations arising almost daily in a rapidly changing environment, it is critical to be able to adapt and be agile.

Also critical is openness and ability to continue learning also called as 'learning to learn' or 'lifelong learning'. Figure 8 provides the response

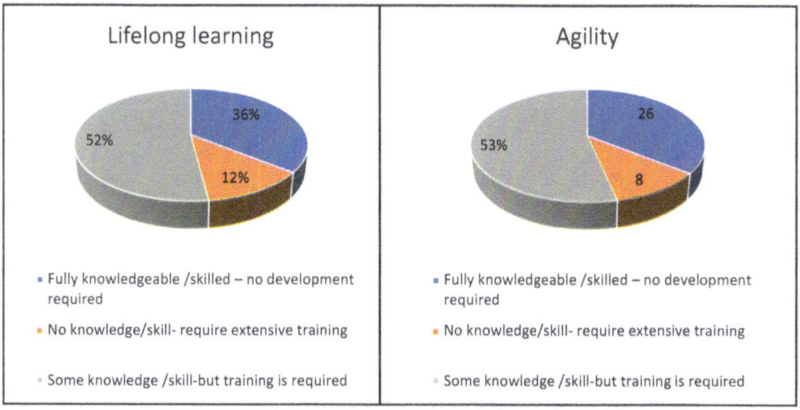

Fig. 8 UAE nationals' response on the level of training required WRT agility and lifelong learning

received from UAE nationals on the level of training required WRT agility and lifelong learning.

Ways of Working

Binkley et al. see 'ways of working' specifically as 'communication and collaboration'.

In a VUCA work where there is increasing connectivity and changing ecosystem, communication skills are critical. Communication skills influence quality of insight and expressive clarity which helps a lot in coordinating action.

Leadership in the current environment is all about discovering the positive energy in every individual and developing and bringing out the best potential in everyone.

Figure 9 provides the response received from UAE nationals on the level of training required WRT communication and collaboration.

Tools for Working

Technology, Digitization and Analytics

In the banking and financial sector specifically, technology-enabled innovation is normally referred to as 'Fintech' (Bofondi & Gobbi, 2017). (At first this term referred to technology applied to the back end of reputable financial institutions but has today developed to include any technological

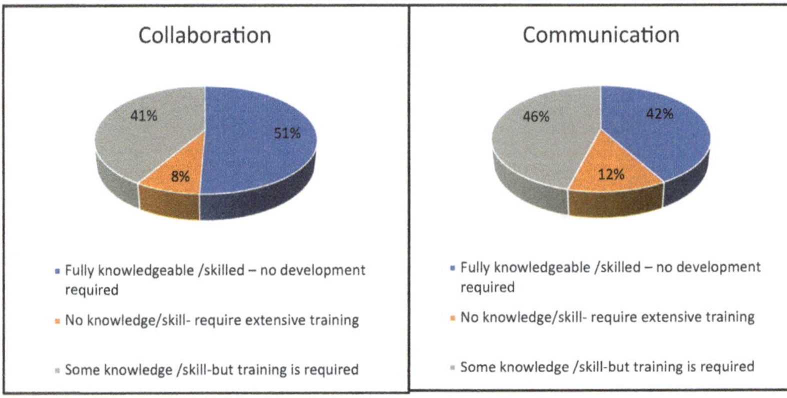

Fig. 9 UAE nationals' response on the level of training required WRT communication and collaboration

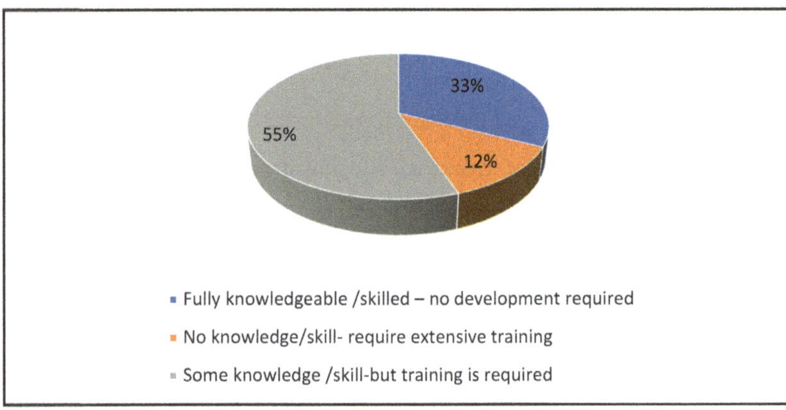

Fig. 10 UAE nationals' response on the level of training required WRT technology, digitization and analytics

innovation in the financial sector.) Fig. 10 provides the response received from UAE nationals on the level of training required wrt technology, digitization and analytics.

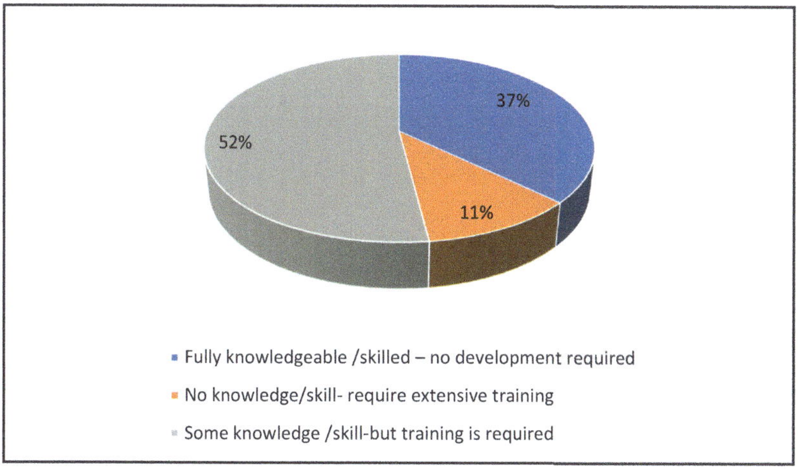

Fig. 11 UAE nationals' response on the level of training required WRT risk management and compliance

Risk Management and Compliance
Guidelines and conformity are fundamental to banking. EY's (2018) concise view is that regulation is the most significant factor defining banks today. EY (2018) states that banks will continue to need good control, a culture of conformity and technology to promote better observance. Another critical and allied area would be risk management. Figure 11 provides the response received from UAE nationals on the level of training required wrt risk management and compliance.

Customer Relationship Management
Where historically service has been considered as a product of capable and dedicated communication, customer centricity is a broader concept, 'keeping clients at the core of strategic intentions' (Coetzee, 2014). Customer centricity's importance moves beyond traditional realms of service. As Coetzee's (2014) study states, consumer centricity must be facilitated by other parts of the banking value-chain. Figure 12 provides the response received from UAE nationals on the level of training required WRT customer relationship management.

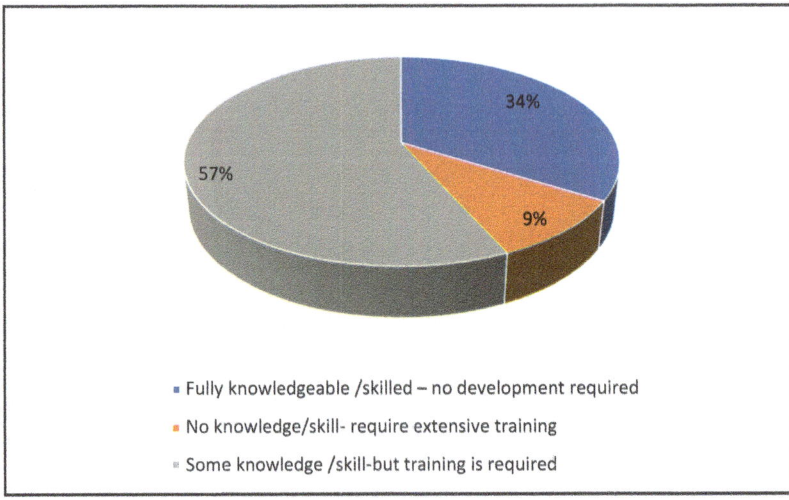

Fig. 12 UAE nationals' response on the level of training required WRT customer relationship management

Core Banking Products/Services and Management and Leadership Skills

Figure 13 provides the response received from UAE nationals on the level of training required WRT core banking products and management and leadership development.

7 Conclusion

This paper is a humble attempt to develop a competency framework for UAE nationals that will help training providers to develop programs that will equip bankers with future skills required for the banking sector. This paper hopes to open dialogue and deliberation among leadership on how they can lead UAE nationals to occupy critical positions in the banking sector.

The framework used in the paper includes skills categorized as ways of thinking, ways of working and tools for working which are critical to develop well-rounded bankers who can navigate the so-called VUCA world with confidence and strength expected of them. We do hope that

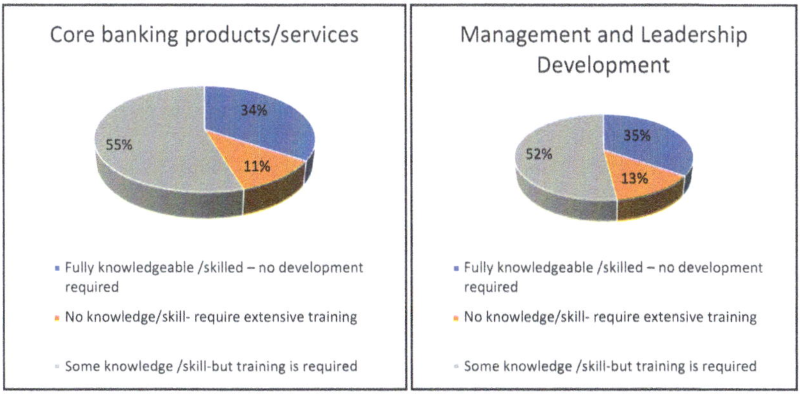

Fig. 13 UAE nationals' response on the level of training required WRT core banking products and management and leadership development

this paper is the start to understand the learning needs of the current generation UAE nationals in banking sector in UAE.

To close few powerful words by 'Barack Obama':

> Change will not come if we wait for some other person or some other time. We are the ones we've been waiting for. We are the change that we seek.

References

Anderson, H.J., Baur, J.E., Griffith, J.A. and Buckley, M.R. 2017. What works for you may not work for (Gen) me: Limitations of present leadership theories for the new generation. The Leadership Quarterly, 28(1), pp. 245–260.

Bessis, J. 2015. Risk management in banking. John Wiley & Sons.

Binkley, M., Erstad, O., Herman, J., Raizen, S., Ripley, M. and Rumble, M. 2010. Defining 21st century skills [Draft White Paper 1]. Assessment and Teaching of 21st Century Skills Project. Available at: http://atc21s.org/wp-content/uploads/2011/11/1-Defining-21st-Century-Skills.pdf

Bloem, J., Van Doorn, M., Duivestein, S., Excoffier, D., Maas, R. and Van Ommeren, E. 2014. The Fourth Industrial Revolution. Things Tighten.

Blundell-Wignall, A., Atkinson, P. and Roulet, C. 2018. The watershed year of 2004: Origins and causes of the crisis. In Globalisation and finance at the crossroads (pp. 87–113). Palgrave Macmillan, Cham.

Bofondi, M. and Gobbi, G., 2017. The big promise of FinTech. European Economy, 2, pp. 107–119.

Brown, P., Hesketh, A. and Wiliams, S. 2003. Employability in a knowledge-driven economy. Journal of Education and Work, 16(2), pp. 107–126.

Chopra, S. and Rajendran, P. 2017. Rethinking client centricity to reinvent business models. In The Palgrave handbook of managing continuous business transformation (pp. 189–211). Palgrave Macmillan, London.

Coetzee, J. 2014. Client-centricity in South African retail banking. The International Business & Economics Research Journal (Online), 13(5), p. 997.

Cowan, R. S. 2018. The "Industrial Revolution" in the home: Household technology and social change in the twentieth century. In The Routledge companion to modernity, space and gender (pp. 69–85). Routledge.

Deloitte. 2018. Banking industry outlook six themes driving banking industry trends. Deloitte. Available at: https://www2.deloitte.com/us/en/pages/financial-services/articles/banking-industry-outlook.html

Everett, N. 2017. Educators learn how to teach the millennial generation (Doctoral dissertation, California State Polytechnic University, Pomona).

EY. 2018. Global banking outlook 2018. EY. Available at http://www.ey.com/Publication/vwLUAssets/ey-global-banking-outlook-2018/%24File/ey-global-banking-outlook-2018.pdf

Friedman, T.L. 2006. The world is flat: The globalized world in the twenty-first century. Penguin, London.

Glowania, S. 2018. Blog. [online]. Available at: https://www.londonschool.com/lsic/resources/blog/vuca-leader-new-world-learning-and-development/ [Accessed 16 July 2018].

Gomber, P., Kauffman, R., Parker, C. and Weber, B. (2018). On the Fintech Revolution: Interpreting the forces of innovation, disruption, and transformation in financial services. Journal of Management Information Systems, 35(1), pp. 220–265.

Houghton, J. and Sheehan, P. 2000. A primer on the knowledge economy.

Johansen, B. and Euchner, J. 2013. Navigating the VUCA world. Research-Technology Management, 56(1), pp. 10–15.

Kapan, T. and Minoiu, C. 2018. Balance sheet strength and bank lending: Evidence from the global financial crisis. Journal of Banking & Finance, 92, pp. 35–50.

Khanna, S. 2014. McKinsey and Company 2014 'The bank of the future'; Somesh Khanna, Interview. McKinsey and Company, November 2014.

Lyons, S. and Kuron, L. 2014. Generational differences in the workplace: A review of the evidence and directions for future research. Journal of Organizational Behavior, 35(S1), pp. S139–S157.

Madara, S.R., Maheshwari, P. and Selvan, C.P. 2018. Future of millennial generations: A review. In Advances in Science and Engineering Technology International Conferences (ASET), 2018 (pp. 1–4). IEEE.

McKinsey and Company. 2015. The fight for the customer; McKinsey Global Banking Annual Review 2015. Financial Services Practice, McKinsey and Company.

Opdebeeck, H. 2017. Rediscovering transcendence behind VUCA and technology. In Managing VUCA through integrative self-management (pp. 149–158). Springer, Cham.

PwC. 2014. PwC Banking 2020: Evolution or revolution? Available at: https://www.pwc.com/gx/en/banking-capital-markets/banking-2020/assets/pwc-retail-banking-2020-evolution-or-revolution.pdf

Rudel, T. K. and Hooper, L. (2005). Is the pace of social change accelerating? Latecomers, common languages, and rapid historical declines in fertility. International Journal of Comparative Sociology, 46(4), pp. 275-296.

Saniee, I., Kamat, S., Prakash S. and Weldon, M. 2017. Will productivity growth return in the new digital era? An analysis of the potential impact on productivity of the fourth industrial revolution. Bell Labs Technical Journal. Available at: http://ieeexplore.ieee.org/stamp/stamp.jsp?tp=&arnumber=7951155&isnumber=7951154

Solomon, M. 2018. Do bank branches still matter? [online]. Available at: https://www.forbes.com/sites/micahsolomon/2014/05/15/do-bank-branches-still-matter/ [Accessed 27 July 2018].

Twenge, J. 2013. Generational changes and their impact in the classroom: Teaching generation me. Medical Education 40(1), pp. 398–405. https://doi.org/10.1177/0098628312465870

Van Laar, E., van Deursen, A.J., van Dijk, J.A. and de Haan, J. 2017. The relation between 21st-century skills and digital skills: A systematic literature review. Computers in Human Behavior, 72, pp. 577–588.

World Economic Forum (WEF). 2017. Beyond FinTech: A pragmatic assessment of disruptive potential in financial service. https://www.weforum.org/reports/beyond-fintech-a-pragmatic-assessment-of-disruptive-potential-in-financial-services [Accessed on 27 June 2018].

Younus, U.M. 2017. Fourth Industrial Revolution. https://scholar.google.co.za/scholar?hl=en&as_sdt=0%2C5&q=fourth+industrial+revolution&oq=fourth+industrial+ [Accessed on 27 June].

PART III

Higher Education and Labour Market in Selected Gulf Countries

CHAPTER 9

A Realist Perspective on Agile Policy for Future Skills in a Digital Age—An Example from the Kingdom of Bahrain

Annamarie Lawrence

1 Introduction

Education reform in the Gulf Cooperation Council (GCC) is driven by the economic development aspirations of the region to move from labour market models built on importing expertise and knowledge to that of indigenous knowledge production and dissemination (Hayes, 2017; Jones and Punshi, 2013; Madbouly et al., 2021). At the core of this aspiration

A. Lawrence (✉)
Tribal Group, Manama, Bahrain
e-mail: Annamariebahrain@gmail.com

A. Mishrif et al. (eds.), *Nationalization of Gulf Labour Markets*,
The Political Economy of the Middle East,
https://doi.org/10.1007/978-981-19-8072-5_9

is human capital development of nationals through a wide range of education and institutional reforms programmes (Karolak, 2012; World Bank, 2017).

In the backdrop of rapid economic and social development in the GCC region over the past 30 years, a vast amount of the expertise needed to deliver these advancements was imported from outside the region (World Bank, 2017). This approach made sense to fast track the ambitious reform projects and ensure the GCC countries had competitive economies capable of attracting foreign investment and participating globally (Donn and Al Manthri, 2013; Kirk, 2014). While traditionally relying on energy reserves to fund economic and social development, GCC governments recognised the need for the private sector to contribute a greater percentage to GDP (EDB, 2021; Jones and Punshi, 2013). It became clear to policymakers that in order to sustain the rapid economic and social development, GCC governments needed a clear strategy for building capacity among nationals.

Each of the six countries that make up the GCC (Saudi Arabia, Qatar, Bahrain, UAE, Oman and Kuwait) took an individual country approach, rather than pan GCC approach, to their reforms (Hayes and Al'Abri, 2019; Kirk, 2014). It is apparent that there are many similarities in these reform pathways including the ambitious development of national strategies and education and labour markets that tended to be based on 'borrowed' international models and policies cited a 'best practice', rather than locally developed models embedded within indigenous systems and structures (Donn and Al Manthri, 2013; Hayes, 2017; Hayes and Al'Abri, 2019).

Adding to the GCC countries challenges of implementing these 'knowledge economy' aspirations, is the growing importance of somehow incorporating emerging technologies and future skills into government agendas. The COVID-19 pandemic has created a new dimension to the urgency and currency of education and skill systems within economies (WEF, 2022). COVID-19 spurred the rapid adoption of digitalisation across most economies which has increased the pace of change needed in education and labour market systems (Amankwah-Amoah et al., 2021).

With strong references to the rhetoric from the World Bank and World Economic Forum (WEF) on the importance of 'future skills' to serve this emerging world of work, each GCC government has responded with its own approach to 'future proofing' its education and labour systems. The WEF's 2020 'Future of Jobs' report was widely cited in regional calls to action by both the private sector and the GCC governments. The report highlights the importance of Government policy for reskilling and upskilling to respond to the impact of COVID-19 and labour market needs (WEF, 2020b). The report states that the key skills needed for future jobs include the ability to think critically, creativity and the ability to learn (WEF, 2020a). This has created an interesting policy dilemma as the private sector calls for a more Agile and speedy response from governments in future proofing skills and supporting the adoption of emerging technologies through their policy mechanisms.

In their white paper 'Agile Governance' the WEF (2018) highlights the importance of applying the principles of Agile to policy making as part of preparing for the fourth industrial revolution. They highlight methods that can be applied by governments and look at ways of ensuring '*adaptive, human-centred, inclusive and sustainable policy*' (WEF, 2018). This policy approach has echoes of customer centric Agile product design such as Design Thinking (Lewick et al., 2018). Agile business concepts such as customer journey mapping and sprint development have found their way into policymaking with aspects of these Agile apparent in some government documentation and practices (Denning, 2020; WEF, 2018).

1.1 The Kingdom of Bahrain

The Kingdom of Bahrain has been a proud investor in educating its citizens since it led the Gulf by opening the first public school in the region in 1919 (Karolak, 2012). With strong historical and political ties to the United Kingdom, much of the early education system was based on British models of education that were popular at the time.

Of Bahrain's 1.5 million residents, just over half are foreign expatriate worker and their families with the other half of the population being 'Bahrainis' (Bahrain Government, 2021). The number of expatriate worker in Bahrain are 535,022 and the number of Bahrainis in the workforce is 152,678. Of the Bahraini population, 47% are under the age of 25 (IGA, 2021). This means there will be a significant number of Bahraini's entering the workforce over the next 20 years. Currently, there are more than 210 public and 70 private schools in Bahrain (Derasat and UNDP, 2018). Education is compulsory ages 6–14. In addition, there are approximately 21 Higher Education institutions in Bahrain. Bahrain is ranked 42 globally and 7th regionally for its economic competitiveness (WEF,

2020b). The economy is one of the most diversified in the GCC with non-oil sectors contributing to just under 80% of the GDP (IGA, 2021).

The 2000s were particularly active for Bahrain policy makers with various economic, labour market, education and social reform initiatives being established to change the reliance on expatriate workers and ensure Bahraini's are the first choice for employment (Hayes and Findlow, 2020; Karolak, 2012). International consultants were invited to partner with Bahrain Government to design and implement these reforms. Many of the resulting agencies, institutions, and ministries established during this time are now in operation for over 10 years. Some of the initiatives included in the education reforms were the establishment of a national qualification and training quality authority, Higher Education Council, the establishment of Bahrain Teachers College, Bahrain Training Institute and Bahrain Polytechnic. All these institutions were set up to better align labour market needs with education and training opportunities for Bahrainis to encourage higher numbers of Bahraini's to be employed in the private sector and reduce the reliance on expatriate workers (Hayes and Findlow, 2020).

Within the context of the need for change driven by the fourth industrial revolution and the desire to change the structure of the labour market, this case study aims to take a closer look at the reform policy approach to new higher education interventions by Bahrain Government. A 'realist' lens is applied to the new Tertiary Action Plan (TAP) reform programme to examine the process in detail and identify evidence of agility.

2 Theory Building—GCC Education Reform, Policy and Complexity

Before outlining the 'new' policy approach of the TAP process, it is necessary to consider education policy and its development in the context of the GCC. This section serves to build theory around the case study to offer analysis and insight (Robson, 2015).

Education policy has always had to navigate the narrow path between political and social paradigms of many institutions, agencies, and individuals (Ball, 1998). This is even more apparent in education reform in the GCC where the shared understanding of the purpose, design and implementation of policy is often missing in the broader political and social systems the policies are relying on for dissemination and implementation (Ball, 1998; Dale, 1999; Kirk, 2014). In all economies, education is inherently a hierarchical system with institutions and agencies responsible for reform often disconnected from the fundamental actors at the core of the system (Gale, 2003). Likewise, it was recognised that the voice of learners as the users of the system needed to be embedded within reform design and implementation (Quinn and Owen, 2016). Addressing this disconnect formed part of the neo-liberal policy levers where deregulated education reforms aimed at encouraging stronger local governance and buy in into education systems (Gale, 2003). Neo-liberal policy makers believed that individual responsibility coupled with deregulation and market friendly policies would lead to positive labour market outcomes (Green, 1997; Greve, 2018). It is within this underlying philosophy of how a postmodern society would assume responsibility for and participate in education that form the philosophical underpinnings of many of the 'borrowed' education policies and models that were imported into the GCC (Hayes, 2017).

Scholars have written about the complex cultural and social systems of the GCC that mean simple economic and labour market theory often doesn't go far enough to capture the deep 'layers' complexities seen in the political economy, social and cultural context of Bahrain (Kirk, 2014; Room, 2017; Walsh, 2017). This means many of the underlying assumptions in academic literature about social and labour market behaviour may not manifest in the same way in the GCC economies. This is particularly apparent when looking at labour market behaviour as an output of education policy, where behavioural economists claim that personal psychology can predict labour market outcomes (Cobb-Clark, 2015; Heckman, 2011). When considering the underlying assumptions of how education policy instruments might lead to labour market impact in the context of developing education systems, these behavioural considerations become particularly pertinent. This is further discussed by Heckman (2011) in looking at how personality psychology predicts labour market outcomes. He states '*Economists need to link the traits of psychology with the preferences, constraints and expectation mechanisms of economics*' (Heckman, 2011, page 3). It is clear that when applying the political and economic paradigms to education reforms in the GCC there is a need to consider the complexities of the context and that traditional linier policy tools may not always be appropriate in the context of the GCC.

2.1 From the Linier to Embedded Complexity—Old Versus New Reform

When analysing Bahrain Government public vision and strategy documents, there is a strong intent to ensure a more 'holistic' civil society approach to reform. Recent rhetoric across GCC governments indicate an explicit understanding of the importance of a more integrated approach embedding principles of civil society to underpin policy and programmes (Hayes, 2017). This rhetoric aligns well to ideas on 'social investment' economic paradigms and aspects of the 'Third Way' that are popular in many Western economies. In the social investment economic paradigm, policy making is seen as a 'live' system, rather than a static linier process (Hemerijck, 2018). This means the need for constant review and feedback is incorporated into the design and that the design and implementation process are part of the same system 'cycle'. The 'policy learning' is an integral part of the effectiveness of policy (Greve, 2018; Moyson et al., 2017).

Early authors of reform highlighted the 'experimental' nature of reforms (Cambell, 1969). This approach saw the design and evaluation of reforms as a 'scientific' process with methodologies that coped with complexity by adding 'controls' and 'measures' (Pawson and Tilley, 1997). Building on some of the popular Management ideas of objectives and KPIs, New Public Management (NPM) saw Western governments implementing 'business-like' standards and measurements to public management (Hood, 1991). NPM is described as being a set of assumptions and value statements that outlines how the public sector should be designed and managed that creates efficiency and standards (Diefenbach, 2009). Also referred to as 'Managerialism' with the key discourse of 'value added' as an important part of modern social policy (Yeatman and Costea, 2018). These neo liberal ideas on running reform and economic development would appear to have been well embraced by the GCC governments (Hayes, 2017). This is evident is in the array of GCC government strategies and programmes that are tracked and measured in accordance with targets and KPIs. The key criticism of this approach has been that reform and policy is designed and implemented with limited regard for the various underlying assumptions, complexities, or outcomes the policy was designed to address (Pawson, 2006), as it is only in the evaluation of the impact of these policies that we can see if they 'worked' or were fit for purpose (Pawson and Tilley, 1997; Pawson, 2006). Economist Joseph Stiglitz (2021) stated that many of the neo liberal policies were '*counterproductive in the long run because they impaired the ability of economies to learn, and even more importantly, to learn how to learn*' (Stiglitz, 2021, page ix). It could be argued that much of the NPM policy approach evident in the GCC is driven within the framework of 'causal explanation' i.e., 'if we do this, then this will happen'. This framework limits the ability to consider the carious complexities and mechanisms that lead to a causal relationship (Room, 2017). Critics of NPM refer to ideas of 'post-NPM' that include digitalisation and Agile concepts to encapsulate the fluidity and social complexity that the strategic objectives and KPI driven policy approach misses (Dunleavy et al., 2006). Criticism extends to the application of NPM on new economies with developing economic and political systems where there is a tendency to apply the standards and metrics popular with NPM without the broader sophisticated systems to manage and contextualise them (Mongkol, 2011).

By contrast, alternatives to this linier approach to policy making focus on policy outcomes within the policy system. When considering the limitations of evaluation of the impact of policy Pawson (2006) says '*evaluation research, in short has reached industrial proportions but remains feudal in its capacity to create change*' (page 7). Instead, Pawson (2006) recommends a continuous cycle of test, revise and refine to build '*explanations*' and create '*realist syntheses*' of the programme system, rather than viewing isolated components of the system. Room (2017) mentions the importance of complexity theories in considering the disentangling of the various mechanisms within a social intervention that might lead to change and impact. He calls this '*transformative realism*' and outlines the evolutionary nature of realism by moving the focus from individual interventions to the '*dynamic interactions*' that develop among various actors in the system (Room, 2017, page 23). In their paper on Agile Governance the WEF also outline the contribution of systems thinking in policy to embrace '*the complexity of an eco-system by providing a methodology that goes beyond immediate problems and addresses foundational principles and patters*' (WEF, 2018, page 8).

Addressing foundational *principles* and *patters* is at the core of defining programme assumptions within Programme Logic models and the Theory of Change (TOC) programme methodology which is used widely by governments as a framework for explaining and measuring the impact of government intervention programmes (UNESCO, 2006).

Building on realist ideas about programme logic and programme evaluation, TOC is a methodology and framework for allowing programme assumptions, learning and complexities to be capture in the design and implementation of development programmes (Valters, 2015). James (2011) defined as '*a Theory of Change is an ongoing process of reflection to explore change and how it happens – and what that means for the part we play in a particular context, sector and/or group of people.*' (James, 2011, page 2). This definition recognises the complexity of change and provides a potential framework to policy design and implementation relevant for a more Agile systems-based approach.

2.2 'Agile' Governance as Part of the 'New'

The term Agile was designed by software developers as a development process that was nimble to respond to change and embedded constant learning and feedback as part of the system. Originally outlined in a document called 'the Agile Manifesto' (Beck et al., 2001), the principles of Agile take a strong emphasis on end user design, encouraging change and learning rather than following a plan and wider participation.

Agile policy or Agile governance is defined by WEF (2018) as shifting the way '*policies are generated, deliberated, enacted and enforced in the Fourth Industrial Revolution*' (page 6). The key different between traditional pan-based policy making and the concept of Agile government is the value of time and responsiveness (WEF, 2018). Build within the Agile policy framework are deliberate mechanisms and sub systems for feedback and reiterations of policy, such as those suggested by the TOC frameworks. Part of the purpose of Agile policy making is to recognise and capture the complexities of the policy systems. Based on ideas of systems and design thinking, this approach recognises that policy making is a complex system that includes elements that interact with each other and the larger environment (Room, 2017).

While developing a theoretical thesis on principles of Agility in a realist framework is an ambition beyond the scope of this paper, there are some clear synergies that could be explored further to identify evidence of Agile policy making in the context of this case study. This is particularly the case when applying a realist framework to social complexity such as that of a reform intervention. This '*transformational realism*' (Room, 2017) allows a starting point for which to collate the systems theory-based concept of 'Agile'.

The following outlines some of the key principles of Agile and considers them within a realist policy making context to support theory building and create a greater synergy between private sector rhetoric and policy rhetoric. The Agile principles in the column on the left are adapted from those outlined in The Agile Manifesto (Beck et al., 2001). While the Agile Manifesto document outlines a total of twelve principles, six have been chosen for the purpose of this study, with the remaining not being relevant to a policy context (Table 1).

3 Data Gathering and Analysis

While realism forms the theoretical lens for the policy process that is the subject of this study, as outlined in the previous section, this realist thread also forms the philosophical foundation for the methodology of data collection and analysis.

As a research methodology, realism addresses the research task differently to more traditional research approaches (Robson, 2015; Pawson and Tilley, 1997). Contrary to the experimental pragmatic approach to research that searches for answers to 'how' and 'why', realism addresses those questions differently by asking '*what worked, in what context, for whom and why*' (Pawson and Tilley, 1997). Realism as an epistemology is less concerned with finding 'truth' but on an evolution of knowledge and learning (Robson, 2015). The underlying ontology is that of a 'real' world that is independent of us but interacts with our interpretation of it. The research aim is to capture what is different about the TAP policy development and consider, if and how, those differences fit within the framework of Agile policymaking.

The realist tradition recognises that the 'real' world is embedded within systems, which are in turn embedded within layers of other systems (Robson, 2015). It is the role of the experimentalist to be a *system builder* through *work* (Pawson and Tilley, 1997, page 60). For the purpose of this study, this *work* is capturing and interpreting data through primary and secondary research in a flexible research design. According to Pawson (2006) '*in the realist model, the primary ambition of research synthesis is explanation building*' (page 74). Another way of describing 'explanation building' is 'theory building' (Robson, 2015). It is the intention of building theory that is central to explaining the 'reality' identified in this research and considering this within the framework of Agile policy making.

Table 1 Agile and its application in education policy making

Agile Principle (adapted from the Agile Manifesto, 2001)	*The underlining paradigm*	*Principle in terms of realist policy making*	*Example of practical application and use in government*
1. End user 'usefulness' and value through customer centric design	End user outcomes over metrics and process	• Focus on the assumptions and outcomes of Policy i.e., 'by what mechanisms, in what context and through what actions' (Pawson, 2006) • The integration of formulation and implementation of education policy (Gale, 2003)	• Logic and Programme Frames • TOC journey mapping • Policy user Journey Mapping
2. Welcome change as part of continuous delivery	People don't always behave the way you assume they will, be prepared to go back to the policy drawing board	• Evidence-based Policy (Pawson, 2006) • Realistic Evaluation (Pawson and Tilley, 1997)	• Regular 'feedback cycles/loops' in Policy journey • Mechanisms for capturing challenges across a wide stakeholder group • Cycle evaluation over end of point evaluation

Agile Principle (adapted from the Agile Manifesto, 2001)	*The underlining paradigm*	*Principle in terms of realist policy making*	*Example of practical application and use in government*
3. Prioritise working outputs in shorter time frames rather than documentation	Focus on delivering policy products to test, iterate and review, not focused on documentation and KPIs	• Transformative Realism and complex systems (Room, 2017) • Policy learning (Moyson et al., 2017)	Policy products that are designed, implemented and tested in a consistent loop with the implementation and impact assessment embedded within the design process as a series of feedback cycles
4. Draw on the wider stakeholder group for participation	Experts and policy 'users' work together for collective learning	• Policy Activists (Yeatman, 1998) • Policy learning (Moyson et al., 2017)	• Policy consultation frameworks • Crowdsourced Policy Making • Co-Created rather than 'top down' policy making • 'Third way' representation
5. Outputs that meet the need they were designed for is the only measure of success	Outcomes are the only measure of success. Outcomes, not inputs need to be measured	• Realistic monitoring and evaluation frameworks (Pawson, 2006)	• Data collected on outcomes, not process. i.e., student outcomes, employer outcomes, labour market outcomes

As this study intends to capture empirical evidence of an evolving phenomenon within a defined context of place and time, it fits well within a case study tradition. Yin (2009) defines case study research as: '*Case study is a strategy for doing research which involves an empirical investigation of a particular contemporary phenomenon within its real-life context using multiple sources of evidence*' (Yin, 2009, page 18).

This case study aims to capture a holistic view of the reality of the phenomena as explained through the data collection about the TAP process. As a holistic case study, a research question helps to drive the overall research design (Robson, 2015).

This research question states the explicit intentions for this research:

In which ways is the TAP process an example of Agile policy?

To address this research question data was collected from multiple sources. First, a documentation analysis was conducted to identify themes that could inform the research question. These documents were all Bahrain Government documents available in English and directly associated with the TAP process. Only documents available in the public domain were used to inform this case study.

The second data collection tool was in-depth qualitative interviews conducted with key experts involved in the development and implementation of TAP. The interviewees were chosen for their seniority and close involvement in the TAP process. They all work for Government of Bahrain, or as consultants to Bahrain Government as part of the TAP reform in various capacities. A total of six people were interviewed in an in-depth qualitative interview. The interviewees were a mixture of both Bahraini nationals and Western expatriates and were all of a senior level with many years' experiences in senior education policy roles of varying capacity.

The expert interviews were audio recorded, then transcribed and manually analysed using thematic coding and analysis to determine common themes of the TAP process. Thematic analysis is described as '*a qualitative research method that can be widely used across a range of epistemology and research questions. It is a method for identifying, analysing, organising, describing and reporting themes found in a data set*' (Nowell et al., 2017, page 2).

This analysis method was chosen to provide real time narrative insight into the TAP process and add richness to the data and identify specific narratives that provided evidence of agility policy making.

4 The Case Study Context—A Brief Description of the Tertiary Action Plan

The following outlines the TAP process to provide context for the case study. The 2030 economic vision for Bahrain provided a high-level overview of the type of economy and society Bahrain aspires to become (Bahrain Government, 2008). To help achieve this a Government Priorities Framework (GPF) document was established for each area of government to outline the key objectives and targets that needed to be fulfilled to achieve 2030 vision. The GPF for education focused on four strategic pillars including: system performance, quality teaching, tertiary success, quality infrastructure. Under each of these headings were a series of objectives and KPIs that were designed to address the required changes within the education system to meet the 2030 Bahraini human capital ambitions.

The Supreme Council for Development of Education and Training (SCET) sits within the office of the Prime Minister and provides high-level oversight and coordination of the education and training initiatives, decisions, regulations and legal frameworks needed to achieve 2030 Vision. In 2019 SCET approved the Tertiary Action Plan (TAP). During 2019 a series of 'readiness reviews' of Bahraini's key higher education agencies and institutions was conducted to highlight good practice and identify areas of change required to ensure the agencies and institutions were able to achieve their objectives. These readiness review recommendations, the 10-year strategic plans of the key tertiary institutions and the GPF were the three key documents that informed TAP. Building on these documents, TAP was designed to address some of the barriers to successful outcomes in the higher education sector and to better align the higher education with the needs of the labour market (Bahrain Government, 2019). While many ambitious higher education reforms had been designed in Bahrain over the past 15 years, the TAP process came out of a recognition that it was necessary to ensure a whole system, integrated approach was taken to addressing some of the challenges and ensure a high-level central point to advocate the required regulatory and legal changes needed to drive the development of the higher education sector.

The TAP processes consisted of a total of ten different working groups whose mandate it was to deliver a design and implementation plans for the workstreams of the revised Bahrain tertiary education system. The ten working groups covered the following areas of the new reform (1)

Governance and Leadership; (2) Funding Formula Model; (3) School Infrastructure Plan; (4) Higher Education Council Reform; (5) Unified Foundation Programme; (6) Unified Examination/Qualification Framework; (7) The Collaboration of Applied Learning Institutes; (8) Skills Bahrain Agency; (9) The Employability and Skills Portal; and (10) Legislation Review (Bahrain Government, 2019).

Each working group was led by a Bahrain Government Minister and supported by a member of the office of the Prime Minister's team. In addition, each working group had a technical expert whose role is to provide advice and guidance from international best practice to support the working group produce an optimal solution. The technical expert was responsible for delivering the necessary content, reports, and presentations to ensure the working groups successfully meet the requirements of their individual briefs.

In addition to Ministerial representation as Chairs on each working group, the whole TAP working group process was under the oversight of a young dynamic Minister for Youth and Sport. Each working group Chair would then report to this Minister, who would in turn provide feedback to the SCET monthly. The working group members were selected from relevant stakeholders in each area so as provide a holistic and informed perspective in each area. Each working group had between 5 and 12 representative agencies, institutions or organisations present. By April 2020 each working group had produced their findings and concluded their work. The implementation of the recommendations of the working groups were to be given to the Ministry of Education and the various relevant institutions for implementation.

5 The Expert Interviews—Findings

The following outlines the findings of the interviews. As discussed previously, the findings are presented across the themes identified from the interviews. While there were a number of potential themes that could be discussed, these have been limited to three core themes for the purposes of reporting and managing the data required in the context of this study.

Where relevant, the verbatim text will be presented. For purposes of clarification or context, there may be additions added in parenthesis to the verbatim text. The term 'respondents' will be used to describe the experts interviewed for this study.

5.1 *Theme One—System Change and a Different Rhetoric*

One of the key areas across all the interviews was that of the intention for TAP to be an education system change, not just designing another set of education initiatives. This 'difference' was often talked about in the context of the different use of terminology to describe the change.

The respondent described the importance of this language in articulating what TAP was trying to do. The first obvious change in narrative is that of calling post-secondary education 'tertiary education' rather than 'higher education', which has been more common in the GCC. When discussing this one respondent said this was done deliberately to move people's thinking away from higher education being about degrees to using a word that incorporates both vocational and academic learning and the word 'tertiary' offers a broader description of post-secondary education and training. This terminology is consistent with the description of post-secondary education used across most of the English-speaking world where there is a trend to move away from the term 'higher education' to describe third level education as tertiary instead. The Organisation for Economic Cooperation and Development (OECD) says '*tertiary education is defined as those having completed the highest level of education, by age group. This includes both theoretical programmes leading to advanced research or high skill professions such as medicine and more vocational programmes leading to the labour market*' (OECD, 2021). The use of the word tertiary is also widely used by the World Bank, United Nationals and other NGOs in their documentation.

The theme of a new rhetoric continued with all respondents outlining the purpose of TAP is to create change in Bahrain in a 'new' way. In part of explaining this new way there was a deliberate use of words other than 'reform' or 'restructuring'. Instead, it was stated by one respondent ... '*we are not going to talk about reform, but they did like (the word) transformation so that was the language used*'. The respondents explained how this helped stakeholders form an agreed understanding that '*it's not about restructuring the University or the Polytechnic*' but rather a whole system change. The language of change and the use of 'transformation' as the terminology of a whole system approach to change was mentioned by all respondents and was clearly very important to how TAP was received by stakeholders.

Descriptions of the 'system' approach were also outlined in general *'we have to take a system approach'... '(there was) not a broad understanding of stakeholders of how this was interconnected at a system level'* ... *'the interconnected approach is new'*.

It was discussed specifically how the working groups were seen as part of this system; they were described as *'levers for change'*. When discussing the working groups approach specifically it was mentioned ... *'we established a term of reference for each working group to establish whole system reform' therefore the working groups were used as a lever for change'* .... *'a few things needed to change at a national level, how they institutions interact with each other, the interconnectness needed to change'*.

Policy scholars have long been interested in the role of the narratives communicated in the policy process (Jones and McBeth, 2010). A narrative is described as a sequence of events with an unfolding plot and characters who are used to demonstrate a moral to the story (Jones, McBeth, and Shanahan, 2014). The policy 'story', or 'policy speak' (Gale, 2003) outlined by our respondents described a deliberate narrative of 'change' and 'different'. The 'unfolding plot' of the story as told by our respondents explains the shift from what *was* (reform) to what *will be* (transformation). The characters in the story are those directly involved in this transformation through their participation in the working groups. The word 'interconnected' was mentioned by four out of the six respondents indicating this as a key theme. The outcome from the working groups concludes the 'moral' of the story in the form of recommendations (Jones et al., 2014). It is important to note that the *process* was as much part of the narrative of 'different' (i.e., the interconnectedness) as the recommendations produced.

5.2 Theme Two—Outcomes not KPIs

Another key theme of the interviews was that of the importance of focusing on outcomes for students, not KPIs or targets. While the GPF document was structured around high-level objectives with KPI targets, the TAP was designed around a common interest in seeing Bahrain's economy grow. One respondent explained the importance of this 'common vision' or 'value proposition' for Bahrainis ... *'too much in education is focused on what the adults want, not what students need'*.

Respondents articulated the importance that the TAP focus should move away from short-term quantitative metrics to longer term impact based qualitative metrics. One respondent said *'this is much more about outcomes, its long term, education is not amenable to short-term KPIs. This is because it is about a learning journey'*. It was recognised that TAP success needed to focus on *'outcomes and student achievement, not KPIs'*. The vision of this was constantly shared with each working group. The outcomes vision was written in the 'value proposition' document that outlined what success would look like for each working group. A couple of the respondent describes how the working groups were constantly kept on track by constantly emphasising the outcomes of the process

> *.... 'Everyone wanted KPIs, but we said we are going to focus on outcomes. What is the picture you have in your head for how Bahrain will be when the economy is working at the level you want?'... 'How are you going to know if your students are doing better because of your activity? this kept in front of them that they need to report on how this will help Bahraini students'.*

It was also mentioned that there is a tendency in Government to think that the task is over once the KPIs are drawn up. This respondent cited the numerous examples of strategy documents and metrics being designed and communicated, but with no real implementation. The designing of the strategy is seen as the end goal. Whereas, by focusing on outcomes there is an agreed understanding of the intention and assumption of what the recommendations (policy) is supposed to achieve.

The trends in business corporate planning was observed by one respondent who said the TAP approach... *'mirrors development in corporate culture where there is an integrated approach to identifying strategy'*.

As discussed previously, the 'managerialism' of the policy process and the use of business indicators is a key of New Public Management (Yeatman and Costea, 2018; Diefenbach, 2009; Mongkol, 2011). An Agile approach to policy making provides an approach to reducing 'policy decay' by '*creating mechanisms to constantly monitor and "upgrade" policies'* (WEF, 2018, page 6). A key difference between NPM and Agile is that of the time value of iteration cycles and review. Agile sees these as shorter and as a result constantly ensuring outcomes and the mechanisms to create those outcomes are constantly assigned (Room, 2017; Pawson, 2006). The more traditional approach to the policy process sees a linier sequence of events with evaluation being the final event (Yeatman, 1998). The Agile policy process sees the evaluation as a constant embedded cycle through feedback loops and mechanisms (Room, 2017; WEF, 2018).

This allows the role of evaluation and impact to be continuous and encapsulate nuances and complexities within the system as the mechanisms, contexts and outputs are explicit and evaluated (Pawson and Tilley, 1997). The ongoing and deliberate cycles of evaluation and iteration of TAP is a key recommendation of this research.

5.3 Theme Three—Integrated Collaboration and Responsibility

This theme overlaps with theme one in considering a systems approach, the focus here is on stakeholder engagement and feedback as a core part of the TAP process.

Respondents described the approach to choosing high-level Ministers to act as Chair to each of the working groups. One of the respondents described the deliberate approach to engaging Ministers who don't have a direct education portfolio by highlighting the common interest that the end goal TAP addressing is *'how do we lift the performance of the Bahrain economy?'*. This 'common understanding' was used as part of encouraging each working group Chair to consider the outcome of their work through constantly linking it back to how it helps lift the performance of the Bahrain economy. This was cited as a key different of the TAP process to other policy interventions because it *'bringing people together in an organised way. Each entity was working in silo, the TAP brought them all together'*. This was further elaborated...(there was) *'not a broad understanding by stakeholder of how this was interconnected at a system level, there were fundamental aspects that needed to be addressed, it wasn't a BTI* (Bahrain Training Institute) *thing or a Polytechnic thing. Getting a common unified vision across the sector to build momentum'*.

When respondents were asked if they believe this was understood by those leading the working groups it was stated that the importance of the Minister level involvement in education was apparent. One respondent said ...*'education was always seen to be a priority... education is not just us it's the entire cabinet... ... Just because you hold a different portfolio in government does not mean that education is a priority that you could be involved in as well'*. There was a recognition that every Bahraini is a stakeholder in education. According to one respondent, this *'prestigious championship'* of Ministerial level oversight and lead allowed *'political levers'* to be aligned and pushed at a national level in favour of moving TAP forward.

This high-level representation was cited as a key difference between the TAP process and other reform interventions ... *'I haven't seen anything like this (the TAP process) in Bahrain or even the whole world'*... *'we had 36 entities and 88 representatives'* ... *'it had national high-level representation'*. The high-level representation was also seen as an important part of addressing the challenges in the education system... *'we knew what the policy problems were and working towards recommendations that are consistent across all'*. The interconnected nature of the representation allowed high-level discussions about the problems and solutions that TAP intended to address across key members of Bahrain Government. By taking this whole systems governance approach to education, TAP created a benchmark for integrated policy outcomes and whole system engagement. While accountability was not explicitly stated as an intention by the TAP process, it could be argued that the consultation process and representation in the working groups lend themselves to higher levels of stakeholder responsibility for outcomes. As stated by one respondent that education is about *'the whole cabinet'*, not just those carrying the portfolio. Ranson (2003) explains that *'accountability is a social practice pursuing particular purposes, defined by distinctive relationships and evaluative procedures. Participating in communities of practice shapes the dispositions of its members'* (Ranson, 2003, page 460). The TAP process indicates evidence of a 'social practice' within Bahrain Government. The 'distinctive relationships' helped to collectively reconsider whose job education is within Government and encourage collective recommendations as a key output of the process.

The intention for implementing some of the TAP's recommendations included sending 'letters of expectation' to leaders of the relevant institutions and agencies to outline the outcomes expected from the institution. Part of this involved ensuring every institution had a clear idea of what success would look like so they knew that they were not just delivering on KPIs but on actual learner outcomes. The monitoring and evaluation of learner outcomes in line with TAP recommendations is a key part of the role of institutional leadership in implementing TAP.

As mentioned under theme one, a key aspect of the integrated collaboration is the feedback and communication cycles. The regular feedback of the working groups, the Chair, the overseeing Minister and other key people ran over a 5-month period and resulted in iterations of the specific working group challenges and recommendations being built upon and refined during the course of the working group process. These feedback cycles allowed for understanding and the recommendations to be continuously reviewed and reiterated as understanding and learning within the working groups grew.

This evidence of 'policy learning' and 'policy dissemination' through the working groups is a core part of Agile principles and transformative realism (Room, 2017). Policy learning can occur at a micro, meso and macro levels within the policy process (Moyson et al., 2017). Micro level policy learning happens between individuals in social settings (Friedmann, 1981). Meso level is within the organisation and recognises that organisations are evolving systems of learning (Argyis, 1999; Senge, 1990). Macro level policy learning looks at learning across the whole policy system and its institutions and agencies (Moyson et al., 2017). There is evidence of this micro level learning by one respondent who told a story of personal engagement by one of the Ministerial Chair who had traditionally not held an education portfolio. According to the respondent '*the Minister demonstrated an excellence in helping disseminate and break down complex policy information to a non-education audience to help create shared understanding, therefore able to gain decision making and consensuses*'. The respondent continued by explaining how this Minister's strength in articulating complex themes allowed different voices and feedback to be brought into the TAP process through the working groups they Chaired. This 'social learning' (Friedmann, 1981) is evident by the explanation of this Chair who identified this policy knowledge and then demonstrated a high level of ability to deciphered and disseminate it within the social learning context of the working groups (Hall, 1993).

5.3.1 Evidence of Agile Policy Making?

This research aimed to answer the research question:

In which ways is the TAP process an example of Agile policy?

There is some evidence from the TAP process case study of Agile principles. While the documentation reviewed for this study doesn't necessarily outline an Agile process, the respondents described many aspects in the process that could be considered as part of the Agile principles. The following outlines the Agile principles mentioned previously and considers the findings and analysis within each of the principles.

5.3.2 *Agile Principle—End User 'Usefulness' and Value Through Customer Centric Design*

The TAP process did not do any formal policy journey mapping as a formal activity in the policy process design. However, respondents describe the repeated importance of 'outcomes' for students as being the priority over process and KPIs. Bringing the 'end user' voice into the TAP process was recognised by the respondents when they explained how too much education policy is about what adults want and not what learners need. The message was communicated throughout the process, in particular when emphasising the importance of outcomes over KPIs.

5.3.3 *Agile Principle—Welcome Change as Part of Continuous Delivery*

Whether explicitly designed purposefully or not, it is apparent that the working group process and the regular meetings and feedback mechanisms are evidence of opportunities for change and iteration in the policy development cycle. While the process could have been designed to finish sooner, the timeframes and series of continuous meetings and consultations allowed for cycles of development to be reviewed, consulted and discussed. There is evidence of space for policy learning and dissemination in the TAP process.

While there is not necessarily evidence of 'continuous delivery' in the sense of policy implementation as this was not the stage of the process during the research, there is evidence of an Agile process of 'continuous delivery' in the development of the working group's collective learning and recommendations. There is some evidence of change from the respondents, especially in regard to policy learning and perspectives on accountability and responsibility. There is also evidence of change towards understanding the importance of outcomes over KPIs within the TAP policy context with actors considering the longer term outcomes as the measure of success over short-term KPIs.

5.3.4 *Agile Principle—Prioritise Working Outputs in Shorter Time Frames Rather Than Documentation*

As this study only looked at the context of the TAP process and not the implementation of that process, it becomes more difficult to identify evidence of working outputs. However, there is evidence of some of the working group recommendations being ratified through Bahrain Cabinet, in particular, the restructure and regulatory changes for the Higher

Education Council into a Tertiary Education Council, and amendment of the progression and articulation regulations to allow for recognition of prior learning and 'stair casing' of lower level to high- level qualifications, the agreement to establish an agency 'Skills Bahrain' to align education, training and labour market needs through career pathways and labour market needs. In addition, new governance structures and Board of Trustees have been appointed at some of the key Bahrain institutions.

The focus of the implementation of the working groups recommendations has been on ensuring the regulatory and legal frameworks are in place to ensure implementation is possible. There has been a definite focus on 'getting things done' over documenting another higher education plan.

5.3.5 Agile Principle—Draw on the Wider Stakeholder Group for Participation

The TAP process and its working group approach provides very strong evidence of wider stakeholder participation. This was a strong theme in the findings of the interviews as discussed in the previous section of this study.

5.3.6 Agile Principle—Outputs that Meet the Need They Were Designed for is the Only Measure of Success

As mentioned in the discussion of the evidence of the first principle, the focus on outputs versus KPIs was a critical part of ensuring the TAP policy design is 'fit for purpose' and able to be measured for outputs. The inputs into the process are not indicators of the success of the process. This is an important point in the context of this study where the realist lens is identifying the extent to which the process appears to be evidence of Agile governance, but this study is not sufficient in itself to determine the success of the TAP process. This principle cannot be achieved until long-term outcomes can be evaluated for their impact. This long-term realist evaluation will determine the true success of this 'new' policy process.

6 Concluding Remarks

Overall, the TAP process remained true to some of the Agile principles and the underlying paradigm of focusing on end user outcomes to develop the future workforce for Bahrain and thereby realising Vision

2030. This Agile approach is also well aligned to Bahrain's national agenda for digitalisation and future skills development.

It was understood change would be part of continuous delivery and by ratifying in Bahrain Cabinet key short-term measures such as career articulation and progression routes, these are now underpinned by the necessary legislation. Another working output for TAP is the establishment of the pilot and set up of a national skills agency who will be tasked with integrating many of the outcomes of TAP and coordinating the skills eco system. Outcomes have also been supported through new key appointments to the Board of governance for the Higher Education Council, Polytechnic and Bahrain Qualifications Authority Boards. These appointments drew on the wider stakeholder working groups who participated in policy formalisation 'co-creating' rather than 'top down' policy making (Greve, 2018)and therefore embedded that knowledge into the system (Room, 2017; WEF, 2018).

There are some areas the TAP process could benefit from future consideration. It would appear that some of the inputs and outputs, within the context of the desired outcomes, had been designed with limited hierarchy and progression. This limits the opportunity for outcomes and the student voice to be central to TAP implementation. The TAP process would benefit from adopting a Programme Logic and Theory of Change frameworks as analytical tool for a formal project-policy-based implementation and measurement of outcomes. This would allow a clear and explicit discussion of the underlying assumptions of what TAP was trying to achieve and high-level conversation about the *context, mechanisms* and *outcomes* as inputs to what worked, for whom and how? (Pawson, 2006; Pawson and Tilley, 1997) and ensure the end users of the policy (students) are achieving what the policy was designed to achieve. Monitoring and evaluation systems are critical to be embedded in the TAP transformation (Pawson and Tilley, 1997). The evaluation should be continuous and draw on various data sources, but needs to focus on outcomes, not process. i.e., student outcomes, employer outcomes, labour market outcomes. This continuous evaluation and the use of Programme Logic models and Theory of Change frameworks will also allow for regular review of the process and reiteration changes to be made as required by determining the degree to which objectives have been achieved and the efficiency, effectiveness, impact, and sustainability of the TAP. The integration of TAP with other related national intervention initiatives, will support the implementation of TAP in providing regular feedback cycles/loops in the policy journey and mechanisms for capturing challenges across a wide stakeholder group.

This study has identified some areas of good practice in the design and consultation of education policy making within the context of Agile principles. As the private sector look towards the 4th industrial revolution, they demand the time value of policy's keep up with market changes and emerging technology, governments will need to find more Agile ways of responding and make Agile systems more explicit. The TAP working group process is a good case study for how this can be achieved, and it is hoped the ongoing implementation of TAP will continue to provide GCC policymakers with an example of good practice Agile policy making.

References

Amankwah-Amoah, J., Khan, Z., Wood, G., & Knight, G. (2021). COVID-19 and digitalization: The great acceleration. Journal of Business Research, 136, 602–611. https://doi.org/10.1016/j.jbusres.2021.08.011

Argyis, C. (1999). On organizational learning (2nd ed.). Willey-Blackwell.

Bahrain Government. (2008). Bahrain Vision 2030. https://www.bahrain.bh/wps/portal/!ut/p/a1/jdDfE4FAEAfwv8VDr-3qqHg7TSlTwyByLybmHKY6k8ifLzz5Efbtdj7f2d0DBhGwLD7vRFzsZBYntzfTl-4Q9aZmagOchg7S4aTl-rZLcGxUYPEECLEroBsjY9bRdBP_y6MWWE2vVYEgQKRmb-xPHQuxT_7M1xT9OX_CM5gDe2HvV9zBtzUfoH6PATCRyNX9Txc0WxFTAMv5huc8V095

Bahrain Government. (2019). The SCET Annual Report 2019.

Ball, S. (1998). Big policies/small world: An introduction to international perspectives in education policy. Comparative Education, 34(2), 119–130.

Beck, K., Beedle, M., van Bennekum, A., Cockburn, A., Cunningham, W., Fowler, M., Grenning, J., Highsmith, J., Hunt, A., Jeffries, R., Kern, J., Marick, B., Martin, R., Mellor, S., Schwaber, K., Sutherland, J., & Thomas, D. (2001). Manifesto for Agile software development. http://www.agilemanifesto.org/

Cambell, D. (1969). Reforms as experiments. American Psychologist, 24(4), 409–429.

Cobb-Clark, D. (2015). Locus of control and the labour market. IZA Journal of Labour Economics, 4.

Dale, R. (1999). Specifying globalization effects on national policy: A focus on the mechanisms. Journal of Education Policy, 14(1), 1–17.

Denning, S. (2020). Who says governments can't be agile? Forbes Magazine. https://www.forbes.com/sites/stevedenning/2020/09/29/who-says-the-government-cant-be-agile/?sh=6e9219c03a6c

Derasat & UNDP. (2018). Bahrain human development report. https://www.derasat.org.bh/wp-content/uploads/2019/07/BahrainHumanDevelopmentReport2018.pdf
Diefenbach, T. (2009). New public management in public sector organizations: The dark side of managerial "enlightenment." Public Management, 87(4), 892–909. https://doi.org/10.1111/j.1467-9299.2009.01766.x
Donn, G., & Al Manthri, Y. (2013). Education in the broader Middle East. Symposium Books.
Dunleavy, P., Margetts, H., Bastow, S., & Tinkler, J. (2006). Digital era governance: IT corporations, the state and E government. Oxford University Press.
EDB. (2021). Bahrain Economic Board. https://www.bahrainedb.com/
Friedmann, J. (1981). Planning as social learning.
Gale, T. (2003). Realising policy: The who and how of policy production. Discourse: Studies in the Cultural Politics of Education, 24(1), 51–65.
Green, A. (1997). Education, globalization and the nation state. Education, Globalization and the Nation State, 130–186. https://doi.org/10.1057/9780230371132_8
Greve, B. (2018). Social and labour market policy. Routedge.
Hall, P. (1993). Policy paradigms, social learning and the state. Comparative Politics, 25(3), 275–296.
Hayes, A. (2017). Deconstructing the 'magnetic' properties of neoliberal politics of education in Bahrain. Globalisation, Societies and Education, 15(2). https://doi.org/10.1080/14767724.2016.1169516
Hayes, A., & Al'Abri, K.M. (2019). Regional solidarity undermined? Higher education developments in the Arabian Gulf, economy and time. Comparative Education, 55(2). https://doi.org/10.1080/03050068.2018.1504884
Hayes, A., & Findlow, S. (2020). The role of time in policymaking: A Bahraini model of higher education competition. Critical Studies in Education, 61(2). https://doi.org/10.1080/17508487.2017.1358756
Heckman, J. (2011). Integrating personal psychology into economics.
Hemerijck, A. (2018). Social investment as a policy paradigm. Journal of European Public Policy, 25(6), 810–827.
Hood, C. (1991). A public management for all seasons? Public Administration, 1, 3–19.
IGA. (2021). Bahrain E-government and information authority—Demographic data. https://www.iga.gov.bh/en/
James, C. (2011). Theory of change review. Asian Development Bank.
Jones, D., & Punshi, R. (2013). Unlocking the paradox of plenty. Motivate Publishing.
Jones, M., & McBeth, M. (2010). Narrative policy frameworks: Clear enough to be wrong? Policy Studies Journal, 38(2), 329–353.

Jones, M., McBeth, M., & Shanahan, E. (2014). The science of stories: Application of the policy narrative framework in public policy analysis. Palgrave MacMillian.
Karolak, M. (2012). Bahrain's tertiary education reform: A step towards sustainable economic development. Revue Des Mondes Musulmans et de La Méditerranée, 131, 163–181. https://doi.org/10.4000/remmm.7665
Kirk, D. (2014). Innovate or replicate: Education reform initiatives in the Gulf Cooperation Council States. The Muslim World, 105(January).
Lewick, M., Link, P., & Leifer, L. (2018). The design thinking playbook. John Wiley & Sons Inc.
Madbouly, A., Reyad, S., & Chinnasamy, G. (2021). Analysis for the knowledge economy in GCC countries (pp. 403–416). https://doi.org/10.1007/978-3-030-62796-6_24
Mongkol, K. (2011). The critical review of new public management model and its criticisms. Research Journal of Business Management, 5, 35–43. https://doi.org/10.3923/rjbm.2011.35.43
Moyson, S., Sholten, P., & Weible, C. (2017). Policy learning and policy change: Theorizing their relations from different perspectives. Policy and Society, 36(2), 161–177. https://doi.org/10.1080/14494035.2017.1331879
Nowell, L., Norris, J., White, D., & Moules, N. (2017). Thematic analysis: Striving to meet the trustworthiness criteria. International Journal of Qualitative Methods, 16, 1–13.
Pawson, R. (2006). Evidence-based policy: A realist perspective. SAGE.
Pawson, R., & Tilley, N. (1997). Realistic evaluation. SAGE.
Ranson, S. (2003). Public Accountability in the age of neo-liberal governance. Journal of Education Policy, 18(5), 459–480.
Robson, C. (2015). Real world research (3rd ed.). Wiley.
Room, G. (2017). Agile actors on complex terrains: Transformative realism and public policy. Routledge.
Senge, P. (1990). The fifth discipline: The art and practice of a learning organization. DoubleDay.
Stiglitz, J. (2021). Forward. In A. D. Bank (Ed.), Powering a learning society during and age of disruption. Springer.
The Organisation for Economic Cooperation and Development. (2021). OECD data: Population with tertiary education. https://data.oecd.org/eduatt/population-with-tertiary-education.htm
UNESCO. (2006). National education sector development plan: A result-based planning handbook.
Valters, C. (2015). Theory of change: Time for a radical approach to learning in development. https://cdn.odi.org/media/documents/9835.pdf
Walsh, C. (2017). Civilisation analysis: Unlocking the social cultural and political context of Arab Civil Society. Asia Pacific Journal of Contemporary Education

and Communication Technology, 3(2), 27–35. https://doi.org/10.25275/apjcectv3i2edu3

WEF. (2018). Agile governance: Reimagining policymaking in the Fourth Industrial Revolution.

WEF. (2020a). Future of jobs.

WEF. (2020b). Global competitiveness report. https://www.weforum.org/reports/the-global-competitiveness-report-2020b

WEF. (2020c). The future of jobs report. https://www.weforum.org/reports/the-future-of-jobs-report-2020c/

WEF. (2022). Catalysing Education 4.0 investing in the future of learning for a human-centric recovery. https://www3.weforum.org/docs/WEF_Catalysing_Education_4.0_2022.pdf

World Bank. (2017). Towards a diversified knowledge based economy. https://openknowledge.worldbank.org/bitstream/handle/10986/29271/122881-WP-EducationSectorEngagementNotefinal-PUBLIC.pdf?sequence=1

Yeatman, J. (1998). Activism and the policy process. Allen and Unwin.

Yeatman, A., & Costea, B. (2018). The triumph of managerialism? New technologies of government and their implications for value. Rowman & Littlefield International.

Yin, R. K. (2009). Case study research: Design and methods (4th Ed.). SAGE. https://doi.org/10.33524/cjar.v14i1.73

CHAPTER 10

High-tech Nationalization of Gulf Employment: A New Labor Market Approach in the United Arab Emirates

Robert Mogielnicki

1 Introduction

Gulf economic development is increasingly taking place in digital spheres. There are high hopes that new technologies can accelerate growth, whether through the future proofing of traditional industries or opening up new segments of the economy. The United Arab Emirates (UAE)—particularly the emirate of Dubai—is at the forefront of efforts to harness technology-focused innovation to enhance economic processes. The Dubai Free Zone Council is studying the feasibility of constructing a free zone for electronic gaming; the Dubai government approved an e-commerce strategy to accelerate the growth of the nascent sector; and

R. Mogielnicki (✉)
Arab Gulf States Institute in Washington, Washington, DC, USA
e-mail: mogielnicki.robert@gmail.com

A. Mishrif et al. (eds.), *Nationalization of Gulf Labour Markets*,
The Political Economy of the Middle East,
https://doi.org/10.1007/978-981-19-8072-5_10

the emirate's 50-year charter envisions a virtual commercial city capable of hosting 100,000 companies. These technology-focused, digital initiatives promise to transform labor market and human capital development trends in the UAE and across the wider Gulf region.

Economic development is closely related to labor market dynamics. Gulf Arab governments have long sought to improve the quality and quantity of employment opportunities available to local citizens. The consequent policies, known broadly as workforce nationalization, and which largely seek to replace expatriate workers with Gulf citizens, tend to adopt a sector-based approach. Governments enforce hiring quotas in certain industries, for example, or prohibit new expatriate work visas in specific professions. Saudi Arabia, Oman, and Kuwait aggressively pursued this policy approach in the aftermath of the oil price crisis of 2014–2015. In many cases, however, these direct labor market interventions have failed to absorb the growing number of local jobseekers entering regional labor markets. At the same time, many traditional professions across the Gulf region, and especially lower-skilled public sector roles, remain vulnerable to automation or other forms of disruption.

Nascent digital industries and the launch of long-term development initiatives based on emerging commercial technologies offer an opportunity to reassess standard approaches to workforce nationalization. Using the UAE as a case study and with a particular focus on Dubai, this chapter aims to update the sector-based approach to workforce nationalization by looking toward future economic activities. The chapter first maps the trajectory of workforce nationalization policies and discusses why a skills-oriented approach to Emiratization may be better aligned with future needs. The chapter then highlights government efforts to promote high-growth areas of the digital economy and other opportunities to implement a high-tech, skills-based Emiratization policy. The chapter concludes with recommendations for how Dubai policymakers can better align workforce nationalization to meet the future needs of a digital economy.

The work follows a multi-disciplinary, political economy approach for tracing the development of a digital economy in Dubai alongside ongoing workforce nationalization policies. The resulting qualitative approach utilizes historical data on Gulf labor markets and case studies to provide an analytical baseline upon which the concluding policy recommendations rest. Government officials, academics, and other stakeholders can use this work as a comparative study when examining the trajectories of workforce nationalization in other regional states. This chapter relies heavily on source materials and data collected as part of the author's research for a technology-focused book chapter in the *Routledge Handbook of China—Middle East Relations*. The research also serves as part of "Next Gen Gulf," a long-term research series launched by the author to explore how advanced technologies shape Gulf Arab governments and economies.

1.1 Workforce Nationalization as Growth Stimulant

Workforce nationalization initiatives across the Gulf tend to focus on specific industries and the positions therein. On April 9, 2021, Saudi Arabia's Ministry of Human Resources and Social development issued new labor directives to localize positions in the country's retail and restaurant sectors ("Only Saudis can work in malls"). In February 2021, Oman's Ministry of Labour extended Omanization regulations to include roles in higher education establishments ("Oman extends Omanisation"). Governments in Saudi Arabia and Oman have long struggled to generate sufficient employment opportunities for new entrants into their respective labor markets. Similar labor market interventions are ongoing in Kuwait. The Kuwaiti central bank announced new regulations that Kuwaitis should comprise at least 70 percent of upper- and middle-level management positions at local banks by the end of 2023 (Elbahrawy 2021).

Despite possessing a much smaller ratio of citizens to total residents than its Saudi and Omani counterparts, the UAE has nevertheless embarked on a similar trajectory of industry-focused workforce nationalization programs. The country's Ministry of Human Resources & Emiratization lists on its website a series of laws issued between 2005 and 2009 concerning national employment quotas in the trade, insurance, and banking sectors (UAE Ministry of Human Resources). Emiratization quotas across the UAE are generally limited to narrow sectors, such as banking or insurance, considered strategic areas of the economy.

The earliest versions of Emiratization initiatives materialized within the banking and finance industry and were driven—in large part—by the desire of newly established governments to safeguard against excessive foreign merchant control over critical industries during the country's early developmental stages. For example, the establishment of the Emirates Institute for Banking and Financial Studies (EIBFS) in 1983 sought to "contribute effectively towards emiratization in the banking and finance sector" (Emirates Institute for Banking). Individual emirate-level governments—in keeping with the high degree of sub-national economic autonomy afforded by the country's constitution—created additional government entities to oversee Emiratization policies within their respective emirates.

More recent Emiratization policies have emerged within a state-society nexus wherein the primacy of the state vis-à-vis foreign residents is not quite a contested sphere. However, the continued existence of Emiratization policies demonstrates the government's genuine desire to protect its citizenry's privileged position in the labor market. Ongoing Emiratization initiatives target improvements in both the quantity and quality of jobs available for Emiratis. Additional laws listed on the Ministry of Human Resources & Emiratization's website involve the Emiratization of specific roles, such as public relation officers in companies with 100 or more employees, or for jobseekers with special needs (UAE Ministry of Human Resources). The ministry likewise contains a cabinet resolution regulating the termination of Emirati nationals working in the private sector as well as a ministerial decree laying out the conditions for training and employment of students. In 2019, a UAE government initiative to create 20,000 jobs for Emiratis over the following three years included directives that managerial positions in the public sector must be reserved for Emiratis (Reynolds 2019). Emirati graduates seeking to gain experience at private companies are also eligible for salary subsidies from the state. As part of the country's 50-year anniversary, the UAE government announced the "Project of the 50"—a series of future-oriented economic development initiatives that included salary subsidies, entrepreneurship promotion, and employment support to enable more Emiratis to enter the private sector (Nasrallah 2021).

The UAE's demographics and the relative strength of its economy, when compared against Gulf Arab neighbors, suggest room for redesigning Emiratization policies beyond the traditional focus on sectors and the positions therein. Emirati citizens constitute approximately 10 percent of the country's total residents, according to United Nations data from 2019 (CIA World Factbook). The UAE likewise possesses substantial sovereign wealth holdings and is one of the Gulf region's most diversified economies, especially outside of the hydrocarbon-abundant emirate of Abu Dhabi (Mogielnicki 2021). The share of hydrocarbon revenues as a ratio of total UAE government revenues reached around

36 percent in 2018, whereas the remaining Gulf Arab countries exhibited ratios closer to 70 percent or more, according to a World Bank Group study.

Indeed, Emiratization is more easily enacted in the public sector sphere. Some UAE government institutions and government-related institutions have sought to tackle Emiratization-related objectives by enhancing the digital and technological skills of Emirati youth. In April 2021, the country's National Service and Reserve Authority announced new directives to equip national service program participants with "future skills…to enhance their contribution to the UAE's digital economy" ("UAE Government Equips National Service Programme Participants"). Emirates Global Aluminium, which is owned equally by the Mubadala Investment Company of Abu Dhabi and the Investment Corporation of Dubai, runs a graduate trainee program that provides recent university graduates with science, technology, and mathematics skillsets with 18 months of training in preparation for leading positions within the organization ("EGA finishes year with highest-ever rate").

Some private multinational companies operating in the UAE view the provision of digital and technology-oriented skills to Emiratis as a means to advance commercial and socioeconomic interests. Under a memorandum of understanding with the Dubai Government Human Resources Department, Microsoft has committed to the digital upskilling of Emiratis through internships, secondment opportunities, and other training programs enabled by Microsoft's Tomoh program (Ndichu 2020). The UAE government encourages these forms of private-sector-led initiatives by presenting an annual UAE Emiratization Award, which IBM won for the high-tech establishments category in 2020. The award is designed to "achieve an Emirati-centered knowledge economy and effective participation of Emiratis in the UAE labor market" (Rizvi 2020). There are a plethora of other training and skills development programs across other areas of the public and private sectors—or functioning jointly as public–private collaborations—for Emiratis. However, the various programs do not constitute a coherent strategy, as each possesses varying lengths and, in some cases, different underlying objectives.

Basing workforce nationalization around technology-oriented skillsets is an alternative approach for organizing Emiratization policies. Such an approach applies well to the evolving nature of regional economies, where new technologies and transactions across the digital economy do not necessarily constitute a sector or industry as such but rather a collection of innovative services and applications cutting across most economic activities. A technology skills-centric Emiratization would likewise split responsibilities between the public sector, which must ensure that students graduating from academic institutions in the country, and private-sector firms that want to innovate.

1.2 *The Digital Economy and Technology-focused Activities*

That the policy design of workforce nationalization initiatives should be better aligned with the skills of cutting-edge, high-potential economic activities is not a controversial statement. In fact, the UAE and its emirate-level governments have rolled out many strategies over the past several years intended to enhance the country's position as a global technology hub. In 2017, the UAE government launched the UAE Strategy for the Fourth Industrial Revolution (4IR). The UAE and Dubai governments have also adopted blockchain strategies. The Emirates Blockchain Strategy 2021 aims to transform 50 percent of government transactions into a blockchain platform (Telecommunications and Digital Gov. Regulatory Authority). An underlying goal behind these strategies and related initiatives involves "creating an environment that fosters computational thinking" (Telecommunications and Digital Gov. Regulatory Authority).

Perhaps nowhere is the push to incorporate advanced technologies into economic activities greater than in the domain of artificial intelligence (AI). The UAE government hopes to position the country as a "global incubator" for commercial projects and ventures that implement AI-focused technologies (Government of UAE Instagram). The commercial stakes associated with government-level interest in AI are high. According to practitioner-led studies, AI could add $15.7 trillion dollars to global gross domestic product by 2030 and facilitate the creation of between $3.5 trillion and $5.8 trillion in value annually, which would equate to between 1 and 9 percent of revenue in 2016 across various industries (PwC 2017).

Various government entities in the UAE oversee the implementation of AI into government processes and enhancing linkages to the private sector. The Minister of State for Artificial Intelligence manages the country's AI portfolio, while the Ministry of Cabinet Affairs and the Future also works closely on AI initiatives. The UAE Artificial Intelligence Strategy 2031—which aims to boost the country's gross domestic product by 35 percent, reduce government costs by 50 percent, and make the country 90 percent resistant to a financial crisis—guides the work of these federal ministries.

Dubai, perhaps more than any other emirate as well as its Gulf Arab neighbors, has identified AI as a central component of its tech-driven economic strategy to enhance government processes and develop a highly skilled private sector. The Dubai Future Foundation and Smart Dubai, a government entity charged with advancing the emirate's "smart" technological transformation, represent two government bodies involved in promoting AI technologies in the emirate. Smart Dubai runs an AI Lab in partnership with IBM to provide the tools and training for government and private-sector actors to implement AI services and applications.

This promotion of AI extends to emirate-level strategies like the Dubai Autonomous Transportation Strategy. Dubai's strategy seeks to transform 25 percent of the emirate's transportation to autonomous modes by 2030—equivalent to around five million daily trips and involving potentially savings of approximately $6 billion per year in transportation costs, according to Dubai Future Foundation (Dubai Future Foundation). Dubai's National Program for Artificial Intelligence hosted a major conference, Ai Everything, in the spring of 2019 under the patronage of Sheikh Mohammed bin Rashid, and the event has become an annual event with the goal of creating a global AI ecosystem.

In a similar vein to the attention afforded to AI, digital services and technology-enabled applications are being applied to traditional economic activities taking place across the country. These emerging economic domains are, according to some viewers, attempts to future-proof more established industries such as finance and banking, retail, and entertainment. The corresponding areas of the UAE's nascent digital economy—including but not limited to fintech, e-sports, and e-commerce—present government-backed growth areas for national citizens to secure employment opportunities. For example, the Abu Dhabi Global Market and its free zone authority are spearheading cryptocurrency policies and regulations, which have permitted a number of cryptocurrency exchanges to operate in a more transparent and responsible manner (Mogielnicki 2019). Dubai contains two e-commerce free zones, CommerCity and EZDubai, which serve to secure the emirate's position as a hub for global e-commerce. According to Bain & Company, annual growth in the e-commerce sectors of Gulf Cooperation Council states and Egypt stands at around 30 percent (Bain & Company). Moreover, the Dubai Free Zone Council is exploring the possibility of establishing a free zone dedicated to e-sports, and the emirate of Dubai has hosted high-profile e-sports competitions and exhibitions.

The UAE's urban hubs are poised to become *smarter cities* over the coming years, requiring even more cadres of skilled professionals to enhance the quality of residential and recreational spaces. Government-related entities such Smart Dubai or Dubai South are actively seeking to improve liability standards for residents—as well as enhancing the visitor experience—through a multitude of smart transformation initiatives. Increasing levels of interconnectivity between commercial, residential, and recreation realms in the UAE's smart cities will require stronger cyber security protocols and more professionals. Given the sensitivities surrounding cyber security, the UAE government will certainly want Emiratis to assume leadership roles within this rapidly expanding field.

1.3 Looking Ahead: Dubai Over the Next 50 Years

An accelerating digital economy and the incorporation of advanced technologies are codified into the UAE's longer-term plans, providing further justifications for restructuring labor market policies in this innovative manner. On January 4, 2019, the ruler of Dubai released his vision for the future of Dubai as part of a 50-year charter containing nine articles. The significance of this charter can be gleaned from the level of elite involvement: the ruler will "personally observe" progress on these articles and tasked Dubai's crown prince, Sheikh Hamdan bin Mohammed bin Rashid Al Maktoum, with the duty of overseeing the charter (Mohammed bin Rashid Al Maktoum). The document is broad in scope and light on implementation details—a pervasive feature of country visions, strategies, and other agendas in Gulf Arab states. Nevertheless, the charter frames Dubai's long-term economic trajectory largely in terms of digital advancement and technological progress.

Through this charter, Dubai's policymakers aspire to further develop the emirate's digital commercial infrastructure. Article three aims to establish a virtual commercial zone capable of hosting 100,000 companies. Part of this virtual commercial city program involves streamlined banking and immigration processes—two service areas wherein physical bureaucracy tends to limit the ease of doing business. The charter also mentions the new concept of e-residencies, which will require the creation and management of an entire digital community complete with the applications and services needed to meet the needs of community members.

Articles four and six focus on Dubai's educational portfolio—specifically the need for a strong commercial dimension to educational attainment. The charter notes:

> *We aim to develop a centralized education database for every citizen to document all the academic degrees obtained, classes and training taken, and conferences attended. It will help us design customized educational plans for our citizens that suit their personal skills. We aim to build an educational and learning system that explores and develops people's skills. Our goal for our citizens is to have a life-long learning so they can continue to improve their skills and capacities to adapt to the rapid global changes in the world.* (Mohammed bin Rashid Al Maktoum)

Like virtual commercial activities, the effectiveness of a centralized educational database depends on the strength of the associated and supporting digital infrastructure. This aspirational educational system simultaneously entails transforming public and private universities into free zones in order to "allow students to carry out business and creative activities, make these activities part of the education and graduation system, and shape integrated economic and creative zones around the universities" (Mohammed bin Rashid Al Maktoum). The objective of this educational strategy is to move beyond simply graduating students and toward generating new companies, employment prospects, and investment opportunities.

The charter likewise proposes smart government applications that would connect citizens—and presumably other legal residents—with global medical professionals. This proposed expansion of the emirate's healthcare accessibility and its consequent personalization for residents entails an enhancement of entail enhancing the healthcare capacity by boosting telemedicine and healthtech. Meanwhile, patients must be proficient users of new technologies and the appropriate cybersecurity safeguards need to be in place and maintained. The creation, implementation, user training, and maintenance of this future-oriented healthcare system demand a specialized skillset.

Article seven addresses the issue of sustainability-oriented technologies and aims to ensure that at least one tenth of citizens' homes are self-sufficient in terms of water, food, and energy. The Dubai Electricity and

Water Authority is responsible for installing solar panels on at least ten percent of Emirati homes, in addition to carrying out the Dubai Clean Energy Strategy 2050, which aims to produce 75 percent of Dubai's total power output from clean energy (Supreme Council of Energy). On the level of large-scale development projects, the Dubai government awarded a contract to China's Shanghai Power and Saudi Arabia's ACWA Power to build a 700-megawatt extension to the Mohammed bin Rashid Al Maktoum Solar Complex—making the Dubai-based solar complex the largest in the world.

1.4 Aligning Workforce Nationalization and Future Needs

There is a clear and recognizable desire to better align workforce nationalization policies with the future needs of labor markets in Gulf Arab states, given the particular trajectory of economic development in the region. Recommendations with strong analytical dimensions are necessary for building a bridge between theoretical ambitions and practical realities. The following list is UAE-centric and proposes suggested starting points rather than a definitive and complete policy prescription.

- **Identify economic policies and development strategies possessing parallel trajectories and seek ways to encourage alignment.** Labor market interventions and supporting technology-driven innovation reflect one such arena. Announcing new policies and strategies is easy, and there is no shortage of economic initiatives in the UAE. Advancing existing policies and encouraging pragmatic overlaps, however, are necessary for progress.
- **Redesign Emiratization policies around the digital and technology-oriented skills that government-related entities and private-sector firms need to remain competitive, profitable, and innovative.** The policymakers behind Emiratization cannot expect Emiratis to support innovation-led growth if they themselves are not innovative in their policy design approaches. Basing Emiratization on specific digital and technology-oriented skillsets would create a more balanced division of responsibilities between government and private-sector actors: The government must produce skilled entrants to the labor market before firms can hire these Emiratis.

- **Clearer inclusion in long-term government visions alongside concrete steps for implementation will give new Emiratization plans a higher likelihood of success.** Dubai's 50-year charter serves as one location wherein such plans might appear. Visions and other long-term planning documents with substantive content not only serve as a commitment device for governments but also provide important commercial roadmaps for firms and investors.
- **Skills related to financial technologies should function as a priority area for early implementation of any skills-based Emiratization policy approach.** Emiratization policies have long focused on the banking and finance industry, and the EIBFS is a ready-made training institute able to help advance newly adjusted policies. Cyber security is another high-priority area for Emiratization-related skills development, as there is strong demand across most commercial sectors as well as in residential and recreational spheres.

2 Concluding Remarks

In various domains of economic development and socioeconomic planning, the UAE government and emirate-level governments have demonstrated a willingness to think outside of the box. Yet their approach to workforce nationalization, though narrower in scope, nevertheless largely resembles that of their regional counterparts. The UAE government is committed to specific workforce nationalization initiatives but also enjoys greater flexibility than its regional counterparts to adapt Emiratization policies to meet the future needs of the country's economy.

Rather than continue to align workforce nationalization with specific industries and professions, Emirati policymakers should aspire to be more creative and associate Emiratization policies with digital and technology-oriented skills. If designed properly, this newly reengineered policy would encourage employers to attract Emirati jobseekers not based on nationality and quotas delineated by industries and professions but rather based on the skillsets needed to remain competitive and innovative.

This chapter reflects an initial, policy-oriented thought experiment wherein the recommendations beg for additional research rather than provide concrete conclusions. Addressing questions of applicability should be at the forefront of forthcoming analytical endeavors. Qatar, with its substantial sovereign wealth resources and manageable demographic constraints, presents a useful and comparative case study. It would be much more difficult for the remaining member states of the Gulf Cooperation Council to make major revisions to their workforce nationalization programs. Indeed, Omani protests emerged across several cities in May 2021, with the key grievance centering upon the persistent unemployment crisis in the country (Al Talei 2021).

The applicability of these initial recommendations listed in this paper also depends on consultation with private-sector actors and an adequate incorporation of their needs assessments into any adjusted workforce nationalization policy design. This preliminary research opted to focus on the region's public sector, given its traditional role in designing and implementing these policies as well as serving as the first mover in this sphere. However, any widespread gains in a technology-oriented Emiratization must ultimately resonate with private-sector concerns, issues, and objectives.

References

Al Maktoum, Mohammed bin Rashid. "The Fifty-Year Charter." https://www.mbrmajlis.ae/50-en/The%20Fifty-Year%20Charter.pdf.

Al Talei, Rafiah. "Oman's Protesters Seek Jobs and Reforms." The Arab Gulf States Institute in Washington. June 11, 2021. https://agsiw.org/omans-protesters-seek-jobs-and-reform/.

Bain & Company. E-commerce in MENA: Opportunity beyond the Hype. Published in 2019. https://www.bain.com/contentassets/2b078686303045ffa1d1207130ab5d79/bain_report__ecommerce_in_mena.pdf.

Central Intelligence Agency. "The World Factbook: People and Society." CIA. Accessed June 10, 2021. https://www.cia.gov/the-world-factbook/countries/united-arab-emirates/#people-and-society.

Elbahrawy, Farah. "Kuwait Asks Banks to Employ Citizens in Top Leadership Positions." Bloomberg. April 14, 2021. https://www.bloomberg.com/news/articles/2021-04-14/kuwait-asks-banks-to-employ-citizens-in-top-leadership-positions?sref=zEzFg8RN.

"EGA Finishes Year with Highest-Ever Rate of Emiratisation." Emirates New Agency. January 17, 2021. https://wam.ae/en/details/1395302901969.

Emirates Institute for Banking and Financial Studies. "About EIBFS." Accessed June 10, 2021. https://eibfs.ae/about-us/.

Dubai Future Foundation. "Dubai's Autonomous Transportation Strategy." Government of Dubai. Accessed June 7, 2021. https://www.dubaifuture.gov.ae/our-initiatives/dubais-autonomous-transportation-strategy/.

Government of the United Arab Emirates. Instagram. May 21, 2019. https://www.instagram.com/p/BxuJkSIDcbf/?utm_source=ig_embed.

McKinsey. Notes from the AI Frontier: Applications and the Value of Deep Learning. April 2018. https://www.mckinsey.com/featured-insights/artificial-intelligence/notes-from-the-ai-frontier-applications-and-value-of-deep-learning.

Mogielnicki, Robert. "Bahrain and Abu Dhabi Compete to be Gulf's Cryptocurrency Hub." Arab Gulf States Institute in Washington. August 14, 2019. https://agsiw.org/bahrain-and-abu-dhabi-compete-to-be-gulfs-cryptocurrency-hub/.

Mogielnicki, Robert. "The United Arab Emirates' Post-COVID-19 Outlook." Journal of International Affairs. March 30, 2021. https://jia.sipa.columbia.edu/online-articles/united-arab-emirates%E2%80%99-post-covid-19-outlook.

Nasrallah, Tawfiq. "UAE Projects of the 50: New Schemes Announced in Abu Dhabi, Plan to Get 75,000 Emiratis into Private Sector." Gulf News. September 12, 2021. https://gulfnews.com/uae/government/uae-projects-of-the-50-new-schemes-announced-in-abu-dhabi-plan-to-get-75000-emiratis-into-private-sector-1.1631418816885.

Ndichu, David. "Microsoft to Upskill UAE Nationals in New Emiratisation Initiative." Gulf Business. September 27, 2020. https://gulfbusiness.com/microsoft-to-upskill-uae-nationals-in-new-emiratisation-initiative/.

"Oman Extends Omanisation by Giving Locals Higher Education Jobs." Yahoo! Finance. February 14, 2021. https://finance.yahoo.com/news/oman-extends-omanisation-giving-locals-173932558.html.

"Only Saudis Can Work in Malls as Local Hiring Drive Accelerates." Arab News. April 8, 2021. https://www.arabnews.com/node/1839156/business-economy.

PwC. Sizing the Prize. PwC, 2017. Accessed May 20, 2019. https://www.pwc.com/gx/en/issues/data-and-analytics/publications/artificial-intelligence-study.html.

Reynolds, Rory. "UAE to Create 20,000 New Jobs for Emiratis," The National, September 29, 2019, https://www.thenationalnews.com/uae/government/uae-to-create-20-000-new-jobs-for-emiratis-1.916607.

Rizvi, Sarah. "IBM Wins UAE Emiratisation Award by MOHRE." ITP. March 17, 2020. https://www.itp.net/channel/90778/90778-ibm-wins-uae-emiratisation-award-by-mohre.

Supreme Council of Energy. "The 50-Year Charter—A Plan for the Happiness and Prosperity of Dubai's Citizens." Government of Dubai. April 7, 2019. https://www.dubaisce.gov.ae/en/press-room/press-and-news/latest-news/2019/04/the-50-year-charter.

Telecommunications and Digital Government Regulatory Authority. "Digital Economy." TDRA. Accessed June 10, 2021. https://u.ae/en/about-the-uae/economy/digital-economy.
"UAE Government Equips National Service Programme Participants with Entrepreneurship, Digital Economy Skills." Emirates News Agency. April 4, 2021, https://wam.ae/en/details/1395302924049.
United Arab Emirates Ministry of Human Resources & Emiratization. "Laws & Regulations: Emiratization Laws." UAE. Accessed June 10, 2021. https://www.mohre.gov.ae/en/laws-legislation/emiratisation-laws.aspx.

CHAPTER 11

Human Capital and Health Education Among Menopausal Emirati Women in Dubai: Implications and Recommendations

Linda Smail

1 Introduction

The United Arab Emirates (UAE) is an example of a rapid and successful developing country in the Gulf region not only in terms of economic terms but also in the progress of its people. Emirati women nowadays constitute a vital part of the nation's workforce and actively contribute to the country's development as they are above 37% of the national labor force. Therefore, in 2015, the UAE government launched the National

L. Smail (✉)
College of Interdisciplinary Studies, Zayed University, Dubai, United Arab Emirates
e-mail: linda.smail@zu.ac.ae

A. Mishrif et al. (eds.), *Nationalization of Gulf Labour Markets*, The Political Economy of the Middle East,
https://doi.org/10.1007/978-981-19-8072-5_11

Strategy for Empowerment of Emirati Women intending to provide a decent living for women and make them motivated and productive in all sustainable and developmental fields. In 2017, the UAE government allocated 8.6% of the federal budget to the health sector (Ministry of Education 2017). Educational programs such as the Physical and Health Education Curriculum (offered in all governmental schools from kindergarten to grade 12) cover topics such as fitness testing and knowledge, diet and nutrition, and psychology to promote personal and social responsibility. In this curriculum, students learn to compute their body mass index and how to keep a healthy lifestyle which will have, in the future, a positive impact on the economy by not only having healthier youth and adults but also reducing health-care costs.

One of the main pillars of the UAE National strategy is to guarantee that all women have access to sexual and reproductive health, and also provide them with health care and educational services that will improve their psychological and physiological health (Women—The Official Portal of the UAE Government 2022). In addition, the UAE's Strategy for the Fourth Industrial Revolution (IR4.0) emphasizes fields such as innovative education and robotic health care. The adoption of robotic health care and artificial intelligence will facilitate the use of telehealth resources and will introduce cutting-edge medical solutions. This strategy will, for sure, open great opportunities in health education services that will enable increased awareness of the various policies as well as issues concerning women's health. Furthermore, health technology solutions are considered the backbone of all health systems and vital tools to address health inequalities (Diño and Ong 2019). However, due to culture, health issues are still considered personal, and thus the need to increase awareness through health education. In fact, health problems are no longer personal matters, because they are linked to the responsibilities of the government, health providers, and productivity at work (Karkoti 2020).

Most Arab women stay away and no longer play their role within their families or society after menopause as if the occurrence of this period is a handicap. Arab women do not try to understand this phase of hormonal change, nor do they adapt and continue to be productive because they consider this period as the "desperate age" as they are no longer fertile (Murphy et al. 2013).

The COVID-19 pandemic has aggravated the situation as it has not only impacted the medical and social aspects, but also the reproductive health of women around the globe.

Women, during the lockdown, did not take care of themselves because, in addition to working from home, they took care of children and their online education.

Despite the end of the lockdown and the availability of vaccines, a lot of women haven't rejoined the workforce and may not anytime soon (Hsu 2021). This has an impact on the IR4.0 strategy toward increasing the number of women in the workforce. Indeed, economists have labeled the impact COVID-19 is having on women in work as a "she-cession" (Alon et al. 2020).

Since the COVID-19 pandemic outbreak, countries turned their efforts toward not only providing health care to their populations but also educating them about continuing their normal life and daily tasks despite the pandemic (Cochrane and Stretton 2022). Indeed, the COVID-19 pandemic showed the world the necessity of health education at all levels. The introduction of new procedures in handling these health-care issues is intended at providing new and unique ways of solving women's health-care issues. Health-care education and awareness among women is vital in eliminating embarrassment or any other form of humiliation women undergo through. The use of qualified health-care workers, which showed its importance since the pandemic, is also needed as it will help deal with embarrassing setbacks and in the long term, lead to increased work productivity.

The UAE Strategy for the Fourth Industrial Revolution should aim at totally improving the services and activities provided to women under the public health-care program. Inclusive health-care provision for women primarily requires a huge focus on need, appropriateness, and effectiveness. The UAE is yet to fully adopt a functional and effective public health-care program dealing with sexual and reproductive health in women (Ministry of Education 2017). The moral and ethical grounds touching on reproductive health, particularly menopause health significantly affect women's psychological health which further affects the human capital output.

The introduction of formal legal entitlements is necessary for the sole purpose of eradicating some of the customary barriers women in the UAE have been undergoing through. A key fundamental role in any health-care system is providing planned training aimed at protecting and improving individual, family, and societal health. Eradicating negative health behaviors in society is a key milestone in solving women's health-care issues.

Health-care service providers must undergo proper training to ensure their success (Slaven and Lee 1997).

The training of health-care workers should be comprehensive dealing with patient training and educational services, especially regarding sexual and reproductive health matters. Accessibility to information and consultation is generally one of the most crucial areas concerning women's health-care issues particularly, the menopause health system.

Patient responsibility and self-care should be reduced to the least minimum levels (Memon et al. 2014). Education in dealing with reproductive and health care among women should be made very accessible to all women in society. The Government's National Strategy for Empowerment of the Emirati Women should put in place laws and regulations that are geared toward the provision of efficient and quality health care (Murphy et al. 2013). The training of health-care providers should mainly focus on offering scientific and systematic training to its health-care workers. It is important for the government to also integrate its health-care system to easily meet all women's health-care matters.

Government training of health-care workers needs to take into consideration, the evaluation of individuals' needs for training, the benefits of this training, and planning. This is very necessary as it helps in evaluating a patient's needs. Patient training, on the other hand, should also be both illness-centered and patient-centered (Bleakley 2010). This ensures that patients provide their real experience of the actual situation affecting them. The effective learning process may be hindered in situations where a patient is not provided with an opportunity to explain her feelings. Training is more active if the patient is granted an opportunity to explain their feelings. The key area of focus in sexual and reproductive health among women needs to focus on patient training and empowering nurse–patient interaction. The life quality of the patient is also an integral part of part training. The main objective of treatment is the care of the patient.

Providing a quality life for all women respective of their social status should be the government's key area of focus. Health-care training offered to patients should specifically focus on different health-care needs. Information sharing to the patient, family, and society on health, illness, pregnancy, aging, menopause, treatment, and lifestyle is key to improving women's psychological health (Memon et al. 2014). Additionally, the health-care providers must also make sure treatment information is clearly explained and learned. Health-care officials are also tasked with the responsibility of evaluating patient progress to allow the setting up of health-care objectives and training methods. A therapeutic approach and information sharing between patients and health-care providers are also necessary for preventing and improving patients' illnesses. The use of monitoring technology is also encouraged as it helps in improving patient recovery in a quality manner. Training, self-monitoring, and psycho-social interventions are crucial in improving the life quality of patients (Cochrane and Stretton 2022).

1.1 Menopausal Emirati Women and Health Education

Health is a kind of human capital as well as an input to producing other forms of human capital (Bleakley 2010). Being unhealthy depresses the ability to work productively and/or the ability and incentives to invest in human capital. Consequently, health education is a major key that is designed to help women and communities, in general, improve their health, by increasing their knowledge or influencing their attitudes.

According to CIPD (Gifford et al. 2021), 60% of menopausal women admit that menopause symptoms affect their work negatively and prevent them from performing well and reaching their full potential. In addition to the physical symptoms, the psychological symptoms can also affect relationships in the workplace. Women going through menopause usually pause or even completely stop their careers when they go through menopause, which has a negative effect on human capital.

Nowadays a lot of companies and governments take into consideration the negative effects that are reflected on their production such as low productivity, absenteeism, and early retirement, as a consequence of the declining health conditions of their employees by either weight gain, diabetes, or menopause (Karkoti 2020; Hardy et al. 2018; Gifford et al. 2021). In fact, the lack of understanding can make women workers feel ashamed and embarrassed at work, but it also costs their companies. A research based on more than 100 papers on menopause found that companies were largely affected in terms of hiring and training costs to find replacement employees if a woman had to leave work permanently, and productivity losses if women's symptoms were disruptive (Brewis et al. 2017).

Health Education is any combination of learning experiences designed to help the general public improve their health, by increasing their knowledge and influencing their attitudes. For this reason, investments in women's health education by increasing health awareness through better access to information and a willingness to change destructive practices is the key factor in empowering women. UAE's IR4.0 strategy is aimed at providing the right medical solutions by amicably addressing women's health-care matters. According to Plan International, women's access to sexual and reproductive health care will go a long way in educating women about their health-care issues individually and at the society level in general. Documenting the extent of health education, particularly on menopause management is a key issue in improving women's participation and performance in any workforce.

Health education is key in empowering women and eliminating embarrassment or any other form of humiliation women undergo through. The use of qualified health-care workers will help deal with embarrassing setbacks and in the long term, lead to increased work productivity (Karkoti 2020). UAE Strategy for the IR4.0 should aim at totally improving the services and activities provided to women under the public health-care program. Inclusive health-care provision for women primarily requires a huge focus on need, appropriateness, and effectiveness. UAE is yet to fully adopt a functional and effective public health-care program dealing with sexual and reproductive health in women (Ministry of Education 2017). The moral and ethical grounds touching on reproductive health, particularly menopause health significantly affect women's psychological health which further affects the human capital output.

It is suggested, based on scientific research using available data from most countries, that health education is one of the important factors that can contribute to the continuing development of societies (Diño and Ong 2019). In particular, the education of young women makes a big difference, in fact, women empowered through health education are in a better position to improve their health and that of their children and other family members (Lutz 2011).

Emirati women participate actively in both the public and private sectors in various roles, they hold two-thirds of the public job market (Women—The Official Portal of the UAE Government 2022). They have equal rights to economic resources and job opportunities, as indicated by the UAE Laws. However, there are challenges and needs of Emirati women in health that are not fully addressed due to the UAE's unique culture and also the fact that the UAE is considered a conservative Islamic society.

Menopause, which is a normal mid-life transition for women, remains inadequately understood and is looked upon differently in various cultures; the Arabic phrase for the menopause phase is "desperate age" because it is considered the end of women's lives as they are no longer reproductive which is the main concern and not the bothersome symptoms or the associated risks that come along with these factors. This is partly due to the lack of education and knowledge of the symptoms during menopause and partly due to the impact imposed by the family and spouse regarding fertility.

With emerging changes in women's education in the UAE, it can be expected that there will be more opportunities for women in the human capital, therefore, educating women about menopause, its symptoms management, and the use of menopausal hormone replacement therapy (HRT) may serve as an important step toward improving women's performance and participation in the workforce. This important task can only be achievable through health-care education.

Based on 2019 UAE Statistics (Dubai Statistics Center 2019), the reported life expectancy in different age groups for Emirati women living in Dubai is above 80 years at birth and above 35 years at 50–54 years. Based on these life expectancies, women are expected to live at least one-third of their lives beyond menopause and will be working during their menopausal transition more than ever before which will have huge implications on the health system.

Many studies have been conducted worldwide regarding menopausal women. Among others (Memon et al. 2014; Donati et al. 2009; Özdemir and Çöl 2004), have explored women's knowledge and attitudes toward menopause and HRT. Unfortunately, interest in the topic in the Arabic world is very limited (Bakarman and Abu Ahmed 2003; Loutfy et al. 2006; Mustafa and Sabir 2012; Erbil 2018). Most of the studies in the Arabic world indicated a lack of women's knowledge and negative attitudes toward menopause. It is important to note that most of the studies in the Gulf region included women from all nationalities living within the country.

Menopause is universal, but attitudes regarding menopause vary by culture (Blount 2021). The diversity of the attitudes toward menopause determines how women describe menopause in addition to how they interpret its effects on their lives. In multigenerational societies, menopause is associated with a bad experience of symptoms such as hot flashes, night sweats, and weight gain, while it is experienced better than expected by women in countries like Sweden, Denmark, and Italy (Slaven and Lee 1997). In the Arab world, menopause is not associated with symptoms or women's experiences, but it is directly associated with the end of fertility.

The UAE government needs to invest more in women's health-care matters (Al-Jenaibi 2015). Physical and Health Education is a great milestone in ensuring women get the necessary support they require, however, more topics related to women's health should be added and taught to both boys and girls as it will help in reducing the embarrassment and fear young girls endure during their menstruation or when faced with any reproductive health issue. The learning integration for all genders is key in lowering what has long been viewed as taboo because society had for a long time avoided openly discussing women's health-care matters such as menstruation. This will give the young women the necessary emotional stability, moral courage, and unlimited social interactions (Al-Jenaibi 2015). The government's efforts to educate women publicly on their health issues are a great milestone and should be supported unswervingly. This will help the population to attain higher levels of knowledge generally and encourage women to stay longer in the workforce.

1.2 Research Scope and Study Objectives

Very few studies have been published in the UAE that surveyed women's knowledge and attitudes toward menopause and HRT in the UAE (Hamid et al. 2014; Ibrahim and Hussein 2016). The studies took place in the Emirate of Abu Dhabi and Sharjah with women from different nationalities. The results of the studies indicate that women's knowledge about menopause was very low and varied significantly with the level of education and nationality. To our knowledge, no studies have been conducted in the Emirate of Dubai.

This study explores the Emirati women's knowledge and attitudes toward menopause, its symptoms, risks, and the HRT knowledge, it also highlights the importance of educating women about menopause. The study results will enable the delivery of better health education, the increasing awareness of health issues which enables health-care policymakers to create and formulate a health-care policy that further increases awareness and has the potential to enhance menopausal women's quality of life and therefore reach their full potential at work.

The study will also benefit companies to support menopausal women as this will increase women's productivity and lower absences and employee turnover, which will help build the human capital of both genders.

We would like through this study to have a closer look at Emirati women's health, which represents an important human capital for the country, and to give some suggestions to the government to implement awareness programs for women and provide them with support to be fully integrated into the industry (IR4.0).

2 Method

The study was conducted among Emirati women from the Emirate of Dubai. The study participants were recruited from five primary healthcare (PHC) centers in Dubai selected randomly from the 25 health centers approved by the Dubai health authority (Dubai Health Authority, n.d.). A random sample of 497 Emirati women aged 30–64 years were enrolled in the study via a multistage stratified and clustered random sampling technique. The first stage was a clustered random sample where five health centers were chosen, while the second stage was a simple random sample from each of the five chosen health centers.

The instrument used in the study was a structured questionnaire that included two major sections after the socio-demographic variables that included the variables: age, level of education, marital, employment, and smoking status.

The second section contained the Menopause Knowledge Scale (MKS), the menopause symptoms knowledge, and HRT practice developed by Appling and colleagues (Appling et al. 2000). The MKS has eight items regarding knowledge of menopause and its health risks and six items regarding HRT knowledge.

The third section was the Attitude Menopause Scale (ATM) developed by Neugarten (Neugarten et al. 1963). ATM includes 34 items specific to attitudes toward menopause. Responses were constructed in terms of what a woman, in general, thinks about menopause. Participants were asked to indicate the degree to which they agree with each item on a 4-point Likert scale ranging from strongly agree to strongly disagree.

The collected data were coded and analyzed using the Statistical package SPSS version 25. Descriptive statistics were computed to describe all items of the questionnaire. One-way Analysis of Variance (ANOVA) and/or the independent-sample t-test will be carried out to test the equality of population means across the categories of each independent variable. Statistical tests with p-values < 0.05 were considered statistically significant.

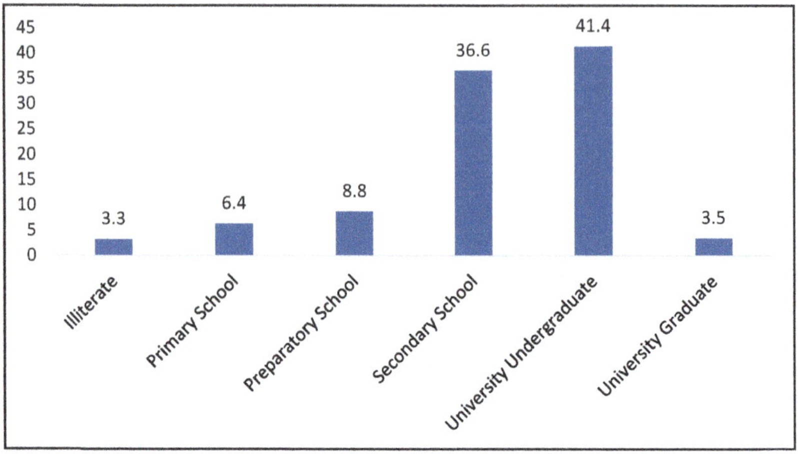

Fig. 1 Women by education level

3 Results and Discussion

3.1 Socio-demographic Data

The mean age of women in this study was 42 years (± 8.7 years). Most of the participants (95%) never used HRT, 96.4% were non-smokers, and 74.3% of them were married.

Over third (36.6%) of the women had completed high school while 41.4% had graduated from university (Fig. 1). Moreover, 44.6% were employed.

The percentage of women who never used oral contraceptive pills (OCP) was 64%, while 32.9% used it in the past. In addition, about two-thirds of the women declared having good health, 32.8% declared having a very good health, 9.7% said their health is not that good, while only 2 women (0.4%) said they have bad health conditions.

3.2 Knowledge About Menopause and HRT

An important part of the study is to check Emirati women's knowledge about menopause.

As it can be seen from Table 1, the majority (81.3%) of women agreed with the fact that menopause is a natural transition in women's lives, while about 9% didn't know anything about menopause. Interestingly, only 8% of the women rated their knowledge about menopause to be very good, while about a quarter (24.5%) declared having little knowledge. Surprisingly, 72.8% of the women admitted to not being aware of any available treatment for menopausal symptoms.

Regarding the source of information about menopause as declared by Emirati women (Fig. 2), the highest percentage was from media (26.6%), followed by family members (25.6%), then doctors 21.1%. This is a small percentage and may be an indication of the weak role played by doctors in this region. The least common source of information was from schools or universities (6.2%) which indicates that there is a gap in this aspect in regards to giving women's information for menopause and HRT. It may explain why 84% of Emirati women said that there is a need for health education about menopause and HRT in schools and universities curriculum.

Table 2 shows the knowledge of women about menopausal hormone replacement therapy (HRT) practices. Over half of the participants, 53.5%, viewed HRT positively. However, out of the 497 women, only 25 were using HRT, 5 of them had prescriptions from a general physician and only 20 women got their prescriptions from a specialist. Moreover,

Table 1 Knowledge of Menopause

Variable	*Level*	*N*	*%*
What do you think of menopause?	It is a natural transition in a woman's life	404	81.3
	It is a medical problem that should be treated as such	49	9.9
	I Don't know	44	8.9
How do you view menopause?	Positively	327	65.8
	Negatively	131	26.4
	Other	39	7.8
How would you rate your knowledge about menopause?	Very Good	40	8
	Good	199	40
	Fair	136	27.4
	Little knowledge	122	24.5
Are you aware of any treatment available for menopausal symptoms?	Yes	135	27.2
	No	361	72.8
	I don't know	1	0.2

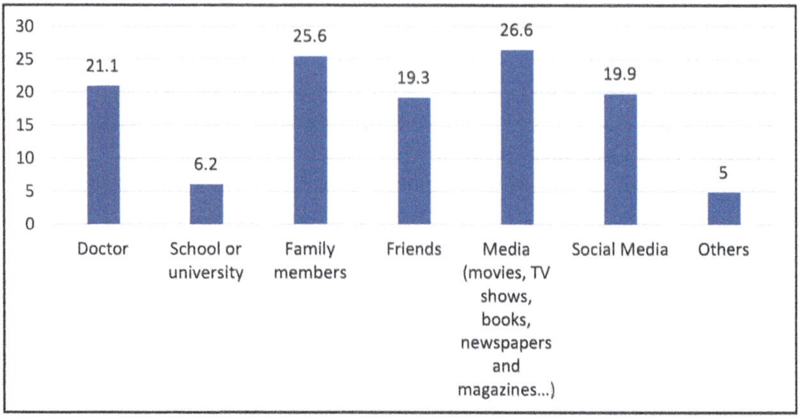

Fig. 2 Source of information about menopause

Table 2 Knowledge and HRT practice

Variable	*Level*	*N*	*%*
Do you think it is necessary to treat menopausal symptoms?	Yes	233	46.9
	No	137	27.6
	Don't know	127	25.6
What are your current views regarding hormone therapy for menopause?	Positive	266	53.5
	Negative	172	34.6
	Don't know	59	11.9
Have you ever used HRT?	Yes	25	5
	No	472	95
Who did prescribe it for you?	General Physician	5	11.2
	Specialist	20	84.8

40.5% of the women declared that their doctors discussed the benefits and risks of HRT with them.

It is important to note that 95% of the Emirati women never used HRT and therefore were not knowledgeable of its benefits and risks, which explains the low knowledge percentage about HRT and related heart diseases. This is similar to what was found in Egypt (Loutfy et al. 2006), where 91% of the women had never heard of HRT.

The menopause symptoms that were acknowledged by more than half of the participants were: hot flash (55.1%), depression (67.4%), mood swings (72.6%), insomnia (56.9%), tiredness (55.1%), weight gain (51.1%), and irritability (61%). About 46% were not aware of vaginal dryness as a symptom of menopause, and 45.5% did not know about the symptom of leak of urine when coughing, sneezing, or laughing (Fig. 3).

These last two high percentages may be explained by the fact that issues related to sexual and reproductive health are usually not taught in schools or addressed by physicians or discussed by family members because of the Islamic religion and the culture as well.

The knowledge of the participants about menopause and HRT and their associated health risks were also low. The fact that the risk of cardiovascular diseases increases with menopause was only known by 23.1% (Fig. 4) and the fact that HRT can increase the risk of heart disease was agreed by only 18.5% (Fig. 5). It is important to note that most women who knew about menopause symptoms are based on their own experience rather than education.

However, 83.3% of women knew that pregnancy cannot occur after menopause, while 79.3% agreed with the fact that menopause occurs

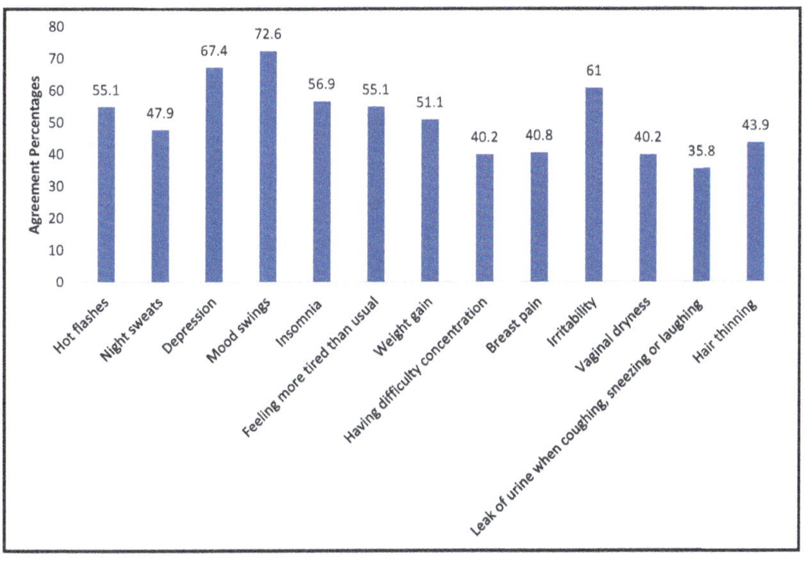

Fig. 3 The percentages of women who knew about menopause symptoms

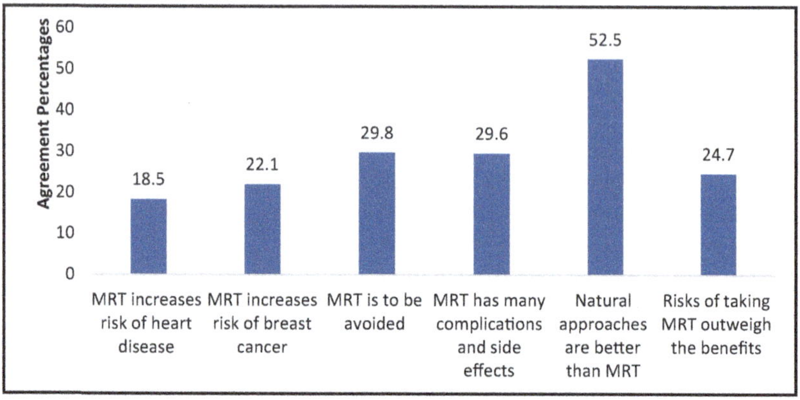

Fig. 4 The percentages of women who knew about HRT risks

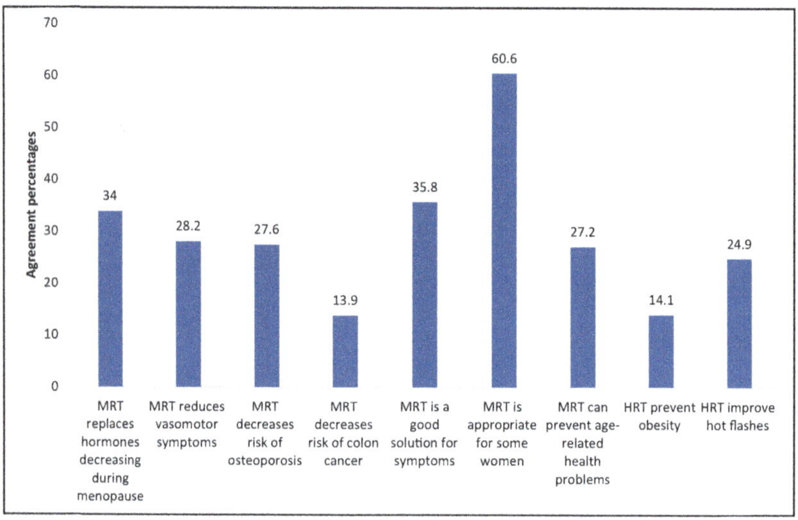

Fig. 5 The percentages of women who knew about HRT benefits

when menstruations stop. Only 40.1% of the women agreed with the statement that menopause can have harmful consequences if not treated.

Only 22.1% of women know that HRT can increase the risk of breast cancer and only 13.9% knew that HRT can decrease the risk of colon cancer. Furthermore, only 27.6% of women were aware that HRT can decrease the risk of osteoporosis. Moreover, 27.2% answered that HRT is good for preventing age-related health problems.

The mean knowledge percentage of menopause and HRT was 40.6% with a standard deviation of 20.7%, this is an indication of a low level of knowledge about menopause and HRT, especially about associated heart diseases.

Using one-way Analysis of Variance (ANOVA) and the independent-sample *t*-test we found significant differences in the mean knowledge percentages among the different categories of education level and employment. Post-hoc analysis results indicated that the mean knowledge percentage for the university undergraduate and graduate were significantly different from the illiterate, primary school, preparatory school, and secondary school groups, respectively. In other words, the higher the education level, the higher the women's knowledge about menopause.

In addition to the low level of knowledge about menopause and the association with education level and employment, the major source of information used by Emirati women is not to be trusted as friends and family members may not have the right knowledge. Moreover, what can be found online and on social media is not always a trusted source of information. Therefore, there is a need to grab more attention to the role of doctors, nurses, and health-care specialists in raising awareness among Emirati women through education and awareness programs about menopause, its challenges to productivity, and also the possible treatment options for a better quality of life.

3.3 *Attitude Toward Menopause*

The results of the Attitude Menopause Scale (ATM) indicate a mean attitude score of 2.42 with an S.D. of 0.26. The lowest score is 1 representing a very negative attitude and the highest is 4 representing a very positive attitude, this indicates a neutral attitude toward menopause among Emirati women. The range of the percentage of agreement for all ATM items was 68.4%, with an average of 55.8% (with a minimum of 21.6% and a maximum of 90%).

With the positive items of the attitude toward menopause, 75.3% agreed with the fact that a good thing about menopause is that a woman can quit worrying about getting pregnant. The minimum percentage of agreements was 21.6% for women who admitted that after menopause, they are more interested in sex than they were before. Again, this may be explained by the culture, as talking about sex life is considered taboo in this Islamic society.

While with the negative items, 90% of women thought that menopause is one of the biggest changes that happen in their lives. The lowest percentage of agreements was 30% which was associated with an agreement with the statement that a woman in menopause is apt to do crazy things she does not understand. Surprisingly, 69.6% of women agreed with the statement "in truth, just about every woman is depressed about menopause."

Using one-way Analysis of Variance (ANOVA) and the independent-sample t-test with the average attitudes score, we found that there were no statistically significant differences in the average attitudes score for educational level and marital status. Statistically, a significant difference was found in the average attitudes score for employment, employed women have better attitudes toward menopause than non-employed women.

Women in different cultures have different experiences and attitudes toward menopause. Some factors may affect beliefs and attitudes such as social background, education, and profession (Memon et al. 2014; Ayranci et al. 2010). In Western societies, where importance is given to women's physical appearance, youth, and also to their reproductive capacity, negative attitudes toward menopause can be observed among women in these societies.

Reporting symptoms by Emirati women was low and this is probably due to the culture which is similar to other women as it was established by a lot of studies around the world (Memon et al. 2014; Donati et al. 2009; Özdemir & Çöl 2004). Moreover, evidence from research indicates that negative impacts of menopause symptoms on economic participation include but are not limited to lower productivity, reduced job satisfaction, and problems with time management (Sarrel 2012; Al-Jenaibi 2015). There were studies about women not being able to look for a job, reducing their working hours, recognizing the negative effects of menopause on their careers, or leaving or losing their jobs due to menopause (Brewis et al. 2017).

There has been an increase in the number of Emirati women living in the Emirate of Dubai who have a university degree or even a higher education in different fields and who are looking for positions especially after their kids are grown up and they decide to come back to the labor market (Nusche 2008). Human capital is a key driver of economic growth, however, the low level of knowledge about menopause and its symptoms is limiting the Emirati women's options for the work they opt for especially if they do not have the needed support during their mid-life phase. Therefore, as in most industrialized countries, health-care education should also become a driver of economic growth (Lutz 2011).

The health education in the UAE does not cover all health issues, in fact, only in 2017, the ministry of education launched the Physical and Health Education Curriculum across all governmental schools (Ministry of Education 2017) with the objective to provide the young Emirati students with the necessary physical education to take care of their health and well-being, however, health education at this stage is more about physical education and is not gender-based health education.

Research showed that health education programs addressing menopause and its symptoms have a positive effect on women's knowledge and attitudes (Orabi 2017). Therefore, menopause should be considered a public health matter and should be dealt with as any major health issue like obesity and diabetes. Health-care education has an important role in enhancing women's health of all ages and education levels, therefore it should be integrated within both the education and health-care systems.

The health education initiative, introduced by the UAE government, should be conducted by qualified health-care workers to ensure its success. It will help in overcoming a long-term health awareness issue that has been present in society caused by the neglect of issues surrounding women's health. The IR4.0 can have a huge impact in improving health education through telemedicine and even mobile health.

The e-health in the UAE is still in the first stages of development. It includes a variety of tools and systems, mobile or internet based, such as prescriptions, patient monitoring, medical records, and medical bills systems.

Telemedicine was the first e-health service to be launched in March 2020 just before the COVID-19 lockdown. It was very beneficial for patients, especially those with chronic diseases who were able to consult their doctors, have a second opinion, and get their medications delivered to their homes without leaving their sofas. It is now used to also monitor elderly and at-risk COVID-19 patients at home. The UAE is working constantly of adding further remote health-care services to its health-care system.

Mobile health or what is called m-health is booming even more now in the UAE due to the IT advancement and great telecommunication infrastructure in the country. M-health is very handy for providing health education and awareness to the public and also training programs to health-care workers. More m-health services and tools need to be added to address more public health issues such as smoking, obesity, and menopause as it is done for diabetes where mobile phones are nowadays used to monitor patient's insulin requirements and provide real-time follow-up.

In 2020, the UK started for the first-time teaching about menopause in secondary schools as part of their new program Relationships and Sex Education (*Relationships and Sex Education (RSE) (Secondary)* 2021). The curriculum will help students to acquire the knowledge that will help them to make informed decisions about their well-being, health, and relationships, to prepare them for better adult life.

Teaching about menopause to young women will give them a great opportunity to learn about menopause, why and when it happens, and its symptoms, and therefore prepare them better for the transition. Moreover, the students will grow up to be a better understanding of general physicians, doctors, and health-care practitioners to other women. Furthermore, educating males will result in raising their understanding of the menopause transition not only as husbands but also as coworkers and managers. This will be the first step in raising awareness about menopause among not only females but both genders. It will also open doors for discussions between daughters and mothers or other women from the family entourage. Adding menopause to the schools' curriculum indicates that UK society attitudes changed and that solutions are being looked for and applied to improve their human capital.

Recently, the UAE started a collaboration with the UK which is one of the leaders in digital health innovation with a lot of tools and solutions that were tested on a large scale (Chaudhury 2021). This collaboration will bring the latest health services to the UAE like the "My Way Digital Health" application to help diabetes patients self-manage their symptoms, and breast cancer diagnosis using AI, and more valuable tools to support decision-making based on data.

One example of the collaboration between the UAE and the UK, that will have a huge impact on women in the UAE, is the Middle East's first digital health library. This will allow access to a range of applications to help customers personally manage their health issues, whether it is to stop smoking or to help reduce obesity, manage issues such as chronic back pain, family planning, and why not to learn about menopause. The access to this information will empower women to take an important role in their health and become better equipped with knowledge that will change their attitudes and improve their productivity.

The use of digital health will be a great opportunity for the UAE to achieve its agenda of transforming its health-care system and improving women's quality of life and therefore strengthen its human capital.

4 Conclusion and Recommendations

The change in women's lives through menopause is an important phase that is associated with physical and psychological symptoms but also has an impact on their quality of life and productivity. The results of this study contributed to the evaluation and understanding of the current knowledge and attitudes of the Emirati women toward menopause that were associated with only education level and employment status.

The study highlighted the fact that Emirati women's knowledge about menopause and HRT-associated health risks are very low, therefore there is a need to improve women's knowledge, so they can cope with the symptoms which will improve their quality of life and therefore stay productive and participate effectively in the workforce.

To the best of our knowledge, there is no health-care policy regarding menopausal women's health-related issues in UAE. Hence, the study findings will enable health-care policymakers to create and formulate a health-care policy that enhances menopausal women's quality of life. It is important to provide proper support to women at this phase of their lives, support could be professional, familial, among colleagues, or even as part of a bigger group including online support groups of women who also went through the same phase. But it is important to make sure that the support is reinforced by experts and specialists in the field.

Hopefully, the study results and recommendations will raise the awareness of women and the general public about menopause by taking a set of measurements such as initiating a UAE Menopause Day to promote awareness about the typical symptoms, running wide educational campaigns about menopause and HRT risks and benefits, and also introducing health education in the curriculum of Emirati schools similar to what was done about obesity. Breaking through the silence by talking about menopause can make a big difference in improving women's quality of life and therefore improve their work performance. In most workplaces women don't get the support needed during this transition of their lives as it is still considered a taboo and personal matter.

Emirati women should be educated and made aware of the importance of medical care and consultancy, in fact, it is important that Emirati women understand that detaching from some of the cultural restraints may be indispensable to have the most suitable health care that will improve the quality of their lives and therefore their productivity.

The fast pace of transformation driven by IR4.0 is pushing countries to update their education systems to be aligned with the needs of industry and economy. Inclusive health-care establishment for women chiefly involves a huge focus on necessity, suitability, and efficiency. UAE is yet to fully accept a practical and operative public health-care program dealing with sexual and reproductive-related issues. In fact, the IR4.0 can have a big impact on health through telemedicine and mobile health applications. Telemedicine can be very valuable not only in monitoring and treating patients remotely, but also in providing health education, guidance, and support to women going through menopause.

The IR4.0 has the potential to place health education at the heart of the health system as it responds to the UAE's vision of being the leader in health-care services. It is recommended that the UAE government puts more emphasis on investing in the digitalized health-care system, especially on women's health-care issues. By doing this, it will increase educational awareness on addressing issues that are concerned with any reproductive health issue. Digitalization will allow health-care providers in serving better with faster and high-quality services, awareness programs, and education-based knowledge, to women in general and those going through menopause specifically.

The UAE government is encouraging women to be part of the IR4.0 by joining the workforce not only in the public sector but also in the private sector, however, Emirati women are also expected to keep fertility rates high, therefore, the government should propose more flexible and favorable laws to ensure women can do so. It is a fact that most private employers refuse to hire women because of the extra needed benefits like maternity leaves, as a consequence, the private sector hires more Emirati males than females to fill the required 15 percent of their workforce with Emirati staff as required by the Ministry of Labor laws.

Employers should take part in the efforts undertaken by the UAE government for the inclusion of women in the workforce by adopting a new organizational culture, diverse training, specialist advisors, personalized absence rules, and more flexible working hours for menopausal women. This will benefit the employer in removing barriers to advancement for women and therefore reduce the gender gap. Furthermore, by supporting women during their menopause, employers will benefit from all skills and talents that all employees, men, and women, of all ages, have to offer to their companies.

Another recommendation from the study is related to education and especially health education. In fact, as jobs in the education sector are on the top list of employment sectors in the UAE, it is important to take advantage of this and direct young Emiratis toward health education. By doing so, we not only educate young Emirati girls but also we educate their families and relatives, we also increase the proportion of women working in health-care education and therefore help their own people. Emirati women will be more comfortable visiting Emirati women doctors or nurses and talking about their health issues.

Women have issues in looking for a suitable job and reduce their working hours to cope with their symptoms. They often feel that their careers are in danger, leave work, or lose it because of the menopause transition period. Companies should be aware of the women's dilemma and review their HR policies and regulations to implement reasonable adjustments, involve managers to support their employees, and break through this taboo by offering support. By having implemented policies regarding the support to women through menopause and open communication about the menopause issue among all employees, companies can be sure that they are able to attract and retain qualified female employees and therefore develop their human capital for a better future.

References

Al-Jenaibi, B. (2015). The Needs and Priorities of Women in the UAE: Identifying Struggles and Enhancing Satisfaction of Employment, Education, Health Care, and Rights. *Contemporary Review of the Middle East*, 2(3), 238–268. https://doi.org/10.1177/2347798915601590.

Alon, T., Doepke, M., Olmstead-Rumsey, J., & Tertilt, M. (2020, September 28). *Shecession: COVID-19 Is Affecting Women's Employment Status Worse Than Men*. World Economic Forum. https://www.weforum.org/agenda/2020/09/shecession-of-2020-causes-and-consequences/.

Appling, S. E., Allen, J. K., Zandt, S. V., Olsen, S., Brager, R., & Hallerdin, J. (2000). Knowledge of Menopause and Hormone Replacement Therapy Use

in Low-Income Urban Women. *Journal of Women's Health & Gender-Based Medicine*, 9(1), 57–64. https://doi.org/10.1089/152460900318975.
Ayranci, U., Orsal, O., Orsal, O., Arslan, G., & Emeksiz, D. F. (2010). Menopause Status and Attitudes in a Turkish Midlife Female Population: An Epidemiological Study. *BMC Women's Health*, 10(1), 1–14. https://doi.org/10.1186/1472-6874-10-1.
Bakarman, M. A., & Abu Ahmed, H. A. (2003). Awareness of Hormonal Replacement Therapy Among Females Attending Primary Health Care Centers in Western Saudi Arabia. *Saudi Medical Journal*, 24(5), 488–492.
Bleakley, H. (2010). Health, Human Capital, and Development. *Annual Review of Economics*, 2(1), 283–310. https://doi.org/10.1146/annurev.economics.102308.124436.
Blount, J. G. (2021). Communication with Women in the Menopause Transition. In *Each Woman's Menopause: An Evidence Based Resource*, 49–68. https://doi.org/10.1007/978-3-030-85484-3_3.
Brewis, J., Beck, V., Davies, A., and Matheson, J. Rep. (2017, July 20). *The Effects of Menopause Transition on Women's Economic Participation in the UK*. Department of Education, London. https://www.gov.uk/government/publications/menopause-transition-effects-on-womens-economic-participation.
Chaudhury, H. (2021, July 20). When the UAE and UK Team Up for Digital Healthcare Solutions. *The National News*. https://www.thenationalnews.com/opinion/comment/2021/07/19/when-the-uae-and-uk-team-up-for-digital-healthcare-solutions/.
Cochrane, T., & Stretton, T. (2022). Enhancing Health Care Education and Practice Post COVID. *Pacific Journal of Technology Enhanced Learning*, 4(1), 8–9. https://doi.org/10.24135/pjtel.v4i1.121.
Diño, M. J. S., & Ong, I. L. (2019). Research, Technology, Education & Scholarship in the Fourth Industrial Revolution [4IR]: Influences in Nursing and the Health Sciences. *The Journal of Medical Investigation*, 66(1.2), 3–7. https://doi.org/10.2152/jmi.66.3.
Donati, S., Cotichini, R., Mosconi, P., Satolli, R., Colombo, C., Liberati, A., & Mele, E. A. (2009). Menopause: Knowledge, Attitude and Practice among Italian Women. *Maturitas*, 63(3), 246–252. https://doi.org/10.1016/j.maturitas.2009.04.001.
Dubai Health Authority. (n.d.). Primary Health Centres. https://www.dha.gov.ae/en/facilities/health-centers.
Dubai Statistics Center. (2019). Population and Vital Statistics. https://www.dsc.gov.ae/en-us/Themes/Pages/Population-and-Vital-Statistics.aspx?Theme=42.
Erbil, N. (2018). Attitudes Towards Menopause and Depression, Body Image of Women During Menopause. *Alexandria Journal of Medicine*, 54(3), 241–246. https://doi.org/10.1016/j.ajme.2017.05.012.

Gifford, J., Maxwell, G., & Young, J. (2021). *Mental Wellbeing and Digital Work: Evidence Summary*. London: Chartered Institute of Personnel and Development. https://www.cipd.co.uk/Images/mental-wellbeing-and-digital-work-evidence-summary_tcm18-98995.pdf.

Hamid, S., Al-Ghufli, F. R., Raeesi, H. A., Al-Dhufairi, K. M., Al-Dhaheri, N. S., Al-Maskari, F., Blair, I., & Shah, S. M. (2014). Women's Knowledge, Attitude and Practice towards Menopause and Hormone Replacement Therapy: A Facility Based Study in Al-Ain, United Arab Emirates. *Journal of Ayub medical college Abbottabad*, 26(4), 448–454. PMID: 25672162.

Hardy, C., Thorne, E., Griffiths, A., & Hunter, M. S. (2018). Work Outcomes in Midlife Women: The Impact of Menopause, Work Stress and Working Environment. *Women's Midlife Health*, 4(1), 1–8. https://doi.org/10.1186/s40695-018-0036-z.

Hsu, A. (2021, June 4). Millions of Women Haven't Rejoined the Workforce—And May Not Anytime Soon. NPR. https://www.npr.org/2021/06/03/1002402802/there-are-complex-forces-keeping-women-from-coming-back-to-work.

Ibrahim, O. M., & Hussein, R. N. (2016). Knowledge, Attitude, and Prevalence of Use of Hormone Replacement Therapy among Women in United Arab Emirates. *Asian Journal of Pharmaceutical and Clinical Research*, 9(3), 154–158. https://innovareacademics.in/journals/index.php/ajpcr/article/view/10810

Karkoti, M. (2020). Al Somna Thaqeela Ala Al Iqtisad [Obesity Is Heavy on Economy]. Al Ittihad. February 16, 2020. https://www.alittihad.ae//article/9661/2020/ السُمنة-ثقيلة-على-الاقتصاد.

Loutfy, I., Abdel Aziz, F., Dabbous, N., & Hassan, M. (2006). Women's Perception and Experience of Menopause: A Community-Based Study in Alexandria, Egypt. *Eastern Mediterranean Health Journal*, 12, S93–S106. https://apps.who.int/iris/handle/10665/117198.

Lutz, W., ed. (2011, September). Population, Education, and Democracy: Refocusing Global Development Priorities. *Population Network Newsletter*. https://iiasa.ac.at/web/home/research/researchPrograms/WorldPopulation/PublicationsMediaCoverage/POPNETNewsletter/POPNET_43.html.

Memon, F. R., Jonker, L., & Qazi, R. A. (2014). Knowledge, Attitudes and Perceptions Towards Menopause among Highly Educated Asian Women in Their Midlife. *Post Reproductive Health*, 20(4), 138–142. https://doi.org/10.1177/2053369114557510.

Ministry of Education. (2017). Ministry of Education Announces a Brand New Physical and Health Education Reform in the UAE. United Arab Emirates Ministry of Education. United Arab Emirates Ministry of Education, January 30, 2017. https://www.moe.gov.ae/En/MediaCenter/News/Pages/sport.aspx.

Mustafa, G. N., & Sabir, J. M. (2012). Perception and Experience Regarding Menopause among Menopaused Women Attending Teaching Hospitals in Erbil City. *Global Journal of Health Science*, 4(3), 170. https://doi.org/10.5539/gjhs.v4n3p170.

Murphy, M. M., Verjee, M. A., Bener, A., & Gerber, L. M. (2013). The Hopeless Age? A Qualitative Exploration of the Experience of Menopause in Arab Women in Qatar. *Climacteric*, 16(5), 550–554.

Neugarten, B. L., Wood, V., Kraines, R. J., & Loomis, B. (1963). Women's Attitudes Toward the Menopause. *Human Development*, 6(3), 140–151. https://doi.org/10.1159/000269714.

Nusche, D. (2008). *Assessment of Learning Outcomes in Higher Education: A Comparative Review of Selected Practices*. OECD Education Working Papers, No. 15. OECD Publishing, Paris. https://doi.org/10.1787/244257272573

Orabi, E. E. (2017). Effect of Health Education Intervention on Knowledge, and Attitude Regarding Menopausal Period among Premenopausal Female Employees. *The Egyptian Journal of Community Medicine*, 35(3), 69–81. https://doi.org/10.21608/ejcm.2017.4100.

Özdemir, O., & Çöl, M. (2004). The Age at Menopause and Associated Factors at the Health Center Area in Ankara, Turkey. *Maturitas*, 49(3), 211–219. https://doi.org/10.1016/j.maturitas.2004.01.013.

Relationships and Sex Education (RSE) (Secondary). (2021, September 13). The Government of UK. https://www.gov.uk/government/publications/relationships-education-relationships-and-sex-education-rse-and-health-education/relationships-and-sex-education-rse-secondary.

Sarrel, P. M. (2012). Women, Work, and Menopause. *Menopause*, 19(3), 250–252. https://doi.org/10.1097/gme.0b013e3182434e0c.

Slaven, L., & Lee, C. (1997). Mood and Symptom Reporting among Middle-Aged Women: The Relationship between Menopausal Status, Hormone Replacement Therapy, and Exercise Participation. *Health Psychology*, 16(3), 203–208. https://doi.org/10.1037/0278-6133.16.3.203.

Women—The Official Portal of the UAE Government. (2022, June 29). The United Arab Emirates' Government Portal. https://u.ae/en/information-and-services/social-affairs/women.

CHAPTER 12

Emiratization: Challenges and Potential Strategies—An Emirati Youth Perspective

Anca Bocanet and Rihab Grassa

1 Introduction

Since 1970, the UAE's rapid economic development has necessitated a massive influx of foreign employees who have played a critical role not just in oil exporting and exploitation, but also in development plans across the whole economy. The UAE government has increased its investments in public services and basic infrastructure projects since the 1970s, thanks to large oil earnings. As a result, non-Emirati nationals make up the majority of the workforce. Due to low native employment rates in the private sector, most Middle Eastern countries are concentrating on localization

A. Bocanet (✉) · R. Grassa
Business Department, Higher Colleges of Technology, Dubai, United Arab Emirates
e-mail: abocanet@hct.ac.ae

R. Grassa
e-mail: rgrassa@hct.ac.ae

A. Mishrif et al. (eds.), *Nationalization of Gulf Labour Markets*, The Political Economy of the Middle East,
https://doi.org/10.1007/978-981-19-8072-5_12

strategies, which involve replacing expatriate workers with competent and skilled local labor. Given the region's growing population, rising unemployment, improving general health, and developing education systems, localization strategies are unavoidable in the Gulf Cooperation Council (GCC) (Swailes et al. 2012).

In the 2000s, following other GCC countries, the UAE government was concerned to increase the participation of Emiratis workers in the private sector and reduce its reliance on foreign workers especially due to the relatively high unemployment among young Emiratis. Indeed, it was expected a relatively 200,000 young Emirati population will enter the labor force by the mid-2010s (representing 25 percent of the Emirati population at that time). Therefore, the UAE government has issued policies known as Emiratization and including some restrictions on the employment of foreign labor force in the public sector.

Emiratization is a program that the UAE government implemented in 2004 to encourage meaningful and efficient employment for its citizens in both the public and commercial sectors. The goal is to lessen the UAE's reliance on foreign labor and ensure that UAE citizens benefit from the country's economic success. The government's concerns about the business sector's significant reliance on foreign labor prompted the policy in the 1990s. When it comes to job hunting, the Labor Law stipulates that Emiratis have precedence over all other nationalities, followed by other Arab nationals. In other words, the Ministry of Labor will not allow non-Emiratis to be hired if its records reflect that unemployed nationals are available to fill the position. The government established the National Human Resource Development and Employment Authority (TANMIA) in 1999 by a decree issued by His Highness Sheikh Zayed bin Sultan Al Nahyan to aid the country's Emiratization drive (Federal Law No. 27). The main goals of TANMIA are to: (i) fully employ national human resources; (ii) reduce the foreign labor component of the total workforce; (iii) increase the supply of qualified and skilled National workforce to meet labor market needs; and (iv) develop practical skills and knowledge of the domestic workforce.

In 2006, the UAE Ministry of Labor issued a decree requiring all private sector companies with 50 or more employees to employ an Emirati human resource manager. The idea behind this law was that Emirati human resource managers would favor the employment of Emirati laborers, thus, boosting Emiratization. This law was canceled less than a year later due to a lack of qualified Emirati human resource professionals

(TANMNIA 2006). As a result, the new Labor Law includes precise criteria for the Ministry of Labor to follow when reviewing employment visa applications from non-UAE nationals, in order to improve the UAE's Emiratization program. This includes determining how many nationals are already employed by a company and whether any of them are qualified to undertake the work. Replacing a UAE employee who has been fired or resigned with a non-UAE national will be a violation of the New Labor Law. The present Labor Law establishes national quotas for all industries, with fines imposed on enterprises that hire non-UAE nationals when local workers are available. Non-UAE nationals should be the first to be laid off if the company has to reduce its workforce. Consequently, the UAE Cabinet decreed that by 2022, there must be at least 20,000 employment openings for Emiratis in a variety of areas, including financial services, aviation, real estate development, and telecommunications.

Despite these efforts, the application of the program of Emiratization remains a big issue, especially for the private sector. Indeed, despite the big success of the Emiratization program in the public sector, today introducing young Emiratis graduate to the private sector present a big challenge for the government. Emiratization has significant challenges, particularly in the private sector, yet it marks a significant shift in employment policy and career development. Following COVID-19, working remotely and autonomously will become the new norm, and the new degree of flexibility added to the UAE's labor market is predicted to have the following effects: (1) increased competition for jobs and talent, (2) increased flexibility of work, space, and time, (3) active support to help people find jobs, and (4) increased investment in talent retention.

In this paper, we are trying to identify the main challenges that impede the Emiratization process in the Private Sector in UAE. Moreover, we are identifying the main factors shaping Emiratization and career development in UAE, including employment policy, education, and labor regulations. Using a survey distributed to more than 3000 youth Emiratis students, this research will first assess the feedback of the young Emiratis toward working in the private sector in UAE and second, will suggest new approaches to accelerate the implementation of an effective Emiratization strategy in the private sector.

2 Literature Review

2.1 UAE Labor Market

In the past ten years, the UAE population has increased slowly every year, from 8.27 in 2010 to 9.89 million in 2021 of which Emiratis account for almost 12%. (World Bank) UAE's unique circumstances, with the majority of the population being non-nationals, foreigners are employed in practically every field, creating a disparity between labor demand and supply. Consequently, the workforce from labor-abundant countries and poor incomes will be appealed to by GCC countries with high fiscal capital, low labor supply, and where salaries are significantly higher than those in their home countries. As such, the UAE features a dual labor market: the public sector, which employs a large number of locals and is recognized for better compensation, flexible working hours, and cultural homogeneity, and the private sector, which employs a large number of expatriates and is known for lower pay and unstable positions (Oakes 2004).

Overall, more than 80% of private sector workers come from low-income nations such as the Indian subcontinent, Africa, and the Philippines, all of which have failing wages and working conditions, and Dubai salaries are significantly higher than those in their home countries. Work permits or residence visas are issued to expatriate workers for the term of their employment; if they lose their job, their work permit and ability to remain in the country are canceled. Private enterprises in Dubai are known for hiring and firing at will, and the fear of being fired, along with the higher pay scales available, means that such employees are often quite cooperative.

A recent study conducted by Emirati postgraduate students from public and private universities found that Male Emiratis rated professional advancement and development as the most significant employment attribute, whereas female Emiratis rated money as the most critical job attribute. The salary was considered the most critical employment attribute by both working men and women, followed by benefits such as housing, child care, and medical insurance. Apart from salary and perks, which are ranked first, the relevance of other employment qualities was shown to vary significantly among both categories. Males place a higher value on professional advancement and job security, whereas non-working females place a higher value on flexible working hours and resource availability (Jabeen et al. 2018).

Hiring UAE citizens has the benefit of broadening the workforce, which improves a company's ability to work with a varied workforce, whether national or international (Aghazadeh 2004). The private sector of the UAE is primarily reliant on international migrant employees, who are supposedly better skilled and equipped than local workers (Al-Qubaisi 2012), and also have lower monetary demands (Waqas 2013).

Although the UAE Ministry of Labor allocates employment quotas and localization targets by sector, the quotas for specific industries appear to be subject to change and are seen as an unattractive way of localizing the private sector, especially given the UAE labor market's institutional characteristics (Barnett et al. 2015). In UAE, Emiratization is a strategy shared by the Ministry of Labor and Social Affairs responsible for policy, and the National Human Resources Development and Employment Authority ("Tanmia"), which provides employment, training, and development opportunities to UAE nationals (Al-Ali 2008). One of the benefits of integrating UAE nationals into the private sector is that businesses can better serve and understand their customers. Not only do UAE nationals gain from the Emiratization process, but so do companies that hire, select, and retain highly skilled employees.

Several industries (for example insurance) have their Emirati salary system, which gives citizens higher pay in order to recruit them. This method is divisive, and there are several points of view. According to some, adding a national allowance to the compensation of people working in the private sector makes positions more lucrative. It would assist the UAE's economy to diversify away from its reliance on oil, tourism, and hydrocarbons in the long term. Others consider a compensation disparity as a barrier (or burden) to the idea of fairness and equality, which could lead to weaker motivation among expatriates conducting similar duties, especially at an executive rank. Private companies, on the other hand, are reliant on expatriate employees as a result of the countries' rapid expansion spurred by the commercialization of their natural resources. Furthermore, as industries are recovering in the post-pandemic era, there is a greater possibility that a sequence of disruptive and inconsistent regulations arising from the pandemic's uncertainties will inevitably impair business analyses (Bocanet et al. 2021).

The World Bank and the International Monetary Fund have long considered unemployment in Gulf countries a major obstacle to progress. Figure 1 distributes the unemployment rate in UAE for the last 20 years.

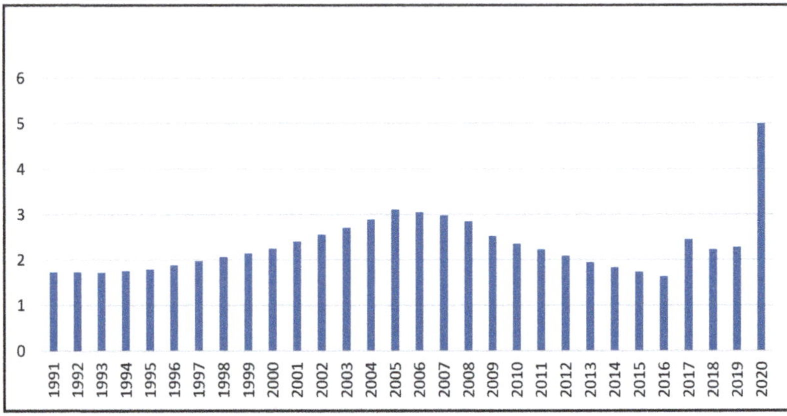

Fig. 1 UAE Unemployment 1991–2020 (% of total labor force)

Management systems and practices that support continuous dependencies on foreign workers at the expense of alienating the national workforce in the private sector, contributed to this phenomenon with social consequences. As a result, getting a job has become more difficult. In response to the challenge of unemployment, the GCC countries, particularly the UAE, implemented economic policies to direct national labor markets and boost work opportunities for their populations. The UAE's council of ministers embraced Emiratization in the early 1990s, which applied to both the public and private sectors, with the former accounting for the great bulk of the workforce (Zeffane and Kemp 2019).

To encourage Emiratization in the private sector, in 2005, the Ministry of Labor introduced a "quota" system for private sector companies, requiring each company to hire a sufficient amount of UAE nationals', No. 43 of 2005. Private enterprises with more than 100 employees had to hire (and keep on payroll) a certain number of Emiratis. If the "quota" of recruiting UAE citizens is satisfied, Order No. 1187 is an incentive to reduce the number of funds required (Ahmed 2011). Other incentives for the private sector for hiring Emiratis and deploying well-being practices are included in the Emirati Salary Support Scheme, comprising merit, pension, and apprentice programs, recruitment targets, and unemployment and childcare allowances.

In addition to the financial incentive, if qualified unemployed UAE nationals are available, the Ministry of Labor has the authority to halt any private sector employer's application for a work permit or a resident visa (Jones 2015). Despite these incentives and enforcements, UAE private businesses continue to try to "get around the system" by recruiting ghost workers which are Emirati nationals employed by firms to meet quotas, or by paying "lip service" and by hiring bare minimum number of nationals to meet the mandatory allocation. The Emirati nationals are paid, but they are not required to work or show up. Recruiting such "ghost" workers is highly penalized by the UAE authorities.

In addition, the Council of Ministers Order No. 26 and Ministerial Order No. 1187 developed a classification system to incentivize organizations that follow Emiratization rules. Companies are ranked into tiers according to the classification system; depending on their status, an organization may or may not be required to "file for the mandatory financial guarantee" (Jones 2015). More recently, the UAE Ministry of Human Resources and Emiratization has set a 10% Emiratization quota for private enterprises to boost their skilled labor workforce, allocating AED 24 billion to generate 75,000 jobs by 2026, in line with the Federal Government's UAE Project of the 50 economic plans.

However, the Emiratization effort has failed to increase national representation, particularly in the private sector. Table 1 shows the workforce distribution by gender and sector in UAE where 40.5% of Emiratis work in the Federal Government, 37.7% in Local Government, 13.7% work either in non-for-profit organizations or are entrepreneurs, and only 8% of Emiratis work in the private sector (Adapted from MoHRE 2019).

2.2 Challenges of Emiratization in the UAE Private Sector

Considering all of the foregoing initiatives, the private sector fell short of the Emiratization targets. The Emiratization policy was met with some pushback from many angles, as discussed below, despite being highly regarded in many places and to some extent successful in the public sector. In a study conducted by Al-Waqfi, M. and Forstenlechner, I. (2014), where managers and HR professionals from various sectors in UAE were interviewed, the majority of participants were unable to provide a clear reporting of their Emiratization targets, indicating an absence of a uniform institutional a clearer Emiratization target, as well as a more transparent reporting structure. The most frequently cited explanation

Table 1 Workforce distribution by gender and sector in UAE in 2019

Sector	*Emiratis*			*Non-Emiratis*			*Total*		
	Males (%)	*Females (%)*	*Total (%)*	*Males (%)*	*Females (%)*	*Total (%)*	*Males (%)*	*Females (%)*	*Total (%)*
Federal Government	44.70	31.00	40.50	2.00	1.60	1.90	3.90	3.40	3.80
Local Government	36.70	40.00	37.70	5.20	3.70	4.90	6.60	6.00	6.50
Private Sector	6.50	11.40	8.00	82.40	46.40	73.90	79.10	44.30	70.70
Others	12.00	17.60	13.70	10.30	48.30	19.20	10.30	46.20	19.00

for the low levels of Emiratization in the private sector is a disparity in compensation expectations leading to a high turnover rate of Emirati employees in the private sector (Al-Waqfi and Forstenlechner 2014).

UAE public and private employment services have been severely impacted by the COVID-19 health emergency and socioeconomic crisis as they have worked to maintain services amidst lockdown measures while also assisting workers and businesses affected by the pandemic to maintain and find jobs and workers, respectively. Thus, the importance of technology-based services in responding to the effects of labor market changes has increased.

The key barriers expressed by many UAE organizations in retaining Emiratis in the workplace are the lack of a career progression path, coaching, and mentoring, which includes further development (The Abu Dhabi Emiratization Forum, 2010). Previous researchers (Lewis and Frank 2002) have highlighted the motivational differences between public and private sector employees and their public sector employment preferences. Such disparity can be attributed to various factors, such as the structural labor market, attractiveness of public sector employment, and lack of professional skills consistent with the demands of the UAE labor market (Tahseen Consulting 2015). While the "appropriateness" of a certain profession and its "lack of prestige" is in part a repercussion of a social agreement, they are also due in part to the nation's cultural landscape, with peculiarities such as the wasta scheme and the role of women in society (Forstenlechner et al. 2012). Emiratis have a significant preference for government jobs, as evidenced by both experiential and public opinion poll data (Forstenlechner 2010; Al-Waqfi and Forstenlechner 2012). Employers think that the types of skills and qualifications they want are in short supply among UAE nationals, particularly with respect to managerial and professional employment, because UAE residents have a high job and income expectations (Al-Qubaisi 2012; Al-Waqfi and Forstenlechner 2014; Barnett et al. 2015). Aside from the monetary benefits, a variety of social and cultural factors promote public sector employment preferences (Sayre and Yousef 2015).

The most common challenges of Emiratization rank from not having the skills standard required for the private sector, followed by lower salary and benefits, longer standard working hours and shorter holidays, and inconclusive job security as compared to the private sector where the job is for life, retention of the national workforce, and language (Aljanahi 2017). Figure 2 illustrates such classification.

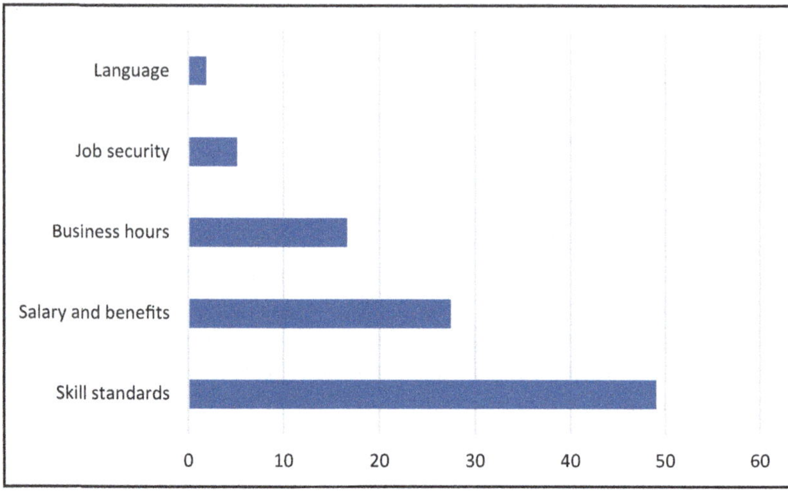

Fig. 2 Top obstacles of Emiratization in the UAE private sector

Not meeting the skills standard required to work in the private sector is the number one challenge of Emiratization in the UAE. This implies a gap between Emirati nationals' academic, technical, and soft skills and the competencies demanded by employers. It is ineffective for private companies to hire Emirati citizens, or any other employee unless the employee possesses the minimal capabilities required by the company. Despite the fact that more qualifications tend to lead to larger wage expectations, there is no reason why a well-educated national with market-oriented talents cannnot still stand out for a government position. Emiratis' low skill standards suggest that the UAE's educational system is inefficient and has to be aligned to address the requirements of the private sector. For the government, private companies, and UAE nationals, low skill levels are a challenge.

The category of income and benefits was the second most commonly mentioned challenge throughout specialized literature. UAE citizens not only appear to have low skill levels, but they also cost more to hire. It is more cost-effective for private companies to hire expats who can execute the job for less money and can be fired quickly if necessary. Moreover, the government sector pays overestimated compensation packages compared to the private sector, which makes localization of labor in the private sector even more difficult. According to research done by "Tanmia," three out of every five Emiratis left corporate roles due to a lack of professional advancement and a mentorship culture (Maktoob 2009) Local employees have seen high levels of turnover also as a consequence of the struggle to integrate into an expatriate-dominated system.

Working hours were the third most common barrier to Emiratization, as the working days are much longer in the private sector as compared with the government sector. One solution is to provide Emirati nationals in the private sector with more flexible or shorter working hours. Another possible option is for the public sector to extend working hours in order to close the gap with the private sector. Business hours are a unique difficulty in the private sector, but modifying public sector business hours policies may provide a solution.

Job security was the second least commonly reported hindrance to Emiratization (Aljanahi 2017). Private companies can fire and recruit expats at will, but Emirati natives are more difficult to fire. Emiratis who do not break labor regulations cannot be fired, hence firing UAE nationals is illegal (Jones 2015). Although job security is not a problem for Emirati citizens per se, it is for the UAE Government as hiring and firing UAE nationals is extremely difficult and expensive; hence, the possibility of job security does not deter UAE nationals from working in the private sector. Emiratis are culturally oriented to prefer working in groups to solving problems and achieving goals through single initiatives, owing to their society's largely collectivist ethos (Goby et al. 2015). This means that rather than seeing themselves as an autonomous force, Emirati workers will seek a group with which to merge.

The language was found to be the least concerning a challenge to Emiratization. While Arabic is the official language in the UAE, due to the population diversity, all sectors have English as the official language of communication, therefore language is neither considered a barrier to UAE nationals working in the private sector nor is it seen as a barrier to employers hiring UAE nationals.

For Emiratis, the public sector is significantly more appealing because it offers superior employment conditions in terms of salary, job security, work hours, work content, and long vacations. Given the government's emphasis on localization and the initiatives, several entities are making to recruit and retain Emiratis by giving them greater possibilities and faster advancements in certain areas, career advancement in government sectors could be deemed to be superior. The option to work in the local tongue (Arabic) is especially appealing, as is the opportunity to practice "wasta" (using networks and relationships) to find work. Also, many local Emiratis, particularly the youth, do not see employability as a top priority. Young Emiratis generally prefer to work in the public sector, despite their willingness to serve as business owners in their own economy (Zeffane and Kemp 2019).

Workdays and working hours play a role in the private sector's reluctance to work. Long and irregular hours, constraints on time spent on cultural and religious observances, limited periods of leave, and a more rigorous attitude toward employee performance may be unsatisfactory to local Emiratis in the private sector. Government offices, on the other hand, usually operate on a Sunday to Thursday schedule (7.30 a.m. to 2.30 p.m.), while offices in the private sector tend to work longer hours. The assumption of higher wages, cultural and social perspectives, the stereotype relation to working specific jobs, such as labor-intensive jobs, as well as a lack of social integration in a multiethnic setting and insufficient qualifications, all contribute to Emiratis' aversion to working in the industry.

3 Methodology

Due to the exploratory nature of this research, we opt for a questionnaire to collect data. The questionnaire allows us to use to collect qualitative information through open-ended questions and quantitative data through closed-ended questions and multiple-choice questions. A mixed type of question allows us to collect, analyze, and combine qualitative and quantitative data in a single study to achieve a complete understanding of a particular research question or area of research (Cresswell 2003; Tashakkori and Teddlie 2003; Johnson et al. 2007). Using this approach in single research offers diverse yet complimentary benefits (Onwuegbuzie and Leech 2005).

The questionnaire used in this paper was developed specifically for this study and took care of the specificities and the culture of the UAE. The questionnaire contained seven items that targeted youth Emiratis' motivations for their work careers. In addition, the questionnaire contained five items that target youth Emiratis' opinions of the current obstacles and the opportunities for Emiratization. In addition to the 12 questionnaire items, the respondents were asked to provide basic demographic information including gender, age, employment status, emirates of living, and monthly income (as there are many working students).

4 Samples

The target population included all students at one of the largest universities in the UAE comprising more than 20,000 Emiratis students from different disciplines and operating on 16 campuses across the UAE. Data for the study was collected through questionnaires distributed in-person to more than 3000 potential graduated Emirati students, in which 2015 were received with a response rate of 67.2%. The students concerned by this survey are level 4 students who will be graduated by the end of the year (semesters for some of them). Consequently, we expect that this survey would provide a representative picture of students' motivations in their work careers and their perceptions of the obstacles that face the Emiratizations of the private sector. The survey has been distributed across the 16 campuses. The reported responses varied by questionnaire items due to non-response on certain questionnaire items.

The 2015 respondents included 57% males and 43% females. Respondents are from different age categories including 30.2% aged less than 20 years; 65.7% aged between 21 and 30 years; 4.5% are more than 31 years. The majority of our respondents are from Abu Dhabi (21.6%) and Dubai (50.6%). Regarding the employment status, the majority of the respondents are unemployed (64.9%), and the remaining are working students (35.1%) where 26.1% of them work for the public sector and only 9% of them work in the private sector. concerning the education level, 66.4% have a high school diploma, and 25.6% will get their bachelor's degree this semester (Table 2).

Table 2 Demographic characteristics of the sample

Demographic characteristics		*No of observations*	*Percentage*
Gender	Male	1151	57.1
	Female	865	42.9
	Total	**2015**	**100**
Age	Less than 20	609	30.2
	21–30	1325	65.7
	31–40	69	3.4
	more than 41	14	0.7
	Total	**2015**	**100**
Emirates living	Abu Dhabi	657	21.6
	Ajman	87	3.2
	Dubai	827	50.6
	Fujeirah	24	7.4
	Sharjah	83	4.6
	Ras al Khaima	329	9.5
	Umm Al Quwain	10	3.1
	Total	**2015**	**100**
Working sector	Public	513	26.1
	Private	177	9
	Un employed	1275	64.9
	Total	**1964**	**100**
Education level	High school diploma	198	66.4
	bachelor degree	3	25.6
	Master degree	1	5.8
	other	44	2.2
	Total	**1982**	**100**
Monthly income	None	1207	62.7
	Up to 3500 USD	175	9.1
	3500–7000 USD	202	10.5
	7000–10,500 USD	52	2.7
	more than 10,500 USD	79	4.1
	Prefer to not answer	210	10.9
	Total	**1925**	**100**

5 Data Analysis

For this study, we collected both quantitative and qualitative data. We used descriptive statistics and comparison to analyze quantitative data.

6 Finding and Discussion

6.1 Work Motivations

We started our survey, by asking our respondents in which sector they are looking to work for/in after their graduation. 61% of our respondents are looking to work in the government sector, only 17.6% of them prefer the private sector and the reaming 21.4% did not decide yet or they keep it for the opportunity that will be offered to them (Table 3). While the rate of potential graduating students looking for working in the private sector is relatively low, it has increased over the last 13 years. Only approximately 10% of students at Abu Dhabi Women's Higher College of Technology wanted to work in the private sector after graduation, according to findings from 2007 research called "Attitudes to the Private Sector" (Randeree 2009). Despite the huge efforts and specific incentives developed by the Ministry of Labor to encourage youth Emiratis to work in the private sector, It is obvious that they are still influenced by the traditional culture to work for government institutions because of the motivations and benefits offered.

It is expected that motivations to work for the public or the private sector would be different from one respondent to another (Table 4). Indeed, the main motivations for our youth respondents who look to work for the private sector are: First, the multicultural difference (22%) as private firms reflect better the UAE society and allow them to gain experience and skills that they could not get in homogeneous Emirati government organizations. Second, the job quality (11%): employees in the private sector usually have better access to international training programs that will help them develop new skills and build on their experience. Besides, multinational and large private firms are more likely to invest in new technologies and industry innovations compared to the public sector. Third, the high compensation in some private sectors such as the banking industry and oil companies (14%). Also, the salary increase

Table 3 Motivations and preferences for work

	No. of Observations	*Percentage*
Private sector	345	17.6
Government sector	1197	61
No preference	420	21.4
Total	**1962**	**100**

in these mentioned sectors is quicker and higher compared to the public sector.

However, youth Emiratis who look forward to work in the government firms believe that the public sector offer: first, a higher opportunity for promotion (23%), as government organization has adopted interesting performance-based promotion schemes to supplement the traditional grade-based system, which is not offered in the private sector. Second, higher salaries (17%), indeed the starting salaries in the government sector are often higher than private sector jobs. Indeed, Emiratis tend to seek high wages and managerial positions while avoiding menial jobs (Grant et al., 2007). Third, more holidays (14%) compared to the private sector. However, it's worth noted that, in 2020, the UAE Cabinet granted equal leaves to the public and private sectors. This decision aims to achieve a balance between the two sectors in the number of official holidays they are entitled to (The United Arab Emirates' Government portal, 2020). Forth, a better work environment (11%) as it is less competitive than the private sector. As well as, unlike the private sector, the working culture tends to be less demanding, with less emphasis placed on long hours and profits. Fifth, higher benefits and allowance (10%): public sector benefits are on average still higher than comparable private sector benefits, as it provides

Table 4 Reasons beyond choosing government of private sector

Sector	*Private*		*Government*	
Reasons	*No. of Observations*	*Percentage*	*No. of observations*	*Percentage*
High salary	186	14	1047	17
Less working hours	83	6	484	8
More holidays	69	5	870	14
Job quality	145	11	109	2
Multicultural difference	290	22	332	6
Opportunities for promotion	83	6	1359	23
Employee investment	108	8	198	3
Fast growth	107	8	366	6
Benefits and allowances	117	9	606	10
Work environment	117	9	656	11
Total	**1305**	**100**	**6027**	**100**

accommodation, good pension schemes, good medical insurance, education for children, a range of discounts from different organizations and leisure memberships, and comprehensive benefits packages.

The main factors of choosing the government sector are mainly influenced by the way they perceive the quality of their work-life (Randeree 2009). Youth Emiratis' interest in working in the public sector is largely motivated by economic factors, high salaries, and benefits might be sufficient to attract youth Emiratis to the government sector, but not sufficient to add quality to their work-life (Baakile 2011). Our finding is aligned with Randeree (2009) who stresses that high salaries and shorter working hours are the main motives why Emiratis choose the public sector.

Besides, our qualitative analysis shows that many respondents mentioned that oppositely to the private sector, working for the public market brings a good work-life balance. Many responders value their capacity to excel at work while also being present for family needs. Moreover, an important advantage to working for the government is the benefits retirement plan created for Emiratis. Retired Emiratis employers would be eligible for these benefits for the rest of their lives, and their spouses may be eligible for the same benefits if the retiree outlived them. Furthermore, unlike private sector workers, public sector workers are less vulnerable to market fluctuations in terms of layoffs and reductions in force. Employees working for the public sector have more job security compared to those in the private sector. Another important reason to opt for working in the government sector is, Emiratis employers frequently receive supplementary advantages. These include cheaper health insurance, vacation days, sick leave days, and holidays, as well as longer maternity leave. All of these advantages, when paired with salaries, boost one's total pay. Most of our respondents rely upon the previous experiences of their parents or relatives in the private sector and compare them with those who worked in the government sector.

Table 5 describes the sector preference of our youth respondents to work in. 24% of them look forward to working in government and public organizations such as municipalities, ministries, and governmental offices; 14% prefer the energy and natural resources firms, 14% in the banking and finance sector; 12% anticipate working in telecommunication, media, and technology. Indeed, these preferable sectors are also subject to Emiratization regulation. In 2005, the Ministry of Labor and Social Affairs Minister's Office has issued 3 ministerial decrees for the banking, insurance, and trade sector. Ministerial resolution No. 41, requires trade sector firms employing 50 or more workers to hire Emiratis at an annual rate of growth of 2%. According to Ministerial Resolution No. 42, enterprises engaged in insurance activities must commit to employing nationals at a rate of 5% per year. Ministerial Resolution No. 43 requires banks in the UAE to hire nationals at a rate of 4% per year. UAE would allocate 40% of banking employment to residents in 2019.

However, only 3% would like to work in the Hospitality and tourism sector. Indeed, Emiratis have tended to avoid working in the hospitality industry as it is seen as unsuitable for them from cultural and religious perspectives (by concerns about alcohol and other issues). Also, only 5% of our respondents consider working in the construction and real estate companies as they found it less advantageous compared to the others sectors. Many job categories are considered culturally inappropriate by Emirati society; hence the locals disregard them. For female citizens, this is even more acute (Baud and Mahgoub 2001; Adam 2003). Also, work preferences varied between females and males. While female look to work for the education and healthcare organizations, these sectors are least favorable for the male.

Table 5 Sector preferences

Sectors	*Overall sample (%)*	*Female (%)*	*Male (%)*	*t-test*
Energy and Natural Resources	14	12	15	1.72[c]
Construction and Real Estate	5	4	7	3.14[a]
Healthcare	9	11	7	3.43[a]
Retail	3	3	3	0.00
Education	7	9	4	2.81[a]
Government and Public Sector	24	23	24	1.03
Banking and Finance	14	12	15	1.69[c]
Telecommunication, Media and Technology	12	12	12	0.00
Hospitality and Tourism	3	3	3	0.00
Transport and Logistics	6	5	6	1.51
Others	1	1	2	1.43

[a]Significant at 1% level and [c]significant at 10% level

6.2 *Obstacles for Emiratization in the Private Sector*

One of the main obstacles for Emiratization is the refusal to relocate. Indeed, only 43.4% (24% male and 18.75% female) of our respondents agreed to relocate to another emirate for work (see Table 6). And those who accept to relocate prefer to move to the big emirates (Abu Dhabi, 43.1%, Dubai 29.8%, and Sharjah 13.8%). Distance and family conditions are the main reasons for this refusal as explained in Table 7.

Table 8 discusses the main obstacles to Emiratization according to our youth respondents. Low salaries and long working hours are the main problems (20.4% and 23.98% respectively). Next, 13.44% of our respondents perceive that work culture is an important barrier for Emiratization.

Table 6 Relocation

	All sample (%)	*Female (%)*	*Male (%)*
Relocation	43.4	18.5	24.0
Relocation City			
Relocation City: Abu Dhabi	43.1	17.3	25.8
Relocation To Dubai	29.8	12.5	17.3
Relocation To Al Fujeirah	4.5	1.5	3.0
Relocation To Sharjah	13.8	8.1	5.7
Relocation To Ras Al Khaiemah	3.9	1.6	2.3
Relocation To Ajman	5.9	3.4	2.4
Relocation To Um Al Quwain	3.2	1.6	1.5

Table 7 Reason for refuse of relocation

	All sample (%)	*Male (%)*	*Female (%)*
Distance	40.8	25.3	15.5
Family conditions	31.4	18.5	12.9
Social problems	5.7	3.7	2.0
Personal problems	9.9	6.6	3.3
Health problems	3.7	2.4	1.3
Expenses	7.0	4.8	2.2
others	1.6	0.9	0.7

Indeed, many of our interviewees, particularly females, argue that social and cultural factors do stand as a major reason for the resignation from the private sector.9.33% of our respondents argue that the English language is a barrier for Emiratis to work in the private sector. 10.66% of our respondents argue that the private sector does not offer carrier opportunities for Emiratis, as many companies recruit Emiratis just to meet quotas. If these companies were hiring Emiratis employees just to meet quotas, the young Emiratis employees will not be able to learn, to develop their carrier and they will not feel comfortable in their jobs and their work environment. Furthermore, our respondents argue that they want a career, not just a job. They shared first-hand accounts of their expectations upon entering the job market for the first time. They are continuously on the lookout for a job opportunity where they can genuinely advance in a firm since they face numerous hurdles in terms of how to advance and uncover their full potential. They are looking for a place to study and grow, as well as a place to put their expertise to use. The work environment atmosphere is also very significant to the respondents. They also do not want to work somewhere where they are hired solely on the basis of their Emirati ethnicity in order to meet a quota.

All in all, when comparing the above reasons in both quantitative and qualitative analysis, it is clear that a lack of experience, training, qualification, English language, low wages, long working hours, and limited opportunities for advancement are the top reasons for low Emiratization in the workforce.

Table 8 Obstacles for Emiratization

	All (%)	*Male (%)*	*Female (%)*
No vacancy for Emiratis	10.66	6.43	4.24
Language barrier	9.33	5.14	4.19
Offshore companies	3.85	2.61	1.24
Low salaries	20.40	11.98	8.42
Low protection	9.28	5.72	3.55
No Law protection for Emiratis	7.96	5.19	2.78
Work culture	13.34	8.01	5.33
Code of conduct	3.38	2.19	1.19
Working hours	23.98	12.56	11.42

7 Conclusion and Recommendations

In this study, we identified the main challenges and barriers to an appropriate implementation of an Emiratization plan that should be addressed to achieve the desired outcomes of this program set by the UAE government in 2004. These barriers include three main elements: (1) work conditions (e.g., lower wages, long working hours, fewer holidays, absence of retirement plan, promotion plan, carrier opportunities, fewer advantages and benefits); (2) inadequate work skills and competencies of youth Emiratis (e.g., poor English language and communication skills); (3) and cultural differences and work ethics that may be incompatible with what is required to succeed in a modern and knowledge-based economy (Al-Waqfi and Forstenlechner 2014).

Some of these limitations are the direct result of the rapid economic growth that caused a transitional transformation of the UAE society. However, many of these limitations are directly related to the deficiencies of the education system and the lack of suitable strategies for national human resources development.

An updated educational system will tolerate a quicker adaptation to the rapidly changing skill demand, preventing both skill disparities and deficiencies. To increase employability across economic sectors and occupations, the UAE workforce must develop new technical skills, particularly STEM-related ones, as well as a combination of non-technical soft skills and transferable digital abilities (such as big data analytics, cyber security, and social media). Implementing an appropriate professional education and training programs for the youth Emiratis job seekers to meet the requirements of the private sector. Employment in the 4.0 industry require tailored educational programs that combine technical and human knowledge, as well as a continual desire to learn. A high level of coordination between the Ministry of Labor and the Ministry of Education is required to revise frequently the majors offered by the universities in the countries and develop new majors that match the requirement of the private labor sector. To enable continuous up- and reskilling, active labor market policies, as well as other initiatives to encourage inclusive lifelong learning and flexible learning pathways, are required.

Revising the national HR policy and rules that govern the Emiratization program is highly recommended. Indeed, a key weakness of the Emiratization plan is that most of the policy govern this program was implemented so far, and the absence of appropriate legislative and institutional mechanisms and processes to guarantee Emiratization targets are met (Al-Waqfi and Forstenlechner 2014). Institutional bodies have to revise old instruments and mechanisms according to the new labor market circumstances and needs.

Another recommendation is the necessity of issuing laws and decrees to protect Emiratis working in the private sector from the abuse and misconduct of the employer. Indeed, Emiratis' younger generation wants a career, not simply a job. Emirati students and new graduates shared first-hand accounts of their expectations when entering the job market for the first time. They are continuously on the lookout for a job opportunity where they can genuinely advance in a firm since they face numerous hurdles in terms of how to advance and uncover their full potential. This study found that young Emiratis are looking for a place to study and grow, as well as a place to put their expertise to use. The workplace atmosphere was found to be very significant to them as well. They definitely do not want to work in a place where they are hired just because they are Emirati to fill a quota.

Revising the current retirement policy plan for Emiratis working in the private service according to the new labor market circumstances and establishing a new mechanism that can help to guarantee pensions and end of service benefits similar to those offered in the government sector, as well as implementing maximum working hours equal with the public sector is also recommended.

It is also recommended to develop incentive plans to encourage private companies to recruit youth Emiratis, as well as incentives to encourage Emiratis to work in the private sector. This incentive system can take the shape of natural incentives or artificial incentives such as allowances, primes, or any other type of benefit. This incentive structure can address the issue of salary disparities between the public and private sectors, as well as the high salaries sought by locals as a result of their exposure to public sector offerings. To ensure a minimal level of salary consistency between the public and private sectors, a wage policy for Emiratis working in the private sector must be developed. As a result of this instrument, the effectiveness of Emiratization in the private sector will improve.

The Fourth Industrial Revolution's approaches must be used to stay up with the concerns influencing today's jobs sector as a result of automation and the development of cutting-edge technology. Accordingly, there is the urge of developing the abilities and competencies needed to manage these risks, keep a healthy working relationship between employees and employers, and come up with creative employment models (Nasser bin Thani Al Hameli, UAE Minister of Human Resources and Emiratization).

While this study offers a comprehensive and interesting analysis of the challenges and barriers to implementing an effective Emiratization program and offers some strategies that can help to achieve the target plan, it suffers from some research limitations. First, our sample size is relatively small. While we believe the data we obtained and the outcomes of our study reflect reality, we recognize that a bigger sample size would considerably improve the findings' reliability and generalizability. Second, our respondents consist of Emiratis students studying in a governmental university. Maybe Emiratis students enrolled in private universities think differently. Third, we are not taking into consideration in our research all categories of UAE society; we are interested only in youth Emiratis students. Future studies are needed to investigate the complexity and the different challenges of the workforce localization in the UAE in greater depth and at a higher scale of analysis.

References

Adam, K. (2003). Women's Empowerment and Leadership in Education: A Key Factor for Emiratisation in the United Arab Emirates. Pretoria: University of South Africa.

Aghazadeh, S.M. (2004). Managing Workforce Diversity as an Essential Resource for Improving Organizational Performance. International Journal of Productivity and Performance Management, 53(6), 521–531.

Ahmed, A. (2011). New UAE Emiratisation Regulation. International Financial Law Review. http://www.iflr.com/Article/2779603/New-UAE-emiratisation-regulations.html.

Aljanahi, M.H. (2017). Challenges to the Emiratisation Process: Content Analysis. Human Resource Development International 20(1), 9–17. https://doi.org/10.1080/13678868.2015.1218661.

Al-Ali, J. (2008). Emiratisation: Drawing UAE Nationals into Their Surging Economy. The International Journal of Sociology and Social Policy, 28(9/10), 365–379.

Al-Qubaisi, O.S. (2012). ICT, Human Capital Development and Emiratisation of the Labour Market in the United Arab Emirates, PhD thesis, Royal Holloway University of London, London.

Al-Waqfi, M.A., & Forstenlechner, I. (2012). Of private sector fear and prejudice. *Personnel Review, 41*(5), 609–629.

Al-Waqfi, M.A., & Forstenlechner, I. (2014). Barriers to Emiratization: The Role of Policy Design and Institutional Environment in Determining the Effectiveness of Emiratization. The International Journal of Human Resource Management, 25(2), 167–189. https://doi.org/10.1080/09585192.2013.826913.

Baakile, M. (2011). Comparative Analysis of Teachers' Perceptions of Equity, Pay Satisfaction, Affective Commitment and Intention to Turnover in Botswana. Journal of Management Research, 3(1), 10–20.

Barnett, A.H., Malcolm, M. and Toledo, H. (2015). Shooting the goose that lays the golden egg: the case of UAE employment policy. *Journal of Economic Studies, 42(2)*, 285–302.

Baud, I., & Mahgoub, H.K. (2001). Towards Increasing National Female Participation in the Labour Force (ARGOS Research Report No. 2). Dubai, UAE: Tanmia/Center for Labour Market Research and Information.

Bocanet, A., Alpenidze, O., & Badran, O. (2021). Business Analysis in Post-Pandemic Era. Academy of Strategic Management Journal, 20(4), 1939-6104-20-4-813.

Cresswell, J.W. (2003). Research Design: Qualitative, Quantitative and Mixed Method Approaches. Thousand Oaks, CA: Sage.

Forstenlechner, I. (2010). Workforce Localization in Emerging Gulf Economies: The Need to Fine-Tune HRM. Personnel Review, 39(1), 135–152.

Forstenlechner, I., Madi, M., Selim, H., & Rutledge, E. (2012). Emiratisation: Determining the Factors the Influence the Recruitment Decisions of Employers in the UAE. The International Journal of Human Resource Management, 23(2), 406–421.

Goby, V.P., Nickerson, C., & David, E. (2015). Interpersonal Communication and Diversity Climate: Promoting Workforce Localization in the UAE. International Journal of Organizational Analysis, 23(3), 364–377.

Grant, J., Golawala, F.S., and McKechnie, D.S. (2007). The United Arab Emirates: The Twenty-First Century Beckons. Thunderbird International Business Review, 49(4), 507–533.

Jabeen, F., Faisal, M., and Katsioloudes, M. (2018). Localisation in an Emerging Gulf Economy. Equality, Diversity and Inclusion: An International Journal, 37(2), 151–166. https://doi.org/10.1108/edi-02-2017-0045.

Johnson, R.B., Onwuegbuzie, A.J., and Turner, L.A. (2007). Toward a Definition of Mixed Methods Research. Journal of Mixed Methods Research, 1, 112–133.

Jones, N. 2015. Emiratisation: A Recap. Dubai: Al Tamimi & Co.

Lewis, G.B., and Frank, S.A. (2002). Who Wants to Work for the Government? Public Administration Review 62(4), 395–404.

Maktoob. (2009). Maktoub Business letter. http://business.maktoob.com/20090000463642/Pay_Gulf_nationals_more_than_expats_-experts/Article.htm, viewed May 2010.

MoHRE. (2019). Workforce distribution by gender and sector in UAE. *UAE Ministry of Human Resources and Emiratisation, 12.*

Oakes, M. (2004). Saudisation: Coming to a Shop Near You. Middle East Economic Digest, 48(13).

Onwuegbuzie, A.J., and Leech, N.L. (2005). On Becoming a Pragmatic Researcher: The Importance of Combining Quantitative and Qualitative Research Methodologies. International Journal of Social Research Methodology, 8, 375–387.

Randeree, K. (2009). Strategy, Policy and Practice in the Nationalisation of Human Capital: Project Emiratisation. Research & Practice in Human Resource Management, 17(1).

Sayre, E.A., and Yousef, T.M. (2015). Young Generation Awakening: Economics, Society and Policy on the Eve of the Arab Spring. New York, NY: Oxford University Press.

Swailes, S., Al Said, L.G., and Al Fahdi, S. (2012). Localisation Policy in Oman: A Psychological Contracting Interpretation. International Journal of Public Sector Management, 25(5), 357–372.

Tahseen Consulting. (2015). Female Labor Market Participation, Available at: http://tahseen.ae/blog/?tag=female-labor-market-participation.

TANMIA. (2006). 'Human Resources Report,' National Human Resource Development and Employment Authority (TANMIA).

Tashakkori, A., and Teddlie, C.B. (2003), Handbook of Mixed Methods in Social & Behavioral Research. Thousand Oaks, CA: Sage.

The Abu Dhabi Emiratisation Forum (2010). Improving retention by harnessing motivation. Post conference report of key findings, ideas, and recommendations. (2010, May). Abu Dhabi, UAE. Retrieved from http://aimevents.net/emiratisation_forum/Docs/EMIRATIZATION.pdf

Waqas, M. (2013). Emiratisation Plan Wanes, Report Blames Business, Arabian Gazette, 12 August, Available at: http://arabiangazette.com/emiratisation-plan-blames-business-20130812.

Zeffane, R., and Kemp, L. (2019). Emiratization: Benefits and Challenges of Strategic & Radical Change in the United Arab Emirates.

CHAPTER 13

Bridging the Gap Between Gulf Higher Education and Labor Market in Industry 4.0

Ashraf Mishrif, Magdalena Karolak, and Cameron Mirza

1 Introduction

The role of education in preparing the nationals to take on jobs within the new era that is technology-driven should be examined in detail. Strengthening the educational system is primordial following the criteria established by WEF (2016, p. 9): (1) expanded access to early-childhood education; (2) ensuring the "future-readiness" of curricula; (3) investing in developing and maintaining a professionalized teaching workforce; (4) early exposure to the workplace and career guidance; (5) investing in

A. Mishrif (✉)
Humanities Research Center, Sultan Qaboos University, Al Khoud, Oman
e-mail: amishrif@squ.edu.om

M. Karolak
College of Humanities and Social Science, Zayed University, Dubai, United Arab Emirates
e-mail: Magdalena.Karolak@zu.ac.ae

A. Mishrif et al. (eds.), *Nationalization of Gulf Labour Markets*,
The Political Economy of the Middle East,
https://doi.org/10.1007/978-981-19-8072-5_13

digital fluency and ICT literacy skills; (6) providing robust and respected technical and vocational education and training (TVET); (7) creating a culture of lifelong learning; and (8) openness to education innovation. The transition to a new economy fueled by technology rather than oil has the potential to create millions of new jobs in the Gulf region. Although World Human Capital Index, which measures the extent to which countries optimize their human capital potential through education and skills, finds that the Gulf countries overall welfare ranges from 68% to 73% against global average of 65%, we can identify four common themes characterizing the Gulf labour markets: low but steady workforce participation of women, high rates of underemployment; large but decreasing share of public sector employment, and hiring criteria based predominantly on academic attainment rather than skills and competencies.

In a number of Gulf countries' dialogue, policy and regulation thinking around crowdsourcing, crowdfunding, virtual work, and changes to cyber regulation is well underway and moving ahead at pace. Nonetheless, there is a scarcity of scientific research on the preparedness of the GCC educational systems with regard to the opportunities and challenges posed by the 4th Industrial Revolution. There has also been limited assessment on how to improve the employability of national workers in light of the technological change. The discussion on this topic is, however, vital for the future of Gulf economies.

2 Rethinking Investment in Higher Education Infrastructure

The GCC countries have made considerable investments in higher education infrastructure, building colleges and universities, and establishing highly equipped laboratories and training facilities. Since the mid-1970s, the number of tertiary education institutions established in the region has reached 88 in Saudi Arabia, 76 in the UAE, 38 in Oman, 32 in Qatar, 19 in Bahrain, and 11 in Kuwait. The growth of the sector was accompanied by a considerable increase in the number of students, researchers, and

C. Mirza
International Research and Exchanges Board (IREX), Washington, DC, USA
e-mail: cmirza@irex.org

academic staff at all levels. The expansion is built on an early investment in primary and secondary education. The total number of students in all education stages in the Gulf region is 12.2 million students, of whom 8.8 million are students in pre-university education and 2.3 million students in higher education in 2020 (AlkhaleejOnline 2021). The expansion is eventually reflected in the growth of the entire education sector, with 0.9 million students in the childhood development, 960,700 teachers, and 43,200 of educational institutions spread out across the GCC countries, of which 73.7% of total educational institutions are governmental.

In addition, some GCC countries, among others, such as the UAE and Qatar strive to become educational hubs and attract more foreign students to relocate and pursue their education in the region. Clear examples exist such as the academic city in Dubai and the Qatar foundation. Nonetheless, there is an urgent need to substantially improve the education system from primary and vocational education to higher education, with the aim of addressing the shortage in the national skilled and high skilled labor force and fulfilling the objective of engaging in Industry 4.0. Evidence from international assessments of students such as PISA (OECD's Programme for International Student Assessment. PISA measures 15-year-olds' ability to use their reading, mathematics, and science) scores of all GCC countries below 500 points. There is theoretically no minimum or maximum score in PISA; rather, the results are scaled to fit approximately normal distributions, which means around 500 score points clearly pointing toward a below-average education system within the GCC.

Modern and relevant curricula are one of the key steps toward estimating and meeting the demand of the current and future workforce. New curricula should match the type of knowledge and emerging skills such as digital literacy, data literacy, critical thinking, emotional intelligence, creativity, collaboration, flexibility, leadership skills, time management, curiosity, and continuous learning (Marr, 22 August 2022). Furthermore, curricula should be more responsive to labor market needs by focusing on branches of science such as applied science, natural sciences, information and communication technology, statistics, economics, mathematics, manufacturing, engineering, and construction. An important step must therefore be taken to evolve curricula toward interdisciplinary and multidisciplinary learning with a shift toward problem-based learning focusing on real-world problems to make curricula more relevant.

The COVID-19 pandemic has accelerated the use of educational technologies as it required a swift shift to online and/or blended modes of instruction around the world. The GCC countries were already well prepared with the existing IT infrastructure and e-systems in place allowing students to continue their education from home and for professors and administrators to carry out their duties using remote systems (Bensaid and Brahmi 2021). The past investments were considerable: as an example, the UAE spent more than 14 billion USD in 2014 on ICT and educational technology (Farid, n.d.). Nonetheless, further investments are required to upgrade the IT infrastructure and to acquire educational technologies to enhance the learning of the skills required by the 4IR jobs, among others, learning through virtual reality, and interactive and collaborative learning. In addition, given the importance of soft skills in the versatile job market, the educators ought to be capable of using the new platforms to train such skills. Consequently, the UAE aims at spending an additional 7.1 billion USD by 2023 to upgrade the e-educational systems (Holland, 21 March 2021).

Furthermore, a change in educational programs to follow the 4IR needs is visible with the opening of the first AI university in the region and in the world altogether, namely, Mohamed bin Zayed University of Artificial Intelligence (MBZUAI) established in the UAE in 2019. Programs in blockchain, robotics, cloud, Internet of Things were established across the region. As such the infrastructure requires hard and soft components including specialized labs. The delivery of continued education to those who are already employed is another aspect of education. Those who are already in positions will require upskilling given the constantly changing labor requirements and therefore closer collaboration is required between the higher education sector and employers. While such opportunities exist online in the form of e-platforms such as Coursera and edX, locally based offerings should be enhanced with courses also offered in Arabic. Among the pioneering initiatives, Industry Champions established in 2022 in the UAE as a partnership between the government and industry leaders, aims at delivering 4.0 modules for chief executives covering lean, six sigma, lean digital, IoT, and analytics as well as upskilling managers in the industrial sector (The National, 16 June 2022). The expansion and availability of such education in locally provided platforms, including in Arabic, and at local educational institutions is another aspect of a continuous preparation of the workforce throughout their working years.

Innovation required for both, the growth of the sectors that are part of 4IR and advanced educational platforms requires adequate funds to support research. It is clear that the GCC governments will continue to be at the forefront of these changes providing investments and creating frameworks for the education and labor markets to be aligned as well as stimulating growth in selected sectors of the economy supporting 4IR. The creation of the Ministry of Industry and Advanced Technology in the UAE is an example of setting such priorities as well as the Ministry of Communications and Information Technology in KSA which aims to build and stimulate a sustainable ecosystem for the development of digital skills and contribute to bridging the gap between supply and demand in accordance with the requirements of the labor market, by increasing opportunities for specific training for national cadres locally, reducing training costs, stimulating and increasing quality partnerships, and thus qualifying distinguished national cadres capable of meeting the requirements The current and future labor market. Given the high cost of the investments needed, careful assessments should be made with regard to short-term and long-term goals as well as modes of outcome assessment.

The investment opportunities in the GCC education sectors should be diverse across all main areas of education, including education delivery, education services, education support services, education infrastructure, and importantly education capacity and capability building. Investments must be stretched across all education levels of delivery from kindergarten, primary education, vocational education, and higher education. Investments in the education services are also fundamental to improving the quality of higher education. This includes curriculum development, professional development, education content development, students' assistance & tutoring, consulting, and student assessment. A more practical approach to investment in education services is to open the door for the private sector to provide the provision of the infrastructure, maintenance of infrastructure, sales, and rental of infrastructure, equipping colleges and universities with IT infrastructure including fiber optic high-speed internet connection and 5G network and other related facilities. Hamalian et al. (2019) reaffirm this argument by highlighting the importance of greenfield investment in higher education, including investment in the services such as management system, tutoring, test preparation, students' assistance, and other services, and purchasing the infrastructure of the education. Private sector collaboration is also needed in curriculum development by allowing private sector companies to participate in the validation of the type of skills needed to be embedded in the curriculum in order to meet the needs of the future job market and importantly in providing real-world experiences of students and involvement in student assessments. Investments in new areas of education services will also improve the quality of the higher education system that is based on the skill set of graduates, digital skills, critical thinking, and vocational training, parameters that have become critical in the development of the Gulf higher education system (Alpen Capital 2018).

3 Preparing the GCC Job Market for Industry 4.0

Statistics show that the size of the GCC labor market is substantially large. According to GCC-STAT (2021), the number of people employed in the Gulf region was 22 million (Excluded UAE) in 2020 (UAE probably did not provide the GCC-STAT with data in that year), 7 million of them were classified as citizens and 15 million were expatriates. From that perspective, the GCC labor market has already tapped into the potential of attracting foreign workers. Furthermore, several initiatives have been made to attract and retain foreign talent in areas pertaining to innovation and 4IR. Such attempts are in line with the recommendation set out by the World Government Summit (2022): provide citizenship and financial support programs for talented foreign nationals to compete effectively for global education talent, students, teachers, and researchers. While citizenship remains difficult to obtain, GCC countries have recently eased long-term residence opportunities as well as opened up new options for stays based on freelance work examples include the recent golden visa introduced by the UAE. The UAE's "Golden visa" is a long-term residency visa that enables foreign talents to live and work or study in the UAE while enjoying exclusive benefits, including an entry visa for six months with multiple entries to proceed with residence issuance and a long-term renewable residence visa valid for 10 years.

As for the geographic distribution of labor, the percentage of employment increased in Saudi Arabia, Kuwait, and Qatar, whereas it decreased in the Sultanate of Oman and Bahrain. Data from the GCC-STAT also shows that 83.3% of the total GCC employees are male. Qatar ranked as the highest of male employment, while Kuwait recorded the highest rank of female employment in the GCC countries. The percentage of female unemployment is high in all GCC countries, with Saudi Arabia recording the highest percentage by 28.2% and Qatar has the lowest by 0.9%, reflecting varying degrees in the cultural, social, and policy approaches toward women's employment between GCC countries. When it comes to categorizing the workforce, we can see that only the UAE and Saudi Arabia have highly skilled employees compared to other GCC countries. According to Leopold et al. (2017), the percentage of the high skilled labor reached 38% in the UAE and 28% in Saudi Arabia of the percentage of total employment. This percentage underlines the shortage of skilled and experienced employees, a challenge that forced the GCC countries to seek foreign experts and high skilled labor from the international labor market as mentioned above.

In the near future, the job market is expected to experience a significant transformation in the types of jobs and skills. To fulfill the needs of Industry 4.0 technologies, we expect several jobs to emerge in the labor market. Industry 4.0 has an incredible role in determining the type of jobs needed in the market as most jobs will require professionals and technicians with advanced skills in big data, AI, web3, and cloud computing. We expect both graduates and employees to be knowledgeable, skillful, and well-trained in data analytics, machine learning, internet of things, artificial intelligence, digital marketing, digital finance, cybersecurity, equipment system engineer, robotics engineering, and control system engineering (TALENTEDGE 2021; NICV, n.d.; Bueno-Delgado et al. 2017).

According to the World Economic Forum (2016), jobs such as telemarketing, title examiner and searcher, underwriter of insurance, library technicians, and mathematical technicians will be shifted automatically by 99%. On the other side, jobs such as the first line of supervisor of installer, mechanics and repairers, human resources manager, director of management emergency, and the first line supervisors of police and detective, firefighting, social media, mental health, and healthcare are expected to be customized with advance technologies and be affected by only 0.66%. The growing trend toward using new technologies especially the internet of things and cloud computing will severely influence the manufacturing sector, as well as the office workers and administrative staff. We also expect significant changes in employment and types of contracts in the next few decades. Chief among these changes is that the labor market will be characterized by short-term contracts, which will be more prevalent than permanent contracts. Employees are likely to adopt job flexibility by seeking employment in more than one company (NICV, n.d.).

Meanwhile, we argue that Industry 4.0 is likely to have detrimental effects on several jobs that are likely to disappear from the labor market. The idea behind replacing workers with automation creates improved efficiency and effectiveness. This is likely to occur in the type of jobs that have repetitive routines and are easily managed by machine learning. The occupations that are likely to disappear over time and be replaced by advanced technologies such as robotics and machinery are in the retail sector, wholesale, manufacturing, logistics, and supply chains. When it comes to manufacturing and processing, using machine learning could improve the productivity up to 20% and reduce the wastage of the raw materials by 4% (World Economic Forum 2016). As for the jobs that are heavily dependent on big data analysis such as financial advisor, mathematical technicians, and credit analysts, we expect them to be performed by computers rather than the human brain as computers can deal with the vast quantity and analysis of big data. When it comes to operational cost-effectiveness, employers are likely to change the nature of secured jobs by shifting work to be done online, so work can be flexible, and employees can work from home in a more blended work mode. Companies can potentially move to smaller offices with lower rent and save the money of purchasing the furniture and office infrastructure (NICV, n.d.).

4 Bridging the Gap Between Higher Education, Labor Market, and Industry 4.0

Bridging the gap between higher education and the labor market is partially evolving around integrating all aspects of information and communication technology in the curricula of higher education, which are so far from the requirements of Industry 4.0. Bridging this gap could be done through reforming both the education sector and labor market, the supply and demand side.

In terms of education, many procedures could be taken to bridge the gap such as updating the curriculums according to the capabilities and skills required in the labor market, adding technical elective courses related to Industry 4.0, giving training courses to the students through specific companies that are highly connected with Industry 4.0 such as cloud computing, and data science, and offering complementary courses (Bueno-Delgado et al. 2017). The educational system could also integrate various skills within all curricula regardless of the subject to make students aware of the needs of Industry 4.0. The emerging skills could vary between critical thinking, creative, problem-solving, collaboration, communication, initiative, curiosity, persistence, adaptability, leadership, emotional intelligence, negotiation, decision-making, and culture awareness (Lase 2019).

Moreover, companies and institutions must develop their own initiatives and adapt to the changes driven by Industry 4.0 and needs in the labor market. Employees must upgrade their own skills periodically to quickly respond to the changes in technology. Specific training programs with the purpose of assessing employee's ability to adapt to changes in the work environment should be regularly introduced, particularly in areas such as augmented reality, manufacturing applications, real time data, and internet of things connected devices (Klaess 2019).

When it comes to skills development, we classify four categories of the skills that are essential in the labor market and aligned to the requirements of Industry 4.0 technologies. The first category of skills is workforce readiness, which includes literacy, numeracy, time management, self-presentation, professionalism, and etiquette. The second category is soft skills, which cover communication, critical thinking, creativity, self-confidence, growth mindset, empathy, collaboration, emotional learning, teamwork, and social awareness. The third category is technical skills, including coding, computer programming, management of the projects, financial management, scientific and machinery function, and technology-based skills. The fourth category is entrepreneurship, which includes innovations, initiatives, resilience, resourcefulness, optimism, risk taking, business acumen, courage, and curiosity. All those skills can be acquired by implementing many programs which could be in the form of team based, practical application, project based, case, experiential, business exposure, coaching, mentorship, and job shadowing (Armstrong et al. 2018).

5 Obstacles to Implementation

Despite the significant expenditure on digital education and required infrastructure within the GCC the educational impact in terms of graduate outcomes is still limited. A significant barrier remains in the quality of instruction students receive in higher education. Teaching, learning, curriculum, and student assessment methods broadly are not providing students with the essential skills to compete in the age of the fourth industrial revolution. The investment in technology is not being matched by investment in pedagogy, instructional design, and relevant assessment methods required to move students from campus proficiency to industry proficiency that is required to be competitive in the age of the fourth industrial revolution. The culture of higher education institutes is routinely based on compliance rather than innovation and enterprise, the lack of vertical innovation arising from the GCC despite significant expenditure is a clear indicator that the higher education sector still requires significant evolution to maximize opportunities arising from technology.

While female academic attainment is broadly higher than males across the GCC this does not currently translate into employment or economic gain. While there has been some progress, national policy should focus on creating opportunities for more females to enter the workforce through policies that support flexible working and conditions that encourage females to create businesses using technology.

Perhaps the most common barrier to overcome is the disconnect and lack of coordination that exists between higher education and industry. A deep sense of mistrust that exists has manifested itself over decades and while some progress has been made in recent years institutions lack the capability or value proposition to ensure that productive and sustainable relations are built with employers. This relationship will be critical to GCC countries seeking to upskill students and the workforce with relevant skills and for creating a culture for collaborative innovation.

6 Conclusion

All evidence points toward a disconnect between higher education in the GCC and the future workforce requirements of employers and the need for both identifying and delivering skills that are required for the Gulf nations and nationals to progress in the Industry 4.0 era. In terms of shaping a way forward and practical steps consideration needs to be given to the higher education regulatory and policy frameworks in addition to the strategic direction of the higher education institutes. Drawing on the book chapters our key recommendations include:

- **Recommendations Related to National Policy**

Human resource policies covering the public and private sector to place greater emphasis on skills, competencies, and professional qualifications rather than rely predominantly on academic attainment. Higher education national policy should gravitate away from the historical triple helix model that refers to the interaction between higher education, government, and industry to a new model and set of relationships that also capture relationships with private equity/venture capital and wider society to support entrepreneurship, innovation, and upskilling of communities with relevant digital skills.

GCC countries should be encouraged to issue all nationals with digital skills vouchers that can be used to upskill and reskill the working population with relevant skills that can be used at approved higher education institutes. These institutes should be considered skills banks that are utilized in evenings and weekends to provide training opportunities to wider society and employees. Improved and relevant career advice and guidance should be developed that alert students and parents to the skills required and future employment opportunities in the age of the fourth industrial revolution. Higher education national systems require further investment into vocational training institutes and support this with national communications and marketing activity targeting young people, parents, and wider society to allow for more practical training and professional certificates in technology-related programs.

A National Digital Competence Framework to include AI and data-related skills should be created by the government and adopted by all institutions. This cross-cutting framework should be led by employers from multiple sectors that articulate skills required for navigating the fourth industrial revolution. The framework needs to go beyond skills and competencies to include attitudes, values, and behaviors required. A national collection of data and a national-level target on student digital skills should be established and findings disseminated on an annual basis to all institutions and employers. Using data collected, a national digital internship program should be established to give higher education students and recent graduates in all disciplines the opportunity to gain hands-on professional experience in digital fields demanded by the labor market. This scheme could provide trainees with the opportunity to strengthen their information-communication-technology-specific skills in fields, such as cybersecurity, big data, quantum technology, and machine learning, and to boost digital skills for businesses in areas including web design, digital marketing, and software development.

GCC countries should develop ethical guidelines on the use of AI and data in teaching and learning for educators to help teachers and educators understand the potential that the applications of AI and data have in education and training, and to help them identify and mitigate the risks AI and data could entail.

- **Recommendations Related to Institutions**

Higher education institutions should conduct a holistic assessment of each student benchmarked against critical skills required in the fourth industrial revolution and develop personalized learning opportunities for students to develop and grow over time to meet the skills and competencies required by industry. These institutes should embed digital skills across all programs, common guidelines for teachers and educators should be developed to foster digital literacy and tackle disinformation through education and training.

The COVID-19 pandemic has led to the sudden and large-scale use of digital learning practices. Institutions should build on this and embrace blended and online learning opportunities for all. Higher levels of digital capacity and experience with alternative and flexible forms of learning have led to faster and more effective responses to emerging skills in demand. To support the quality delivery of blended or online learning institutions should invest in rigorous and regular professional development of faculty to enhance their own digital skills and ensure that they are able to ensure a high-quality blended/online learning experience for students.

Program design should place greater emphasis on experiential learning for all students with employers having a greater role in the assessment of students. Assessment should move toward establishing a greater balance between formative and summative assessments and move away from high stakes exams with a greater focus on assessment of digital and soft skills, application of knowledge and employability skills. Institutions should move toward a blended faculty with more adjunct professors and industry professionals as part of the teaching workforce.

Institutional governance such as the Board of Trustees should have representation from industry and in particular the technology sector to provide timely advice, strategic direction, and challenges regarding the institution's transition to digital transformation and the role of the institute in the face of the fourth industrial revolution.

References

AlkhaleejOnline. (2021). Infographic. Statistics and Figures on Education in the Gulf States [Online]. Available at http://khaleej.online/xmZmxy (Accessed 3 July 2022).

Allpin Capital. (2018). GCC Education Industry, November 13, 2018. Available at https://argaamplus.s3.amazonaws.com/9e55ad53-477f-48f0-b202-2c2f03d6a03d.pdf.

Armstrong, K., Parmelee, L., Santifort, S., Burley, J., & Van Fleet, J. W. (2018). Preparing tomorrow's workforce for the Fourth industrial revolution for business: A framework for action. *Deloitte & The Global Business Coalition for Education.*

Bensaid, B., & Brahmi, T. (2021). Coping with COVID-19: Higher Education in the GCC Countries. In A. Visvizi, M. D. Lytras & N. F. Aljohani (Eds.), Research and Innovation Forum 2020: Disruptive Technologies in Times of Change (pp. 137–153). Springer.

Bueno-Delgado, M. V., Romero-Gázquez, J. L., Cañavate-Cruzado, G., & Melero-Muñoz, F. J. (2017). Gaps between Skills Required by Industry 4.0 and Academic Programs Focused on ICTs: A Case Study of Computer Science Degrees in a Spanish University. In *Annual International Conference of Education, Research and Innovation (ICERI)* (Vol. 10, pp. 7329–7337).

Farid, S. (n.d.). UAE Top Performer in EdTech. Edarabia. Retrieved on September 1, 2022 from https://www.edarabia.com/uae-top-performer-edtech-innovation/.

GCC-STAT. (2021). Labour Statistics in the GCC Countries for the First Quarter of 2020, Quarterly Report April 2021. Available at https://gccstat.org/images/gccstat/docman/publications/Quarterly_Report_on_labour_Statistics_in_the_GCC_Countries_-_First_Quarter_of_2020.pdf.

Hamalian, M., Sfeir, R., & Mikati, B. (2019). Investment Opportunities in the GCC Education Sector, Middle East, Strategy & Part of the PwC Network.

Holland, K. (2021, March 21). EdTech Is the Silver Bullet to the Middle East's Education Sector Post-Pandemic. Arabian Business. Retrieved on August 30, 2022 from https://www.arabianbusiness.com/opinion/comment/462597-edtech-is-the-silver-bullet-to-the-middle-easts-education-sector-post-pandemic.

Klaess, J. (2019). Employee Training to Fill the Industry 4.0 Skills Gap [Online]. Available at https://tulip.co/blog/how-industry-4-0-is-training-tomorrows-workforce/ (Accessed 4 July 2022).

Lase, D. (2019). Education and Industrial Revolution 4.0. *Jurnal Handayani Pgsd Fip Unimed*, 10(1), 48–62.

Leopold, T. A., Ratcheva, V., & Zahidi, S. (2017). *The Future of Jobs and Skills in Middle East and North Africa: Preparing the Region for the Fourth Industrial Revolution*. In World Economic Forum.

Marr, B. (2022, August 22). The Top 10 Most In-Demand Skills for the Next 10 Years. Forbes. Retrieved on September 9, 2022 from https://www.forbes.com/sites/bernardmarr/2022/08/22/the-top-10-most-in-demand-skills-for-the-next-10-years/?sh=3addaa9a17be.

NICV. (n.d.). The Impacts of the Fourth Industrial Revolution on Jobs and the Future of the Third Sector [Online]. Available at https://www.nicva.org/sites/default/files/d7content/attachments-articles/the_impact_of_the_4th_industrial_revolution_on_jobs_and_the_sector.pdf (Accessed 3 July 2022).

TALENTEDGE. (2021). Careers: Best Jobs in the Era of Industry 4.0 [Online]. Available at https://talentedge.com/articles/careers-best-jobs-era-industry-4-0/ (Accessed 3 July 2022).

The National (2022, June 16). UAE Collaborates with '4IR Champions' to Boost Tech Adoption in the Industrial Sector. Retrieved from https://www.thenationalnews.com/business/technology/2022/06/16/uae-collaborates-with-4ir-champions-to-boost-tech-adoption-in-industrial-sector/.

World Government Summit. (2022). The Future of Higher Education in the Knowledge Economy. KPMG. Retrieved on March 1, 2022 from https://home.kpmg/ae/en/home/insights/2022/04/the-future-of-higher-education-in-the-knowledge-economy.html.

World Economic Forum. (2016). The Future of Jobs: Employment, Skills and Workforce Strategy for the Fourth Industrial Revolution. Global Challenge Insight Report.

Index

A

Academic achievement, 132
Academic Bridge Program (ABP), 134
Accounting, 9, 63, 133, 182, 298
Achievements, 11, 37, 38, 40, 87, 113, 144, 145, 181, 188
Activities, 7, 10–12, 16, 28, 32, 36, 41, 51, 60, 77, 87, 92, 101, 107, 108, 115, 133, 143, 150, 153, 157, 160, 163, 168, 184, 185, 247, 256, 260, 261, 263, 271, 274, 310, 329
Agile, 45, 53, 216, 229, 233–236, 243, 246–250
Agile Governance, 229, 233, 234, 248
Agile policy, 17, 18, 234, 235, 243, 250
Analysis, 3, 14, 16, 18, 40, 45, 65, 73, 74, 85, 128, 152, 156, 157, 195, 216, 230, 235, 238, 246, 283, 309, 312, 315, 326
Application, 13, 29, 36, 42, 46, 47, 60, 70, 115, 126, 155, 167, 204, 210, 233, 260, 261, 263, 286, 288, 295, 299, 327, 330
Arabian Gulf region, 7
Artificial intelligence (AI), 3, 13, 28, 51, 115, 150, 151, 154, 156, 166, 206, 260, 261, 270, 286, 322, 325, 329, 330
Automation, 3, 7, 14, 43, 45–47, 53, 115, 152, 207, 256, 314, 326

B

Bachelor's degree, 133, 182, 192, 305
Background, 19, 85, 142, 160, 203, 204, 284
Bahrain, 2, 4–7, 11, 17, 32, 34–36, 49, 92, 94–99, 101, 102, 104, 106, 108, 110, 113, 114, 228–231, 239, 241, 242, 244, 248, 249, 320, 324
Banking and financial services, 17, 203, 209

A. Mishrif et al. (eds.), *Nationalization of Gulf Labour Markets*, The Political Economy of the Middle East,
https://doi.org/10.1007/978-981-19-8072-5

Banking sector, 17, 204, 205, 211, 212, 220, 221, 257
Benefit, 10, 41, 43, 47, 48, 51, 53, 55, 71, 75, 92, 95, 111, 141, 158, 159, 166, 179, 183, 249, 272, 276, 280, 282, 287–289, 294, 296, 297, 301, 302, 304, 307–309, 313, 314, 324
Business, 5, 12, 16, 31, 40, 41, 48, 63, 69, 70, 91, 115, 123–129, 132, 133, 137–140, 142–146, 150, 151, 156, 181, 193, 204, 206, 229, 243, 262, 263, 294, 297, 299, 301, 303, 304, 327, 328, 330
Business Administration program, 133
Business environments, 133
Business hubs, 13
Business management, 133, 141
Business schools, 60, 62, 69–71, 73, 78, 133, 138–140

C

Campus, 39, 65, 127–129, 132, 135–137, 139–142, 194, 305, 328
Capabilities, 16, 17, 35, 43, 44, 49, 61, 63–65, 92, 114, 144, 150, 151, 153, 156, 157, 161, 163, 165, 166, 171, 180, 188, 217, 302, 323, 326, 328
Career, 46, 47, 64, 65, 69, 75, 77, 86, 133, 137–139, 163, 170, 204, 248, 249, 273, 284, 289, 295, 301, 303–305, 312, 314, 319, 329
Challenges, 4, 7, 9, 10, 12, 14, 18, 19, 28, 32, 37–39, 41, 43, 52, 63, 69, 77, 93, 98, 124, 127, 135, 150, 155, 157–161, 163–165, 167–170, 181, 184, 189, 191, 194, 196, 205, 228, 236, 239, 245, 250, 274, 283, 295, 298, 301–303, 313, 315, 320, 325, 331
Citizens, 2–5, 12, 16, 18, 19, 29, 30, 34, 45–49, 53, 95, 112, 181, 183, 191, 229, 256–258, 261, 263, 294, 297, 298, 302, 303, 310, 324
Classroom, 41, 44, 45, 60, 69, 133, 164
Cloud computing, 3, 13, 115, 325, 326
Collaboration, 18, 44, 48, 135, 152, 157, 164, 166, 212, 217, 218, 245, 259, 286, 321–323, 327
Commercial sectors, 265, 294
Competition, 37, 50, 78, 127, 262, 295
Consultation, 77, 237, 245, 247, 250, 266, 272
Contract, 111, 181, 185, 264, 325
Country, 4, 9, 11, 17, 30, 35, 39, 50, 52, 91–96, 101–103, 111–114, 116, 127, 129–132, 134, 135, 137, 140, 142, 146, 155, 156, 161, 162, 164, 166, 182, 183, 187, 190, 193, 194, 196, 204, 228, 257–262, 265, 266, 269, 275, 277, 286, 294, 296
Course, 47, 50, 68, 71, 92, 128, 132, 133, 144, 145, 156, 165, 167, 190, 193, 196, 210, 216, 245, 322, 326
COVID-19, 4, 8, 15–17, 19, 40, 41, 43, 52, 54, 56, 65, 115, 116, 152, 158, 168, 270, 271, 285, 295, 301, 322, 330
Cultural perceptions, 132
Cyber security, 206, 262, 265, 313

D

Data analytics, 3, 13, 44, 49, 206, 313, 325
Decision-makers, 134, 189, 193, 196
Degree, 2, 12, 32, 34, 44, 60, 61, 65, 74, 96, 103, 104, 113, 128–133, 182, 186, 188, 210, 241, 249, 258, 277, 284, 295, 306, 325
Department, 123–127, 132, 133
Development, 2, 3, 8–19, 28, 29, 33, 34, 38, 39, 43–46, 48, 49, 51–54, 62, 63, 70, 75–78, 81, 82, 85, 86, 88, 91–93, 96, 101, 103, 105, 107, 111–116, 123–126, 130, 136, 141, 142, 144, 149, 150, 153, 157, 158, 160, 161, 163, 166–168, 170, 180, 181, 183–185, 187–190, 192, 194, 195, 203, 204, 227–230, 232, 234, 235, 238, 239, 247, 249, 255–259, 264, 265, 269, 274, 285, 293, 295–297, 301, 313, 314, 321, 323, 324, 327, 330
Digital health sector, 16, 149
Digital skills, 16, 149, 150, 153–158, 160, 161, 170, 171, 323, 324, 329, 330
Digital transformation, 3, 155, 158, 159, 331
Digitization, 17, 42, 44, 48, 207, 212, 218
Dubai, 96, 134–140, 157, 163, 255, 256, 260–265, 275, 277, 296, 305, 306, 311, 321

E

E-commerce, 255, 261
Economic growth, 2, 4, 7, 18, 29, 30, 43, 51, 53, 112, 133, 159, 285, 313
Economics, 2–6, 8, 10, 11, 13, 16–19, 28, 30–32, 34, 40, 41, 43, 46, 47, 51, 53, 54, 56, 92, 96, 102, 104, 107, 108, 111, 113, 116, 123, 125, 133, 135, 141, 142, 146, 152, 156, 180–183, 188, 194–196, 208, 227–233, 239, 255, 256, 258, 260–265, 269, 274, 284, 293, 294, 298, 299, 309, 313, 321, 328
Economy, 4–6, 8, 10–12, 14, 15, 27, 28, 30, 32–35, 39–41, 43, 45–47, 51–54, 94, 95, 98, 107, 115, 116, 125–127, 129, 135, 140, 146, 152–154, 180–183, 190, 191, 195, 203, 208, 210, 228, 230–233, 239, 242, 244, 255–259, 261, 262, 265, 270, 288, 293, 297, 304, 320, 323
Ecosystem, 11, 158, 166, 170, 171, 207, 217, 261, 323
Education, 2, 3, 6–10, 13, 16–19, 28–32, 34, 35, 37–55, 59, 61, 63, 65, 73, 91–93, 95–99, 101, 103, 104, 113–115, 123, 125–129, 131–135, 138, 139, 143–146, 150, 154, 156, 157, 163, 164, 166, 167, 169, 180, 183, 185, 189, 191, 192, 195, 210, 228–231, 239, 241, 244–246, 248, 263, 270, 271, 273–279, 281, 283–289, 295, 305, 309, 310, 313, 319–324, 326, 327, 330
Education City, 39, 128, 131–133
Education policy, 230, 231, 236, 238, 247, 250
Education system, 4, 7–10, 13, 15, 27, 29, 30, 32, 41–43, 53, 56, 99, 100, 124, 135, 137, 142,

153, 212, 229, 231, 239, 241, 245, 288, 294, 313, 321
Element, 16, 40, 49, 53, 67, 73, 91, 144, 161, 234, 313
Emiratisation, 297, 299, 303
Employment, 2, 5, 6, 13, 14, 17, 28, 29, 31, 32, 40, 50–54, 61, 63–65, 69, 74, 103, 107, 109, 113, 114, 124, 126, 153, 180, 183, 187, 188, 191, 192, 194, 195, 203, 230, 256–258, 261, 263, 277, 283, 284, 287, 289, 293–297, 301, 303, 305, 310, 313, 315, 324, 325, 328, 329
Entity, 11, 141, 184, 191, 258, 260–262, 264, 303
Entrepreneurship, 5, 10–12, 41, 193, 258, 327, 329
Environment, 4, 8, 14, 37–39, 48, 52, 60, 61, 65, 70, 95, 134, 138, 140, 141, 182, 185, 216, 217, 234, 260, 308, 312, 327
Export-Oriented Industrialization (EOI), 12

F

Facility, 134
Features, 42, 44, 52, 63, 66, 125, 126, 152, 154, 192, 206, 210, 262, 296
Finance, 8, 9, 14, 32, 70, 133, 135, 139, 142, 185, 208, 257, 258, 261, 265, 309, 325
Findings, 19, 72, 85, 87, 127, 144, 145, 208, 235, 240, 246, 248, 287, 307, 309, 315, 329
Fintech, 204, 206, 209, 217, 261
Foreign Direct Investments (FDI), 33, 142
Formulation, 92, 164, 236
Foundational principles, 233
Fourth industrial revolution (4IR), 28–30, 43–46, 48–50, 53–55, 115, 192, 193, 229, 230, 260, 270, 271, 314, 322–324, 327–331
Free trade zone, 140
Free zones, 13, 135, 141, 142, 255, 261, 263

G

Gap, 14, 16, 17, 19, 28, 37–39, 41, 42, 55, 88, 96, 113, 150, 155, 180, 182, 205, 210, 212, 279, 289, 302, 303, 323, 326
Generations, 13, 19, 39, 43, 56, 104, 111, 127, 135, 151, 154, 167, 168, 194, 209, 221, 314
Global business, 138, 139
Governance, 37, 231, 245, 248, 249, 330
Government, 2, 4, 6, 7, 9–12, 15, 28, 30, 32, 34, 35, 41–43, 46–55, 92, 93, 100, 101, 103, 108, 109, 111, 112, 116, 125, 132, 135–137, 151, 153, 154, 187, 189, 190, 203, 228, 229, 232–234, 236, 237, 239, 243, 245, 250, 255–265, 270, 272, 273, 276, 277, 285, 288, 293–295, 301–304, 307–309, 313, 314, 322, 323, 329
Graduates, 5, 7, 31, 65–68, 79–85, 130, 139, 192, 259, 283, 295, 327
Gross domestic product (GDP), 8, 9, 34–36, 54, 95, 98, 104, 105, 131, 183, 192, 228, 230, 260
Gulf cooperation council (GCC), 2–17, 19, 27–43, 49–56, 60, 71, 87, 92–107, 109, 111, 113, 114, 124–126, 128, 146, 152, 156, 161, 163, 164, 170, 181,

227–233, 241, 250, 261, 266, 294, 296, 298, 320–325, 327–330
Gulf industrialization, 8
Gulf labour market, 116

H
Healthcare, 7, 14, 16, 18, 52, 100, 105, 116, 149–171, 195, 263, 270–274, 283, 285–289, 310, 325
Higher education, 1, 3, 4, 7, 9–13, 16, 17, 19, 28–30, 37–40, 43–50, 52–55, 59, 62, 63, 73, 100, 123–126, 128–130, 134–137, 141, 180, 182, 183, 230, 239, 241, 248, 257, 284, 320–323, 326–329
Higher education institutions (HEIs), 8, 14–16, 28, 29, 37–40, 43, 46, 50, 53, 55, 60, 71, 124–128, 134, 135, 146, 152, 154, 170, 229, 328–330
Higher education system, 9, 12, 15, 97, 128, 134, 135, 146, 324
History, 156, 185, 187, 188
Human capital, 4, 7, 10, 11, 15, 16, 29, 30, 40, 51–54, 91–93, 96, 98, 113, 116, 128, 144, 146, 150, 156, 239, 271, 273–277, 285–287, 289
Human capital development, 2, 228, 256
Human capital production, 16, 123, 124, 126, 127, 144, 146
Human resource (HR), 6, 34, 75, 91, 92, 96, 98, 105, 107, 113, 114, 116, 160, 194, 203, 204, 294, 313, 325, 329
Human resource management, 16, 123–126, 139, 140, 143–145

I
Impact, 1, 14, 19, 29, 30, 40, 42, 56, 73, 115, 116, 125–127, 133, 146, 151–153, 157, 161, 165–168, 170, 185, 192, 194, 210, 229, 231–233, 237, 242, 244, 248, 249, 270, 271, 275, 284–288, 301, 327
Implementation, 18, 19, 43, 53, 112, 150
Industrial cities, 12, 13
Industrial internet of things (IIoT), 3, 115
Industrial policy, 8, 12, 19, 156
Industry 4.0 (I4.0), 3, 4, 7, 9, 10, 12–15, 17, 19, 28–30, 50, 51, 53, 54, 115, 150–154, 156, 170, 321, 324–328
Information Systems, 14, 133, 143
Initiatives, 5, 10, 18, 28, 31, 35, 40, 43–48, 50, 51, 53, 55, 66, 78, 80, 81, 86, 95, 182, 185, 188, 192, 204, 230, 239, 241, 249, 256–260, 262, 264, 265, 285, 299, 303, 313, 322, 324, 327
Innovation, 3, 7–12, 15, 16, 18, 19, 28, 34, 35, 44, 51, 52, 54, 113, 129, 145, 153, 154, 158, 162, 163, 167, 169, 186, 189, 195, 205–208, 212, 213, 215, 217, 218, 264, 286, 307, 320, 323, 324, 327–329
Institutions, 9, 10, 12, 14, 28, 36–39, 42, 45, 47, 49, 50, 54, 55, 59, 60, 86, 88, 124, 125, 127, 128, 130–132, 134–136, 138, 140–143, 146, 167, 189, 191, 194, 206, 217, 230, 231, 239, 240, 245, 246, 248, 259, 260, 307, 320–322, 327–331
Integration, 13, 19, 61, 70, 111, 236, 249, 276, 304

International institutions, 128, 135, 186
International Monetary Fund (IMF), 4, 29, 125, 297
Internet of things (IoT), 3, 13, 47, 115, 151, 152, 322, 325, 327
Internships, 60, 63, 69, 70, 77, 86, 133, 259, 329
Investment, 2, 3, 7, 9, 11, 15, 16, 19, 30, 34, 41, 51, 52, 96, 112, 133, 180, 182, 183, 208, 228, 232, 263, 273, 293, 295, 320–324, 327–329
Iran, 100, 141, 150, 152, 157, 158, 160–162, 166, 170
Islamic Banking, 139

J
Job market, 5, 15, 17, 19, 31, 65, 116, 126, 137, 180, 182, 274, 312, 314, 322, 324, 325
Job satisfaction, 284
Job security, 296, 301, 303, 309
Jobseekers, 256, 258, 265
Journalism, 130, 133

K
Knowledge-based economy, 7, 10–12, 313
Knowledge economy, 228, 259
Kuwait, 2, 4–6, 30, 32, 34–36, 49, 92, 94–99, 101, 102, 104–106, 108, 110–113, 228, 256, 257, 320, 324

L
Laboratories, 9, 45, 134, 320
Labour, 8, 9, 13, 14, 19, 45, 47, 52, 54, 91–94, 104–109, 111–116, 153, 228, 299, 324, 325
Labour market, 1–4, 7–9, 12–19, 30, 50–56, 109, 152, 153, 156, 183, 190–192, 196, 227–231, 237, 239, 248, 249, 321, 324–326, 329
Labour migration, 108, 112
Landscapes, 8, 44, 49, 141, 142, 153, 156, 301
Leadership, 4, 16, 17, 48, 51, 67, 71, 79, 86, 125, 133, 138, 139, 144, 145, 153, 166, 179, 180, 191, 217, 220, 245, 262, 321, 327
Leadership development, 78, 79, 220, 221
Localization, 93, 108, 116, 293, 294, 297, 302, 303, 315
Location, 12, 127, 142, 265
Logistics, 13, 142, 194, 326

M
Management, 9, 16, 33, 37, 38, 47, 63–65, 73, 75, 77, 82, 85–88, 111, 124, 133, 139, 141–143, 155, 158, 160, 187, 193, 194, 204, 205, 208, 210, 219–221, 232, 257, 262, 274, 275, 298, 323, 325, 327
Market behaviour, 231
Marketing, 70, 133, 137, 139, 188, 194, 204, 325, 329, 330
Master's programme, 131
Mechanisms, 19, 47, 55, 112, 149, 162, 170, 229, 233, 234, 236, 243, 244, 247, 250, 314
Memorandum of understanding, 259
Middle East, 35, 133, 134, 140, 142, 286
Middle eastern region, 135
Ministerial Resolution, 309, 310

N

Nationalities, 130, 131, 138, 275, 276, 294
Nationalization, 2, 3, 6, 9, 13–15, 27, 28, 30, 31, 37, 40, 50, 53–55, 93, 116, 124, 204
National workforce, 2, 3, 19, 31, 294, 298, 301
New era, 319
New York University, 135, 136
North Africa, 134

O

Oman, 5, 6, 32, 34–36, 39, 41, 49, 92, 94–102, 104–106, 108, 110, 113, 114, 150, 157, 228, 256, 257, 320, 324
Omanization, 14, 257
Operations, 10, 133, 136, 143, 150
Opportunities, 7, 9, 12, 14, 15, 17, 28, 29, 38, 40, 44, 46, 47, 50, 54, 55, 60, 70, 71, 77, 86, 109, 124, 137, 138, 144, 150, 152, 156, 157, 159, 161, 165, 167, 168, 180, 183, 184, 187, 188, 190, 192, 193, 204, 230, 247, 256, 257, 259, 261, 263, 270, 274, 275, 297, 298, 304, 308, 312, 313, 320, 322–324, 328–330
Organizational learning, xiv
Organizations, 10, 92, 125, 143, 150, 299, 301, 307, 309, 310

P

Partner, 42, 104, 140, 141, 144, 171, 184, 207, 230
Partnership, 125, 128, 131, 154, 185, 194, 207, 261, 322, 323
People, 7, 12, 15, 29, 38, 40, 43, 51–53, 66–68, 92, 93, 101, 102, 105, 112–115, 130, 132, 133, 136, 150, 154, 160, 193, 210, 236, 238, 241, 245, 269, 289, 295, 297, 324, 329
Platform, 41, 42, 137, 139, 152, 162, 167, 208, 260, 322, 323
Policy, 2, 3, 5, 6, 9–11, 14, 16–19, 31–35, 38, 61, 93, 100, 108, 114, 125, 150–154, 156–164, 170, 171, 228–238, 242–250, 256, 260, 264–266, 276, 287, 294, 295, 297, 299, 313, 314, 320, 325, 328, 329
Political economy, 231, 256
Population, 4–6, 8, 10, 15, 28–33, 43, 45–55, 71, 91–96, 100–109, 111–114, 116, 125, 126, 131, 135, 137, 158, 161, 164, 182, 195, 196, 229, 271, 276, 277, 294, 296, 298, 303, 305, 329
Possibilities, 16, 150, 152, 165, 303
Postgraduate, 2, 60, 131, 137, 296
Priorities, 144, 145, 156, 160, 165, 190, 323
Private sector, 2, 3, 5–7, 9, 11, 19, 28, 31–34, 36, 40, 49–52, 54, 132, 161, 162, 182, 183, 194, 195, 228–230, 235, 250, 258–261, 266, 274, 288, 293–299, 301–305, 307–309, 312–314, 323, 329
Process, 3, 13, 15, 17–19, 32–34, 38, 40, 41, 48, 62–64, 70, 71, 92, 111, 114, 124, 126, 127, 135, 143, 144, 146, 153, 155, 156, 167, 168, 212, 230, 232, 234–240, 242–250, 272, 295, 297
Production, 3, 11, 13, 15, 33, 34, 36, 44, 49, 103, 115, 123, 227, 273
Program, 19, 40, 44, 47–49, 61, 69, 79, 86, 111, 127, 129, 130, 134,

137–139, 142, 186, 188–191, 193, 259, 262, 271, 274, 286, 288, 294, 295, 313, 315, 329, 330
Promotion, 46, 150, 258, 261, 308, 313
Public Investment Fund (PIF), 17, 180, 185, 194, 195
Public policy, 134
Public sector, 2, 5, 6, 9, 17, 31, 33, 52, 165, 191, 195, 232, 256, 258–260, 266, 288, 294–296, 299, 301, 303–305, 307–310, 314

Q
Qatar, 2, 4–6, 11, 16, 32, 34–36, 39, 49, 92, 94–99, 101, 102, 104, 106, 113, 114, 123, 124, 126, 128–134, 144, 145, 228, 265, 320, 321, 324, 325
Qatar Foundation, 129–132, 321
Qatar Investment Authority, 133
Qatar Museums Authority, 131
Qatar Petroleum, 133
Quality assurance, 38, 96, 135, 169, 170

R
Realism, 233, 235, 237, 246
Reforms, 6, 7, 17, 18, 32, 137, 164, 227, 228, 230–232, 234, 238, 239, 241, 242, 245
Regulation, 208, 219, 261, 309, 320
Reputation, 27, 53, 136, 139, 169, 180
Requirement, 67, 77, 108, 169, 191, 204, 212, 214, 313
Research and development (R&D), 3, 7, 9–12, 16, 131, 156
Research centres, 132
Research methods, 131
Residents, 47, 112, 229, 257, 258, 262, 263, 301, 310
Resources, 4, 5, 11, 12, 30, 32, 37, 42, 44, 47, 49, 92, 131, 133, 163, 217, 265, 270, 274, 297, 309
Results, 34, 41, 47, 49, 101, 113, 165, 168, 169, 192, 243, 286, 293, 295, 297, 298, 313, 314
Retail Management, 143
Robotics, 28, 51, 151, 152, 322, 325, 326

S
Salary, 258, 296, 301, 303, 307, 308, 314
Sales, 194, 207, 323
Saudi Arabia, 2, 4–6, 9, 16, 17, 28, 32, 34–36, 39, 41, 49, 51, 92, 94–102, 104–108, 110, 113, 114, 124, 134, 150, 157, 160, 179–184, 186–189, 191–196, 228, 256, 257, 264, 320, 324, 325
Schools, 2, 41, 42, 49, 64, 73, 82, 88, 96, 97, 99, 111, 129–134, 136–140, 142, 170, 185, 189, 229, 240, 270, 278, 279, 281, 283, 285–287, 305, 306
Science, 13, 27, 39, 97, 100, 130–133, 136, 141, 153, 190, 259, 321, 326
Secondary education, 96, 99, 127, 132, 191, 241, 321
Secured Information Technology, 143
Social media, 283, 313, 325
Society, 4, 5, 7, 12, 15, 18, 28, 29, 39, 40, 43, 46, 48, 52, 54, 92, 100, 114, 115, 130, 231, 232, 239, 258, 270–272, 274, 276,

284–286, 301, 303, 307, 310, 313, 315, 329
South Asia, 134
State, 4, 5, 30, 34, 35, 46, 48, 54, 110, 113, 125, 131, 140, 151, 162, 168, 181, 194, 196, 258, 260
Strategic management, 143, 153
Students, 2, 5, 14, 15, 18, 27, 28, 31, 32, 37–45, 47–50, 53, 55, 56, 59–65, 69–72, 74, 75, 77–82, 85–88, 99, 100, 111, 124, 127–129, 131–139, 141–145, 161, 186, 188–190, 192, 196, 242, 247, 249, 258, 260, 263, 270, 285, 286, 295, 296, 305, 307, 314, 315, 320–324, 326–330
Supply, 2, 8, 9, 19, 55, 111, 116, 154–156, 161, 164, 165, 209, 294, 296, 301, 323, 326
Supply chain, 3, 13, 326

T
Technical skills, 3, 8, 63, 186, 193, 204, 212, 313, 327
Technique, 64, 73, 74, 138, 139, 277
Technological developments, 11, 28, 29, 36, 51, 54
Technological transformation, 261
Technology, 3, 7, 10, 11, 14, 27, 28, 33, 36, 39, 46–49, 51, 96, 115, 127, 131, 132, 136, 142, 151–154, 156, 159–161, 163, 167, 170, 194, 204–210, 212, 217–219, 259, 260, 264, 270, 273, 307, 309, 310, 314, 319–323, 326–330
Time management, 284, 321, 327
Tourism industry, 16, 17, 180, 183, 192, 194–196
Traditional education, 42, 61
Transparent, 162, 169, 261, 299

U
Undergraduate universities, 132
United Arab Emirates (UAE), 4, 10, 16, 32, 34, 35, 49, 73, 92, 94, 98, 99, 101, 102, 107, 108, 114, 124, 134, 135, 140, 142, 150, 255, 269, 308
United Kingdom (UK), 98–100, 136, 141, 154, 155, 188, 229, 286
United Nations (UN), 10, 29, 103, 258, 306
United States (US), 55, 99, 100, 131, 132, 142, 185, 188
University, 5, 9, 11, 31, 38, 39, 42, 49, 50, 126–128, 131, 132, 134, 136–139, 143, 185, 189, 212, 259, 278, 283, 284, 315, 322
University campuses, 132, 196
User, 155, 231, 234, 236, 248, 249, 263

V
Variable, 71–73, 85, 87, 104, 277, 279, 280
Various capacities, 238
Various mechanisms, 233
Various programs, 73, 259
Various sectors, 131, 299

W
Workforce, 2, 5, 6, 8, 9, 14–16, 27–29, 31, 34, 40, 50, 53, 54, 56, 59, 60, 96, 106, 107, 113–115, 150, 153, 154, 158, 159, 161–163, 191, 193, 204, 209, 229, 248, 269, 271, 274–276, 287, 288, 293–300, 312, 313, 315, 319, 321, 322, 325, 327, 328, 330

Workforce nationalization, 17, 18, 256, 257, 259, 260, 264–266
Work Integrated Learning (WIL), 15, 60, 62, 87
World, 4, 5, 7, 9, 11, 13, 28, 29, 31, 32, 39, 43, 44, 50, 51, 53–55, 67, 69, 93, 95, 98, 102, 103, 107, 115, 125, 127–129, 132, 133, 136–141, 151, 180, 183–187, 189, 191, 195, 196, 205–208, 211, 212, 216, 220, 228, 235, 241, 264, 271, 275, 284, 322, 324
World Economic Forum (WEF), 155, 206, 228, 325, 326
World Economic Human Capital Index, 52
World Intellectual Property Organization (WIPO), 36

Y

Year, 41–44, 61, 64, 72, 73, 93–95, 98, 102, 103, 108, 129, 130, 132, 136, 139–142, 157, 180, 186, 188, 191, 204, 207, 256, 259, 261, 262, 294, 296, 305, 310, 324
Youths, 132, 182

The manufacturer's authorised representative in the EU is Springer Nature Customer Service Centre GmbH, Europaplatz 3, 69115 Heidelberg, Germany. If you have any concerns regarding our products, please contact ProductSafety@springernature.com

Printed and bound by CPI Group (UK) Ltd, Croydon, CR0 4YY
30/09/2026
02225254-0008